HONDA
CB750
Gold Portfolio
1969-1978

Compiled by
R.M.Clarke

ISBN 9781855204669

 BROOKLANDS BOOKS LTD.
P.O. BOX 146, COBHAM,
SURREY, KT11 1LG. UK

HN7BGP
Printed in China

Brooklands Books

MOTORING

BROOKLANDS ROAD TEST SERIES

Abarth Gold Portfolio 1950-1971
AC Ace & Aceca 1953-1983
Alfa Romeo Giulietta Gold Portfolio 1954-1965
Alfa Romeo Giulia Coupés 1963-1976
Alfa Romeo Giulia Coupés Gold Port. 1963-1976
Alfa Romeo Spider 1966-1990
Alfa Romeo Spider Gold Portfolio 1966-1991
Alfa Romeo Alfasud 1972-1984
Alfa Romeo Alfetta Gold Portfolio 1972-1987
Alfa Romeo Alfetta GTV6 1980-1986
Allard Gold Portfolio 1937-1959
Alvis Gold Portfolio 1919-1967
AMX & Javelin Muscle Portfolio 1968-1974
Armstrong Siddeley Gold Portfolio 1945-1960
Aston Martin Gold Portfolio 1948-1971
Aston Martin Gold Portfolio 1972-1985
Aston Martin Gold Portfolio 1985-1995
Audi Quattro Gold Portfolio 1980-1991
Austin A30 & A35 1951-1962
Austin Healey 100 & 100/6 Gold Portfolio 1952-1959
Austin Healey 3000 Gold Portfolio 1959-1967
Austin Healey Sprite Gold Portfolio 1958-1971
BMW 6 & 8 Cyl. Cars Limited Edition 1935-1960
BMW 1600 Collection No.1 1966-1981
BMW 2002 Gold Portfolio 1968-1976
BMW 6 Cylinder Coupés & Saloons Gold P. 1969-1976
BMW 316, 318, 320 (4 cyl.) Gold Port. 1975-1990
BMW 320, 323, 325 (6 cyl.) Gold Port. 1977-1990
BMW M Series Gold Portfolio 1976-1997
BMW 5 Series Gold Portfolio 1981-1987
BMW 6 Series Gold Portfolio 1976-1989
Bricklin Gold Portfolio 1974-1975
Bristol Cars Gold Portfolio 1946-1992
Buick Automobiles 1947-1960
Buick Muscle Cars 1965-1970
Cadillac Allanté 1986-1993
Cadillac Automobiles 1949-1959
Cadillac Automobiles 1960-1969
Checker Limited Edition
Chevrolet 1955-1957
Impala & SS Muscle Portfolio 1958-1972
Corvair Performance Portfolio 1959-1969
El Camino & SS Muscle Portfolio 1959-1987
Chevy II & Nova SS Muscle Portfolio 1962-1974
Chevelle & SS Muscle Portfolio 1964-1972
Caprice Limited Edition 1965-1976
Chevrolet Muscle Cars 1966-1971
Chevy Blazer 1969-1981
Camaro Muscle Portfolio 1967-1973
Chevrolet Camaro & Z-28 1973-1981
High Performance Camaros 1982-1988
Chevrolet Corvette Gold Portfolio 1953-1962
Chevrolet Corvette Sting Ray Gold Port. 1963-1967
Chevrolet Corvette Gold Portfolio 1968-1977
High Performance Corvettes 1983-1989
Chrysler 300 Gold Portfolio 1955-1970
Imperial Limited Edition 1955-1970
Valiant 1960-1962
Citroen Traction Avant Gold Portfolio 1934-1957
Citroen 2CV Gold Portfolio 1948-1989
Citroen DS & ID 1955-1975
Citroen DS & ID Gold Portfolio 1955-1975
Citroen SM 1970-1975
Cobras & Replicas 1962-1983
Shelby Cobra Gold Portfolio 1962-1969
Cobras & Cobra Replicas Gold Portfolio 1962-1989
Crosley & Crosley Specials Limited Edition
Cunningham Automobiles 1951-1955
Daimler SP250 Sports & V-8 250 Saloon Gold P. 1959-1969
Datsun Roadsters 1962-1971
Datsun 240Z & 260Z Gold Portfolio 1970-1978
Datsun 280Z & ZX 1975-1983
DeLorean Gold Portfolio 1977-1995
De Soto Limited Edition 1952-1960
Charger Muscle Portfolio 1966-1974
Dodge Muscle Cars 1967-1970
Dodge Viper Muscle Portfolio 1990-1998
ERA Gold Portfolio 1934-1994
Excalibur Collection No.1 1952-1981
Facel Vega 1954-1964
Ferrari Limited Edition 1947-1957
Ferrari Limited Edition 1958-1963
Ferrari Dino 1965-1974
Ferrari Dino 308 & Mondial Gold Portfolio 1974-1985
Ferrari 328 348 Mondial Gold Portfolio 1986-1994
Fiat 500 Gold Portfolio 1936-1972
Fiat 600 & 850 Gold Portfolio 1955-1972
Fiat Pininfarina 124 & 2000 Spider 1968-1985
Fiat X1/9 Gold Portfolio 1973-1989
Fiat Abarth Performance Portfolio 1972-1987
Ford Consul, Zephyr, Zodiac Mk. I & II 1950-1962
Ford Zephyr, Zodiac, Executive Mk. III & IV 1962-1971
Ford Cortina 1600E & GT 1967-1970
High Performance Capris Gold Portfolio 1969-1987
Capri Muscle Portfolio 1974-1987
High Performance Fiestas 1979-1991
High Performance Escorts Mk. I 1968-1974
High Performance Escorts Mk. II 1975-1980
High Performance Escorts 1980-1985
High Performance Escorts 1985-1990
High Perf. Sierras & Merkurs Gold Portfolio 1983-1990
Ford Automobiles 1949-1959
Ford Fairlane Performance Portfolio 1955-1970
Ford Ranchero Performance Portfolio 1957-1979
Edsel Limited Edition 1957-1960
Falcon Performance Portfolio 1960-1970
Ford Galaxie & LTD Limited Edition 1960-1973
Ford Thunderbird 1955-1957
Ford Thunderbird 1958-1963
Ford GT40 Gold Portfolio 1964-1987
Ford Torino Limited Edition 1968-1974
Ford Bronco 1966-1977
Ford Bronco 1978-1988
Goggomobil Limited Edition
Holden 1948-1962
Honda CRX 1983-1987
Hudson Limited Edition 1946-1957
International Scout Gold Portfolio 1961-1980
Isetta Gold Portfolio 1953-1964
ISO & Bizzarrini Gold Portfolio 1962-1974
Jaguar and SS Gold Portfolio 1931-1951
Jaguar C-Type & D-Type Gold Portfolio 1951-1960
Jaguar XK120, 140, 150 Gold Portfolio 1948-1960
Jaguar Mk. VII, VIII, IX, X, 420 Gold Port. 1950-1970
Jaguar Mk. 1 & Mk. 2 Gold Portfolio 1959-1969
Jaguar E-Type Gold Portfolio 1961-1971
Jaguar E-Type V-12 1971-1975
Jaguar S-Type & 420 Limited Edition
Jaguar XJ12, XJ5.3, V12 Gold Portfolio 1972-1990
Jaguar XJ6 Series I & II Gold Portfolio 1968-1979
Jaguar XJ6 Series III Perf. Portfolio 1979-1986
Jaguar XJ6 Gold Portfolio 1986-1994
Jaguar XJS Gold Portfolio 1975-1988
Jaguar XJS Gold Portfolio 1988-1995
Jaguar XK8 Limited Edition
Jeep CJ5 & CJ6 1960-1976
Jeep CJ5 & CJ7 1976-1986
Jensen Interceptor Gold Portfolio 1966-1986
Jensen Healey 1972-1976
Kaiser - Frazer Limited Edition 1946-1955
Lagonda Gold Portfolio 1919-1964
Lancia Aurelia & Flaminia Gold Portfolio 1950-1970
Lancia Fulvia Gold Portfolio 1963-1976
Lancia Beta Gold Portfolio 1972-1984
Lancia Delta Gold Portfolio 1979-1994
Lancia Stratos 1972-1985
Land Rover Series I 1948-1958
Land Rover Series II & IIa 1958-1971
Land Rover 90 110 Defender Gold Portfolio 1983-1994
Land Rover Discovery 1989-1994
Land Rover Story Part One 1948-1971
Fifty Years of Selling Land Rover
Lincoln Gold Portfolio 1949-1960
Lincoln Continental 1961-1969
Lincoln Continental 1969-1976
Lotus Sports Racers Gold Portfolio 1953-1965
Lotus Seven Gold Portfolio 1957-1973
Lotus Caterham Seven Gold Portfolio 1974-1995
Lotus Elan Gold Portfolio 1962-1974
Lotus Elan Collection No. 2 1963-1972
Lotus Elan & SE 1989-1992
Lotus Europa Gold Portfolio 1966-1975
Lotus Elite & Eclat 1974-1982
Lotus Turbo Esprit 1980-1986
Marcos Coupés & Spyders Gold Portfolio 1960-1997
Maserati 1965-1970
Matra Limited Edition 1965-1983
Mazda Miata MX-5 Performance Portfolio 1989-1996
Mazda RX-7 Gold Portfolio 1978-1991
McLaren F1 Sportscar Limited Edition
Mercedes 190 & 300 SL 1954-1963
Mercedes G-Wagen 1981-1994
Mercedes S & 600 1965-1972
Mercedes S Class 1972-1979
Mercedes 230 • 250 • 280SL Gold Portfolio 1963-1971
Mercedes SLs & SLCs Gold Portfolio 1971-1989
Mercedes SLs Performance Portfolio 1989-1994
Mercury Limited Edition 1947-59
Mercury Comet & Cyclone Limited Edition 1960-1970
Mercury Muscle Cars 1966-1971
Cougar Limited Edition 1967-1973
Messerschmitt Gold Portfolio 1954-1964
MG Gold Portfolio 1929-1939
MG TA & TC Gold Portfolio 1936-1949
MG TD & TF Gold Portfolio 1949-1955
MGA & Twin Cam Gold Portfolio 1955-1962
MG Midget Gold Portfolio 1961-1979
MGB Roadsters 1962-1980
MGB MGC & V8 Gold Portfolio 1962-1980
MGB GT 1965-1980
MGC & MGB GT V8 Limited Edition
MG Y-Type & Magnette ZA/ZB Limited Edition
Mini Gold Portfolio 1959-1969
Mini Gold Portfolio 1969-1980
Mini Gold Portfolio 1981-1997
High Performance Minis Gold Portfolio 1960-1973
Mini Cooper Gold Portfolio 1961-1971
Mini Moke Gold Portfolio 1964-1994
Morgan Three-Wheeler Gold Portfolio 1910-1952
Morgan Plus 4 & Four 4 Gold Portfolio 1936-1967
Morgan Cars Gold Portfolio 1968-1989
Morris Minor Collection No. 1 1948-1980
Shelby Mustang Muscle Portfolio 1965-1970
High Performance Mustang IIs 1974-1978
High Performance Mustangs 1982-1988
Nash & Nash-Healey Limited Edition 1949-1957
Nash-Austin Metropolitan Gold Portfolio 1954-1962
Oldsmobile Automobiles 1955-1963
Oldsmobile Muscle Portfolio 1964-1971
Cutlass & 4-4-2 Muscle Portfolio 1964-1974
Oldsmobile Toronado 1966-1978
Opel GT Gold Portfolio 1968-1973
Opel Manta Limited Edition 1970-1975
Packard Gold Portfolio 1946-1958
Pantera Gold Portfolio 1970-1989
Panther Gold Portfolio 1972-1990
Barracuda Muscle Portfolio 1964-1974
Pontiac Tempest & GTO 1961-1965
GTO Muscle Portfolio 1964-1974
Firebird & Trans-Am Muscle Portfolio 1967-1972
Firebird & Trans-Am Muscle Portfolio 1973-1981
High Performance Firebirds 1982-1988
Pontiac Limited Edition 1949-60
Pontiac Fiero 1984-1988
Porsche 356 Gold Portfolio 1953-1965
Porsche 912 Limited Edition
Porsche 911 1965-1969
Porsche 911 1970-1972
Porsche 911 1973-1977
Porsche 911 SC & Turbo Gold Portfolio 1978-1983
Porsche 911 Carrera & Turbo Gold Port. 1984-1989
Porsche 911 Gold Portfolio 1990-1997
Porsche 924 Gold Portfolio 1975-1988
Porsche 928 Performance Portfolio 1977-1994
Porsche 944 Gold Portfolio 1981-1991
Porsche 968 Limited Edition
Range Rover Gold Portfolio 1970-1985
Range Rover Gold Portfolio 1986-1995
Reliant Scimitar 1964-1986
Renault Alpine Gold Portfolio 1958-1994
Riley Gold Portfolio 1924-1939
R.R. Silver Cloud & Bentley 'S' Series Gold P. 1955-1965
Rolls Royce Silver Shadow Gold Portfolio 1965-1980
Rolls Royce & Bentley Gold Portfolio 1980-1989
Rolls Royce & Bentley Limited Edition 1990-1997
Rover P4 1949-1959
Rover 3 & 3.5 Litre Gold Portfolio 1958-1973
Rover 2000 & 2200 1963-1977
Rover 3500 & Vitesse 1976-1986
Saab Sonett Collection No.1 1966-1974
Saab Turbo 1976-1983
Studebaker Gold Portfolio 1947-1966
Studebaker Hawks & Larks 1956-1963
Suzuki SJ Gold Portfolio 1971-1997
Vitara, Sidekick & Geo Tracker Perf. Port. 1988-1997
Avanti 1962-1990
Sunbeam Tiger & Alpine Gold Portfolio 1959-1967
Toyota Land Cruiser Gold Portfolio 1956-1987
Toyota Land Cruiser 1988-1997
Toyota MR2 Gold Portfolio 1984-1997
Triumph Dolomite Sprint Limited Edition
Triumph TR2 & TR3 Gold Portfolio 1952-1961
Triumph TR4, TR5, TR250 1961-1968
Triumph TR6 Gold Portfolio 1969-1976
Triumph TR7 & TR8 Gold Portfolio 1975-1982
Triumph Herald 1959-1971
Triumph Vitesse 1962-1971
Triumph Spitfire Gold Portfolio 1962-1980
Triumph 2000, 2.5, 2500 1963-1977
Triumph GT6 Gold Portfolio 1966-1974
Triumph Stag Gold Portfolio 1970-1977
TVR Gold Portfolio 1959-1986
TVR Performance Portfolio 1986-1994
VW Beetle Gold Portfolio 1935-1967
VW Beetle Gold Portfolio 1968-1991
VW Beetle Collection No.1 1970-1982
VW Karmann Ghia 1955-1982
VW Bus, Camper, Van 1954-1967
VW Bus, Camper, Van 1968-1979
VW Bus, Camper, Van 1979-1989
VW Scirocco 1974-1981
VW Golf GTI 1976-1986
Volvo PV444 & PV544 1945-1965
Volvo Amazon-120 Gold Portfolio 1956-1970
Volvo 1800 Gold Portfolio 1960-1973
Volvo 140 & 160 Series Gold Portfolio 1966-1975
Forty Years of Selling Volvo
Westfield Limited Edition

BROOKLANDS *Road & Track* SERIES

Road & Track on Alfa Romeo 1964-1970
Road & Track on Alfa Romeo 1971-1976
Road & Track on Alfa Romeo 1977-1989
Road & Track on Aston Martin 1962-1990
R & T on Auburn Cord and Duesenburg 1952-84
Road & Track on Audi & Auto Union 1952-1980
Road & Track on Audi & Auto Union 1980-1986
Road & Track on Austin Healey 1953-1970
Road & Track on BMW Cars 1966-1974
Road & Track on BMW Cars 1975-1978
Road & Track on BMW Cars 1979-1983
R & T on Cobra, Shelby & Ford GT40 1962-1992
Road & Track on Corvette 1953-1967
Road & Track on Corvette 1968-1982
Road & Track on Corvette 1982-1986
Road & Track on Corvette 1986-1990
Road & Track on Ferrari 1975-1981
Road & Track on Ferrari 1981-1984
Road & Track on Ferrari 1984-1988
Road & Track on Fiat Sports Cars 1968-1987
Road & Track on Jaguar 1950-1960
Road & Track on Jaguar 1961-1968
Road & Track on Jaguar 1968-1974
Road & Track on Jaguar 1974-1982
Road & Track on Jaguar 1983-1989
Road & Track on Lamborghini 1964-1985
Road & Track on Lotus 1972-1983
R & T on Mazda RX-7 & MX-5 Miata 1986-1991
Road & Track on Mercedes 1952-1962
Road & Track on Mercedes 1963-1970
Road & Track on Mercedes 1971-1979
Road & Track on Mercedes 1980-1987
Road & Track on MG Sports Cars 1949-1961
Road & Track on MG Sports Cars 1962-1980
R & T on Nissan 300-ZX & Turbo 1984-1989
Road & Track on Pontiac 1960-1983
Road & Track on Porsche 1951-1967
Road & Track on Porsche 1968-1971
Road & Track on Porsche 1972-1975
Road & Track on Porsche 1975-1978
Road & Track on Porsche 1979-1982
Road & Track on Porsche 1985-1988
R & T on Rolls Royce & Bentley 1950-1965
R & T on Rolls Royce & Bentley 1966-1984
Road & Track on Saab 1972-1992
R & T on Toyota Sports & GT Cars 1966-1984
R & T on Triumph Sports Cars 1953-1967
R & T on Triumph Sports Cars 1967-1974
R & T on Triumph Sports Cars 1974-1982
Road & Track on Volkswagen 1951-1968
Road & Track on Volkswagen 1968-1978
Road & Track on Volkswagen 1978-1985
Road & Track on Volvo 1957-1974
Road & Track on Volvo 1977-1994
R & T - Henry Manney at Large & Abroad
R & T - Peter Egan's "Side Glances"
R & T - Peter Egan "At Large"

BROOKLANDS *Car and Driver* SERIES

Car and Driver on BMW 1955-1977
Car and Driver on Corvette 1978-1982
Car and Driver on Corvette 1983-1988
C and D on Datsun Z 1600 & 2000 1966-1984
Car and Driver on Ferrari 1955-1962
Car and Driver on Ferrari 1963-1975
Car and Driver on Ferrari 1976-1983
Car and Driver on Mopar 1956-1967
Car and Driver on Mopar 1968-1975
Car and Driver on Mustang 1964-1972
Car and Driver on Pontiac 1961-1975
Car and Driver on Porsche 1955-1962
Car and Driver on Porsche 1963-1970
Car and Driver on Porsche 1970-1976
Car and Driver on Porsche 1977-1981
Car and Driver on Porsche 1982-1986
Car and Driver on Volvo 1955-1986

RACING

Le Mans - The Bentley & Alfa Years - 1923-1939
Le Mans - The Jaguar Years - 1949-1957
Le Mans - The Ferrari Years - 1958-1965
Le Mans - The Ford & Matra Years - 1966-1974
Le Mans - The Porsche Years - 1975-1982
Mille Miglia - The Alfa & Ferrari Years - 1927-1951
Mille Miglia - The Ferrari & Mercedes Years - 1952-57

A COMPREHENSIVE GUIDE

BMW 2002

BROOKLANDS *Practical Classics* SERIES

PC on Austin A40 Restoration
PC on Land Rover Restoration
PC on Metalworking in Restoration
PC on Midget/Sprite Restoration
PC on MGB Restoration
PC on Sunbeam Rapier Restoration
PC on Triumph Herald/Vitesse
PC on Spitfire Restoration

BROOKLANDS *Hot Rod* 'MUSCLECAR & HI-PO ENGINES' SERIES

Chevy 265 & 283
Chevy 302 & 327
Chevy 348 & 409
Chevy 350 & 400
Chevy 396 & 427
Chevy 454 thru 512
Chrysler Hemi
Chrysler 273, 318, 340 & 360
Chrysler 361, 383, 400, 413, 426, 440
Ford 289, 302, Boss 302 & 351W
Ford 351C & Boss 351
Ford Big Block

BROOKLANDS RESTORATION SERIES

Auto Restoration Tips & Techniques
Basic Bodywork Tips & Techniques
BMW 2002 Restoration Guide
Classic Camaro Restoration
Chevrolet High Performance Tips & Techniques
Chevy Engine Swapping Tips & Techniques
Chevy-GMC Pickup Repair
Chrysler Engine Swapping Tips & Techniques
Engine Swapping Tips & Techniques
Ford Pickup Repair
Land Rover Restoration Tips & Techniques
MG 'T' Series Restoration Guide
MGA Restoration Guide
Mustang Restoration Tips & Techniques

MOTORCYCLING

BROOKLANDS ROAD TEST SERIES

AJS & Matchless Gold Portfolio 1945-1966
BMW Motorcycles Gold Portfolio 1950-1971
BMW Motorcycles Gold Portfolio 1971-1976
BSA Singles Gold Portfolio 1945-1963
BSA Singles Gold Portfolio 1964-1974
BSA Twins A7 & A10 Gold Portfolio 1946-1962
BSA Twins A50 & A65 Gold Portfolio 1962-1973
BSA & Triumph Triples Gold Portfolio 1968-1976
Ducati Gold Portfolio 1960-1973
Ducati Gold Portfolio 1974-1978
Ducati Gold Portfolio 1978-1982
Honda CB750 Gold Portfolio 1969-1978
Laverda Gold Portfolio 1967-1977
Moto Guzzi Gold Portfolio 1949-1973
Norton Commando Gold Portfolio 1968-1977
Triumph Bonneville Gold Portfolio 1959-1983
Vincent Gold Portfolio 1945-1980

BROOKLANDS *Cycle World* SERIES

Cycle World on BMW 1974-1980
Cycle World on BMW 1981-1986
Cycle World on Ducati 1982-1991
Cycle World on Harley-Davidson 1962-1968
Cycle World on Harley-Davidson 1978-1983
Cycle World on Harley-Davidson 1983-1987
Cycle World on Harley-Davidson 1987-1990
Cycle World on Harley-Davidson 1990-1992
Cycle World on Honda 1962-1967
Cycle World on Honda 1968-1971
Cycle World on Honda 1971-1974
Cycle World on Husqvarna 1966-1976
Cycle World on Husqvarna 1977-1984
Cycle World on Kawasaki 1966-1971
Cycle World on Kawasaki Off-Road Bikes 1972-1979
Cycle World on Kawasaki Street Bikes 1972-1976
Cycle World on Norton 1962-1971
Cycle World on Suzuki 1962-1970
Cycle World on Suzuki Off-Road Bikes 1971-1976
Cycle World on Suzuki Street Bikes 1971-1976
Cycle World on Triumph 1967-1972
Cycle World on Yamaha 1962-1969
Cycle World on Yamaha Off-Road Bikes 1970-1974
Cycle World on Yamaha Street Bikes 1970-1974

MILITARY

BROOKLANDS MILITARY VEHICLES SERIES

Allied Military Vehicles No.2 1941-1946
Complete WW2 Military Jeep Manual
Dodge Military Vehicles No.1 1940-1945
Hail To The Jeep
Military & Civilian Amphibians 1940-1990
Off Road Jeeps: Civilian & Military 1944-1971
US Military Vehicles 1941-1945
US Army Military Vehicles WW2-TM9-2800
VW Kubelwagen Military Portfolio 1940-1990
WW2 Jeep Military Portfolio 1941-1945

27048

CONTENTS

ACKNOWLEDGEMENTS

Honda's reputation grew enormously during the late 60's and one of the reasons for this leap forward was the magnificent 4 cylinder CB750 which has gone on to become one of the most sought-after Japanese motorcycles and which is now a confirmed classic.

Regular readers of Brooklands books will know that titles like this one are an attempt to create a living archive and to make available to enthusiasts literature about their bikes which, due to time, has become hard to find. In compiling such books as these we depend on the generosity and understanding of the original writers, photographers and of course the publishers of the original journals whose copyright material is reprinted here. In this instance our thanks go to the management of *Bike, Classic Mechanics, Cycle, Cycle Australia, Cycle Buyers Guide, Cycle Guide, Cycle World, Motor Cycle Mechanics, Motorcycle Sport, Motorcyclist, Motorcyclist Illustrated, Popular Cycling* and *Two Wheels* for their continued support.

R M Clarke

The Honda Motor Company was founded in 1948 in Japan by Soichiro Honda who was the son of a blacksmith. He was the manufacturer of piston rings and saw the opportunity to manufacture cheap powered bicycles for a transport starved public. The piston ring company was sold and bicycles fitted with a 50cc clip-on engine that ran on turpentine were put into production by the new company. These motorised bicycles were a great success, so the ambitious and forward thinking Soichiro began to have ideas for even larger machines.

During the 1950's, he produced a variety of very good machines that were influenced by German technology, and for the time, looked incredibly old fashioned. There was a good deal of NSU ideology to be seen in the mid to late fifties products but by 1958 significant changes were taking place in Honda's ultra modern factories. The machines coming off the assembly lines were now more advanced than many a European design and Soichiro Honda decided to go motorcycle racing, in particular on the Isle of Man at the TT.

During the first part of the 1960's, ultra modern roadsters of 50cc, 124cc, 250cc and 305cc were produced in huge numbers and exported all over the world. A range of fabulous racing bikes of multicylinder configuration were developed with the fours and sixes, with their in-line across-the-frame layout, beating all the opposition and setting the style for the roadsters of the future. A twin cylinder double overhead camshaft twin called the CB450 Dragon appeared in 1965 hinting at racing technology. It alarmed European manufacturers but it was rather expensive and did not sell very well, much to their temporary relief.

The future truly arrived in 1968 at the Tokyo Motor Show when, after some three years of speculation, Honda announced not a 500/4 as had been expected, but a 750cc 4 cylinder model. The machine had the air-cooled in-line across-the-frame engine layout that was to become a classic with overhead camshaft and a hydraulically operated disc front brake. The world gasped as this was the stuff of which racing bikes were made of and yet it was affordable although not cheap.

In twenty short years, Soichiro Honda had not only moved on from antiquated mopeds to four cylinder technological marvels, but had now written a new chapter in the history of the motorcycle. From now on, motorcycling would never be the same again and where Honda led, the rest of the world would follow. It couldn't afford not to.

Tony Eldridge

Not for the kiddies

Production due to start "mid-March": Honda U.K. expect to import probably not more than 100 a year: Initial batch will number about 12: Distribution of 750 (and 450) through restricted number of dealers

THE long-awaited four-cylinder Honda 750 will be displayed to the British public for the first time at the Brighton Motor Cycle Show which opens on Saturday, April 5. There will be two machines on the Honda stand, one being part of a mobile display, the other standing at floor level. After its appearance at the Tokyo Show last November the 750-4 has had frequent mentions in the motor-cycle enthusiast and trade press, but only now has one been made available in the U.K. for close inspection.

The first impression is of formidable size—such as to make one of the new 450s standing alongside appear almost of mini-bike dimensions. The engine, of course, is the most interesting feature of the bike. Honda's knowledge acquired in the production of multi-cylinder racing engines has been put into this new power unit. The four cylinders are set across the frame, the whole of the engine bay being quite tightly packed, the cam covers close to the lower edge of the fuel tank, while the four Kei-Hin carburettors plus air box fill in the space back from the engine to the glass-fibre battery cover and tool box.

Power output from the 736 c.c. (61mm x 63mm) o.h.c. unit is claimed to be 67 b.h.p. Compression ratio is 9:1 and maximum r.p.m. quoted are 8,500. In top gear, speed of the 750-4 at 8,000 r.p.m. is said by Honda Tokyo to be 125 m.p.h. This engine has plain steel-backed shell bearings for the five main-bearing crankshaft, with dry-sump lubrication, the oil reservoir being situated

on the offside just below the dual seat. Capacity of the system is six pints. Four separate exhaust pipes curve smoothly beneath the crankcase and gearbox (two going each side) and merge into two megaphone silencers, one above the other, that angle up along side the rear hub.

The five-speed gearbox has a left-foot-operated shift. A massive 12in disc brake on the front wheel is operated by handle-bar ball-ended lever coupled to a small reservoir and master cylinder mounted alongside the brake lever on the handle-bar. This gives direct mechanical action throughout the operating system to the master cylinder; from there the hydraulics take over to apply the pads to the disc. Rear-wheel braking is taken care of by an 8½in drum with single leading shoe operated by right-foot pedal.

The double-cradle frame carries a pivoted rear fork with coil-spring damper units angled slightly forward. Front forks are telescopic with rubber gaiters preventing ingress of dirt or water. The wide, sweeping handlebars on the machines shown at Brighton are fitted in the U.S. market, but before deciding on whether or not these will be the ones for this country some discussion will take place between Honda U.K. and dealers and prospective owners.

A pear-shaped fuel tank with large filler is finished in a special paint with contrasting lines on the base colour (most of which are a metallic paint). The quilted dual seat, which on "stationary" test at least proves to be very comfortable, has a chrome trim strip around its lower edge; the rear edge tilts up slightly to give the pillion passenger better location.

Large-face (5in diameter) instruments are angled towards the ride; the speedometer, on the left-hand side, reads up to 150 m.p.h., the matching tachometer registers to 11,000 r.p.m., the red band starting at 8,500. Car-size winkers are placed front and rear, with small reflectors in two positions on each side of the machine.

6

THE ULTIMATE

Well finished castings are used throughout the engine. The oil filter can be seen between the center pipes.

A 150 mph speedo and an 11,000 rpm tach are standard equipment on the four. Both are easily read.

WHENEVER A NEW model comes to the surface, everybody quickly jumps on the bandwagon and wants to see, feel, ride and talk about it. Without a doubt, the new 750 Honda will be the center of attention for some time to come.

Although produced in Japan, the 750 is an American motorcycle. It's big, it's fast, and it's flashy. It would seem these are the prerequisites for success in the U.S. motorcycle market today. Americans like big machines, and make no mistake about it — the Honda four is big. It doesn't fall into the H-D 74 category, but it is nonetheless a very large motorcycle.

As might be expected, the four is not light, it tips the scales at over 500 pounds. This immediately takes it out of the bike-for-the-little lady category. However, it has muscle and large quantities to boot but more about this later. This over 500 pound figure doesn't come as any big shock when you see the machine, as the bike looks so large. Regardless of what the Honda weighs,

you wouldn't guess the weight once you're under way.

A good portion of the weight vanishes the minute you release the clutch and move away. The factory has done an excellent job of keeping the major portion of the weight low. The end result is a machine that feels quite comfortable both at high speed on the freeway, and at the same time manageable in heavy traffic.

The decision to install four cylinders is

a natural one. Honda has had a great deal of experience in working with motorcycles that utilize a transverse four-cylinder layout. There are those who will question the wisdom of using that many cylinders. One thing remains very evident. In order to extract more power from a given displacement, the choice to go to more cylinders is a wise one.

By keeping the reciprocating parts as light as possible, the rev limit can be raised. Obviously, the pistons, rods and

7

All four carburetors are operated through this series of shafts and rods. Much better than conventional cables.

With the seat raised, the electrics are exposed for checking or servicing. Oil tank cap can also be seen.

After removing the tank and seat you can see just how neat and compact the entire powerplant installation is.

valve gear on a twin are going to weigh more than those used in a four. Not half perhaps, but still substantially less. It is also quite obvious that Honda has done an admirable job in reducing the reciprocating weight to a very low figure. The four will rev quite happily to 9500 RPM should the occasion demand it.

The sound the engine makes while doing this sort of thing can only be compared to what you might hear on a recording of the Isle of Man during TT week. It's out of sight. A real mind bender. If you like motorcycles, the sound will fascinate you.

Like us, you too will sit there blipping the throttle just to hear that works-racer-like sound. Silky, throaty and vibrant, all at the same time — if you can imagine that. In the future perhaps this sound will be commonplace and for this we're sad. For this is one of the most exciting sounding machines to be offered to the public in many years.

The four has been in the works for quite awhile. They are still licking their wounds after the 450 episode. We won't go into this now, just to say that Honda

has not forgotten the experience with the early 450. (The later 450's were as desirable a machine as any we've ridden, but unfortunately the die had been cast in most people's minds.)

They have waited until the machine was right before exposing it to the American public, and press, for our evaluation. While subsequent machines may have a slightly different gas tank shape, or perhaps the color scheme may be a wee bit different, you can bet the old heirlooms that the Honda factory is going to deliver a bike to your local dealer that is pretty well identical to the machine we rode.

Contrary to many so-called "expert" opinions, the four is not merely two bored out 350 twins stuck together. It is a brand new engine from the ground up. The output is rated at a whopping 75 horses at 9500 RPM. Honda has enjoyed the reputation of being far more factual in their advertising data than a goodly number of other manufacturers, both Oriental and otherwise.

Due to limited time we had the 750, we didn't have the opportunity to get drag strip ET slips, or run the machine flat out; however, we'll go out on a limb and say that the 750 will run a strong 120 to 125 MPH (possibly more) anytime the rider wishes to do so.

Now, a lot of people may be thinking, "Big deal. My bike will go that fast."

These four mufflers make beautiful music. They are raised to prevent grounding while cornering.

The hydraulic front disc brake is operated from the usual place. Check that extremely compact unit.

The large front disc is bolted to the attractive aluminum hub. Brake does an excellent job, even though it needs to!

You're right, but you're forgetting one very important fact. While the Honda 750 will top out somewhere in the 120 range, what is really shattering is just how fast it will get you there. We'll go out on our limb even further and say the 750 will run in the middle to high twelves, providing (spelled with a capital P), the machine is in tune and the rider knows what it's all about.

Like a number of other Honda products, the valves are operated via a single overhead cam layout. Upon removing the seat you'll immediately notice four 26 mm carburetors that are opened and closed simultaneously through the use of a cross-shaft and connecting rods. This is far more practical than having four individual cables. Once adjusted, the carburetors stay adjusted. This is no small accomplishment considering all the hassle we see created trying to keep just two carburetors in adjustment!

Externally the powerplant is quite clean and uncluttered in appearance. Honda has done an excellent job in keeping the overall appearance of the four so smooth looking. We frankly expected to find more plumbing and cables than we did. This cleanliness in design extends to the rest of the machine as well.

At first glance, the front disc brake is of Gargantuan proportions. When you consider the performance of the Honda 750, you quickly realize that with something this fast you had better have something in the way of some pretty good stoppers. This is why the need for a large front brake (it's almost twelve inches). It's a hydraulic unit that has the master cylinder and filler incorporated into the handlebars.

It does its job quite well. A rider on a

machine weighing over 500 pounds, hurtling down the road at over a hundred must be confident that his brakes will haul him down to a safe stop. Honda brakes have always been first rate, so we have no reason to believe the new one will be any different.

One thing that is different is the use of a separate oil tank. Up to now Honda has used a wet sump design, but with the four cylinder 750, more oil was needed to take care of the engine's innards. If Honda had chosen to continue with the wet sump design, the bottom of the engine would have been considerably lower. Ground clearance would have been substantially reduced.

Contrary to what many think, the addition of a separate oil tank will do very little, if anything at all, toward keeping the oil any cooler. A number of people have the mistaken idea that a dry sump engine is a cool running proposition. Not so. With the separate oil tank, you're taking that hot lump of oil from the bottom of the engine and putting it into another container. The addition of an oil cooler in warmer weather wouldn't be a bad idea.

We're looking forward to seeing what John Everyman thinks of the new 750. We liked it very much, but then we like big, fast, flashy roadburners that will cruise at an honest hundred, handle like they're on rails and stop well in the bargain.

Our guess is that one ride on the four will hook you. If touring is your bag, or if you're just looking for a machine that you can cruise through the local drive-in with, then look no further. (You custom fans should have a ball with this one.)

The Honda four is impressive, standing still, or at a hundred packing double. It even has an electric starter — status seekers, thrill seekers and motorcycling enthusiasts look no further — the Ultimate has arrived. ■

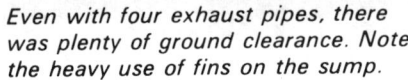

Even with four exhaust pipes, there was plenty of ground clearance. Note the heavy use of fins on the sump.

We found the starter lurking under a cover behind the cylinders. Starting was instantaneous.

Riding the four is a unique experience. Lots of power, good handling and adequate brakes are the 750's hallmark.

Honda 750 Four

Honda performance. Honda styling. Honda warranty. 24 models. Biggest line in the business. And now the Honda 750 Four. Nobody else offers so much. And what about all those nice people?

Honda 750 Four Specifications			
Engine	736cc single overhead cam Four cylinder	Max. Speed	125 mph
Horsepower	68 @ 8,500 rpm	Quarter Mile	12.6 sec.
Weight	445 lbs.	Compression	9.0:1
Trans/Ratios	5-speed, 13.4; 9.2; 7.1; 5.9; 4.9	Tires	3.25/19 front 4.00/18 rear

See the "Invisible Circle" film at your Honda dealer's. Pick up a color brochure and safety pamphlet or write: American Honda Motor Co., Inc., Box 50, Gardena, Calif. 90247.

HONDA

Honda 750cc Four

At last someone's done it and it's as good as it should have been. No factor in fast, comfortable, safe cycling has been overlooked in making the Four.

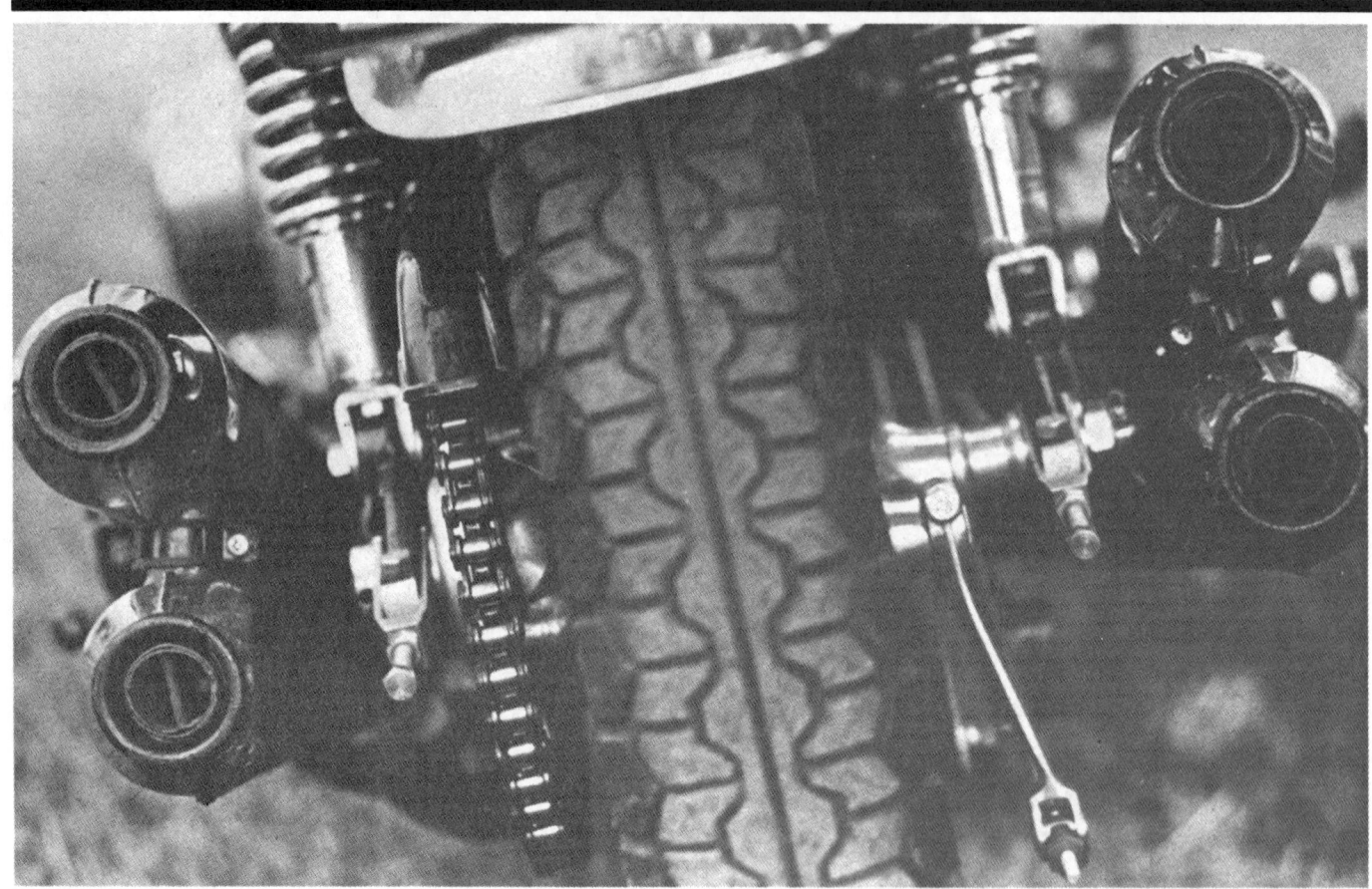

● Sometimes we get the feeling that in the ten years or so that they've been producing motorcycles for this market, Honda has been groping—trying to find the kind of motorcycle that would make the motorcycle enthusiast *really* enthusiastic, and trying without much success. Each successive model has been better than the one before, and there is not much in the performance of Honda's components that one can reasonably fault. But Honda has not, until now, built a real grabber. Their CL77 sold in vast numbers, and started the whole "street scrambler" trend, *without* making anyone really jump for joy. Those high pipes looked jazzy, and you could use the bike out in the rough if you didn't try to push too hard, but while the CL77 gave good service, it somehow lacked that old zing. Maybe because the CL77 tried to be all things to all men.

No effort is made to make the 750 seem like something it isn't. The 750 Four, very definitely is made to travel long distances—fast, safely, and comfortably. No high pipes, skid plates, puny gas tanks or any of that.

What the Four has is refined, functional engineering features—features that were developed to perform first, and then made acceptable in terms of styling. There's nothing really startling in the first visual impression of the Four. Nothing jumps immediately forward to grab you by the lapels and scream Living-Theater shock words. No hard sell. It's real, *all real.*

Two things made me suspect the nature of this new Honda from the first "sneak" photos that fluttered across my desk: that big disc brake on the front wheel and the uncommon amount of ground clearance. The clearance isn't all vertical, either. If you look at a

head-on photo of the front or rear of the bike, you'll see that the hardware such as exhaust pipes, stands, pedals, and footrests are tucked around the frame tubes and against the engine cases as tightly as possible. A silhouette view from the front would show that the hardware is contained within the legs of a shallow *V*, with an apex just below the crankcase. Imagine going around a sharp off-camber bend at 80 mph or so and running over a bump or drainage culvert. On most big touring bikes you wouldn't even have to hit the bump before the center stand or exhaust pipes would be dragging. On the 750, you've got to be well into racing speeds before you can get the side stand and left footrest to touch on fast bumpy curves; I never touched anything on the right side.

I didn't know what to expect when I walked up to the Four for the first time. It

12

Honda's Gran Prix experience with cycles and formula 1 cars has given rise to the techniques needed to develop and build this ultimate bike.

Incredible smoothness and flexibility coupled with the most powerful standard engine made.

could have felt heavy and awkward with a soft, squashy suspension, despite visual hints to the contrary. There could have been no authority behind the exciting specifications. I sat on that wide soft seat and eyed the electric turn signals suspiciously while Honda Service Rep Bob Young filled me in on the machine's development history and technical features. By the time it was opportune to take a first ride, the suspense had set off a flight of butterflies in my stomach.

You reach down with your right hand to turn on the double-spigoted fuel valve, just under the rear of the tank. If the engine's cold, lift the choke lever on the left carb. The ignition main switch is mounted on a frame gusset under the left front edge of the fuel tank. All the way counter-clockwise is off: back one click to start the engine. Up on the throttle grip assembly, there's another ignition control switch with three positions. Either way from the middle position is off. Push the little starter-button under the throttle housing, and out comes the sweetest motorcycle sound you'll ever want to hear. Like a street-tamed Offy with mufflers. As with most Hondas, this one's a little cold natured; she likes to warm up before the engine seems eager. A couple of minutes on half choke for a cool spring morning and the idle becomes velvety smooth.

Throttle response is absolutely instantaneous: twist the grip slightly, and the tachometer needle swings wildly around the dial. With four cylinders to provide the power pulses to the crankshaft at every 180 degrees of its rotation, not much flywheel is needed—or provided. Clutch lever operation is very light and smooth. Push down one notch on the left-mounted foot pedal for first gear and feed the clutch lever back out as you gingerly

open the twist grip. All clumsiness caused by the 750's weight vanishes once you begin to roll.

We headed north out of Los Angeles on 101 and then took Coast Road 1 at San Luis Obispo. In the group were the Four, a Kawasaki Three, and a Kawasaki 350 Twin. You might be interested to know that the Three is faster up to 90 mph, to the tune of about 50 feet in a 0-90 run, but then the Four overtakes and continues to pull away from 100 mph up to its maximum of 130. It was getting dark by the time we got to San Simeon and the road began to look and feel like a roller coaster track. What else could we do but settle into a road race on the deserted highway?

Difficulties arise in describing how well the Four handles while going very fast on twisting, unfamiliar roads. It takes a while before the senses really believe what you can do with a bike that is as heavy as the 750. For me, it was like drinking a stout shot of Dr. Jekyll's magic juice. Only instead of hairy Mr. Hyde crouched in the saddle, there emerged a more Hailwood-like demon with a plastic Buco chin jutting into the black night. The speedo-needle climbs incredibly quickly to 90 in third gear at the slightest hint of a straight section in the pavement, until the farsighted automotive sealed-beam headlight (SAE #6012) reveals another one of those dead-snake-in-the-road-type curve warning signs At 8600 rpm, those four muffled reverse-cone megaphones wail maliciously. I came closer and closer to each sign as I learned to trust the disc brake and feel its grip on the road through the tire.

You have to pull very hard on the lever to obtain maximum braking. Even with the front wheel moaning slightly as it hits small ripples

in the road, the feel through the lever is so direct that you can roll the throttle with your palm to facilitate down shifting without fear of locking the wheel. The rear brake is very sensitive to pedal pressure during panic stops. Since the front brake is so powerful, even more weight than usual is transferred to the front wheel under heavy braking. Until I got used to pulling very hard on the front brake and pushing very, very softly on the rear brake, the rear wheel would lock and bounce violently.

Releasing the brakes, handle-barring the bike into the turn, and winding the throttle back open produces no surprises: no wobbles or lurches or sudden bursts of power to the rear wheel. Nothing of the machine distracts from your attention to the road. Noticeable vibration is almost nil. None of your parts that touch the footrests, seat, gas tank, or handlebars are numbed to sleep.

Riding along that tortuous road, I began to experiment with steering techniques. The Four is a different motorcycle. Its weight distribution and steering provide handling that I have never before found in a big road bike. But there's more weight to distribute than on a light, powerful bike, and you have to ride it differently. When you're ready to enter a turn, say to the right, you push directly horizontal and forward on the right handlebar grip and pull directly back on the left. Try that on a light bike at high speeds and sooner or later you'll get the front wheel into a terrifying wobble or slide.

More than a small share of the Four's cornering power must be derived from the use of excellent tires. They're new Dunlops, made in Japan. The front is designated F-3; the rear K-87. The tires are obviously designed to withstand sustained high speeds. The bike was virtually new (200 mi) when I picked it up in Gardena. The rubber was scarcely touched, but tread depth on both front and rear was only three-sixteenths of an inch. This is done for two reasons: at 130 mph, a thick-treaded heavy tire will build up tremendous amounts of heat from the internal flexing of the rubber and when the heat reaches a critical level, the tread will separate from the cord and be flung off from the centrifugal force; also, under hard acceleration, the Honda's 44 lb/ft of torque is multiplied by a factor of 14 in low gear. If one makes many second-gear power shifts with a normal tire, the tread cleats would start to fold under and be torn away from the carcass. But if normal tire rubber were used in the Four's special tires, the thin tread would wear too fast. To regain the traction lost in using hard rubber, Dunlop has resorted to using a very intricate tread pattern. On the rear where forward traction is required, there are lots of very thin, shallow, W-shaped slits on the tread blocks. Each slit presents an edge to grip the pavement. With

Soundly conceived, ingeniously designed and meticulously developed, this newest multi opens a new era in really satisfying road/sport bikes.

all these edges, the hard, thin tire works wonderfully well.

Suspension on the Four is firm without being rough. Since the unsprung weight is no higher than on bikes weighing 200 lb less, the proportion of suspension movement to chassis ditto is very high. That way, you don't feel the bumps as much. I never felt any shock absorber or fork oscillation caused by insufficient damping rates. The shocks are the DeCarbon type first seen on the 450 KL models, and have the shock-absorbing fluid separated from the volume-compensating gas by an elastic membrane. This keeps the fluid from becoming aerated, which would lead to erratic shock action and bad handling. I haven't had a chance to look inside the front forks yet, but by their superb reaction to road irregularities, I'd say that Honda has been doing lots of basic research in this area; perhaps the days of Honda's notoriously poor bump control are over.

With a 210-watt generator and a 14 amp/hr battery, Honda could have chosen any lighting system they wished without fear of straining the system. The sealed-beam they used is the automotive type that throws a flat, wide pattern. This is fine for cars since they don't ever lean—not temporarily at least, I found when I threw the bike from one direction to the opposite on the twisty road, the lean of the machine would direct the beam half that was on the inside of the turn up in the air and leave a dark spot. One of those sealed-beams with a plain, sharp-focusing spot in the center of the lens would probably work better.

When we pulled into the Big Sur to let the two-strokes gas up again, the station proprietor warned of high winds and deer and police ahead. So we cooled it on into the populated area to spend the night. Just before Pacific Grove, where the road runs along a high bluff over the sea, we found the high wind. The big Honda's extra weight really adds to stability in strong side winds. The guys riding the lighter bikes definitely had to fight the strong gusts.

Cruising along the next morning, we passed through Hollister on Route 156. This is the town that was terrorized by a couple of motorcycle gangs years ago and prompted the movie *The Wild Ones*. We didn't even get any really hard looks, so I guess it's all blown over. I did keep an eye peeled all the way through town, though. The Four's standard equipment mirrors are good for keeping track of overtaking traffic. I never had used dual mirrors before, but wouldn't be without them now. The 750 is one of the few machines on which vibration doesn't render the mirrors useless at highway cruising speeds.

Another of the Four's standard features that I was at first dubious of is the flashing turn signal. While looking for the Infamous

Byron Black's place in Fresno, we got a little lost in rush-hour traffic. Those signal lights seem to reassure car drivers. You can almost feel the anxiety in the look of a hostile motorist. It may be a slight fear of the cycle's extreme mobility. At any rate, drivers seemed to be much more relaxed around the Honda with its signals working than when I was riding one of the other bikes.

That night at Black's place, conversation naturally centered around the Four. A lot of Black's students of Linguistics at Fresno State College are motorcyclists and, at word of the Four's arrival, a group arrived—fairly bristling with questions about what went on inside all those aluminum cases.

Although basically quite straightforward and orthodox in principle, the single overhead cam engine and five-speed gearbox show fresh new answers to layout problems and painstaking development in making the answers work reliably.

Following the Honda twin cylinder cycling and automotive practice, the Four's crankcase is split horizontally with the seam running through the centers of the crankshaft and transmission mainshaft. Thirty capscrews pull the crankcase halves together top to bottom, with lots more holding the side-mounted breaker points, starter-generator, clutch, and gear-selector mechanism covers.

Whatever problems kept Honda's Gran Prix car from success apparently had nothing to do with its plain-bearing crankshaft, for the practice is continued in the Four. Beside vastly simplifying the assembly and lowering the cost, the plain-bearing crank proved virtuous in performance as well.

By using modern forging techniques, Honda is able to make the crankshaft from one piece of steel and, by carefully developed tool design, arrange the granular structure of the steel to pre-conform to the mechanical stresses that it will get in the engine. The connecting rod journals are arranged so that the four cylinders are a pair of 180-degree twins: the outside cylinders are at top center, and fire on alternate strokes, with the middle pair in a like relationship. The five main bearing journals are carried by thin-wall bearings in massive webs cast in the aluminum alloy crankcases.

By using a forged instead of cast crankshaft, the main bearing and rod journals can, in the interest of low friction, be held to their rather small 36mm diameter to maintain the needed strength. The plain-bearing rods are surprisingly thin *H*-sectioned forgings with the big-end split along its center line, giving a detachable cap. By using the very strong lightweight crankshaft and rods rigidly supported as they are in the five main bearings, the Four lives happily at its 8500 rpm peak.

Dual primary transmission and single camshaft drive sprockets are machined into the

Compact forged steel crankshaft with five main bearings allows engine to live happily at 8500 rpm peak

Flexibly mounted individual carburetors and carefully tuned inlet port flow capacity boost the Four's power

Handlebar-mounted front disc brake master cylinder is biggest contribution to sensitive feel of hand lever

Big twelve-inch disc and self-adjusting caliper give fantastically powerful braking to nearly 500-pound bike

dical shape of combustion chamber is the result sophisticated research in power/emission control.

The valve-train: more moving parts than ever before, yet compact, easy to service, and very strong.

Heavily finned crankcase provides great rigidity. Removed sump cover shows bottom of oil pump

Primary drive chains are at center of crankshaft. Bottom case in foreground shows gear selector.

here's only one way to know the real effect of even the most carefully calculated engineering scheme: ke the machine out on the road and try to get from one place to another as fast as possible, safely.

Powerful 210-watt alternator rotor is vented to pass magnetic field of DC exciting charge coil.

ew ball-and-ramp throw-out bearing and faster rning clutch give easier, more gradual control.

Handily-mounted micronic oil filter is fast and easy to change. Being in air stream helps cool oil.

Breaker points and condensers are mounted on end of crank for easy checking of ignition timing.

15

The Four gives no bogus thrill: no emotional noise,
Visual or audible. There aren't any distracting performance
Substitutes. The Four's joy is quickest found by the expert.

crankshaft between the center main bearing and number-three crank web. The cam-drive chain goes straight up through a passage between the center cylinders to the camshaft drive sprocket. This sprocket is bolted to the one-piece camshaft casting. Four plain pillow bearings support the camshaft, one at each end and one at both sides of the drive sprocket. Each pair of support bearings is actually part of an integral casting that is bolted to the cylinder head and carries the rocker-arm pivot spindles as well. Rocker-arm and cam lobe rubbing surfaces are lubricated by oil squirted from orifices drilled in a supply gallery in the bearing housing. Camshaft support bearings are pressure-fed.

In an effort to keep engine width as narrow as possible, the cylinder bores are kept to a relatively small 60mm (stroke 63mm). In order to use valves big enough to develop the desired power, some trickery was required to keep the inlet and exhaust valve heads from hitting each other on "overlap." The problem was solved by offsetting the valves slightly each way from the center of the combustion chamber.

It is fairly well known that Honda Research and Development has some quite sophisticated basic research equipment to inquire into the mysteries of cylinder breathing and combustion. Test engines are rigged on a dynamometer with electronic pressure sensors attached to such critical spots as inlet and exhaust ports, combustion chamber, and crankcase. Amounts of gasoline and air entering the engine and qualities of gas leaving are carefully metered. A high-speed movie camera takes pictures inside the combustion chamber through a quartz window. All of this information is fed to an integrating computer which breaks down the process into quantitative data for each degree of crankshaft rotation in the power cycle. By having such instant feedback, Mr. Yagi and his staff can make developments in days that would take years in a less well-equipped lab.

Once the one-piece cylinder head casting is removed, it is extremely difficult to guess where cause gave over to effect in the development of the combustion chamber. The side-stepped valve heads seat down in very smoothly funneling pockets that flair slowly from concavities to convexities as their loci meet. The pockets are obviously gas flow directors, but the effect of the shallow ledge that locates the sparkplug position only Dr. Yagi and his Magic Box know for sure. A sharp-lipped ridge separates the valve heads and runs from the sparkplug hole across

Continued on next page

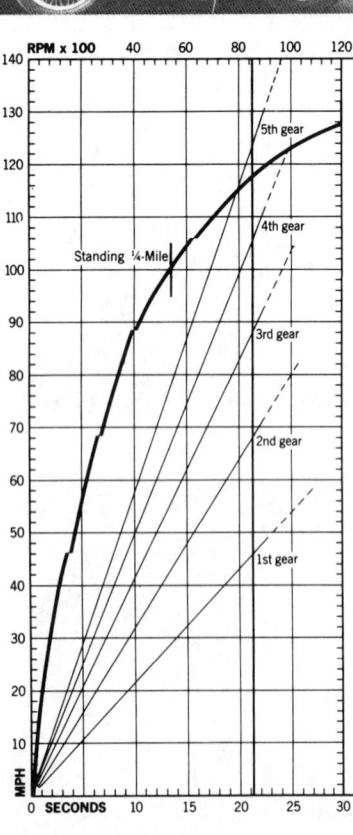

750cc SPORTS TOURER

Price, suggested retail	$1495 East Coast, POE
Tire, front	3.25 in. x 19 in. Dunlop F-3
rear	4.00 in x 18 in. Dunlop K87
Brakes, front	1.625 in. x 11.7 in.
rear	6 in. x 8.75 in.
Brake swept area	73.75 sq. in.
Specific brake loading	8.75 lb./sq. in.
Engine type	Single overhead cam 4-cylinder
Bore and stroke	2.401 in. x 2.480 in., 61 mm x 63 mm
Piston displacement	44.93 cu. in., 736cc
Compression ratio	9:1
Carburetion	(4) 28 mm, Kehin-Seiki
Air filtration	Micronic element
Ignition	Battery-coil
Bhp @ rpm	67 @ 8000
Mph/1000 rpm, top gear	14.6
Fuel capacity	5 gal.
Oil capacity	8 pt.
Lighting	210 watts
Battery	12v, 14 AH
Gear ratios, overall	(1) 14.0 (2) 9.55 (3) 7.45 (4) 6.13 (5) 5.25
Wheelbase	57.3 in. max.
Seat height	34 in. static with rider
Ground clearance	9 in.
Curb weight	485 lb.
Test weight	645 lb.
0-60 mph	5.3 seconds
Standing start ¼ mile	13.496 seconds, 100.11 mph
Top speed	131 mph

between the valves before it dips back up to blend with the chamber side. This lip development contrasts strangely with the currently popular theory that there is a lot of cross flow between the inlet and exhaust valves in a high performance engine. Conspicuously missing are the typical Honda iron skulls cast into the combustion chambers. The valve seats are shrunk into the aluminum.

Feeding each 32mm-diameter inlet valve is a 28mm Keihin standard cylindrical-slide carburetor. Apparently the "idiot-proof" constant velocity carbs were of little benefit on the Four. The carbs are connected to the head stubs with very carefully shaped rubber tubes and to the molded fiberglass air-cleaner box by rubber air-flow bells. Separate control cables lead from each carb to a bobbin-type junction, where a single cable connects them to the twistgrip.

Taking the exhaust gases from the head ports are four individual pipes that sweep gracefully back to their own upswept reverse-cone megaphone. The megaphones are equipped with muffling baffles, and the pairs on each side are connected together with a pressure-sharing tube. Word has it that a lot of experimentation went into the exhaust system development. Sparkplug location was even changed several times to control emission gas quality. Wall thickness on the header pipes was increased to prevent discoloration. The baffles are removable, and that mill makes a genuine R-model sound with them out.

Like the head, the cylinder is a single shell-mold casting. The cylinder liners can be pressed out for replacement. Neoprene-coated rollers and slippers guide the cam chain as it passes through the center of the cylinder block.

The ignition breaker points and condensers are mounted on a backing plate at the right end of the crankshaft under the shiny chrome cover. There are two sets of points, and the breaker cam is driven right off the end of the crankshaft. That means that two plugs fire on every revolution: each cylinder fires a wasted spark on the breathing stroke at bottom center. The points for cylinders one and four are mounted directly to the adjustable backing plate and the other set of points fits on an independently adjustable sub-plate. The method assures spot-on timing for each pair of cylinders. Provision is made to set the timing either with a continuity light, statically; or with a strobe light. The points complete a conventional battery and coil ignition system.

Under the alloy cover on the left end of the crankshaft is the alternator and starter ring-gear. The alternator is unique in the motorcycle field in that it is of the excited field variety. With this setup, the battery regulates the charging rate, much like the automotive system. There are actually two sets of coils, one inside the rotating core and another outside. When battery voltage drops below 12, the regulator charges the inner coil, activating the magnetic field and boosting the charge rate. This alternator is power-rated at a

Power is transmitted to the gearbox countershaft through a pair of primary chains. One side of the countershaft is a neoprene shock-mounted chain sprocket. The countershaft goes through a large roller bearing and connects directly to the outer clutch hub, under the chrome-plated cover that you can see behind the kickstart pedal. The comparatively small speed reduction of 1.7:1 between the crankshaft and clutch permits weak springs to be used, resulting in the Four's light hand-lever pressure. The ball-and-ramp-type throwout bearing is an improvement over the spiral-gear variety found on other Hondas. Clutch engagement is smoothly progressive.

The low gearbox and clutch reduction ratios which allow the use of light components, require further reduction gearing ahead of the output sprocket. A third shaft is mounted behind and driven by the layshaft. This third jackshaft protrudes through to the outside of the gearbox case and turns the drive sprocket.

All of the juggling with the power transmission speeds and torque may sound complicated, but it was necessary in order to fit all of the Four's features into such a compact package and have it all perform so well.

Only four bolts fasten the engine directly to the frame, once the exhaust pipes, carbs, cables, and wires are removed. With a little practice, a couple of mechanics can have the engine out of the frame, and apart, in an hour. At 176 lb the engine is extremely light for its capabilities, but it still takes two guys to wrestle it up on the work bench.

Several small features on the Honda make it evident that servicability was a design factor. To change the sparkplugs or adjust the tappets, you first have to remove the gas tank. Two minutes is all it takes. Just pull off the fuel hoses, pivot the seat up on its hinges, and slip the tank out of its rubber locating pouch at the rear and off the slotted nubs at the front. Each sparkplug wire is numbered with a plastic band so that it can't be put on the wrong plug. Synchronizing the carbs on the 750 could have been a tedious and agonizing task if it weren't for a handy provision. At the mounting flange of each carb, there is a small screw that covers up a hole in the carb bore. By placing a small vacuum gauge over the holes, one at a time, the idle and cable adjustments can be quickly made to coincide on all four carbs.

Triangular fiberglass covers are quickly detachable, by means of rubber snap-fasteners. The right-side cover forms a heat shield for the oil tank. On the left, removing the cover reveals a clump of electrical components: the voltage regulator, starter solenoid, fuse box, and rectifier. With the gas tank and side panels removed, the entire electrical system is exposed.

With the tank and side covers off, it's easy to see one of the main reasons for the Four's stability and good handling. The massive frame contains enough tubing and box-sectioned gussets to support a small automobile.

In developing the frame and suspension

Honda has used a section of test road that has washboard ripples of varying height and spacing. Weeks of testing on the ripple road destroyed numerous frames before the present layout was settled upon.

Another interesting destruction test was used on the Four, this one developed by Mr. Nakajima, who was over at American Honda for a few years and knows the American rider well. This test involved taking the bike up to 7000 rpm in each gear above first, and then jamming the gearshift lever back into the next lower gear. They cycle was repeated for hours until something failed. When the final prototype was subjected to the Arikawa Skid Test, the rear drive chain was the ultimate failure point in repeated instances. Interestingly enough, an American Diamond chain lasted longer than all the other brands tested.

Several bothersome items came to my attention during a photography trip on the Four through Yosemite. The 750 is a purple thing to get up on the center stand. You have to pull up quite stoutly on the handle near the top of the left shock absorber. Apparently the chain oiling system isn't quite worked out yet, for the oil gets thrown on the mufflers while you're cruising and leaves a big puddle in the drive at night. A totally enclosed chain will probably be the final solution to the problem.

Despite the minor gripes, the Four gave no trouble during the 1300 miles of hard riding that I gave it. The only adjustment necessary was to tighten the rear chain a couple of times. Gas mileage was 27 mpg racing up the coast road and 42 mpg when cruising at a constant 70 mph on route 99. One quart of oil was used, and most of it was lost out of the chain oiler.

The Honda 750 Four is truly *the* motorcycle for the person who wants big bike road stability and the smoothness that only a four-cylinder machine can give. The Four handles like a road racer, is comfortable, and has fantastic brakes. If you don't care about any or all of those qualities, a lesser bike may be what you need—maybe even what you deserve. ◉

HONDA'S FIRE ENGINE

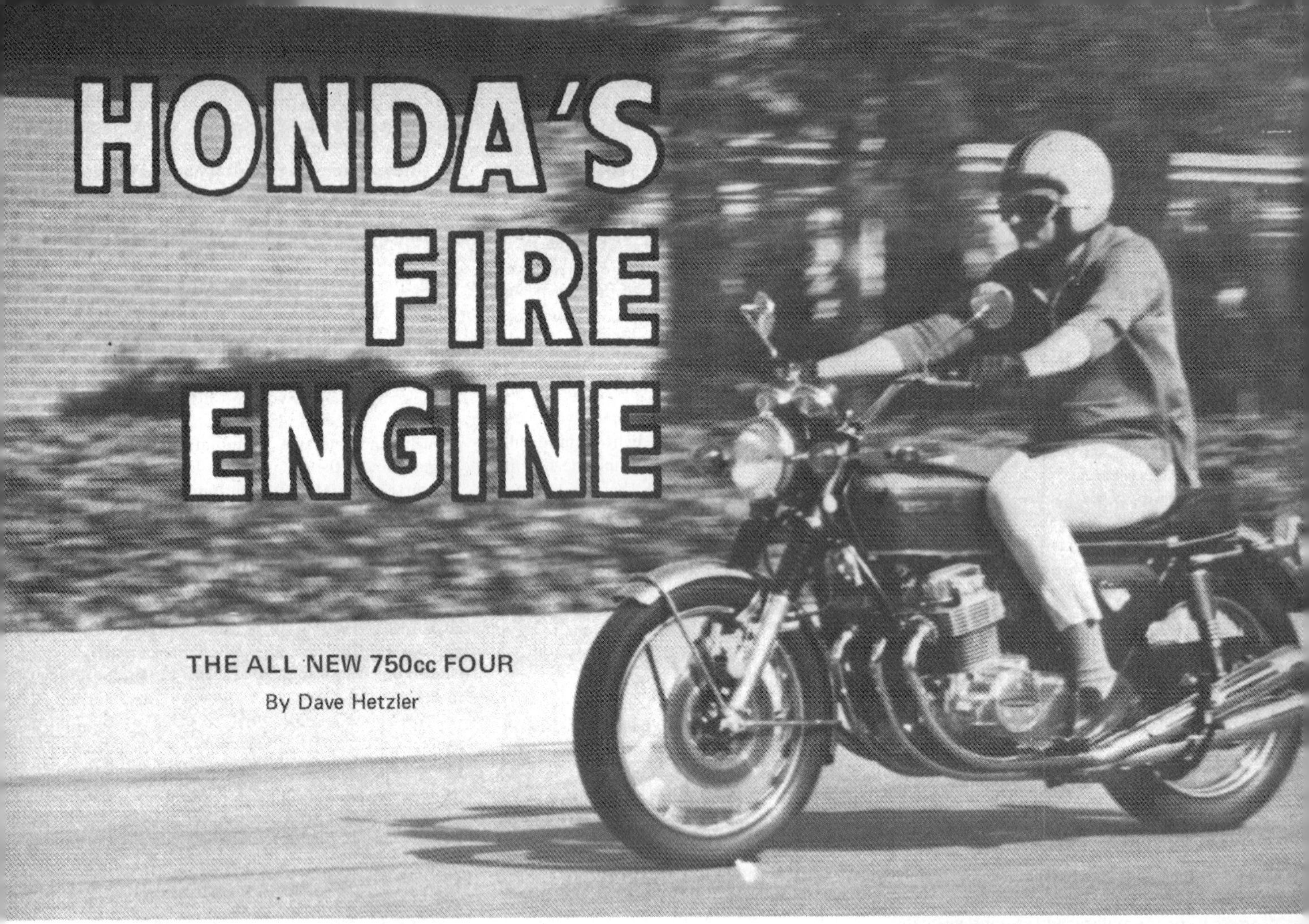

THE ALL NEW 750cc FOUR
By Dave Hetzler

I'm one of the old timers that can remember when the English motorcycles reigned supreme. If you were a member of the "in" group you rode one of the 40 inchers from across the pond. I also remember when in the late '50's the bikes from the land of the rising sun started to hit our shores the word went out, "How can anyone buy that Jap junk". Most motorcycle dealers didn't want the "stuff" in their store. They told their customers not to buy the oriental junk because it would fall apart in less than 5000 miles. We all know now just how wrong they were. On the whole it could be said the Japanese motorcycle industry is by far the most advanced cycle industry in the world. Their automation is comparable to that of Detroit and their product is every bit as good as that coming from the mid-west city.

The industries culmination, to this point, has to be the recently introduced Honda 750cc four cylinder. Without a doubt this is the most advanced street machine ever offered to the motorcycle riding public. Five speed transmission, four cylinders mounted transversely in the frame, overhead cam, you name it, the Four has it. Whether it's the best bike ever built remains to be seen, but it wouldn't surprise us if it turns out to be.

Of course the most interesting part of the bike is the engine, four cylinders, inline and mounted traversely across the frame. For the first time in Honda's history they've gotten away from the ball and roller crank. The four has babbit bearings on both the mains and rods. The reasons for this are twofold. They wanted to use a pressure system of oiling and plain bearings lend themselves to this type of system better than rollers. The other reason for the babbits is the heat factor. Many people don't realize that oil, besides lubricating, helps to carry some of the heat from the engine surfaces and to do this the oil flow must be optimal. The oil is carried in a separate reservoir and is not, as it's reported elsewhere, the first time Honda has used this system, the early CE-71's 250's also used a separate oil tank.

The cam drive for the overhead cam is taken from between the number two and three cylinder. In typical Honda fashion the drive is an endless chain (no master link).

Because of the fact that the transmission shares the engine oil and all shafts run on rollers, it has to be lubricated on the scavenge side of the system.

The cylinders are actually split into

All four carbs are rubber mounted but as smooth as this engine runs it seems to be unnecessary.

At the widest point of the engine the Four is not as wide as some 250cc two-stroke twins we've seen.

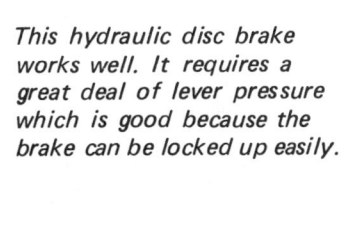

This hydraulic disc brake works well. It requires a great deal of lever pressure which is good because the brake can be locked up easily.

To our knowledge Honda is the first company to include an oil pressure warning light. More manufacturers should do this.

As complicated as the Four is all adjustments can be made easily and quickly. Don't get the carbs out of sync though.

Under the seat is the battery and tool kit carrying case, plus all the connectors for the rear wiring.

two halves, two right hand cylinders and two left hand. Between the two is the cam drive chain. The two cylinders in each half have a space between them for cooling and the Four needs all the cooling it can get. During our test we had an opportunity to pack double up some fairly steep hills and while the machine didn't even know it was pulling two, the heat radiated from the engine was enough to make the driver place his feet on the very outside edge of the footpegs.

The frame is a conventional double downtube unit that is extra hefty; the

Four's engine is no lightweight at 176 pounds. During our test it didn't flex and being as strong as it is, breakage should be no problem at all.

One of the more interesting features on this machine that's loaded with new and exciting things is the disc front brake. Before I go any farther I want to say that most motorcycle manufacturers should have done this many years ago. Almost every 40 inches built today is capable of speeds faster than what its brakes can handle. With the rear brake it's not much of a problem but the front brake does 85

per cent of the work under hard braking and it's a bit disconcerting to feel the brake fade as you're using it. The Honda's unit is hydraulically operated with the master cylinder mounted on the right handlebar. The brake lever itself takes quite a bit of pressure to operate and that's a good thing. A hydraulic brake has a great deal more mechanical advantage over the more conventional mechanical unit and so it would be much easier to lock up. Locking the front wheel of a machine that weighs 480 pounds dry is an experience not to be forgotten so it's

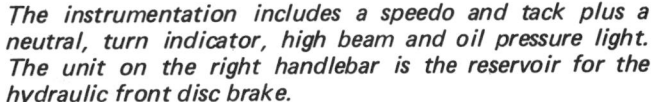

The instrumentation includes a speedo and tack plus a neutral, turn indicator, high beam and oil pressure light. The unit on the right handlebar is the reservoir for the hydraulic front disc brake.

The passenger footpegs are bolted to the exhaust pipes. Hopefully this will hold up under hard riding.

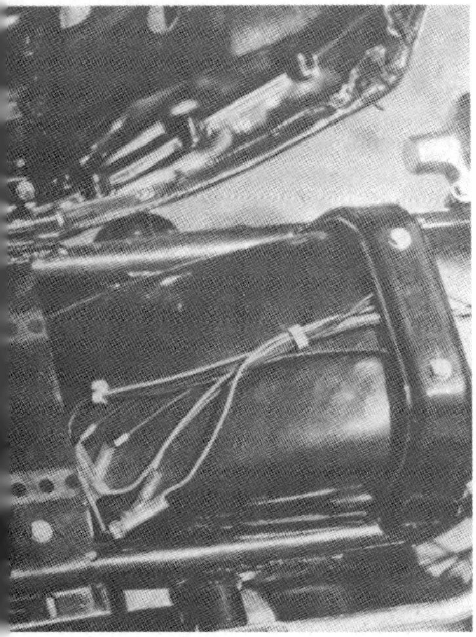

best it never happens. On our test machine the brake did squeal when the brake was applied lightly but this sound went away when the brake was used hard. We'll put up with the noise just as long as the brake works, and in this case it works — well.

With any machine eye appeal means a great deal and the Four scores here in spades. One night before the bike had been released to the public we took it down to Van Nuys Blvd., where it's happening in California, and the reception was not to be believed. Guys driving their 427 whatever, their 'Vettes, or whatever, pulled over to the side and yelled out they wanted to look at the machine. Those who wanted to race took one look at the four exhaust pipes sticking from the rear of the bike and had second thoughts. Other bike riders pulled along side and slobbered until you were embarrassed. Suffice it to say the Four is an eye catcher wherever it goes.

The only tricky thing about the Four would be the syncing of the four carbs. They're the standard round slide unit used on most of Honda's ma- chines but getting them to work in unison could be a time consuming job.

Getting the carbs to sync is about the only tricky thing on the bike. It starts easily with either the electric or kick starter, it has turn indicators that are visible from a long distance away, the riding position is comfortable, gas mileage is good and with a five gallon tank the cruising range is over 250 miles. In short, the Honda Four is the ultimate road bike for anyone who wants that sort of thing. I can't think of anyone who wouldn't.

Easy Riding
ACROSS THE CONTINENT ON A HONDA FOUR
BY FRANK CONNER

From the canyons north of Los Angeles down across the desert. Through Navajo country, Yosemite and Royal Gorge. Then across the mountains and onto the long Eastern freeways into the smog of New York City. The Honda Four was made for it all.

• For a whole mile down the road from American Honda I resisted the temptation, but then I couldn't stand it any longer. Leaving the bike in low gear (a 25 mph speed limit), I flicked my right wrist and watched the tach needle whip around to the 8500 rpm red line. I sat a bit taller in the saddle then, listening to those four exhaust-pipes, pipes that sing the most beautiful song that you can own for less than $20,000. Because the 750cc Honda Four was such a rarity during those middle days of August, the rest of Los Angeles listened just as carefully as I did.

The Four was tall, and it was heavy. I had to tilt it over to one side before I could plant a foot flat on the pavement at red lights. But once its wheels were rolling, the thing turned into a racehorse. You could operate the controls with light, positive motions. Pulling the clutch required only two fingers. The gearshift had a short, positive throw. The brakes were the best I'd encountered on anything that didn't carry permanent number plates. With only a touch of throttle, the bike would sit up and get gone. It would go exactly where you pointed it, and pointing it required almost no effort at all. Riding the Four was like flying a fighter; each generates a feeling of elegance. I was glad that I was wearing leather gloves, and I wished for a long white scarf.

I entered the freeway on-ramp much too fast, but was able to relax halfway through the sharp turn even though the horizon was still tilted up on its side. The Four wasn't a bit bashful about hooking over way past the point where alarming things usually happen to a big bike. Still heeled over, the machine responded instantly to small steering corrections, and then we were upright again in a mad rush of speeding cars flitting from lane to lane to jockey for each others' draft. Reading my two handlebar mirrors as if my life depended upon them (it did), I grabbed a handful of throttle and joined the battle.

Since the Four's 67 horses are fed into a close-ratio five-speed box, there are no awkward riding-speeds. If the engine began to lug or scream in a particular gear, all I had to do was go up or down one gear, and the engine was perfectly content. The bike and I fitted each other nicely, and wonder of wonders, there was no vibration.

Leaving the freeway network, I redlined the tach needle in low gear again, and from the corner of my eye watched the pedestrians' heads snap around. I was in hog heaven; unless the Four melted itself somewhere en route, my ride on this bike from Los Angeles to New York was going to be the kind of ride that most people dream about.

Sunday morning, I strapped my pack on the back of the saddle and left for U.S. 395, and Yosemite. Off through innocuous hills and valleys to Palmdale; and then the broad sweeps of crazily-

PHOTOGRAPH: LARRY WILLITT

forest-ranger camp nearby. Steve was absolutely enchanted with the Four. He liked it so much that I offered him a ride into Bishop, 50 miles away. We took off at sundown. Paying no attention to the speedo, I was using about the same amount of throttle that it took to go 80 mph solo, figuring that we'd be doing about 60 mph riding two-up. Steve shouted that the Highway Patrol was following us. I glanced at the speedo. 80 mph. What a motorcycle! I eased off to 65, and the fuzz sailed on by. That was a cold ride, but the sky was full of stars, and the silhouettes of the mountains, still dimly visible, made it all worthwhile.

The next day, I backtracked down U.S. 395, and the Sierra Nevadas looked completely different in the early morning sunlight. At Lone Pine, I took off for Death Valley. There was no traffic on the road except for a few lizards. As I bombed along, I wondered if Death Valley had anything worth seeing. Then the road climbed up to a pass, where superb ranges of mountains and valleys stretch away from horizon to horizon. As the road fought its way down from the pass, waves of hot air rolled against my face, and the distant desert shimmered in the heat.

The narrow, twisting road was poorly surfaced, and drifting dirt had piled up in a few of the blind corners. The edge of the road hung over sheer drops; there were no guard rails, no shoulders, no nothing—just space when the pavement ended. The bike drifted a bit on a patch of sand in one of those blind corners, got real close to the edge, and scared me badly. I gritted my teeth and crawled the rest of the way down the mountainside, hating myself for having taken fright so easily. At Panamint Springs I stopped for gas, a beer, and a sandwich, all served up by a twelve-year-old boy, and afterwards felt much better.

In Death Valley itself, I was surrounded by the most spectacular geological formations that I have ever seen. In the distance, off to my right, was a lake. "Aha," said I, "a mirage." After a while I caught up with my mirage, which didn't go away as all good mirages are supposed to do, because it was an alkali salt-flat of immaculate and eye-searing whiteness.

Enjoying myself thoroughly, I smiled at the fears of many people about riding the deserts in August. The heat wasn't even affecting me slightly. Then, at Furnace Creek, I turned off into the museum parking lot and found myself about to ride right into a big pile of rocks at one side. Doing all of 10 mph, I could have stopped the bike easily, but my mind was sluggish and refused to function. I just stared stupidly at the rocks ahead. At the last moment, I gave a mighty heave and the bike wobbled

tilted valleys, where stark mountain ranges grow straight out of the ground with no foothills or trees to soften them.

At Lancaster, there was a stretch of concrete four-lane that had been grooved while wet into wavy patterns. The bike danced around on it uncomfortably, but soon I noticed that the machine only moved a few inches at a hop, so I relaxed. Always before on long trips, my butt would start aching about halfway through the first day, and it wouldn't become properly numbed until the second day. Now was the time for my tail to get sore, but it didn't. In fact, it never did. The saddle on the Four doesn't seem all that great if you just sit on it for a moment, but it's really Super Saddle in disguise.

Gradually, the road became clogged with traffic. It seemed as if there were millions of campers, either going to or returning from Yosemite. Cars and campers crawled along and got in each other's way; for them, this journey was a nightmare. For me, the traffic had overtones of fun. I'd overtake a long line of traffic, and as soon as the oncoming car had passed the car ahead of me, I'd punch the gearbox down into fourth, grab a big handful of throttle, and peel off to the left. I'd sail over into the left lane, get everything available in fourth, and then catch fifth. Still accelerating like a wild thing, I'd tear past the line of cars on my right and before

anybody got unduly worried, I'd ease in between a couple of cars to let the next oncoming car whiz past me.

The desert country was magnificent. The road led me through great flows of lava, some of it smooth and some jagged. It was easy to understand why the Spaniards had called it "mal pais" ("badland"). Past Bishop, the Sierra Nevadas on my left suddenly became huge and craggy, with snowcapped peaks, but in the valley the August heat was ferocious. Then the road began to climb, and soon I found myself riding through pine forests. The air turned chilly, and ominous thunderheads loomed ahead. I left U.S. 395 and entered Yosemite from the west. At Tioga Pass (almost 10,000 feet) the Four seemed to have just as much power as it did at sea level. That amazed me.

In places, I was above the treeline, and it seemed strange to be riding along in the middle of summer with patches of permanent snow and ice only a few hundred yards away. The rain finally came, and I got drenched. My teeth were chattering, and I was shivering uncontrollably. I should have remembered that whenever you go riding in the real mountain country—even in August—you should take along plenty of warm clothes.

That night I found a motel about 20 miles back down U.S. 395, and there I met Steve—a big, husky, cornfed Iowan who was working for the summer at a

and brushed past the largest rock. I parked, looking around guiltily to see if anybody had noticed my awful error. Nobody had.

Leaving Death Valley, I emerged into the flat, empty roads of western Nevada. This seemed to be a good time to find out if the Four would hold together at speed, so I rolled on some throttle and ran it up to 100 mph. I held it there for half an hour, as tar patches in the pavement rushed toward me and the wind played with me, and the bike felt good. My arms began to tire from holding on, but the bike seemed perfectly happy to run at that speed. Many, many motorcycles would have melted their engines at that speed in the August heat on the desert.

I stopped at yet another out-of-the-way filling station, and a whole collection of off-road bikes materialized out of nowhere to look at the Four. This happened wherever I stopped. Everybody had heard of the Four, but at that time few were on the road; the rider would study the lines of the bike, and then tell me—with passion in his voice—that someday he was going to own a Four. Before finishing the trip, I came to the conclusion that Honda is going to sell an awful lot of those bikes.

My editor had told me that a bike shop in Las Vegas had a sanitary operation, so I took the Four over there to get the scheduled service-check and to get a loose rear chain tightened. The editor was right: it *is* a sanitary operation. I listened as the mechanics cheerfully shouted insults at each other while they worked. My mechanic was Rocky, and the Four was in good hands, because Rocky was not about to turn it loose until he had checked everything on it. As he worked, he told me about riding the dry lakebeds, and a near miss with a sailcar on his last ride. "Never heard a thing; I was just idling back across the lake at about 70 when I looked over to the left, and there it was, just sailing along with its windward wheel in the air. It passed me, and I was so surprised that I didn't even catch up with it again."

Then an incredible character came into the shop. You could tell right away that he was a character because he wore Levis several sizes too large, a well-worn Italian knit shirt, and an unassailable cool. He turned out to be the legendary Paul Pratt, who recently completed his longest journey: two and a half years of riding through Mexico, Central America, and South America on a detuned 650cc Triumph twin. We talked about the real long distance riding, and Paul said that you can only digest so much scenery; after that the pleasure (or dissatisfaction) of the journey comes from the people you meet along the way. All of the long distance travelers he had met had developed considerable sensitivity in sorting out the people they were meeting.

Paul believed that his Triumph was the ideal machine for the type of trip that he liked. He didn't need or want a lot of top speed. He valued reliability, a wide powerband, and smooth throttle response for negotiating rocky dirt roads carved into mountainsides. His current Triumph had 35,000 miles on it, with no catastrophic failures.

It was midafternoon when Paul Pratt and I parted company. I wanted to spend another three or four days talking with him, but the editor was making impatient noises back in New York, so I fired up the Four and headed for Kingman. I dropped out of the pass down to Hoover Dam and Lake Mead, which was not real. It was simply a gigantic painted backdrop, a movie set, and I half-expected to see Nelson Eddy and Jeanette McDonald in a canoe in the middle of the lake.

Afterwards came strong gusting crosswinds. Whenever a big blast of wind hit us, the Four simply leaned into the gust a bit and then righted itself when the wind was done. A lighter bike would have been blown all over the road, but on the Four I could relax.

Overnight in Kingman, Arizona, and on the road again at seven in the morning, I was going east on Route 66. The Santa Fe tracks ran alongside the highway, and a passenger train caught up with me. I wondered how fast it was going, so I turned on the Four and matched speeds with the train. 98 mph; that train wasn't fooling around.

For the first time during the trip, I got involved with a number of semitrailers. As I approached one of the big trucks, its turbulence would shift the helmet around on my head, and wobble me around on the bike, but the Four would keep going straight. As I pulled up even with the rear of the trailer, the draft would suck me forward and give me another eight to 10 mph. Alongside the tractor, another blast of turbulence would hit me, and then I'd be past.

Route 66 in Arizona could never make up its mind what kind of highway it wanted to be. First would come good pavement; then a mediocre stretch; and finally some awful road, with lots of potholes and frost heaves. The Four took all but the worst of the stuff in its stride, but it would dive off into the potholes. I guess that anything on two wheels would have done the same. Somehow, though, the Four never did deliver that spine-jarring crash of bottoming suspension that takes the starch out of you so quickly.

At Holbrook I left 66 and wandered up into the Four Corners country and the Navajo reservation. The road is unfenced, which means that when you top any hill you can expect to see the road dead ahead covered with congregations of cattle, sheep, horses, or goats. I had several interesting experiences with the assorted livestock, proving once and for all that in a panic stop, the Four's brakes work like champions.

The horses and cows seemed to know about motorcycles, and as I'd come thundering at them, brakes working frantically, they'd amble off to the side. But the calves and sheep didn't seem to get the message. They'd see me coming and look up, mildly interested, but they wouldn't move until I was only about 20 feet away. Then, in utter panic, they would scatter in all directions. After awhile, I could begin to guess where the next collection of animals would be hidden, so I'd slow down a bit.

Later, on one of the overlooks at the Canyon de Chelly, I was admiring the secret pocket-canyons carved out of the sandstone by the river over the centuries. Cliff dwellers had lived in these canyons, growing their crops in them and building their houses in natural caverns high in the sheer walls of the cliffs, so as to make it very difficult for their enemies to get to them. A busload of Navajos from nearby Chinle, and a couple of other tourists were standing beside me, also enjoying the view. One of the tourists struck up a conversation about bikes. He told me about his adventures in riding a BMW on the Alcan Highway. The other tourist (who was a stranger to us both) listened for awhile and then joined in with some of *his* experiences on motorcycles on the

Alcan. Both tourists became deeply interested in comparing notes about a particularly nasty (when muddy) stretch of the road near Yellowknife. I left them there engrossed in conversation.

In Shiprock, New Mexico, I made a friend. A nine-year-old boy, a Navajo, smiled a huge smile at me, calculated to warm the hardest heart, and asked if I would give him a ride on my bike. I started to give him the brushoff, changed my mind, and told him to go ask his folks if it was okay with them. Whether or not he asked their permission I don't know, but after a convincing length of time he returned and said it was okay with them.

We went for a 15-minute ride, and he held on tight all the way, shouting his pleasure and waving at his friends.

The next morning I worked my way north to Durango, Colorado, where I picked up U.S. 160. The road twisted and turned its way through the gorgeous San Juan mountains, and there was a lot of traffic. The Four and I played Pass the Cars again, while I enjoyed those wonderful curves. Some of the enjoyment went out of it temporarily when a car going the other way slung a rock the size of a walnut, which got me, THOCK, right on the kneecap. For the next five miles I rode crouched over, massaging my left knee

At Alamosa, I left U.S. 160 and went north to look at the Sand Dunes National Monument. There, in the lush part of Colorado is a vast basin that gets almost no rain and is therefore a desert, complete with sand dunes 700 feet high.

North up a flat and fast road to Salida, and then I joined a number of tourists heading east on U.S. 50. Sections of the road were wide, with paved shoulders, which turned out to be a Good Thing, because I came around a blind corner, and there I was face to face with one car passing another. I took to the shoulder. Five minutes later, the same thing happened again. Ten minutes after that, it happened a third time. If the drivers who did their passing in those blind corners were lipreaders, they may have noticed that I called them some hard names.

Just this side of Canon City, I stopped at the Royal Gorge. Not even the three-ring tourist traps set up on the rim could dim the wild beauty of that sheer canyon, with the Arkansas River rampaging angrily so far below.

The next day I visited the Four Seasons in Denver to get the 2000-mile inspection on the Four. While there, I called the editor to see how things were

going, and he said, "Come home, come home, wherever you are. This month's deadline is here." Then I made a big mistake. Looking at a roadmap, I saw that I-80 runs from Denver to New York, and I decided to ride it. I had forgotten the basic rule: superhighways are no place to ride motorcycles, because on superhighways motorists and riders alike get lulled into carelessness.

Interstate 80 aimed me right for the middle of a big thunderhead, but the highway veered just in time. Now I was headed toward another thunderhead; surely it was going to get me. But again the highway angled around and missed it. All morning long, the highway dodged patches of rain, and never once did I get wet. The highway engineers had been thoughtful, laying out the road between the thunderheads.

As I rode, I learned that you can hear yourself sing inside a Bell Magnum; in fact, the helmet lends a pleasing echochamber effect to rusty voices like mine. So I rode and sang songs like "John Henry", "Frankie and Johnny", "The Wreck of the Ol' 97", "Hobo Bill", and "If You're Goin' to San Francisco", and sang them all in the same key. I stopped for the night at a friendly motel way out in the middle of nowhere, and sang some more in the shower. Mr. Bell's helmet gives you a better tone.

The sun was out early on Sunday morning, and so was I. Since the mist didn't burn off until midmorning, I rode for awhile with my headlight burning. At my cigarette breaks in rest areas and filling stations, I met a dozen or so of my fellow travelers. These people had watched me pass them six or eight times, and they were curious about the bike, so they talked with me. All were impressed by the Four. One driver, a music teacher en route to New York from Denver, said, "You seem to be having a ball; it must be a very good motorcycle." He was right on both counts.

Morning passed pleasantly, and then I got to the Valley of the Shadow: the variously-numbered superhighways that serve as I-80 from Chicago to the Ohio border.

In the suburbs of Chicago, I was riding in the right lane. Beside me in the center lane was a Buick, driven by a middle-aged man with a supercilious smirk pasted to his face. He decided to join me. I had been watching his right front tire, and as soon as it began to turn I grabbed my brakes. The Buick's rear bumper just missed my front tire. I

was infuriated, more by the man's smirk than by his action, and I pressed the horn button to blow a mighty blast of displeasure. The horn would yield no more than a pitiful croak. This enraged me even more. I whipped into the center lane, positioned the bike a couple of inches from the Buick's front fender, turned my head to stare at the driver through his front windshield, and bellowed at the top of my lungs. When aroused, I can make lots of noise. The driver never lost his smirk, but he did turn white.

As I rode on, I brooded about motorcycle horns. Motor vehicles are fitted with horns for use when the other traffic fails to see them. Industry concensus is that most riders who get hurt on street bikes do so because other traffic failed to see them. Logically, then, the street bike should be equipped with a horn at least as loud as the one on an automobile. What kind of horn does the motorcycle actually get? Hah!

Monday morning on the Ohio Turnpike was delightful. There was little traffic, and I was passing through rich farm country, and the air was cool, not cold. One truckdriver whom I was passing stuck his head out of the window and shouted so loudly that I could hear him through the helmet, "THAT'S A GREAT MOTORCYCLE!"

Pennsylvania's turnpike was something else. At the bottom of a long hill, both lanes of traffic came to a stop, and I was at the end of the line. I looked in my mirror and saw a car and a truck sailing down the hill, side by side. They hadn't perceived that the traffic was stopped. The skin on my back crawled as I frantically punched the Four into gear and headed for the space between the two cars ahead of me. For the next few moments there was much squalling of tires and squealing of brakes, as I cowered on the bike, and then everything became quiet. Both the car and the truck had gotten stopped, but the truck now occupied the space where I had been. *Continued on page* **101**

CB750

A connoisseur's dream

TEN years ago the chances of any manufacturer producing a machine such as the Honda 4 would have been remote. Or even five years ago . . . Then, just when motorcyclists the world over were despairing for their sport, the great American public came to the rescue. They found that bikes were fun to ride! Encouraged, the Japanese lost no time in establishing a stranglehold on the small bike industry, leaving the big bike scene, for the while, to others. This was too good (for us) to last, and soon most of the big Japanese manufacturers had a full-size roadburner on the stocks. Yamaha were there with a 650 vertical twin, Honda started with the 450, Suzuki with a 500 and Kawasaki with a 650 twin and, later, the 500 three. It was perhaps inevitable that Honda, with its tremendous resources and racing experience, would sooner or later cap the lot. The weapon they chose was the 750 c.c. four. So sophisticated was the specification that as details began to reach this country there were many who were inclined to dismiss the model as a publicity stunt. Four cylinders? Overhead camshaft? Disc front brake? Electric starter? And selling at £600 in this country? "Too good to be true" and "We'll believe it when we see it" were typical reactions.

The dream took a little longer to realize than anticipated. The first four was circulating Brands Hatch over a year ago at a pre-show test day, but it has only been during these last few months that the big Honda has been in (some) showrooms. The price, too, has risen to £680. The first batches into this country sold immediately. The machine that I have had the opportunity of riding was supplied from those early batches by Reads of Leytonstone to Pat Patterson of Sutton, who kindly offered it to us for an impression test. I must stress that it was an impression test, for the machine had done a mere 300 miles when we took it over.

My first reaction to the Honda? It's a connoisseur's dream. It is every bit as good as it promised to be, and gave me some of the most enjoyable motorcycling possible. My only complaint is that it had to arrive at a time when the weather was far from clement and opportunities to ride it were somewhat restricted. Can you imagine anything more frustrating than to have a bike like that in the garage and snow on the ground?

The Honda 4 is a large machine. Now, there is an obvious statement! Everyone knows it's a large machine but just how large is not fully appreciated until one has swung a leg across it. Sinking into one of the most luxurious dualseats that

I have ever sampled, I was surprised to find I could not place both feet firmly on the ground. This was not so much due to the seat height, at 31in about average, as to the fact that my legs were being forced out by the oil tank and air filter housing. These measure a full 16in across. The petrol tank, too, is broad on the beam, and the rider is obliged to sit rather wide-legged. It will not bother many riders; it didn't bother me once the initial surprise wore off, but there are those who prefer a tighter, knees-in, feel. To return to that dualseat. It is 26in long, 12in across at its widest point and 4½in deep. It is finished in a quilt pattern in synthetic leather (that is as much like the real thing as it is possible to get), with a raised rear and a grab strap behind the rider. One feels it would be the greatest of pleasures to sit there for mile after mile, wallowing in its luxury.

Just as one does not take a thoroughbred and set off at full gallop, so it is with the Honda. It needs to be gently warmed up. The drill is: petrol on, ignition on, choke closed, throttle set at ⅛th open, press the starter button. Provided the procedure has been faithfully followed, the engine will always burst into life immediately with a roar that may wake a few sleeping dogs, but that will make the blood run quicker in the veins of motorcyclists. Can you imagine the thrill of hearing those four pipes chiming in? All who have enjoyed the glorious sound of the racing fours will be able to recapture something of it with this road-going Honda. And yet it is not really

noisy. At least, not once it is on the move, but this machine did need a minute or two to warm up. As soon as the engine has fired the choke lever must be released just a little, then the revs kept at about 2,000 r.p.m. until it is willing to accept the choke fully open. This takes a little while and on the odd occasion I short-circuited this system (rather than become the target for old boots and things late at night) it was a mile or two before the engine would chime in happily on all four pots.

This may sound rather a chore—indeed, no doubt it is—but it's all part of the thrill of getting to ride this machine, and few owners will begrudge the time involved.

The controls all fell beautifully to hand and foot on this Honda. The relationship of bars, footrests and seat was just about right for me, although whether it is on the standard version is debatable, for the owner had wisely opted for the flatter Honda 450 handlebars in preference to the massive American-style bars that are fitted as standard. Riding a machine of the proportions of the Honda is not without its difficulties. The controls were very heavy, especially the throttle, with a single cable pulling four separate cables from a junction under the tank (one to each Keihin carburettor). It had the added disadvantage of not having a friction adjuster, understandable in view of the heaviness already, with each carburettor having a spring doing its best to close the slide. The slightest relaxation of the rider's grip, especially if he has heavy gloves on, and it succeeds! This was a particular problem when operating the dipswitch with the right thumb. My thumb just would not reach without a slight shift sideways and the movement was often enough to have the throttle snap shut on me. Control of the six-plate clutch suffered slightly less by comparison but was still on the heavy side. The hydraulically-operated

Honda four—£680 worth of motorbike—what every suburban drive-in should have . . .

CB750

disc front brake was the lightest control on the handlebar. It had a feel not unlike a drum brake with hard linings. It was sensitive enough for town use in the wet without problems and from high speeds quite an asset in stopping the Honda's 517 lb. The rear brake was a good one but the pedal was tucked in a little too well and was a mite difficult to reach with a hefty boot. The other handlebar controls include a flashing indicator operated by the left thumb. It is one of the better switches for this task and had a positive feel about it. The flashers themselves were excellent, the first ones that I have had no hesitation in using in daylight. The horn button, also part of the left-hand clutch unit, operates a horn that was in keeping with the bike—loud and powerful. On the right-hand throttle assembly is the dipswitch with a lip preventing the switch going to the "off" position accidentally. The parking light is *between* the dip and main beams.

The instrument panel has a superb layout, with dials mounted in just the right position for a rider's perusal. The speedometer, on the left-hand side, has a red main-beam warning light and a yellow flashing-indicator warning light, plus the odometer and tripmeter, while the tachometer on the right houses the neutral-indicator light and the oil-pressure warning light. At night the instruments are illuminated with a soft green light, shining through the digits. A most soothing panel that needed the merest flick of the eyes for the rider to take in all the information.

A kickstarter is mounted on the right side, for emergency use. It was not needed, but out of interest we started the Honda first kick using it. The gearchange, on the left side, *looks* a little flimsy, but this may be doing it a disservice. The five-speed gearbox is one-down, four-up.

Engaging first gear from rest always produced an audible clunk and the gear-changing was, if you will excuse the term, BMWish. By that I mean that the revs had to be carefully balanced to road speed. If this were done the gears slid

in with ease, but merely prodding with the boot produced a clunk very much like you hear from a BMW driven badly. The neutral-warning light, indicating that one is between first and second, was very necessary, for on "our" machine neutral was very difficult to locate from bottom, and not easy from second. It usually paid to make sure that neutral was engaged before one rolled to a stop. It is only fair to say that I have had the opportunity to talk to a few other owners of the 750 Honda since, and they all claim no difficulty at all in this operation, so it seems possible that this particular machine's gearbox was a little stiff.

Having established some sort of understanding of the layout of the Honda, I prepared to ride it. It would be cheating to say that I wasn't just a little bit nervous as I put it into bottom gear. After all, here was nearly £700 worth of the most sophisticated and potent machinery on the market. One could not help but be impressed by the thought of 67 (?) b.h.p. burbling away below—even if they are Japanese. The very quick action throttle didn't help acclimatisation, for trying to settle at 2,000 r.p.m. for warming up I found that a movement of less than ₁/₁₆ in lost me 1,000 r.p.m.! In the

event I gently fed in the clutch, having been warned that it all happened in the last half-inch. The clutch bit, the revs rose and the biggest Honda took off with as little fuss as the smallest. What a feeling of majesty this machine induces! My ride home included the city and at every stop bowler-hatted businessmen gathered in droves to admire the beautiful red and gold machine. I grinned smugly back at them, dying to tell all those poor car-bound sufferers that here was *the* way to travel.

All my apprehension about the Honda melted as I purred along. Once out of town, remembering that we were running in with a r.p.m. ceiling of 4,000 (about 60 m.p.h.), I let the needle creep up and, for a short time, enjoyed the surge of power as the 4 strained at the leash. Nowhere in the rev range we were restricted to did the Honda betray the slightest trace of vibration and the engine made as little noise as one could imagine. It sat on the road with a solidity and comfort that left the rider tingling with pleasure. Here, in the country, was the environment that the 750 was intended for. It had negotiated the city streets without protest or tantrum, but it was making its weight felt at my wrists by

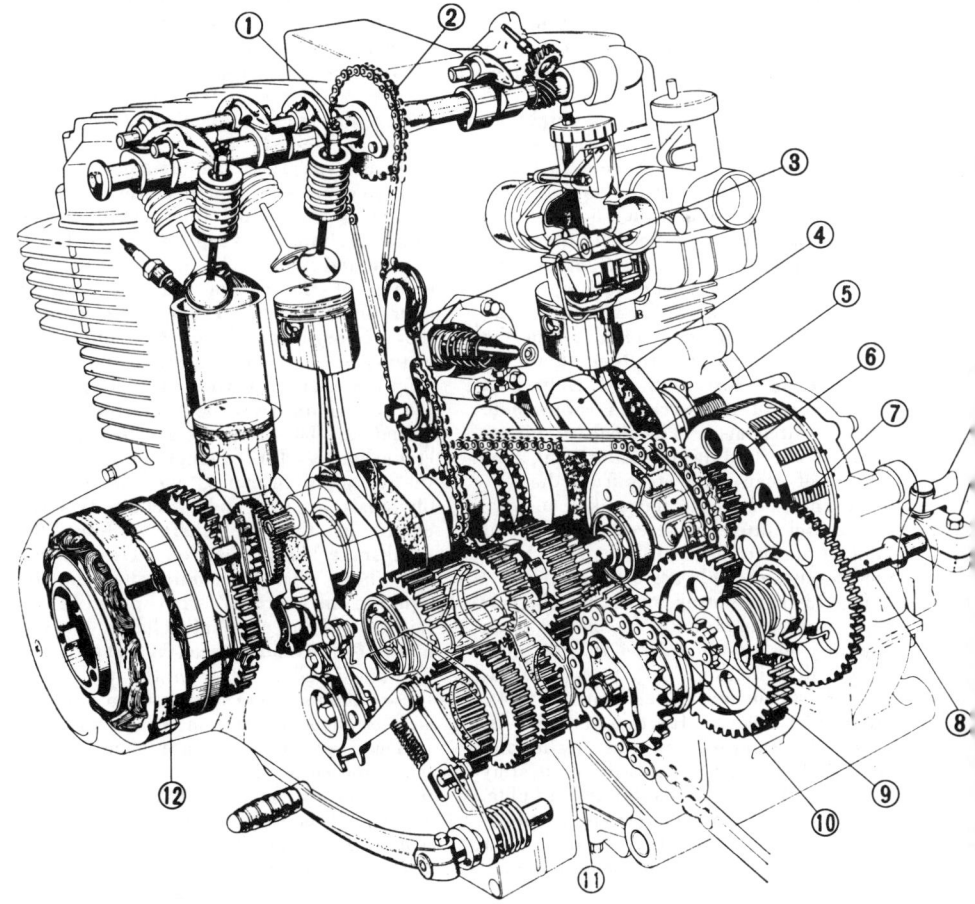

① Camshaft	⑦ Clutch
② Camchain	⑧ Kick starter spindle
③ Camchain tensioner	⑨ Final driven shaft
④ Crankshaft	⑩ Mainshaft
⑤ Primary chain	⑪ Countershaft
⑥ Primary driven sprocket	⑫ A.C. generator

the time fields began to appear. The handling had that solid feeling, of substance. The bike sat on the road with a certainty and security that made the rider feel that it would never be so ungentlemanly as to twitch at the back. The only time the 517 lb could be felt was in changing direction through a series of bends. To swing from side to side needed a positive effort; it wasn't enough merely to "think" the machine through a bend. When we have had the opportunity to try one on our test track we will find out how much this impression is bourne out by fact. As it was, so solid did the Honda feel that one had the distinct impression that were a small car foolish enough to collide with it, the car might be capsized!

What a pleasure to accelerate away from the lights and hear those four exhausts in chorus. It is a chorus that can easily get out of tune on downward changes as the throttle is quick enough to make the gentle roll needed a matter of some delicacy. Performance was, for us, a hypothetical question, but I have no doubt that the four will get pretty close to that claimed 125 m.p.h. Fuel consumption cannot be taken too seriously, running-in tending to give a false reading, as you will see from our figure of something over 70 m.p.g.! It just shows what *can* be done, though. The four-gallon tank is a respectable size but the reserve of one gallon might be considered a little generous. It is a pity that rubber knee grips are not included in the specification for, although these are usually "anti-vibration" fittings, and in that sense are not needed, they also perform a useful service in preventing a worn patch on the paintwork.

One would not normally relish heaving all the weight of the Honda on to the centre stand but the roll-on stand required little effort, with the right foot doing most of the work. A robust side stand is fitted also. The dualseat hinges to reveal the toolkit and battery top, plus a maze of snap connectors from the wiring harness. I would have liked to have seen a lock fitted to the seat for it is not difficult to lift the seat, once you know the secret, and tools are a temptation.

The 12-volt lighting one expected, perhaps unreasonably, to be better than anything else with a 50/40w bulb supplying illumination. As it was, it was very good but no better than on most other big bikes. Ignition is by AC generator mounted on the right-hand crankshaft end and enclosed by an alloy housing. A trifle vulnerable in a tumble, I fear. Two contact breakers supply sparks to the four plugs. The starter motor is beneath a chrome panel mounted immediately aft of the cylinders. Although the 14 ah battery does not look very large it did its job with ease, spinning the engine without trouble on the coldest day. The starter made a metallic screech when used, which was a bit worrying at first, until I found that they all do it!

Dictates of the American market are obvious in many of the items on the machine, such as side reflectors, folding footrests and front-brake stop light. A notable absentee is a headlamp flasher. Essential on a machine of this calibre, in my view. The petrol tank is rubber mounted and could be rocked backward and forwards, which suggests that even with four cylinders there is still a problem of high-frequency vibration, though it certainly was not apparent to the rider. It seems that Japanese manufacturers have a penchant for putting the ignition key under the nose of the tank, but the four at least has the benefit of a separate light switch on the handlebar. Only the parking light is operated by the key, which could be removed when it was in that position.

Rider protection on the big Honda is above average, with 6½in-wide chrome mudguards shielding one admirably. These, unfortunately, did not protect the machine from road dirt, as I found out when cleaning the bike before returning it to the owner. It must be one of the most awkward machines made when it comes to cleaning. I have never seen so many nooks and crannies and there is not even the temporary relief of a large sweep of alloy. Particularly difficult parts to reach were the front cylinders behind the exhaust pipes and the "inside" silencers. Owners will have to take special care to ensure that these difficult-to-get-at parts are not neglected.

On the subject of maintenance . . . It is to be expected that a machine as sophisticated as the Honda four would not be quite so simple to keep on the road as a "bread-and-butter" bike, but there *are* **aspects of the design that are a little worrying . . . For example, to replace the primary-drive chain** (two single-row chains) or the camshaft chain one has to strip the engine/gearbox unit completely, for the chain runs between the centre cylinders. This is necessary because the crankshaft is a forged single unit, running in five plain bearings, and one cannot, obviously, pass an endless chain over the centre of the crankshaft without the crankshaft being removed. Owners can only hope that the chains have a life equal to the bearings'! It is possible that failure of the camshaft chains on two of the four Hondas raced at Daytona can be considered a straw in the wind, but these chains were subject to greater stresses than any Honda would normally undergo and their failure shouldn't be taken too seriously. Of a more mundane nature is the matter of rear-wheel removal. It is rather surprising that the wheel is not of the quickly detachable type and one wonders why a manufacturer with the technical resources of Honda does not fit the q.d. wheel. At least the owner attempting repairs on his engine has the benefit of a handbook whose only fault is that it makes all the operations seem more simple than they can possibly be!

Much has been said about the four-cylinder Honda engine and we can only echo that which has been said before. It is a vertical four-cylinder in line across the frame. Each cylinder has two valves actuated by a single shaft driven from a sprocket on the crankshaft. Adjustment of the chain is by a cam tensioner, which can be removed without dismantling the engine. Valve springs are conventional double-coil items. Running at a compression ratio of 9 to 1, each cylinder has a bore of 61mm and stroke of 63mm. The pistons have three rings. As already stated, the crankshaft is a forged unit running in five plain bearings. The big-end is of the split type in plain bearings; the small-end has no bushing. Oil is delivered at a maximum pressure of 57 lb (above that a relief valve incorporated in the delivery side of the oil pump bypasses the oil to the crankcase sump). Delivery is by a rotor-type trochoid pump mounted on the bottom of the crankcase and driven through the kickstart gear. Oil is filtered through a replaceable cartridge filter element. Oil capacity is six pints.

Transmission is by two single-row chains running from a sprocket at the middle of the crankshaft. The clutch has seven cork mould discs, bonded to the plates. It has four springs and is of the wet type, running in an oil bath which, it is claimed, also serves to dissipate the heat generated by the clutch. The clutch can be removed from the engine assembly without need for dismantling the rest of the engine.

Tyres are Japanese Dunlop and are the new fat type, 3.25 x 19in on the front and 4.00 x 18in. rear. Suspension is of conventional type with telescopic oil-damped front forks and adjustable rear-suspension units of a single-cylinder double-acting type. Following current fashion, the chrome-plated rear springs are exposed. The frame is of double-cradle type with extra rigidity provided by a triple down tube head section. With 67 b.h.p. at 8,000 r.p.m. the makers no doubt considered the extra strength necessary.

We enjoyed our time with the Honda CB750. It is one of the delights of motorcycling to sit astride a machine such as this and, although a price tag of £680 will prevent many riders indulging in its pleasures, we are sure that those who do will be as impressed as we were. Anyone who buys a bike such as the CB750 should have a full understanding of what is involved before laying out hard-earned cash and for this reason we have been at pains to point out the drawbacks as well as the advantages. Most of the drawbacks are due to the complexity of the design, and prospective purchasers will probably buy the bike *because* it is a complex design and, therefore, cheerfully accept the problems, if any, that arise. Whatever the cost and whatever the complexity there are going to be a fortunate handful of riders who will be sampling the delights of motorcycling in a way undreamed of a decade ago. B. P.

Honda has more to move you

Take all the superlatives you've heard about other big bikes and forget them. All the new Honda 750 Four needs to prove itself is you on the seat.

Face it. If you're ready for a 750, this won't be your first bike. But it could be the last you ever need to buy.

The Honda 750 Four is built to take it. For as long as you like. Give the command and it will take you to speeds in excess of 120 mph. Acceleration? The 750's got it. It'll go the quarter in under 13. Smoothly.

This is the one all the bike books have flipped over. The one you can stay with. But don't take our word for it. Read the test reports. Any of them. They'll convince you.

The 750 has four carbs, a five-speed gearbox, a hydraulic disc brake on the front wheel. Yes, *disc*. And best of all, there's a four-cylinder overhead cam engine that runs smoother and quieter than anything you've ever been on before.

The 750 Four. A 67-horsepower masterpiece from the master maker. Honda.

The new
750 Four
HONDA

29

HONDA'S

The fastest accelerating roadster ever tested! Charles Deane reports on the CB750 . . .

In all its glory . . . the Honda CB750. It was quite easy to lift on to the stand in spite of its weight. Note oil filter between exhaust pipes

Easy to read instruments and a very neat, uncluttered handlebar layout made the CB750 easier to ride. Note quick-filler fuel cap on petrol tank

The single-disc, hydraulic front brake is a very effective stopper from any speed. It also has no grabbing or locking tendencies, unlike a twin-leading-shoe

Four carburettors, four cylinders 736 cc capacity make one very powerful motor producing 67 bhp at 80 Ignition key and gearchange on

HEAVYWEIGHT

▶ **Meet Honda's heavyweight champion, the CB750! Winner of the French 24-hour Bol d'Or production machine race, the coveted Daytona 200 and . . . will the Production TT be next?**

We will know the answer to this question next month, but having just finished testing this incredible four-cylinder 750, I would say that the Honda CB750 must stand a very good chance.

Unlike the majority of works specials at Daytona, most of which were built especially for the race with racing frames, brakes and numerous other non-standard items, the Honda used was basically the roadster model with a tuned motor producing around 90 bhp.

In standard trim, the CB750 engine develops 67 bhp and its specification reads like a race motor with four cylinders in-line across the frame, a five main-bearing crankshaft revving to a safe limit of 8500 rpm.

The crankcase splits horizontally and also houses the five-speed gearbox. With this number of gears, one would imagine that the high-performance four was lacking in tractability, but this is not the case. It simply means that maximum use can be made of the 67 horses produced to give searing acceleration.

In fact, the motor has such a wide power band that one need only use three of the five gears around town and providing the throttle wasn't wound hard against the stop, the CB750 would pull happily away from 20 mph in fifth gear with under 2000 rpm showing on the tachometer.

Starting

Starting the Honda 4 was no trouble using the electric starter. A single lever with linkages to all four carbs closed the chokes and with ignition on showing a red oil warning and green neutral indicator lights, one simply pressed the button on the right handlebar to bring the motor to life.

The one criticism was the length of time taken in warming up the motor. Only by playing with the choke lever for some minutes was it possible to get the motor running sweetly on all four cylinders when starting from cold.

However, I suppose one has to make allowances for the vast amount of metal which has to be heated up to correct running temperature and once warm, the four responded instantly to the throttle.

Considering the weight of four carbs on the end of the twistgrip, it was reasonable in operation. But I think that the quick-action twistgrip should be changed to slow as the throttle response is too sharp for wet riding conditions in traffic. Rear wheel spin in first, second and third gears was a problem unless extremely careful use was made of the throttle in the wet!

Clutch action was beautifully light but rather fierce. After "clonking" first gear home, it needed fine control of both throttle and clutch to avoid a screaming motor or a "dying" one as the clutch dropped very sharply home.

Gearchanging was always positive, but rather noisy. There was no grating, but certainly a solid clonk. A certain amount of whining also emanated from the transmission.

Attractions

The CB750 is laden with "extras" like a Christmas tree—electric starter, flashing indicators, handlebar cut-out switch, oil and neutral warning lights, handlebar mirrors, stoplight operated by hydraulic, disc front brake and the snazziest speedometer and tachometer are among the many attractions offered on this "super-bike".

The weight of the Honda is approximately 480 pounds plus fuel, oil and road dirt. In other words, once you're on the move you're controlling a fair hunk of metal. Surprisingly, at anything more than walking pace, it is extremely controllable and can be used comfortably in weaving through traffic or for flicking through bends at speed.

I think the low centre of gravity helps a great deal in making this machine light to handle and

in mega-silencers on either side the rear wheel give the CB750 a ... y appearance. Note pillion rest is ...unted directly on the silencer

Kickstart, clutch, cb points and four-pint oil tank are all on right-hand side. Note rear brake is on right, gearchange on left

The rear mudguard is not deeply valanced and a fair amount of spray covers rear of bike. Note flashers and adjustable springs

This is the end . . . which annoys envious E-type owners as it disappears rapidly away from them! Note angular rear tyre

HONDA CB750

'Fantastic'

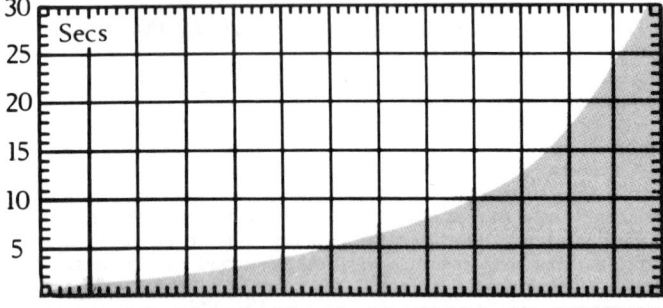

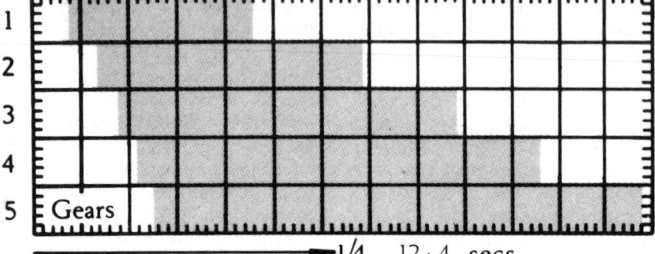

1/4 12·4 secs

SPECIFICATION

Engine: Overhead camshaft, transverse, in-line four-cylinder, bore and stroke—61 × 63 mm. Capacity—736 cc producing 67 bhp at 8000 rpm. Crankshaft: five plain main bearings, with plain big-ends and unbushed small-ends. Single camshaft driven by central single-row chain with spring-loaded tensioner. Dry-sump lubrication, six-pint oil capacity.

Transmission: Primary drive by duplex chain from middle of crankshaft to gearbox. Secondary transmission by gears from gearbox output shaft to countershaft. Final drive: ⅝ × ⅜ in. chain. Multi-plate clutch running in oil. Five-speed constant mesh gearbox, ratios: 14.01, 9.57, 7.47, 6.25 and 5.26 to 1.

Electrics: Ignition by 12 volt battery and twin coils. Charging by 210 watt alternator to 14 amp/hr battery 7 in. headlamp with combined pilot light. Flashing indicators, oil and neutral warning lights.

Brakes: Front—11½ in. disc with hydraulic calliper. Rear—7 in. single leading shoe. Wheels and tyres: 3.25 × 19 front, 4.00 × 18 rear.

Suspension: Honda telescopic front forks, two-way damped. Rear swinging arm with gas-filled spring damper units.

Dimensions: Ground clearance, 6½ in. Saddle height, 31 in. Wheelbase, 57½ in.

Price: £679 19s. including PT.

Concessionaires: Honda (UK) Ltd, Power Road, London, W.4.

---

only the angular rear tyre, which is a Japanese Dunlop, makes one feel a little uncomfortable as it changes from flat to angled tread in the wet.

The steering lock was good for town riding, but a damper is needed for high-speed motorcycling. This we discovered at around 80 mph on a bumpy bend, when the front end seemed light and gave one or two heart-stopping twitches as the power was poured on through the bend.

Top speed of the CB750 in a comfortable, sitting-up position was approximately 110–115 mph with the rider wearing a Barbour suit.

However, with racing leathers and crouched, chin-on-tank position, 125 mph was attained. No doubt, with higher gearing and a racing fairing, 135 mph would be possible.

With 70 mph limits on main roads and motorways, it isn't really the top speed of a motorcycle which counts. Even the most mundane 250 can exceed today's maximum.

The CB750 merely laughs at 70 limits as in top the motor is spinning gently at around the 4500 mark on the tacho. Where this super machine does score is, of course, acceleration.

Without a doubt, this four-pot Honda is the fastest "stock" roadster over the standing quarter-mile. A mere 12.4 seconds elapse from blast-off before you're hitting the end of the quarter strip. The "ton" is achieved in a fraction under the 12 second mark.

Blurred

One of the beauties of using the motor to the red limit is the almost complete lack of vibration. The only sign that the engine is starting to work hard is that the wing mirrors become blurred and the four mega-silencers take on a fairly healthy bark.

From the riding point of view, the CB750 offers almost armchair comfort with its deep, padded dual-seat. Both rider and pillion passenger have ample space and long-distance touring is a dream.

The only sounds as you sit back in comfort at 90 mph is the rustle of the overhead cam valve gear and the wind. This is a motorway road-burner at its best.

Braking from high speed is good using the single disc, hydraulic front unit as there is no tendency for the wheel to lock as with twin-leading shoe drum brakes. Braking is progressive and directly related to the effort placed on the lever.

However, the rear brake was fierce and care had to be used to avoid locking the rear wheel. This applied even more on wet, greasy London roads.

Electrics

Lighting or rather the electrics on the 750 are all 12-volt. To cope with the huge demand from flashers, warning lights, electric starter, etc, there is a 12v/14 amp hr battery supplied by a powerful 210 watt generator.

Night riding on dark country lanes is comfortable up to 60 mph and a maximum of 70 mph is possible on open roads.

One of the thoughtful devices on the bike was the light controls operated by the right thumb switch next to the twistgrip.

The four-position switch gave off, dip-beam, pilot light and main beam without having to take your hand from the throttle. A park position was also available on the ignition switch, which meant you could leave the lights on after removing the ignition key and nobody could turn them off.

Lighting on the instruments was also excellent as the dials were in black with light green figures. At night, the instrument lights shone through the figures to give a luminescent glow.

The finish of the CB750 is good and at the end of the test, there wasn't a trace of oil to be seen on the machine other than in its right place . . . in the oil tank and on the rear chain.

One pint of oil was used to top up the oil tank in 600 miles of road testing and we poured in a gallon of fuel approximately every 38 to 42 miles. This could be stretched to around 54 miles if we used the throttle carefully, but who wants to use this bike like a plonking tourer?

Obviously, if I could afford the cost of spares and maintenance, plus the high initial price, this would be my "get out of town" machine for going places fast!

THE ONLY WAY IS THE RIGHT WAY

A quarter of a turn makes an awfully big difference

by Bob Braverman

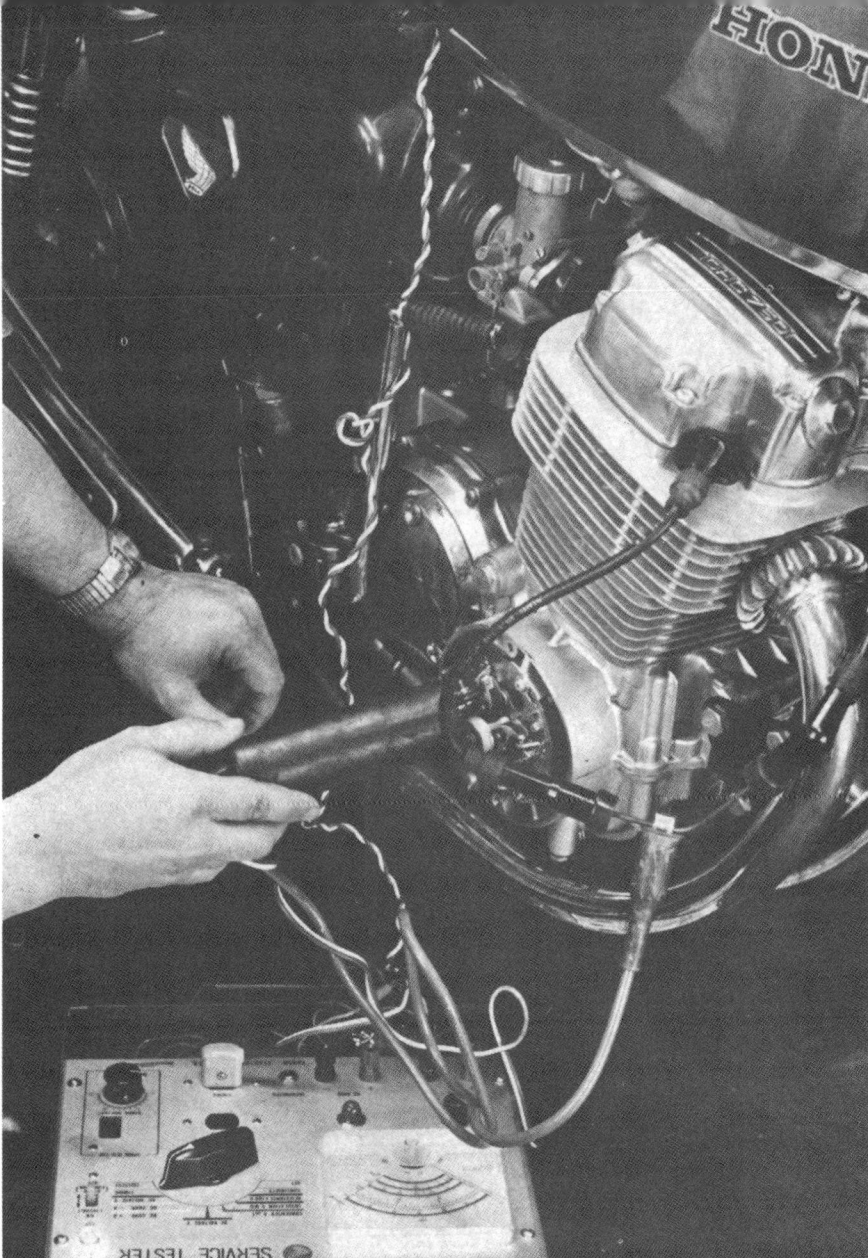

As it comes out of the box, the Honda-4 is a delightful motorcycle, but once properly tuned up and adjusted correctly, it can be a joy forever.

The difference between average servicing and really good servicing is like night and day. We found this out very recently after one of the staff members purchased one of these jewels, and the Honda Motor Company offered to show us just how to go about tuning up our little beauty, thereby extracting as much performance and enjoyment as possible. The rather interesting thing about it, is that you don't need a lot of specialized equipment to get the job done. There are only a few phases of the operation where it would be necessary to bring the motorcycle to your local dealer. This is in the area of ignition timing.

Since everybody doesn't have a strobe light or an ohm meter, we found it far cheaper and more convenient to bring the motorcycle to our local Honda Service representative for this phase of the work.

By following the simple step-by-step instructions all you Honda 750 owners are in for a delightful surprise. I would venture to guess that maybe one out of ten is really tuned properly. I have ridden a number of these machines now, and the only one I've run across that really runs great is the one we tested, after

being tuned up by Honda Motor Company, here in L. A.

The use of the vacuum gauge is an absolute necessity, since without this instrument, it's impossible to tell just when the carburetors are set correctly. We used four vacuum gauges, but you can use one. It takes longer to do it this way, but if you're careful, the end results will still be the same. If you have no tools whatsoever in your possession, and you intend to keep your 750 for a long time, it would be worthwhile spending the $50 to $75 to purchase the vacuum gauges plus a few screwdrivers and wrenches. Also, let's not forget that feeler gauge.

There is nothing tricky or unusual about tuning up the 750, but if there is one word needed to sum up the whole operation, it must be "care." It takes a good deal of care when setting up ignition and carburetion, not to mention the valve train in order to let the 750 engine perform as it was designed to do.

Also we found that, once properly tuned, it stayed tuned far longer than any of the other ones we had tested.

In going through the tune-up procedure, we found nothing tricky or complicated. All of the procedures are rather straightforward. In order to insure trouble-free performance, it is important that you follow the procedure outlined here. Don't, under any circumstances, skip any of the steps, since this will result in less than satisfactory performance. I also hope this procedure will be adopted by some of the agencies now selling the 750's. In some of the service departments we have visited, they do not do it this way and we have had it proven to us quite conclusively that unless the four-cylinder machine is tuned up in this manner, the owner is going to come out on the short end of the stick.

You Honda Four owners will be just as surprised as I was when you see what a difference it makes when the job is done right in the first place.

1. Using a 17 mm wrench, remove all of the valve adjusting caps.

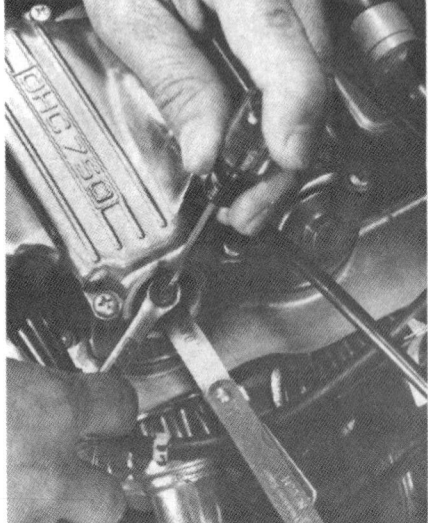

2. Using a 10 mm wrench and a small screwdriver, set all of the exhaust valves at .003. Once this has been accomplished —

3. Using the same screwdriver and 10 mm wrench, set the intakes at .002. Before adjusting any valves, be sure that it has returned to its seat.

4. Both sets of points should be adjusted between .012 and .016. This is fairly critical, so work carefully and be sure the setting is within the indicated tolerance.

5. When the engine is timed properly, number one and number 4 cylinders will be running correctly when the "F" mark shows in the window just at the points break. There is an additional mark ("F") on the rotor for cylinders two and three.

6. Check of the ignition system with the use of a Strobe light is the only accurate way of determining whether or not the engine is correctly timed. This can be done by your local shop.

7. By loosening these three screws (arrow) the entire base plate can be turned, thereby enabling the tuner to time cylinders one and four at full advance.

8. Once the screws have been loosened, grasp the plate in this manner and turn it in both directions until the "F" mark shows in the proper position.

9. For setting the advance on cylinders two and three, merely loosen these two screws and repeat the same performance only instead of rotating the whole base . . .

10. With the aid of your small screwdriver, rotate the forward set of points so the "F" mark again shows in the window.

11. A short extension for the high tension lead is a desirable item for cylinders two and three, since the plugs are hard to get at with the wire clipped from the Strobe light.

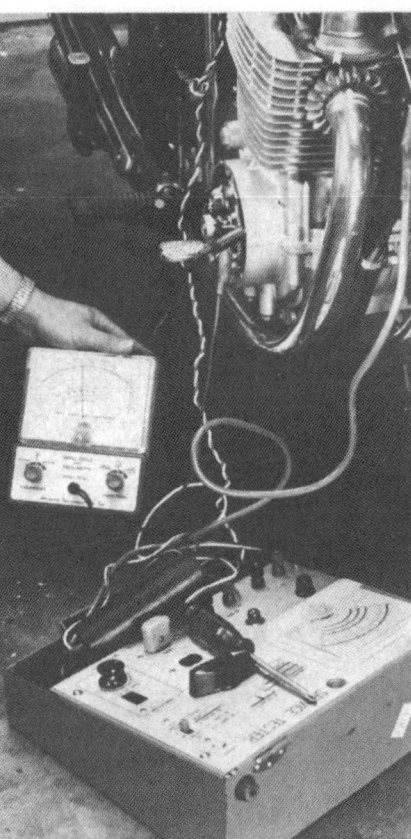

12. One very important phase of the tune-up procedure here is setting the dwell at 98° being sure that the setting is as close as possible. A degree or two one way or the other makes quite a difference in the overall performance. Most dealers can do this for you.

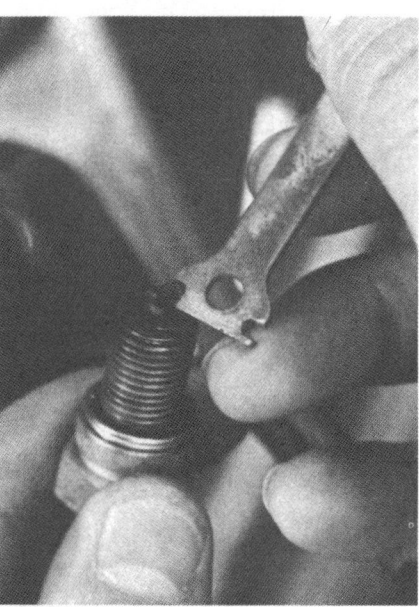

13. All plug settings should be between .024-.028. If the plugs look a little bit seedy, replace them at this point.

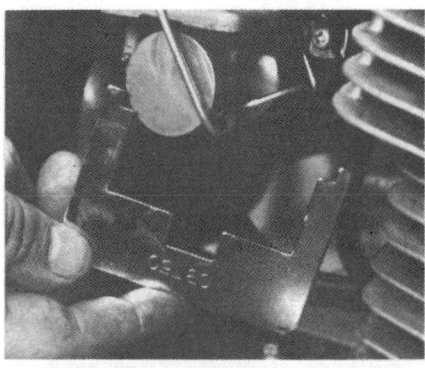

14. Another thing you may want your dealer to do is to set the float level for you. Set all four floats at 26 mm. You can get this handy gauge for float setting from Honda.

15. One item often overlooked is checking to be sure the ring clamps holding the rubber induction sleeves to the carburetor and cylinder head are tight enough. Be sure these are all tightened up, thereby eliminating any possible air leaks.

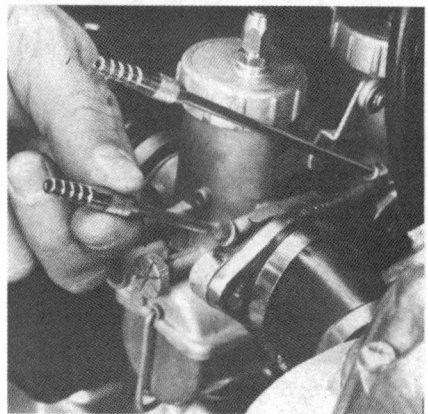

16. Remove the threaded plug in each carburetor and insert a C100 (Honda) main jet with a short tube soldered to it.

17. Loosen all four cable adjusters at the top of the carburetors and run the adjustments all the way down until there is plenty of slack in the cable housing.

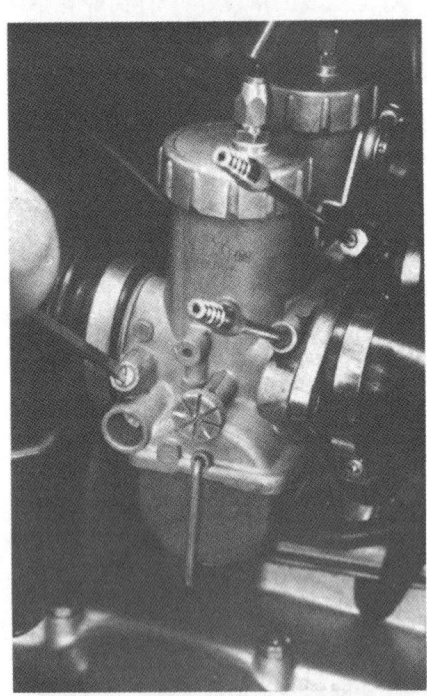

18. With a small screwdriver, very carefully turn all four low speed circuit adjusting screws all the way in until they bottom. Don't tighten them down, but stop when the screw reaches the bottom. Then back out each screw one turn.

19. Now start the engine and set all four idle screws until the engine runs at 1,000 rpm with the tubes running up to the vacuum gauges.

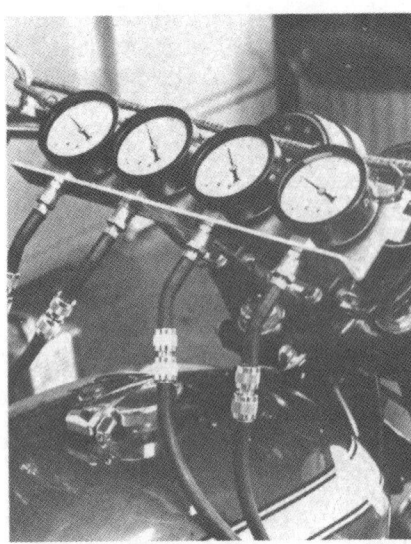

20. Chances are, under normal circumstances, this is about what you'll be seeing. The readings will vary from one gauge to another.

21. Adjust each gauge so it reads between 8 and 9 lbs. psi. Take all the flutter out with the bleeder valve with no more than 1 lb. of needle bounce. These gauges sell for about $10 each.

22. Up at the throttle set this adjustment so that the engines runs at approximately 2500 rpm and then —

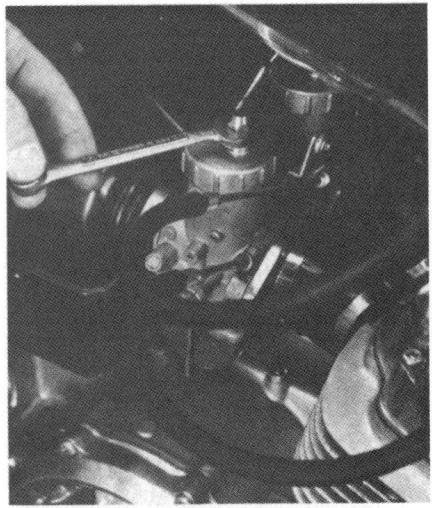

23. Go back and set each cable adjuster at each carburetor until there is zero slack in it. Then go back to the throttle adjuster and set the idle down between 850 and 950 rpm. Now remove the metal tubes and replace the plugs in each carburetor.

AT 100 MPH IT ISN'T EVEN BREATHING HARD

How many motorcycles do you know that start to flex their muscles at 80 mph? The Honda Four does.

We're used to seeing lots of them now. The big fours humming down the street aren't nearly the rarity they were several years ago. You used to look up every time you heard one go by. Occasionally you still do, although you're getting quite accustomed to having them pass you on the freeway or drive by in the dark of the night. When one passed under your window at 11 or 12 at night you automatically know it's a Honda four. No other machine sounds like it and for that matter, no other machine rides like one either.

Riding a four is a unique experience, unlike anything else. There are certain things you couldn't duplicate, no matter how many scheckles you were willing to spend, and in some cases it has a few traits you really wouldn't want to duplicate.

From all indications, it was Honda's concept to design a super-smooth high-powered roadster capable of traveling great distances at high speed with no more effort than going to the corner store for the evening paper. And they've done it. Without a doubt the four represents what some consider the ultimate in high speed transportation, but with

Styling and finish is absolutely first cabin. How Honda can offer this much machine for the price is really something.

Those four pipes really make beautiful music. There is no machine that sounds like the Honda Four.

You'll find the speedo and tach at just the right angle, so reading those large instruments at any speed is easy.

reservations. After riding several Honda fours over several thousands of miles, we feel the 750 is much more at home over 60 mph than it is plugging along in heavy traffic. The fact is, it doesn't seem to like low speed operations too much at all. It feels heavy and with a certain degree of awkwardness at slow rush hour speeds. Stopping and starting in heavy traffic is not fun. The truth of the matter is, it's not fun on any motorcycle, but it's less fun on the Honda four. It's a big bike and it's heavy. Tipping the scales at slightly over 500 pounds (512 to be exact) the rider gets the distinct impression a good portion of this weight is located up in the gas tank area. It really feels top heavy. Perhaps this is one of the reasons why the rider always feels somewhat uneasy about riding the big four at in-town traffic speeds. But just hit that freeway and wick it up a bit, and the machine suddenly changes its

personality as Jeckle and Hyde did. It suddenly becomes a precise handling completely predictable piece of equipment that installs a tremendous amount of confidence in the rider. But it still feels heavy. Regardless of how fast you ever ride the motorcycle, you never completely lose this feeling of massiveness. We got used to it, true, but we never got to the point where we actually liked it.

In designing any machine there are a certain number of concessions that must be made. Regardless of what you want at the outset, you're never going to get it 100 percent, regardless of how much money you plan on spending. Because of this, the concessions made in the case of the four were made with production, manufacturing and consumer costs uppermost in the designer's mind. Honda has done a superb job.

One of the things that we especially liked about the four was the braking system that comes as standard equipment. While a few of our acquaintances own fours and occasionally make noises about adding a second disc to the front end, we can only ask why. It certainly isn't necessary. When completing the

brake tests we found that at 120 mph you can get on the brakes pretty hard and literally lock the front wheel, watching the smoke rolling off the bottom of the tire where it comes in contact with the pavement, and at the same time watch the forks bending back under the great pressure. The forces generated by trying to stop at these speeds are fan-

Nary a drop of oil anywhere and the engine is the smoothest multi to date, but it is heavy.

Right next to the throttle you'll find a convenient ignition kill switch. This is a fine idea for emergency situations.

This is the best front anchor in the business. It's no trouble to lock the front wheel at 100 m.p.h., if it should become necessary.

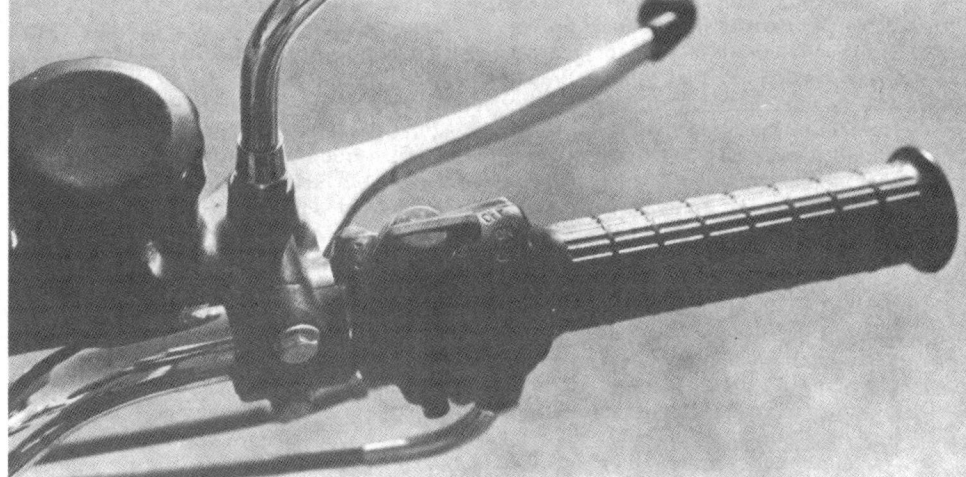

tastic, and yet the four will do this repeatedly with virtually no fade. The hydraulic front anchor is without a doubt, the best front brake we have ever run across on any motorcycle anytime, anywhere, and that's saying a lot.

Because of the fantastic smoothness of the engine, the rider is often tempted to let the revs run down lower than is good for the bike. We found that under 3,000 rpm our test machine had a tendency of gas fouling the plugs. We would suspect, that the low speed circuit in the carburetor was overly rich to help facilitate starting and early morning, cold-weather running.

The engine itself, is fairly orthodox Honda design. It is a single overhead cam arrangement not unlike those that have come before in smaller sizes. One change Honda has made for 1971 is in the area of better carburetor control. Instead of four cables, one running to each carburetor, Honda now utilizes a mechanism that ties all the carburetors together and uses only one cable to operate this entire mechanism. It's a far more satisfactory arrangement since it eliminates the old bugaboo about cable stretch and subsequent carburetor maladjustment.

Starting is a simple painless operation that takes place instantly when the choke lever is raised and the starting button is pushed. Warm up is a slow process on the four. We found that it took almost 10 minutes before the engine came up to normal operative tem-

peratures on cool fall mornings. Once the temperature started to come up however, it was no longer necessary to leave the choke on and thereby preclude any possibility of fouling the plugs. We found that just a few minutes running time and you could flip the choke off and forget it.

Hustling along a narrow twisty road is work. This is not what the Honda four was meant to do and it lets you know this quickly and positively. It is a high speed touring machine that is much happier about being ridden on freeways and fairly straight highways. Another item that could use improvement is the poor damping of the rear shocks. Make

no mistake, the machine is stable enough going around corners. It's just that it takes a certain amount of work on the part of the rider, and after 15 or 20 minutes it gets to be a bit of old news.

One really nice thing about the four is its power output. The bike doesn't seem to really care whether or not there are one or two people on the saddle. It does whatever you ask of it with the engine just kind of loafing along, never seeming to breathe hard regardless of the demands placed on it by the rider. Unlike a lot of other 750 roadsters, the power does not tend to drop off at high road speeds. A lot of the modern day super bikes rocket up to 70 mph, or even

All four carburetors are hooked together positively (arrows) and only use one cable, instead of four individual ones.

The first time you start bending the four around a corner, you'll really appreciate the large amount of ground clearance.

The seat and rear suspension are fine for two up riding. The only objection is the seat is rather high.

some go to 80, after which performance starts to ebb away. Not so with the Honda. At 70 and 80, it's still picking 'em up and laying 'em down in much the same manner as it did at 40. At 100, the rider starts to feel acceleration dropping off, but unless you're racing, who cares?

Like all Hondas, the finish is impeccable. The only thing we could find fault with was the rather crude looking welding exhibited on the chassis. Most of this is hidden however, and with the frame being painted black, you don't notice this unless you really get down there and look for it.

One thing we never have liked and still don't, is the rather sudden throttle response especially·in low gear. There is a slight lag from the time the throttle is opened until something happens. And when it does happen, it happens quick. We would much rather see some sort of cam type throttle assembly that allows the throttle to be opened more slowly, just off of the idle position. This would make riding in traffic far more enjoyable and a lot less nervewracking. The gear box is ultra smooth, and the more you ride it, the smoother it gets. Likewise with the clutch. The interesting thing is that repeated beatings at the local dragstrip did not seem to take any edge off of the clutch or gearbox operation. It operated silky-smooth and positively every time. Although the last Honda four we road tested was capable of turning e.t.'s in the twelves, this one wouldn't. The best we could get was 13.04. We would suspect that something was lacking as far as the state of tune was concerned. Also the quarter mile speeds never got much over 100. The best we got was 100.97. The bike should run at least two to four miles faster. The actual top speed by the way was 121 flat.

One thing we would like to see Honda change are the tires. There are certain freeways here in southern California that have road surfaces looking for all the world as though someone had taken a giant comb and run along the concrete before it had a chance to set up. The reason for this is to help the rain run off during the wet season, but it does tend to play hob with certain types of motorcycle tires. The Honda four is afflicted with this problem. The rider soon learns nothing is going to happen, but this very slight amount of wiggling that takes place is similar to the sensation encountered when running over a steel lattice type bridge with knobbies. Anybody out there who has ever done this will be quick to understand exactly what we're talking about.

It's truly incredible that you can buy such a superb piece of machinery at such a low price. How Honda has been able to offer the consumer this much equipment and performance at so modest a figure is amazing. The degree of finish and performance is certainly out of the ordinary, and we can remember times when it would cost you three to four times as much to get something not even close to what Honda represents. One thing that is not quite so obvious when the rider first starts riding the Honda is just how much ground clearance it has. This fact is driven home once the pilot becomes familiar with the handling characteristics and starts pushing the machine harder. This game seems like a natural on the four since the looks and sound are not unlike a number of special GP bikes seen and heard only a couple of seasons ago. Because everything is tucked up and in close, the chance of dragging anything on the pavement is pretty remote. This

is a pretty comforting thing to know when you're suddenly faced with having to stuff the machine down another three or four degrees because you misjudged a corner.

One thing we definitely did not like was the rear stand. You're practically inviting a hernia everytime you lift the bike up on to the rear stand. As a result we found ourselves avoiding this at all costs.

Although the engine stays in tune for a long time and servicing is quite simple, we have found through experience that tuning up the 750 is not slap-dash operation. It requires a great deal of care. The fact is, a lot more care than the majority of other motorcycles we have come in contact with. Once tuned properly the 750 is a superb thing from an engine standpoint, but improperly tuned up, it's disappointing. It would be well worth any perspective buyer (or any present owner for that matter) to go out of his way and find himself a mechanic who knows and understands these power plants. It will make a remarkable difference in just how your Honda four performs. There's nothing tricky or dodgy about tuning the four, but it must be done carefully.

A large degree of engine smoothness can be traced to the five main bearing forged crankshaft. By having five main bearings in a four cylinder engine (plus a careful balance job) this goes a long way towards insuring a smooth, flex-free vibrationless engine. Also it might be worth mentioning here that those five main bearings also mean bearing life is increased considerably since inhibiting crankshaft flexure means far less bearing wear.

Although there are a few niceties Honda has introduced in 1971, the four is still basically the same machine it was last year only with a few refinements. For the masses, it has few equals. It is economically priced, beautifully finished, well constructed and the sound is out of sight. The power plant is extremely flexible and given half way decent, service will reward its owner with thousands of trouble-free miles with maximum enjoyment. *Bob Braverman* **CG**

HONDA CB 750 FOUR

ENGINE

Type . . . . inline, four cylinder, ohc four cycle
Bore and stroke . . . . 61 x 63mm
Displacement 736cc
Compression ratio 9.0:1
Max. Horsepower . . . . 67 at 8,000 rpm
Max. torque . . . . 44.12 ft/lbs.
Ignition . . . . alternator/battery
Carburetion . . . . 4-constant velocity concentrics
Lubrication . . . . wet sump

DIMENSIONS

Length . . . . 85.0 in.
Wheelbase . . . . 57.3 in.
Ground clearance . . . . 5.5 in.
Dry weight . . . . 522 lbs.

WHEELS AND BRAKES

Front tire size . . . . 3.25 x 19 in.
Front brake type . . . . hydraulic, disc
Rear tire size . . . . 4.00 x 18 in.
Rear brake type . . . . internal expanding

TRANSMISSION

Type . . . . constant mesh, five speed
Clutch . . . . wet, multi-plate
Internal gear ratios 1st, 2.500:1; 2nd, 1.708:1;
         3rd, 1.333:1; 4th, 1.097:1; 5th, .939:1
Final ratio 2.667:1

PERFORMANCE

Indicated highest one-way speed 121.5
Acceleration 0-60 . . . . 5.6
Braking distance 30-0 . . . . 30.0
Quarter-mile acceleration:
   Top speed 100.00
   Elapsed time 13.05

GENERAL

Air filtration . . . . dry paper
Battery type 12V-14AH

CAPACITIES

Fuel tank . . . . 4.5 gal.
Fuel reserve . . . . 1.3 gal.
Oil tank . . . . .53 gal.
Engine/Gearbox (total) . . . . .93 gal.

FRAME AND SUSPENSION

Front suspension . . . . telescopic, double damping
Rear suspension . . . . spring over shock,
                     pneumatic damping
Frame type . . . . tubular, double cradle

COLORS: Red, Gold, Green or Brown

PRICE AS TESTED — $1600.00 FOB GARDENA

DISTRIBUTOR

American Honda Motor Co.
P.O. Box 50
Gardena, CA. 90247

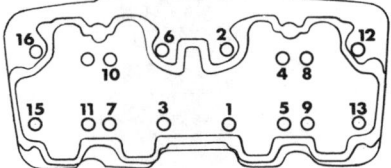

EXHAUST

INLET

With such a large alloy head distortion can be a big problem. Tighten down the nuts evenly in the order shown, to right torque

Check oil pump body for cracks. Clearance between the inner rotor and outer rotor, and the outer rotor and casing is .0138 in. max

HONDA

HONDA'S MIGHTY 750 UNDER MM'S MICROSCOPE

■ Although Honda's four-cylinder engine is straightforward in design, because of its high power output great care is needed in preparation and maintenance.

As long as everything is set up within the tolerances given all should be well.

Note that the pistons should be installed with the arrow stamped on the crown facing the exhaust and that the rings must be fitted with the maker's marking uppermost.

One point which does require great care on assembly is the crankshaft bearings.

These should be checked for wear, using a press gauge available from Honda agents, and the shell bearings must be selected according to the crankshaft/crankcase size.

There are three sizes of crankcase cap, denoted by A, B or C, and these are shown by the letters stamped on the front of the lower crankcase half, in order from left to right.

The crankshaft journals also

have three sizes, shown by letters and numbers stamped on the flywheel. The letters refer to the main bearing journals and the numbers to the crankpin journals. Connecting rods also have a number stamped on them to denote the size of the big-end eye.

To obtain the correct oil clearance the shell bearings are colour coded, so knowing the size of the bearing cap and journal according to the stamped letters and numbers, the shell colour can be found from a table available at your Honda dealers.

Because of these size variations it is essential that all bearings are replaced in their original positions and correctly torqued down.

special tools

07001-30001	inlet seat cutter
07002-30001	exh seat cutter
07003-30001	inlet top cutter
07004-30001	exh top cutter
07005-30001	inl lower cutter
07006-30001	exh lower cutter
07007-30001	seat cutter holder
07008-30001	valve guide reamer
07031-30001	valve remover
07031-30010	valve remover body
07046-30001	valve guide drift
07087-30001	tappet locknut wrench
07050-30001	rocker shaft remover
07078-30001	head bolt wrench
07032-30001	piston ring clamp
07033-30001	piston support
07011-30001	alternator rotor puller
07094-30002	spark plug wrench
07022-30001	drive sprocket holder
07086-30001	clutch locknut wrench
07048-30020 ⎫	countershaft
07048-30025 ⎭	bearing drifts
07065-30001	oil pressure gauge
07068-30001	gauge adaptor
07068-30007	vacuum gauge adaptor
07068-30012	vacuum gauge adaptor
07024-30001	vacuum gauge set (4)
07064-30010	vacuum gauge (1)

ENGINE DATA

lubrication

Dry sump. Rotor displacement type feed and scavenge pumps driven from kickstart idler pinion.

relief valve blow-off pressure	57 lb./in.^{2}
warning lamp cut-in	7 lb./in.^{2}
pump rotor clearance (maximum)	.0138 in.

engine

bore	61 mm
stroke	63 mm
capacity	736 cm^3
number of cylinders	4
compression ratio	9:1
engine unit weight	176.3 lb. (with oil)
maximum power output	67 PS at 8000 rpm
maximum torque output	44.12 lb. ft. at 7000 rpm
compression pressure (at starting speed)	170 lb./in.^{2}
ignition timing at 1000 rpm	6 deg. btdc
at 2500 rpm	40 deg. btdc
contact breaker	Hitachi
cb gap setting	.012–.016 in.
spark plug, hot	NGK D-7ES

normal	D-8ES
cold	D-10E
gap	.024–.028 in.
thread size	12 mm × 12.7 mm reach
cylinder head warpage	.002 in. or less

valve timing:

intake opens	5 deg. btdc
intake closes	30 deg. btdc
exhaust opens	35 deg. bbdc
exhaust closes	5 deg. atdc
valve clearance, intake	.002 in.
exhaust	.003 in.
cam lift, intake	.314–.316 in.
(minimum	.3132 in.)
exhaust	.295–.296 in.
(minimum	.2925 in.)
cam base circle	1.102–1.103 in.
(minimum	1.1 in.)
camshaft runout	.002 in. or less

valve springs:

free length, inner	1.50 in.
(minimum	1.457 in.)
outer	1.622 in.
(minimum	1.575 in.)

valve guide clearance

intake	.003 in. max.
exhaust	.003 in. max.
valve seat angle	90 deg.
valve seat width	.04–.05 in.
correction cutter, inner	40 deg. intake
	26 deg. exhaust
outer	radiused

piston:

skirt clearance, minimum	.0004–.0016 i

fitted ring gap:

top and second ring	.0079–.016 in
(maximum	.028 in.)
oil control ring	.004–.0012 in
(maximum	.028 in.)

ring groove clearance:

top	.0016–.0028 i
(maximum	.007 in.)
second	.001–.0022 in
(maximum	.0065 in.)
oil	.0004–.0016 i
(maximum	.0045 in.)
maximum bore wear	.002 in.)
rebore oversizes	+.25, .50, .75
	1.00 mm

bearings

ankshaft supported in five main bearings.
ains and big-ends are all shell bearings.

ains clearance	.0008–.0018 in.
aximum	.0032 in.)
ax. journal wear	.002 in.
g end clearance	.0008–.0018 in.
aximum	.0032 in.)
ankshaft runout	.002 in. or less

B. Big-end and mains bearings are available
differing sizes and are coded according to
e size of the journal and bearing cap.

el system

rburettor (4 off)	Keihin piston valve
minal bore	28 mm
ain jet	120
edle jet	.102 × .15 in.
edle	.098 in.
rottle valve	2.5
ot jet	.047 in.
jet	100
screw opening	$1 \pm \frac{1}{8}$
w jet	40

transmission

5-speed crossover gearbox driven through
multiplate clutch. Primary and final drive by
chain.
clutch:

driving plates	7 (bonded)
driven plates	6 (plain)
number of springs	4 (coil)
spring load	214–227 lb./
	.984 in.
minimum	198 lb./.984 in.
free length	1.258 in.
minimum	1.20 in.
driving plate thickness	.135–.141 in.
minimum	.122 in.
maximum plate warpage	.012 in.
primary reduction	1.708
secondary reduction	1.167

gear ratios (internal)

1st	2.500
2nd	1.708
3rd	1.333
4th	1.097
5th	.939

electrical equipment

12 volt a.c./d.c. system, coil ignition.
Separately-excited field 3-phase a.c. generator,
charging battery via rectifier and voltage regulator. Negative earth.

battery	Yuasa B64-12
capacity	12 v, 14 a-h
alternator	Hitachi LD 113-01
output	156 W
regulator	Hitachi TL1Z-38
rectifier	Hitachi SB6B-7
starter motor rating	.6 kW
reduction gear	22.04:1
fuse rating	15 amp.

torque wrench settings

camshaft bolts	6.5–9.4 lb. ft.
big end bolts	14.5 lb. ft.
main bearing bolts	14.5 lb. ft.
crankcase bolts, 8 mm	16.6–18.1 lb. ft.
a.c. generator bolt	72.3 lb. ft.
cylinder head nuts	13.7–15.2 lb. ft.
clutch centre nut	32.5–36.2 lb. ft.

STAGE TUNING THE HONDA 750

PT. I - INTRODUCTION

Getting the Maximum Performance from Your 750 Engine and Chassis
by Bob Braverman

Not since the Harley-Davidson Sportster was introduced in 1957, has any motorcycle captured the American motorcyclists the way the Honda 750 has, and with good reason. First of all, the idea of being able to buy a four cylinder engine that hosts the features the 750 does is certainly worth looking at. Also, the chassis can boast of a number of innovations not found on many production motorcycles, when it was first introduced.

The front disc brake is probably the most powerful stopping component in the motorcycle industry, except perhaps for some of the racing versions. Although you may not be aware of it, the frame on this motorcycle is quite light. It would be difficult to save more than a few pounds in constructing a new mass of tubing to connect all of the parts together. The results you would get would not justify the expense or effort. However, there are still a number of things that can be done to the chassis to further improve the handling and increase the riding enjoyment.

To prove or disprove any modification to a power plant, it would be foolhardy to trust a seat-of-the-pants evaluation. So we contacted Exhibition Engineering, and they agreed to construct a special dynomometer just for the Honda 750 engine. These people are capable of providing the type of components a performance minded 750 owner can use.

The next installment will contain information on a kit any rider can purchase and install. It is a bolt-on operation, and the difference in performance is surprising, while the cost is quite low.

We have been in contact with the Honda Four Owners Club, as well as other people providing services and products for this motorcycle, and they are willing to work with us in any way possible to make this series of articles a success. We are enthusiastic about the potential of this series, and we believe that even with the limited amount of research and development work we have done so far, there is a vast untapped potential in this power plant yet to be discovered. We

The large duct carries away the exhaust fumes from the four exhaust pipes.

Instrumentation is simple but complete. Only the necessary instruments and controls are used.

A nylon shoe (from a Sportster primary) is used to keep tension in the rear drive chain.

Along with a torque scale there's a dual cylinder head temperature indicator and a vacuum gauge.

The actual loading device is a dual caliper disc brake unit. This arrangement works out fine.

think you'll be as surprised as we were, as we uncover these things one by one.

There are certain factors working against us, like the cylinder head design. There are some serious drawbacks in this area that unfortunately we cannot rectify, but with some careful work, we can minimize these problems.

A lot of things can be done with the Honda Four without spending a great deal of money. Most of the changes are simply learning what to do and how to do it. If you follow our instructions, you'll be rewarded with a better motorcycle than you can buy from a dealer. Whatever prob-

lems the Honda 750 Four has can either be eliminated or minimized to the point where they are no longer bothersome. Stay tuned in. It will be worth it. *CG*

STAGE TUNING THE HONDA 750

PART 2

The more effort we put into this stage tuning series, the more respect we have for this four cylinder Honda. **by Bob Braverman**

It would seem there is no load too great for the engine to handle. Big bore kits don't seem to faze the reliability, and of course the performance increase is noticeable. So noticeable, in fact, that a recent trip to the dragstrip with a stock out of the box bike, a somewhat hotted up machine, and an all-out full blown street chassis dragster, proved to us there is gobs of performance for the asking. Another fine byproduct of our test was proof that while the increase is substantial, the powerplant is by no means fussy.

We found it quite easy to become consistent, with the ET's never varying more than 1/10th of a second. The box stock machine, while it was fairly tuned up, did have a lot of hard miles on it. As a result, 13.50's were about average, with one run dropping down into the low 13.40's. Speeds, by the way, were just about 100 mph flat. For an average, this is just about what we expected.

Moving on to the Stage I machine, (824cc's) we found the ET's dipping down into the 11's, 12 flat or 11.95 being the average. Miles per hour were slightly over 115. Unfortu-

nately, a new front wheel had been installed, but not balanced. Also, some fork work had been done at the last minute, and there was a slight problem with the front suspension. The results produced a high speed gallop that was disconcerting for this rider. Only a few runs were made, because with the front end problem, the machine was not as safe as it should have been.

The real fun came with the last one, the highly tuned 890cc job. This bike would run about 11.70 flat, with the mile per hour clock reading just about 118 (117.90 was par for the course). We feel sure that anybody with some experience on the dragstrip could take this motorcycle and within the first few runs turn 11.90 to 12 seconds flat. It is comparatively easy to ride, and like most dragsters, the first few feet determine whether the run will be an 11.70 or a 12 second performance.

We found the best way to bring the bike out of the gate was to whip the revs up to 7000, drop the hammer and turn the throttle wide open. An examination of the photographs will show a very pronounced weight

transfer, with adequate bite as the rear end of the bike got a good hold of the ground. The bike does not rocket out of the chute, because of the all up weight of 500 pounds. This is a great deal of mass for the engine to get moving quickly. To reduce the weight any further would require a large amount of extensive chassis modification work, with many special pieces having to be fabricated. This was not our idea in conducting this test. The idea was to take three motorcycles that resembled something you could ride on the street, do the job to them and check their performance against one another. This we feel we have done, and the results are interesting.

The semi-modified and full race jobs weigh within a few pounds of each other, while the box stock one was noticeably heavier. Since completing the test, the highly modified version has been stretched to a full 910cc's. We have not tested this and cannot report on the difference in performance, although we suspect the extra 20cc's would not make that noticeable a difference.

The difference in displacement is

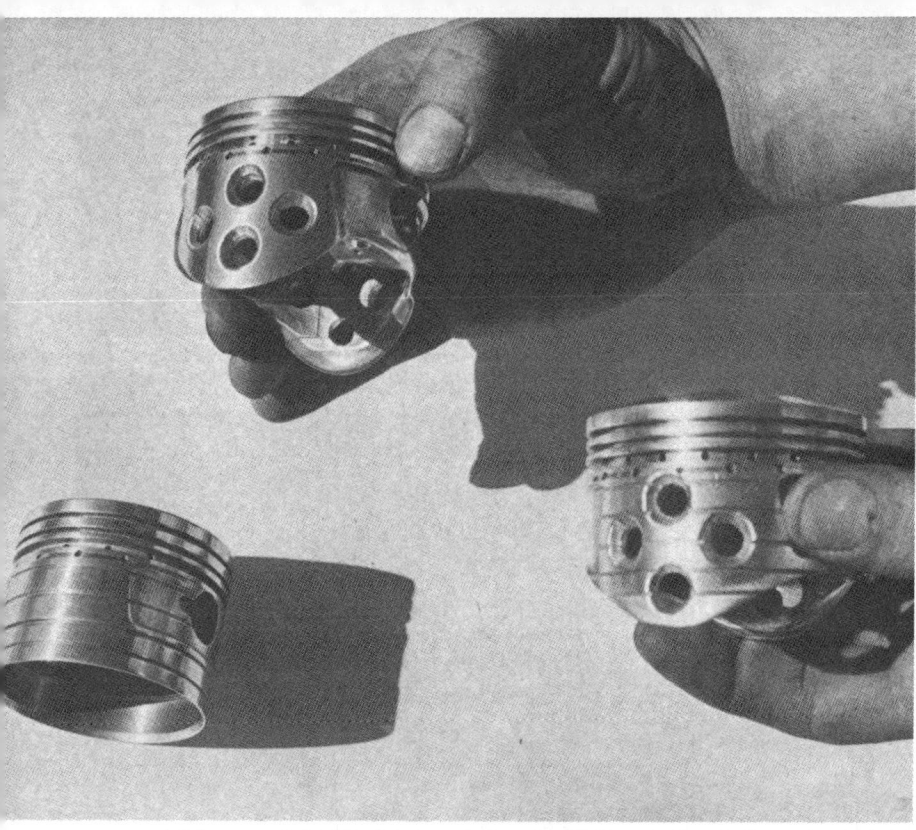

The alternator is balanced on the crankshaft once the main crank assembly has gone through the entire balancing process. The alternator is marked so that it can be installed the same way every time.

The modified street piston (upper left) is virtually the same as the racing version (lower right). Both types are machined from the same castings the stock pistons are made from (lower left).

With increased bearing loads it's vital that additional oil be fed to the bearings in the manner shown. A simple channel cut to each side of the oil feed hole handles the job nicely.

Several pounds of weight are machined off of the individual crank throws after which it is necessary to go back and rebalance the entire lower end assembly.

made up entirely with the boring bar. There was no effort made to change the stroke or the bottom end, other than making it better. R. C. Engineering, who supplied the motorcycle and did the work on all of the bikes run at the dragstrip, uses cylinder sleeves of a special steel alloy that is stronger than the standard items. They claim it also provides longer cylinder life. The sleeves come as a casting and must be machined to accept the new pistons. The cylinder

casting must also be bored out to receive the new liners. The four cylinder holes in the aluminum casting are bored .003 of an inch oversize and heated to 400°, at which time the new liners will be slipped in place. After the whole assembly has been allowed to cool, the top of the cylinder is milled .003 to insure that the mating surfaces are perfectly flat, and also to improve the deck height of the pistons.

With this phase of the job out of the way, each cylinder is finish bored,

and head gasket 'O' ring grooves are cut in the steel flange on the top of each cylinder. This is done to eliminate the standard head gasket, since the additional cubic inch displacement has led to a number of head gasket problems when using the standard parts. The 'O' ring is nothing but a piece of copper wire that is tapped into the groove and provides a seal against the cylinder head when it is torqued down in place. It should be mentioned here that automotive dragster engine builders employ the same technique, to insure no loss of compression in those supercharged large displacement V8's found on dragstrips across the country.

Before the completed reworked cylinder can be utilized with the standard bottom end, it will be necessary to

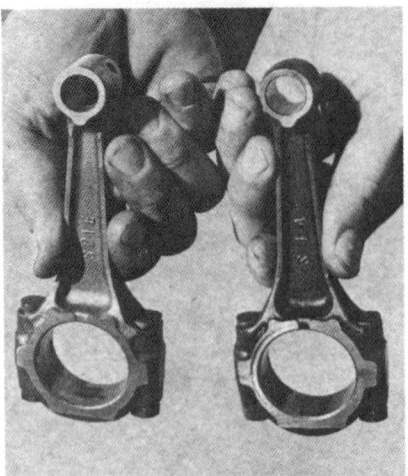

The modified rod (left) has been heat treated and shot peened to greatly improve reliability and strength. The earlier stock rods (right) do not stand up well in modified engines.

Soft copper wire is then tapped into the circular channel so as to provide a proper seal and in that way eliminate any further head gasket trouble. This system works like a charm.

After boring the cylinders, a fly cut is made across the top to level up the casting, at which time O ring grooves are machined into the top of each steel sleeve. At this point the sleeves themselves are finished, bored and honed.

remove the top crankcase half and bore out each spigot hole, so that the sleeves may drop down and register in the top casting.

The pistons used in the basic big bore kit are Honda 350 SL units. The piston crown is machined to clear the cylinder head, and valve pockets are built to provide piston to valve clearance, eliminating any possibility of the valves crashing into the piston head at 9 or 10,000 rpm. Then the skirts are cut down and slippered, to reduce weight and frictional drag. This is important, since a larger displacement means more piston weight. In order to keep piston weight at a minimum, this reshaping and cutting is necessary. Also, the reduction in friction is a reasonable goal.

Although the pistons may vary

Before the reworked cylinder can be installed in the crankcase halves, it will be necessary to machine out the spigot holes to receive the new larger diameter sleeves. These holes should be a close fit.

slightly, depending on what they're being used for, they all look pretty much the same, except on the full race job. These have holes drilled in the piston skirts, and grooves machined in to help provide extra oil, since additional lubrication is needed on these highly loaded items at the upper rev limits. Each top piston ring

Since most of the horsepower is generated in the head assembly, it is necessary to clean up the ports and combustion chamber. It is not a good idea to recontour the head, but instead merely clean it up.

It is necessary to install a double spring setup on the ignition points to prevent floating at high rpm. This one modification makes a considerable difference in the performance of the entire ignition system.

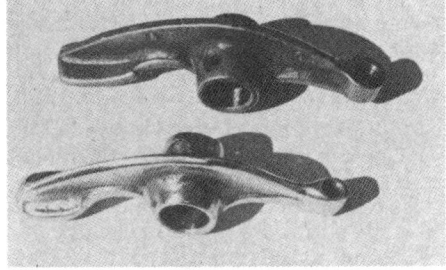

Since it is vitally important to reduce the valve train mechanism mass, judicious work with a grinder can almost cut in half the weight of each rocker arm. Be careful not to overdo it, as this will weaken the components.

A four-into-one header, collector, and megaphone add greatly to the machine's mid-range and top end performance. Needless to say, its use should be discouraged for street use because of the noise.

lip is machined back .015, to reduce piston to cylinder wall scuffing. Since the 750 connecting rod is bigger than the 350 twin, it is necessary to mill an additional .125 on the inside of each piston pin boss. This will accommodate the wider top end of each rod and also provide the necessary side clearance. After all the machine work is finished, the pistons are balanced to 1/10 of a gram and highly polished.

The basic cylinder head also receives attention. The standard inlet valves are replaced with .100 oversized stainless steel items that are stellite tipped, with hard chrome stems. Although the standard intakes are substantial, these new stainless steel units fare better for sustained high rpm use. The stellite tipped stems hold up considerably longer when used with a modified cam shaft. The hard chrome plating on the stem provides a slick surface, and one that is more resistant.

After the valve machine work has been completed, it is polished to improve strength as well as air flow. The new valve when completed is 3½ grams lighter than stock. This is surprising in view of the fact that it is larger and considerably stronger. The top portion of the inlet valve stem is tapered back slightly to reduce port restriction and provide less blockage to the incoming fuel/air charge. The complete inlet tract is shaped and polished to provide maximum flow and velocity.

The combustion chamber is also cleaned up and polished. While on the subject of combustion chambers, it may be worth mentioning here that it would be foolish to remove those

In conducting our three machine test, the first bike we rode was a stocker which ran in the low to middle 13's. This is about par for this type of motorcycle.

With the all up weight of 500 pounds the addition of the larger rear tire is an absolute necessity. Notice what the weight transfer has done to the tire the instant the clutch has been released.

little pockets and ridges found in the original casting. In flow testing a standard cylinder head, it was discovered that although it looks racy to remove these little ridges, it disturbs the flow necessary to high efficiency. It's better to clean them up and polish the head out.

The cylinder head on the Honda Four is one of the problem areas. In order to put the spark plug and valves in a convenient spot, a certain sacrifice had to be made in performance. As a result, the combustion chamber design is not the optimum. Unfortunately, to remedy this would require a completely new casting, and this represents a huge sum of dollars and much work, and a lot of R&D time.

As a result of these problems in cylinder head design, it is difficult to really fill the cylinders adequately at high rpm with the big bore kits. The fact that they put out as much power as they do is amazing, since it is evident that by repositioning the valves

We found that coming out of the gate was relatively easy with the full blown job since all that was necessary was to wick on the throttle and drop the hammer.

and spark plugs, a noticeable increase in power would result. However, this is not possible under the present arrangement, so we make do with what we have. It is doubtful that anybody would be willing to pay several thousand dollars for a new cylinder head.

Like the intakes, the exhaust valves are polished and undercut, to provide less restriction to the spent gases exiting through the exhaust port. The exhaust valve guide is left at the standard height, but all sharp edges are removed from the guide and the port, to reduce hot spots and improve heat transfer. Inlet and exhaust valve guide seats are carefully cleaned up and kept at .045 width. Each seat is cut at a 45° angle, while the valve is ground at 44° degrees to provide a good seal.

Holding the valve springs to the head, we found standard springs have a .030 shim under each one for street use. For high performance work, an S & W spring is installed, with alloy collars and keepers. This increases the seat pressure from 70 to 90 pounds, and the light collars and keepers reduce the valve train weight another 8 grams. Every bit counts.

Although the rev limit seems to be the same as a standard engine (10,000 rpm), the modified job gets there a lot quicker. Standard rocker arms are utilized, but are lightened and polished to reduce weight and increase strength. Our opinion is that

HONDA CB 750 RACING ENGINE

	MODIFIED		STANDARD	
Displacement	54.5 cu. in.	910cc	44.93 cu. in.	736cc
Bore	2.639	67mm	2.401	61mm
Stroke	2.480	63mm	Same	
Compression Ratio	12½–1		9–1	
Compression Pressure	215 lbs.		170 lbs.	
Horsepower	90 @ 9,500 rpm		51 @ 7,000 rpm	
Camshaft	Kenny Harman "F"		Std. Honda	
Valve Lift	.393 in.	.339 ex.	.314 in.	.294 ex.
Valve Timing	48°–74°	81°–38°	5°–30°	35°–5°
Valve Clearance	.005	.007	.001	.0015

The fully modified machine produced ET's in the 11.70 bracket, although more performance is there for the asking providing the owner is willing to settle for less reliability and higher maintenance costs.

STAGE TUNING THE HONDA 750

while the polishing looks good, it would be better to have the rocker arms and connecting rods shot peened, to improve strength and longevity. The valve adjuster bolt is drilled ¾ of its length, and the standard lock nut is replaced with a titanium counterpart. Total rocker arm weight is reduced by 21 grams.

Interestingly, standard connecting rods from the late model 750 K1 series have proved to be adequate. The earlier units, though lighter, were also weaker and had a tendency to bend under average racing conditions. Each rod is magnafluxed, along with the rod bolts, and then both are heat treated and shot peened to reduce any possibility of failure.

After extensive testing, we found that the rod web thickness and width are at a minimum for most racing applications. For this reason, it would be a good idea if no polishing or lightening is attempted, as it would remove vital material from a very critical load area and reduce the strength.

It may be worth mentioning here that the turbocharged Honda Hawk engines, while utilizing standard connecting rods that have been thinned down slightly and reheat treated, have thus far proved quite reliable; so reliable, in fact, that the horsepower of the original engine has been tripled with no adverse effects. You can't ask

New stainless steel valves in alloy collars replace the stock items for that last little bit of high rpm horsepower. Also, the new valves provide less restriction and improve flow.

for much more than that. In a forthcoming issue, we will pass along the special heat treating information for those of you who contemplate doing this sort of thing.

The small end of the rod is fitted with a special bronze bushing to reduce friction, while the big end is surfaced to increase side clearance .010 on the crankshaft journals. The bottom rod bearing clearances are set at .002, after carefully torqueing them down. Each rod is then carefully balanced.

Before R. C. Engineering does any work to the crankshaft, each unit is first magnafluxed and then checked for alignment and wear. If the crank checks out okay, the outer diameter of each counterweight is cut approximately half an inch, and all edges are radiused and polished. This one operation reduces the rotating mass by 3½ pounds, and greatly improves throttle response and acceleration. With this out of the way, all oil transfer holes are relieved to improve oil flow across the bearing surface and aid in cooling. The bearing surfaces are micro polished, and then the crankshaft is carefully balanced and readied for installation.

If the bike is being used for street use, the alternator must also be balanced and indexed. For dragstrip use, the alternator can be removed and an alloy cover plug fitted in its place. Main bearing clearance is .0025-.003 of an inch.

To provide lubrication in a reworked engine, the oil pump must receive some attention to be sure it will handle the increased load. The pressure release valve spring is shimmed .060 of an inch, bringing the oil pressure to a full 85 pounds. A small oil hole

is drilled in the oil transfer line of the cylinder, to spray oil on the cam chain roller. This seemingly small detail aids cam chain roller life.

That about sums up the details needed to produce an 11 second street dragster. Although we have reports on the collector pipes and megaphones, we cannot pass judgment on them, since none of the bikes we rode were fitted with them at the time of testing. From previous experience, we have found that a collector system with a megaphone does increase the power range and put plenty of beans on the ground.

Performance is not cheap, and the more performance you get, and the more cylinders you have, the higher the price will be. If you need any further information, we suggest writing to R. C. Engineering at the address listed below.

In the next installment, we have some interesting facts about improving the handling of the 750 Four chassis. Believe it or not, you can make several significant changes in the motorcycle's personality without even lighting up the torch. Everything can be handled in your garage, or by the local bike shop down the street. You won't believe the difference in handling until you've tried it. *CG*

Race-Test: 750cc PRODUCTION HONDA FOUR

An electric starter really can make the difference. Witness Graham Wylie's . . .

High, wide and handsome

by Ray Knight

THERE ARE SOME interesting stories behind how we get our hands on 'bikes for race testing. Sometimes the offer is made because a dealer has an interest in getting publicity for a particular model, or we make the suggestion because the 'bike in question is one that is "in the scene" at the time, and is obviously of general interest to readers in comparing the performance of a race prepared version with other makes, under the ultimate testing of race conditions, to see which is the quickest when the chips are down.

The CB750 was a little different. Obviously it's an excellent subject for testing, but there are not many around the circuits. None is obviously sponsored, so there weren't any to get our hot little hands on anyway. But then the Editor received a letter from Graham Wylie who had one, was preparing it for production racing with goodies like twin discs and Girlings and, what is more, actually wanted yours truly to hammer it around a circuit to see how it went. Couldn't really refuse, could we?

The Honda is a couple of years old now and has served Graham well on the road. But like many of us he'd been bitten with the idea of racing, and, with a quick sports machine, that was the obvious thing to race. It says well for the 'bike that it has never been overhauled or needed it, and is now serving Graham well in making his racing debut in the production class. He's had a fifth at Gaydon and was leading at Cadwell Park, but slid off – so he and the machine are hardly outclassed on riders' circuits. The scene of this particular action was Snetterton, and the fact of riding there so often gives a

useful yardstick of performance against personal and other machines' performances on a circuit where top-end performance counts rather more than the ability to ear 'ole to the maximum, something that can vary quite a lot, and introduces factors not relevant to comparative testing.

The Honda is a big 'bike in every respect. I'm far from short, but found that my feet only just went squarely on the ground. It's possibly taller than the 1971 Bonnevilles, and they are ridiculous for anyone with short legs. So it was high; that was in part due to the 19 inch rear wheel that Graham has fitted to give extra ground clearance for racing. And looking down at the engine one was impressed by the way it stuck out on either side of the 'bike, at crankcase level that is. So it was wide. That it's handsome no enthusiast could deny.

In fact, the 'bike is immaculate for a two-year-old job and the only difference that one could see from the standard model was that there were two discs with which to stop it – the extra one is a listed optional extra on the homologation list. There were no air cleaners. Substituted were "Read" induction trumpets with gauze covers to keep out the termites. There was a steering damper to assist navigation and, of course, the riding position was suited to racing, with rearsets and bolt-on 'bars – yes, not clip-ons, but the Dunstall type that bolt through the top of the forks.

Graham practised to qualify for his ride in the production race and I did likewise on the Trident, then came my turn to practise on the Honda with the 1000cc open racers with whom I would be competing. It was really being thrown in at

lightning getaway (No. 40) as he picks his way . . .

through the pushers.

the deep end and perhaps a little unfairly, you might think. But I'd argue that one by saying that the race was won anyway by the same lad who won the production race, Tony Smith on a Norvil Commando, and if the racers could not keep up with him, then the rest were fair game for another racing roadster.

A prod on the starter button produced a well ordered rustling from the four cylinders under the tank and the motor ticked over at an indicated 1000 revolutions. Left foot under the two inch long gear

pedal and with "one up" and a touch of throttle we were rolling. Now that was going to be a problem, to remember that the gear and brake pedals were "arsy-tarsy"

It's rather like sitting over a large Hoover.

with the conventional British set-up, so I'd better keep that in mind even in the heat of a dice. So out with the racers to see what we had to play with for today.

Buzz to eight thou in first, second and third, heel into the first corner (Riches), and I was pleas-

antly surprised with the steadiness provided by the damping in the forks and by the Girlings fitted to the rear. When we went over the bumps it came down straight and no further hops, skips or jumps resulted. Down the straight and a few racers went screwing by, their open exhausts drowning the comparatively quiet whirring from down under.

The red line appears at eight and a half thousand, but it was an extremely windy day and that gale was right behind the 'bikes. Graham had said that he had seen the needle come right out of the other side of the red band in top gear, but since it wasn't mine, or even a "trade" machine, I'd no intention of doing it a damage and eased when it got to eight and a bit. And then the wind started to catch

Race-Test: 750cc PRODUCTION HONDA FOUR

Only 7828 registered on the clock. Still a while to go.

it and the passage down the straight became a slight weave; nothing nasty but enough to make you think.

Now to try the twin discs at the Hairpin. Curiously for discs, the action was on the spongy side, though Graham said that they had been firmer before he dropped it at Cadwell. Anyway, in spite of the action they stopped well enough for a first try. Screwing away from the Hairpin a most interesting comparison presented itself in the shape of Peter Darvill on his production racing 750 and as standard as he says it is, it was a fair bit quicker than the "Wyliemobile".

Well – practice was completed with no particular problems showing themselves, apart from the fact that the wind was causing some bother. In particular, braking for the Esses with a strong side wind was something to watch. I could not really fathom this aspect of the navigation as the wind caused my Trident no bother, apart from being aware of it. Ground clearance had been no problem so far, but on a strange machine, and a private one at that, I'd not really "bent" it yet and in any case was leaning out to prevent anything touching – or at least minimise the possibility.

The production race was first in the programme and Graham had his ride and came in grinning, obviously having enjoyed himself, with graze marks on the bottom of the fairing where he'd been "scratching". The going had been rapid for the conditions and he'd finished in 20th place. Now for mine.

The draw for grid positions gave a fifth row back and on the outside, which fitted in rather well with a plan that I had in mind, remembering that the Honda is fitted with an electric starter. Now the start of open races, unless it's of the clutch variety, is by push. At least, initially. I'd seen Hondas paddled away from the line in the T.T. and when moving the starter was used. If it was good enough for a Grand Prix event then it was good enough for a club race, especially when I did not feel that I was likely to rob anyone of any silverware. Some of the stuff out there had been a fair bit quicker than the Honda.

So the flag twitched, I pushed three paces, pressed the go button, leapt aboard and pointed the, by then, howling Four up the outside of the grid and made ground fast. Well, it was a good idea and was working fine as I made four rows quick, but then the character on the outside at the front wanted some more road on my side and that put paid to that idea, but the rush up the road under the bridge was not so bad, in about ninth place I'd guess, and you can be a lot farther back than that.

Down the straight a couple of twins went by, the Honda passed a couple itself and the revs rose to 8500 in each gear after a faultless selection. Grab that curiously spongy front brake lever – for a disc set-up that is – but spongy or not, it certainly worked. Remembering to shove the left foot instead of the right at the gear stick, it was second for the Hairpin as someone rushed under the front wheel. I was in the middle of a gag-

a-raa . . . a bugle call like you never heard before.

Twin discs – a little on the spongy side.

gle of machines all being screwed to the utmost up the road. There was a production Commando just getting away, though once the motor is howling in fourth the Honda seems to hold the situation. But there was that side wind again and the 'bike weaved about a bit as the brakes went on for the sharp left/right.

There's the feeling of a lot of machinery under you when it comes to throwing that 'bike about, and some of the more agile racers got by. It's fitted with two of the big Dunlop 4.10 tyres and I can't help thinking that a smaller section on the front might help that a little. Out of the Esses and into Coram's long curve the suspension coped admirably with the bump on the way in as I climbed off to make sure that I didn't wear away some more of Graham's fairing, but I never did really get the feeling of scratching hard. Even so, few machines came by on the corners.

I soon found the Honda on arguing terms with a couple of racers and, while chasing one down the straight, found the rev-counter needle going well into the red. I had to let them go while the wind buffeted the fairing and I really put the brakes to the test to regain a few yards. That was not too good an idea as the Hairpin rushed up ultra-fast, and I had to get right down to first to assist braking, though it was really too low to be useful coming out. I'd found that particular limit.

As the eight laps went by familiarity was gained and a little more manhandling the 'bike was

indulged in, but at such short acquaintance I never did lose that feeling of rather a lot of 'bike. Neither could I figure out why the wind affected the Four and not the Three. The fairings look not too dissimilar; there's no more apparent side area for it to catch.

I quite enjoyed those eight laps. The result was 15th, I believe. When you remember that the Honda has a two-year-old motor "bog standard", it compared creditably with, for instance, a production Commando with all its goodies. It's not surprising that they are faster. The brakes stop a lot of 'bike rather well and I'm ready to believe that they could be improved – Graham says that they're been better. The rear with its very short pedal could work too well and lock the wheel if you had an insensitive right boot.

It's rather like sitting over a big Hoover with those four cylinders buzzing away underneath. Under the prevailing conditions it could have pulled a higher gear too, and been a bit quicker on top speed I'd bet. The test proved that the 'bike is quicker than a lot, but not as quick as well prepared production racers. It steers well over the rough but that wind was a problem, though since the weaving manifested itself under heavy braking as well, I'd wonder if there were not another cause – even the hydraulic steering damper. I've cured high speed weaves on 'bikes before by removing them. Disregarding the action of the twin discs, they stopped well enough but just lacked the final edge for pushing your luck.

To summarise: the 'bike gave the impression of a first-class roadster that had yet to receive the final "sorting and sharpening" to make it really competitive in racing. The motor can be made faster – Peter Darvill's is. After dicing with him on the Trident I know it

can be made to steer and stop well enough, too.

Just as a follow-up: riding in after the race I let it idle along in top and it was everything that you would expect of a Four – dead smooth, quiet and very, very tractable – but that doesn't win races.

COME ALONG QUIETLY, PLEASE SIR

From the green-with-envy department comes the argument that some people have more luck than others. Take f'rinstance Sgt. George Saunders and P.C. Frank Hill of the Metropolitan Police who have just had a brace of BMW R75/5s forced upon them. The idea was conceived by the ever imaginative BMW Concessionaires in Chiswick, and the aim of the whole thing is to set off from Newcastle and go thence to Norway, Sweden, Denmark, Germany, Holland, Belgium, Luxembourg, France, Switzerland, Liechtenstein, Austria, Yugoslavis, Italy, Andorra and Spain. 15 countries in five days, all expenses found. Other credits: Machine preparation by Read Titan, clothing and pocket money by Rivetts, food and drink by the German Food Centre.

By John M. Larsen

There have been few cycles in American history that have captured the fancy of the buying public like the Honda Four. This dependable scooter is popping up on about any road you travel. But, like all good things, maintenance is required to keep them that way.

A lot of cycle owners, who have worked on their own bikes, get a lump of fear in their innards at the thought of doing an overhaul on one of these Swiss-watch Multis. The biker who is used to hassling two-stroke Singles immediately feels "NO WAY." Just how formidable is an upper end overhaul on one of these Fours? We pried one apart to find out.

Our machine is a 1970 model 750E. The later models of this machine are identified by the further designation K-1 and K-2. For the purposes of overhauling they are all the same with the exception of throttle linkage and O-rings at the base of the cylinder, which are not found on the later manufactured engines.

Before we get the engine strung all over the garage and living room floor, let's be certain that the engine really needs to come apart. There is a long list of things that can make a Four miss and/or lose power but some of them can be cured without tearing the engine down. A compression check should show you if an overhaul is in order. Take a compression gauge and with the spark plugs removed and the throttle open, each cylinder should pump not less than 140 psi of compression when the engine is spun with the electric starter. The cylinders should not vary more than 15 psi from each other. If one of the cylinders is weak, next remove the caps covering the rocker arms and be certain that one of the adjusting screws has not worked tight, thereby not letting the valve seat which could cause low compression. If the valves are adjusted properly and compression is still below par, then you will have to take a deeper look.

If excessive oil consumption and a lot of exhaust smoke is the reason you are concerned, you might need new piston rings, but be certain to carefully inspect the cylinder head for any defects and check for worn valve guides as well as going after the rings. Don't be like the dummy who tore his scoot to iddy-bittys because of exhaust smoke only to find that his little brother has put lawn mower two-stroke mix in the tank.

1

OVERHAUL:
750 HONDA FOUR
DO IT CORRECTLY AND YOU'LL SAVE A LOT OF LOOT

1. *Begin teardown by removing the tank and air cleaner air box, side covers and the slides from the carbs. Drain oil and remove the filter.*

2. *All four carbs are removed by loosening the hose clamps either at the carbs or the manifolds. The two rear footpeg bolts hold the mufflers on either side and the exhaust headers are clamped onto the cylinder heads. Remove by loosening the 12-mm bolts and slipping the exhaust pipes off. Remove tachometer drive from cylinder head.*

3. *Prepare the left side of the engine for removal by unsnapping the wiring harness and removing the starter cable from the solenoid shown at upper right in photo. Remove shift lever and drive chain as shown.*

4. *Prepare the right side of the engine by removing the kick start lever, clutch cover and cable. Take off the footpegs by withdrawing the lower mounting bolt. Remove the oil supply and return lines and the oil tank and breather hoses. Unsnap the blue and yellow wires which feed the breaker plate.*

5. *The engine will only come out of the right side of the frame; remove the bolts and three-cornered brackets. The engine will now slip free. Two men will accomplish this much quicker than one.*

6. *The parts needed for the overhaul are four sets of piston rings and a complete upper end gasket set as shown here. The cost will be about $30.00 to $35.00 depending on the dealer and type of gasket set.*

2

3

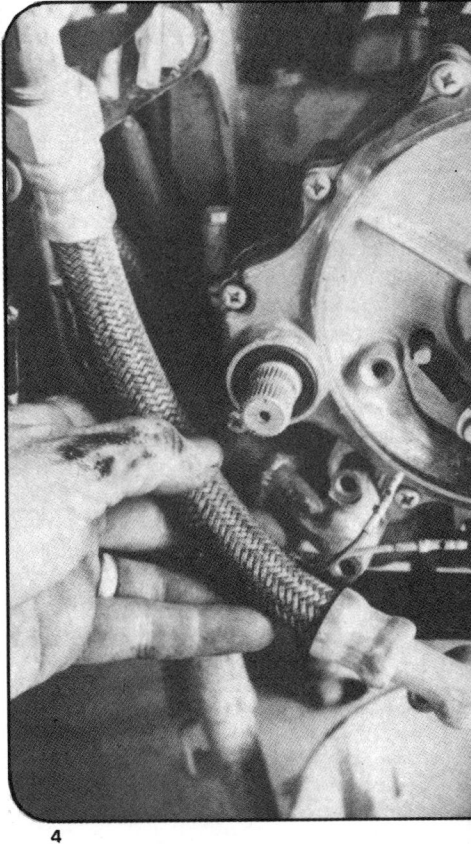

4

5

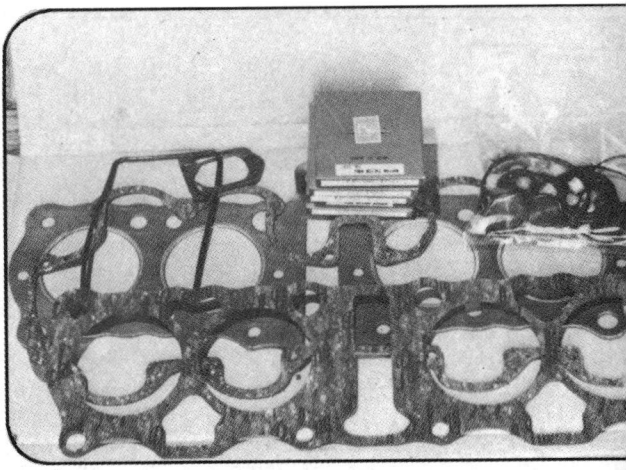

6

HONDA FOUR

7. The rocker cover is held on the engine by 19 screws. Remove with an impact driver.

8. Remove the cam chain tensioner as shown.

9. To remove the cylinder head, the rocker arms and cam holder caps are removed. Take notice of the stamped code shown here as G9 which is found on upper and lower halves of the cam holders. These are set in pairs and must be replaced matched as shown.

10. The rocker shafts will have to be pushed from the mounts after the 10-mm headed bolts have been removed from the mount tops. Use Honda tool no. 07050-30001 for this purpose. We found a ¼-inch socket extension or a 39¢ screwdriver will do the same job.

11. The cam chain has no master link. The cam is removed by taking the two 10-mm headed screws from the cam sprocket and then rolling the sprocket free. Now withdraw the cam from the sprocket and chain.

12. The cylinder head is held in place by 16 12-mm nuts and six 10-mm bolts. The four bolts in the center of the head are located by removing the gasket-material plugs so the bolts may be reached as above.

13. The head should come free with a couple of taps with a soft-head hammer. If it does not, check for the bolts or nut you overlooked. Tie a piece of mechanic's wire onto the cam chain to aid in reassembly.

14. A quick check of the valves is made by turning the cylinder head over and then filling the combustion chambers with solvent. There should be no leakage for at least 60 seconds. If a valve shows up faulty, check for a carbon particle or other foreign body which may be holding it open. Do this by turning the head rightside up and rapping the top of the stem of the valve with a hammer so to cause the valve to snap open and shut. Check again. If the valve, or valves, still leak, the valve will have to be reground or replaced.

7

8

10

9

15. The cylinder block will now come free with no further removal of any fastenings. They tend to stick so rap with a soft-head hammer. Resist the urge to drive a screwdriver blade into the crack between the cylinder and the block, as this will damage the mating surfaces and no doubt cause a leak after reassembly.

11

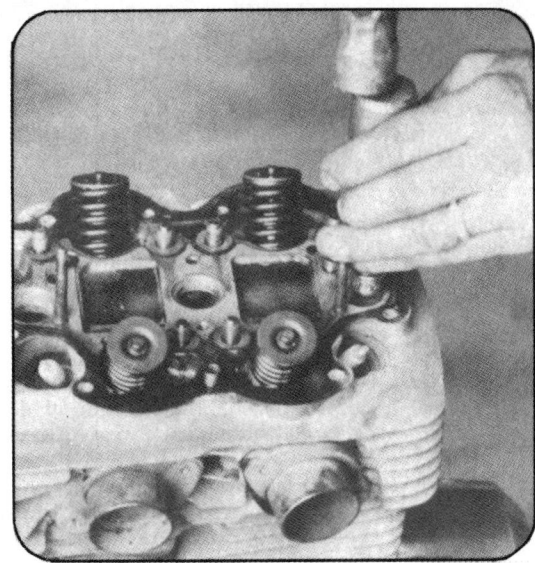

12

13

14

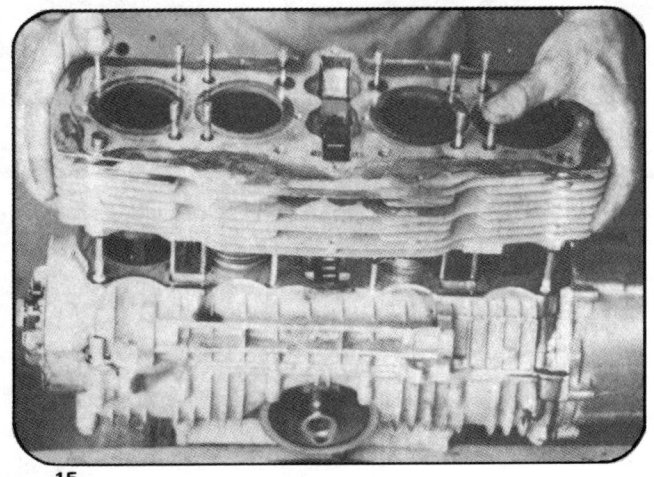

15

HONDA FOUR

16. Remove the pistons by taking the spring clips from the end of the wrist pin and then push out the pin. Take a sharp instrument and scratch the number of the piston on its top, (number four shown here) so you can put the pistons back into the same hole on reassembly. They are not perfectly identical.

17. Carefully clean the carbon from the head of the piston, and take an old piston ring and break it to form a scraper to clean any deposits from the ring grooves. Check the pistons by replacing them in the block and by using a feeler gauge. Measure the clearance between the piston and cylinder by sliding the piston up on the gauge starting with .001 in. If clearance is more than .006 in. the piston should be replaced with the next over size and the block rebored.

18. Place the new rings in the cylinder and check the end gap with the feeler gauge as shown. The rings should not have less than .018 in. or more than .028 in. end gap. If there is any ring ridge in the top of the cylinder, it will have to be reamed out or new rings will break.

19. The new ring will usually have a gap less than the above so the end of the ring must be filed out to the required gap. A small point file will do.

20. Install the new rings on the piston and take care that the triangular mark on the piston faces the front of the engine.

21. When the pistons are ready for installation, you will find that hose clamps make good piston ring compressors. The old Honda trick of placing the pistons in the block before attaching them to the rods will not work on the Four due to the short stroke and the number of cylinders. Oil the pistons well before installing in block. Place the base gasket on the block rather than on the case. Before installing the cylinder block be certain that the two back center studs have new "O" rings in place. Later models do not use "O" rings at the base of the cylinder barrels. Squirt ½ teaspoon oil into each cylinder before replacing head to keep new rings from galling the cylinder walls.

22. Before installing head be certain that the two rear center studs have new O-rings in place. All repair instructions tell you to use a torque sequence on installing a cylinder head, but on the Honda Fours they mean it. If you cannot beg, borrow or steal torque wrench, we strongly recommend you buy one as a last resort. This is a $118.00 head and you can mess it up if you do other than torque the head down in the sequence noted in the photo. All the nuts take 15 ft/lb except the 10-mm headed bolts (No. 2, 7, 15, 19, 21, 22) which should not have over 6 to 8 ft/lb.

23. Now thread the cam through the chain and then the sprocket. If you have the cam on the timing marks, install the chain on the sprocket (see next photo). Install the rocker assemblies.

24. The trick on cam timing is to have the camshaft located as shown in the top of the photo and then rotate the crank until the mark on the rotor T 1-4 appears in the hole in the breaker plate as shown at the bottom of the photo. Now work the sprocket around in the timing chain until the two sprocket bolts will slip through the sprocket into the cam without moving either the crank or the camshaft. If the T 1-4 mark shows and the cam looks like the above when you are done, you know you have done it right.

25. Set the valves so that the exhaust has .003 in. clearance and the intake has .002. Turn the crank and recheck because if the rocker arm is partly up on a cam lobe when you adjust it you will get a false reading.

Now you are ready to replace the rocker cover and slip the engine back in the bike. As anyone who has worked on the modern Hondas can tell you, the Fours are just more of the same. Just as the principles of cam timing are the same as other models and the general successful idea has been proven again.

With the info we have given you here we have one thing in mind, namely to make sure that the throttle will have four willing bangers going so you still have all of that power in the palm of your right hand.

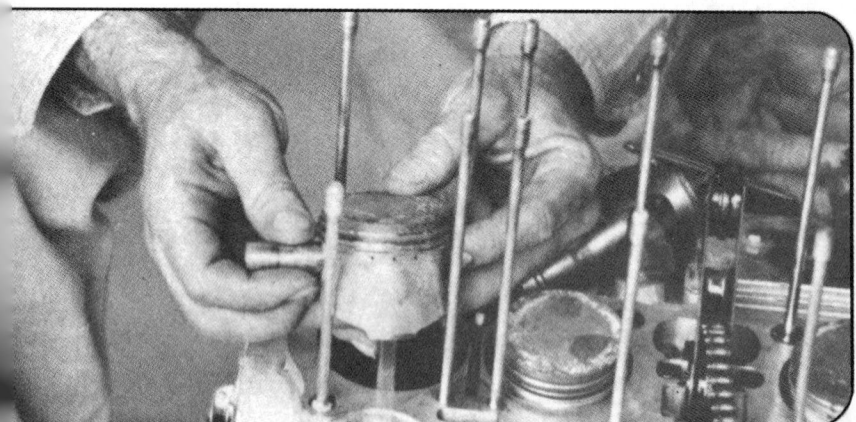

16

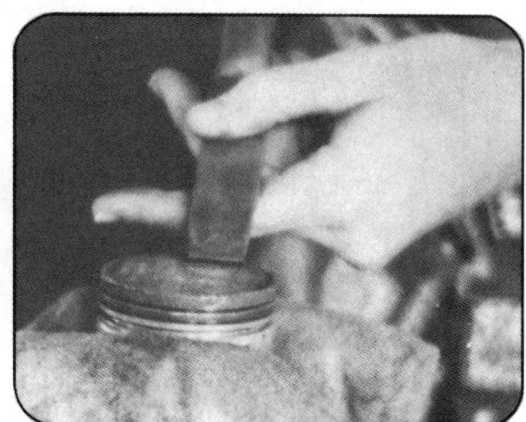

17

18

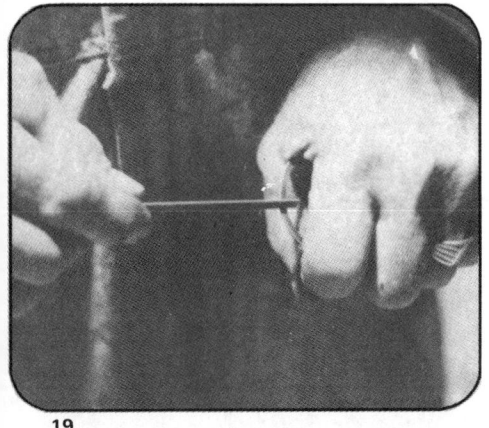

19

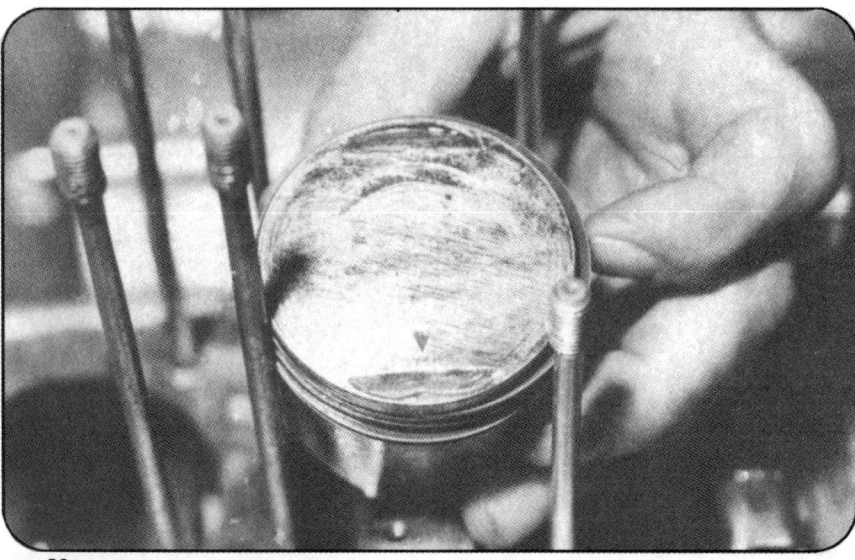

20

21

22

23

24

25

Riding a "great big teddy bear"

Warming up the pregnant egg: the bulge is for a Krober ignition system

LAST year a couple of CR750 Hondas arrived in the UK, purchased by Bill Smith for his own use and for his rider—John Williams. These machines were hardly cheap, and if you recall the very high prices quoted for racing 750 parts after the 1971 TT you would have a good idea of the cost of genuine Honda racing parts. The "CR" parts that appeared at that time in the parts books had prices attached, and although it is generally considered that orders for such parts could never be filled, the blossoming of really fast Hondas in France and the USA started before Yoshimura had his special components widely distributed. Some of the racing parts are a reasonable price: pistons at about £6 and special cam chains—shared with CR350s—at about £4.60 demonstrate this. The prices of gearbox components, camshafts, and cycle parts are less acceptable. The "Honda Racing Service Club"—which must surely be the works under a thin veneer—are the source of these special Honda parts, and clearly work under the same constraint as the Production Racer parts of Yamaha Works fairings for Yamahas come out at over £200 now, and similar labour-intensive, short-run parts in the Honda catalogue reflect the high cost of such work.

Complete race-kitted engines can be ordered, and in fact a first delivery of five units duly arrived at Chester this winter with no units short. Consequently there are several such engines around now. No one should confuse these HRSC racing components with the full works equipment. The Honda that Bill Smith rode at Daytona this year went through the speed traps at 148 m.p.h. The works machine managed over 160 m.p.h. and had the aid of just about anything that Honda could think of to improve its performance. The HRSC parts are rather more closely related to those on the production machines, and it is surprising to see just how much of the CR750 is from the road machine. The front wheel is standard, and the usual duplication of the calipers has been carried out. The thickness of the steel discs has been reduced almost by half, so as to cut down the substantial unsprung weight that they incur. The front forks are also standard, both lower legs and stanchions coming straight from the road machine. The fork crowns are not standard, and are special components. The frame is visibly standard. From a detailed investigation one can see that it has simply been pulled off the line at a certain stage and then worked on. Minor lugs have been either cut off or left off, and a few extra brackets welded on. In fact the CR750 frame bears precisely the same relationship to the CB750 unit as is

borne by the TZ350 watercooled Yamaha to the RD350 road machine. The swinging arm also remains unaltered from the road machine. The rear wheel is definitely different; the massive twin-leading-shoe drum brake appears to be the same as that fitted to the Honda Racing Service Club 350 twin owned by John Skellern and described in *MCS* last year. Some of the parts used are surprising: the clutch springs come from the old CB77 305 c.c. road machine, and the primary chain is the normal CB750 component: both of these parts are likely to be heavily stressed, and it speaks volumes for the much criticized primary chain that it bears up under the strain. The twin disc front brake is the same as can be seen on many road machines, and apart from the thinned discs the only alteration is the use of Ferodo disc pads as may now be obtained from Joe Dunphy.

The critical parts are the cranks, pistons, camshafts and carburettors. The crank is altered for racing use and has a slightly longer stroke. It is polished, lightened, and selectively assembled and is not directly replaceable by a standard crank as the taper on the generator output stub is totally different, to match the CR93 energy transfer ignition fitted at the factory. The little generator is far smaller and lighter than the massive CB750 unit, but throughout the 1972 season Bill Smith and John Williams had repeated difficulties with the ignition system. Although it works well up to 14,500 r.p.m. on a CR93, the idle spark system on the four is too much for the system as it stands. The two fours at Silverstone were fitted with

different systems: Bill Smith's had two batteries in the vast seat fairing, and no provision for charging them. This was the system used in the Bol d'Or last year, where the Honda ran well up. The other machine, ridden regularly by John Williams, was fitted with a Krober battery-less ignition system. This required a blister to be grafted on to the lower part of the fairing.

The distinctive appearance of the Smith Hondas is produced by the special fairings fitted to the machines. Bill Jakeman has now retired from his business, and was therefore able to spend a considerable amount of time over the winter sorting out the airflow requirements for these machines. Throughout 1972 the key problem was overheating: on many occasions the bikes ran really well, only to overheat severely. At Silverstone last year this happened even when all the streamlining had been torn off. These problems didn't stop John Williams lapping at over 102 m.p.h. in the Isle of Man, still the fastest lap set up on a production framed machine, so the potential was continually reaffirmed without the success that seemed to be reasonably within their grasp. There were many lessons to learn last year, and much trouble could have been avoided if they had known that the CR750 engines had to be run in for 500 miles before being raced! As no one had told them this, much of the sorting out process was unnecessarily difficult. The two cams for the CR750 produce 90 and 96 b.h.p. respectively: compare this with the standard 67 b.h.p., and consider that Honda designs for full reliability at 67 b.h.p., and the rough early life that the engines were given can be seen to exacerbate all sorts of reliability and heating problems.

I was interested to hear that they had used NGK D8 plugs last year, and only now moved on to the D12 rating that I used on my Honda CB750 for both road and track!

The anti-overheating campaign included an oil cooler and comprehensive MIRA wind tunnel testing. The ordinary fairing shape is just the start of this airflow programme. The huge tail section, the engine enclosure casings, and the slight duct shaping at the end of the engine casings all had a critical effect on the coefficient of resistance. The key objective of the programme was to get the heat away from the engine. The negative pressure and turbulence regions behind any such unaerodynamic device as a motorcycle were harnessed to aid the airflow past the engine. The function of these casings was to channel the airflow, and the shape at the rear fairing below the rider's thighs gave access to the pressure depressions at those points. Consequently the air is pushed in the front, guided along the engine finning, past the carburettors, and then sucked out the back. These fibreglass casings are all single skin mouldings, and before painting are clearly translucent. Bill Jakeman would have preferred them to have been left in their raw state, and having seen them in that condition I can see why he thinks so. His efforts seem to have been successful as the oil cooler was hardly warm after a session on the track.

It is, however, difficult to avoid thinking of these Jakeman-faired Hondas as lowflying pregnant guppies.

The Hondas are not all that easy to start when cold, and three-man relays rushed up and down the paddock before the single megaphone started howling. Both John Williams and Bill Smith took the fours out

for a few laps circulating a few yards apart: both sounded impressive.

Bill Smith then handed over his machine: apparently there were only a few miles to go before the cam chain was due for replacement, consequently I was asked to keep the r.p.m. down to 8-8½. "It's easy to ride—it's like a great big teddy bear". Getting on board the beast, it was pretty hard to believe it: the sheer bulk of the machine is intimidating. Once aboard and moving the usual transformation occurs, and the machine feels immediately manageable in spite of its still substantial impression of size. The clutch is a bit delicate, and I was not encouraged to slip it when pulling away as it could well burn out.

The CR750 feels only slightly less flexible than the CB750, once one allows for the taller gearing. The riding position is comfortable which is hardly surprising in view of the fact that the machine was tailored for Bill Smith who is much the same size as I am. The bulbous front of the fairing shields one's hands and forearms so that the feeling of being "in" rather than "on" the machine is enhanced. The smooth and effortless manner in which the four accelerated is in dramatic contrast to the frenetic urgency of a racing Yamaha. A lap or two at a singularly sedate speed, at r.p.m. well below 8,000 allowed me only to discover that the Honda was quite easy to ride at such speeds, and that the steering was remarkably good. The brakes felt just like my road Honda CB750, singularly effective and sensitive. As they had the same Ferodo pads as I had in my road machine this was only to be expected. After the sidecars had had their session I took the Honda out again: there were only a very few laps allowable before the cam chain was due for replacement, so when it persistently misfired on two cylin-

Bill Smith on board the 750 with "total loss" ignition system

ders I came in: one plug proved to be oiled up, but this was not enough. Still, it was quite fast, but not terribly dramatic. The steering still felt as good, but the back end weaved about on Maggott's ripples.

As a last check, I was allowed to try John Williams' Krober-equipped four: what a contrast! This four gathered itself and stretched forward to grasp each corner as it was barely out of the apex of the last. Down the straight in fourth gear the back wheel found one of those longitudinal ripples, and the four shrugged a good few feet sideways: the light crosswind became distinctly noticeable as this four's high top speed came up. The braking and steering remained excellent, but the handling was not nearly so good: I am far heavier than John Williams, and this showed up in the squirming that went on at Maggotts. The acceleration was good, but not as impressive as that of a 350 Yamaha, and the overall performance felt a bit down on that phenomenal two-stroke. At Daytona Bill got only 148 m.p.h. on the speedtrap, and Martin Sharpe reported little difficulty in getting by on his air-cooled 350 Yamaha. The great contrast was in the manner in which the performance was delivered: the CR750 was far nicer to ride, and I can only repeat Bill Smith's comment: "It's a pity about two-strokes".

This machine is surely what F750 is all about: exciting to look at, distinctive exhaust note, and a real mass of powerful machinery for the rider to master, all based firmly on standard components. Much the same could be said about the Yamaha, but somehow the four-stroke has a greater grandeur than the nervous and devastatingly fast little two-stroke. The supporters of 350 Yamahas in F750 ought to try a CR750—or a well set up racing Trident—or a Derimead 750 before speaking out in favour of handing over this class to the thoroughbred whippets from Yamaha. Perhaps more dealers could be tempted to follow Bill Smith's Honda and Bennett's threes if the International class became 501-750. Our thanks are due to Bill Smith for opening the eyes of even this Yamaha owner!—M. R. W.

The writer's CB750 as transformed by Dresda Autos

HONDA CB-750 K3

● Hidden away under the Honda CB-750 Four's fuel tank, flanked by its quadruple carburetors, you'll find the secret of this Superbike's success. Don't look in there expecting to find cabalistic symbols, mathematical formulae or a message for your Captain Midnight decoder ring. What you'll see is that part of the throttle return spring is now covered by a short neoprene sleeve, placed to protect a pair of rather unimportant carburetor vent hoses from pinching or chafing. Nothing of any great consequence would occur even if the return spring chaffed through both vent hoses. But the protective sleeve is there, just as a refinement, and it is typical of the kinds of refinements that make the Honda CB-750 what it is. Other Superbikes are faster and at least a couple handle better, but none are as slick, as steadfastly reliable, as the big Honda. None but the Sportster and the Norton have been in production as long but more important, none have had the incredible attention to detail typified by that little sleeve on the Honda's throttle return spring.

Oddly enough, none of the refinements worked on the CB-750 since its introduction in 1970 seem to have been intended to make the bike any faster—and it is certain that none have had that effect. Considering that Honda created one of the first *true* Superbikes (and thus set an example that brought all the others) one might have expected more attention to the performance side of things. But the main thrust of the CB-750's evolution has been in the opposite direction. It is widely known that early pre-production prototypes were quicker and somewhat less civilized than the Fours actually delivered into customers' hands back in 1970, and subsequent development has moved the bike further away from the pure performance concept. Smoothness, silence and reliability have been paramount considerations. Those fired with the sporting spirit may find Honda's approach regrettable, but with total CB-750 sales now closing in on 100,000 units it would be hard to convince the firm's directors that they are making a mistake.

Now we have the 1973 CB-750 K3, which is a slightly slower but more refined version of the CB-750 K2—which had about the same relationship with its predecessor. Some of the CB-750's decline in absolute performance probably is attributable to subtle changes in its valve-lift specifications. There also has been a power loss incurred

with the introduction of more efficient, and more restrictive, mufflers. With the 1973 model the CB-750 becomes even quieter—and slower—due to a restricted inlet for the air-cleaner housing that more effectively silences intake roar. The net result is that there is little racket emerging from either the inlet or exhaust sides of the engine, and careful work inside has squelched what can be a lot of clatter from pistons and valve gear. The CB-750 K3 is *quiet!*

None of these measures has done a thing for absolute performance, as has already been noted, but they actually do not have much effect in terms of daily operation. Those exhaust and inlet restrictions do shave the peak off the CB-750 engine's power curve, and that definitely reduces the kind of performance you'd get at the drag strip. However, most riders will hold the engine well below its 8,000 rpm redline, shifting up at perhaps 6,500 rpm, and the restrictions mentioned do little to depress performance in the lower portion of the engine's powerband.

Another series of changes have been made in the CB-750's final drive system. Like all Superbikes the big Honda sends a lot of pressure to the rear wheel through its sprockets and chain, with deleterious results to the service life of both. This was a severe problem in the beginning, when the bike had a 16-tooth transmission sprocket and a 45-tooth sprocket on the rear wheel. That proved an unsatisfactory arrangement, and the sprocket sizes were increased to lower chain tension under load as well as provide larger wrap-over radii at the sprockets. Today an 18-tooth transmission sprocket is used in combination with a 48-tooth rear wheel sprocket, which has improved chain life and yields a taller overall drive ratio (originally 5.61:1, now 4.99:1). This obviously does little for flat-out acceleration. On the other hand it makes highway cruising less busy for the engine, which pays dividends in smoothness, fuel economy and reliability. It is a change entirely in keeping with the other CB-750 developments.

Most of the other changes over earlier models found in the CB-750 K3 have nothing to do with speed or lack of same. For example, there are the wear indicators on the bike's disc brake pucks. Because the wear adjustments with hydraulic disc brakes are entirely automatic it is possible to scrub away the puck's friction material right down to the steel backing pieces before there is any indication of wear and impending trouble. This difficulty has been resolved very neatly with the addition of a little red tab to each brake pad. The tab marks the limit of the friction material, and indicates how much is left to anyone who takes the trouble to glance into the brake caliper. It's a service/safety measure, and a good one.

Safety is also served by other changes in the CB-750 K3. It now has bigger rear-view mirrors, and the turn indicator lights now have double-filament bulbs that make them clearance lights as well. Turn on the headlights and you also light one set of turn-indicator filaments. You won't be as likely to hit the high/low-beam switch instead of the headlight switch, or vice versa, with the revised control layout—which now has these switches on opposite ends of the handlebars. Also, the emergency kill switch has been turned 90 degrees so that you are not as likely to accidentally bump it into the off position while riding. And finally, the turn-indicator switch has been redesigned to permit a partial actuation for signaling lane changes. Push the switch over gently with your thumb and the lights start to blink, but the switch will pop back off unless it has been shoved over hard into its locked-on position.

Some of the changes are hidden, like the fuse box located behind the left sidecover. Previously the CB-750 has had its fuses placed in-line in little plastic holders, positioned much more for the manufacturer's convenience than yours. In the CB-750 K3 all the fuses are in a single box, just like a car, which certainly will make troubleshooting less a chore. Just like a cat, too, is the device that stops actuation of the starter unless the transmission is in neutral.

Other hidden changes are in the CB-750's forks and rear suspen-

Red-tabbed pucks help to prevent the unaware from wearing the pucks down to backing metal.

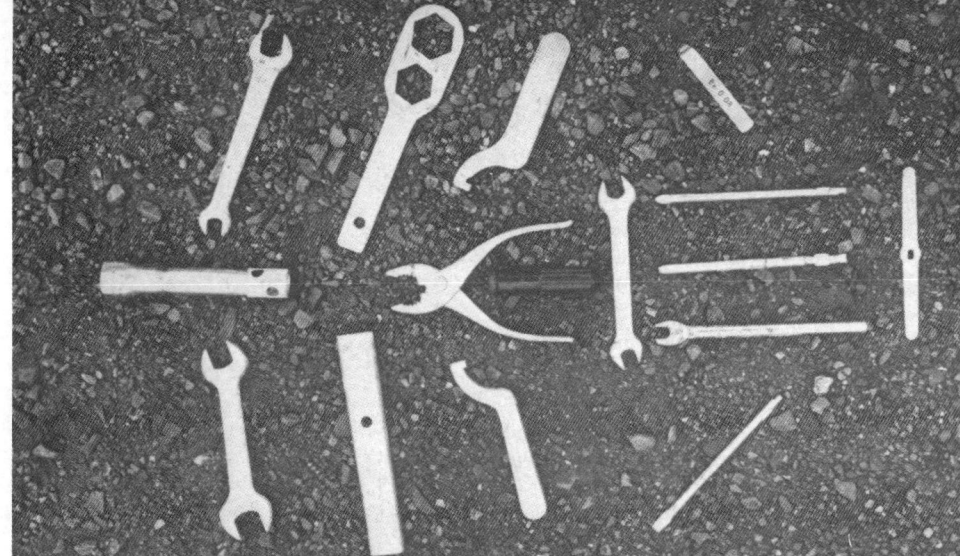

There are enough tools for small chores, but for the most part the tools will just stay bagged up.

Refinement is the name of the game, and the number of warning/idiot lights always figures in the score.

The fuse box and other electrical components live rubber-mounted under the left sidecover.

sion units. The nitrogen-filled DeCarbon rear shocks have been replaced with those of a more conventional pattern—with a five-position adjustment for spring preload instead of the earlier three-notch arrangement. The forks have also come in for a change: last year's CB-750 K2 used fork damping virtually identical to that of the CB-500, but there has been a change back to the original damper valve configuration. Both spring rates and damping for the forks and rear suspension struts have been revised to improve the CB-750's ride—though we are not at all certain this "improvement" is a reality. In plain fact, the CB-750 neither handles nor rides as nicely as its smaller brother. Road surface irregularities are far more unsettling for the CB-750: it twitches when running over freeway rain grooves, and has a comparatively harsh ride. Other Superbikes are generally worse in these respects and we might not even notice the Honda's ride/handling shortcomings but for the extraordinary quality of both in the CB-500—which presumably was produced by the same design team. Perhaps such anomalies exist just to remind us that motorcycle suspension engineering still is more art than science.

One of the CB-750 Honda's best features is its front disc brake, which it has had from the beginning. The only difference we can detect between then and now is the complete absence of brake squeal—a big source of aggravation with most discs, including those on other Hondas—and a splash guard wrapped over the disc itself to keep the thing from spitting rainwater in your eye. All the

near-incredible stopping power of the modern motorcycle disc brake (another Honda first, introduced on the CB-750) is of course still there.

Unfortunately the Four's rear drum-type brake is nothing like as effective and agreeable as the one up at the front wheel. The Honda's rear brake locks far too easily, and this problem is compounded by a disagreement between the arcs described by the swingarm and the brake rod: the lack of coincidence in these arcs makes the brake pedal jiggle up and down, unless you are using the brake, in which case the tendency to jiggle is converted into jagged changes in braking pressure. With all that happening it becomes almost impossible to avoid locking the rear wheel unless the rear brake is used very lightly. Obviously the fact that the front brake does most of the stopping for the motorcycle effectively reduces this problem to a mere annoyance, but it is sadly out of character for the otherwise wonderfully refined CB-750 and one hopes that Honda will have corrected this in the K4 model.

As mentioned previously the CB-750 K3 falls somewhat short of the CB-500 in handling, but it still is pretty good judged by broad-spectrum standards. The big Honda will carve around turns *very* well, as long as the road is reasonably smooth. Rough spots set off more wheel hop and fork waggle than is comfortable in such a large and heavy motorcycle, and the CB-750 definitely is a dou-

ble handful under those conditions. Even so, with experience you'll find that the bike can be pitched around vigorously, and the only thing you must remember is that this Honda always has you outnumbered. It's big, heavy and needs both time and muscle to get it from hard-right to hard-left. And you really wouldn't *ever* want to get the Four into a big slide. You can ride it hard, as it has excellent tires and rates high in terms of fundamental stability. Thus, serious trouble will only be encountered after serious brain-fade has overcome the Honda rider's judgment. There's plenty of warning when you've gone far enough. You can use the right footpeg and the centerstand extension on the left as limit gauges, and you certainly won't run out of tires at the cornering angles those things permit.

Ride, like handling, falls short of the CB-500's refined behavior but still puts the CB-

750 right up there with the best. The bike feels like maybe its springs are a bit too stiff and the damping too limp by about the same amount. That doesn't keep it from being comfortable. Its seat is broad and soft, and there is enough distance from the seat down to the pegs to prevent your legs from getting cramped. This last may account for the CB-750 lending the impression that it is very tall, which it isn't. The difficulties those with short legs have in keeping the bike upright at a stop are due more to seat width than seat height, which is not much greater than the average for all motorcycles.

Riding comfort gets a boost from the engine's power output characteristics, which derive from a torque curve that is virtually a straight line. It is much like those of Honda's various SL engines, with lots of raw torque available anytime you whack open the throttles. You can indulge in a flurry of

The need for lots of wrench-twisting and chain adjusting has been diminished by a change in gearbox/rear-wheel sprocket ratio.

upshifts and downshifts if that is what pleases you; it won't make a terribly big difference in your rate of progress down the road. Indeed, this is one of the CB-750's principal charms.

Serviceability may not be a big thing with the high-rollers who can afford new CB-750s; it will be appreciated by mechanics and their appreciation should be reflected in the bill they present to the owner. Also, high-rollers as well as lesser mortals can encounter minor problems out on the road and it should comfort them to know that there is easy access to nearly all the ancillary jazz on the Honda. Lift the seat and pull the side-covers (which plug into place) and you can get at most of it. And in the unlikely event you have to fix something underneath the bike you can flop it over on its side without having oil and fuel run all over the place.

Fuel doesn't even run through the carburetors nearly as rapidly as you might sup-pose. We found that whipping the CB-750 hard would pull the mileage down to about 41 mpg, and that mixed-conditions riding gave us an average of about 45 mpg. That translates into a maximum cruising range, between service stations, of 200 miles, running 144 miles on the 4.5-gallon tank's main supply (3.2-gallons) and then switching to the 1.3-gallon reserve.

And would that all motorcycles were as basically refined as the Honda CB-750 K3 Four, and as reliable. Our test bike had been thoroughly thrashed by a variety of test riders by the time we finished, and apart from developing a slight jangling in its clutch the Honda showed not the slightest distress at having been so harshly used. It wasn't puffing or leaking oil, didn't develop any tendencies toward hard starting or an uneven idle, and in general displayed a willingness to continue happily along in the face of our best (worst?) efforts.

Best of all, while the CB-750 is out there on the roads in numbers too large to give it any eye-appeal as a curiosity, it will boost the prestige of its road-rider owner at every coffee stop just because it is so incredibly well-finished. The Four sparkles and shines and gleams, and its every detail is just so tremendously tidy you can't help but admire the bike even if you're riding something else. You look at that "K3" designation and consider the CB-750's three-year history and you know that it is to some extent the creature of afterthought, but nothing in its broad layout, appearance, or smallest detail suggests anything except meticulous advanced planning. Or maybe what you get in the CB-750 K3 is more nearly the result of meticulous afterthought. Either way it has produced in the Honda CB-750 an uncommon degree of refinement—and for the Honda company a hundred thousand pretty well satisfied customers. ◉

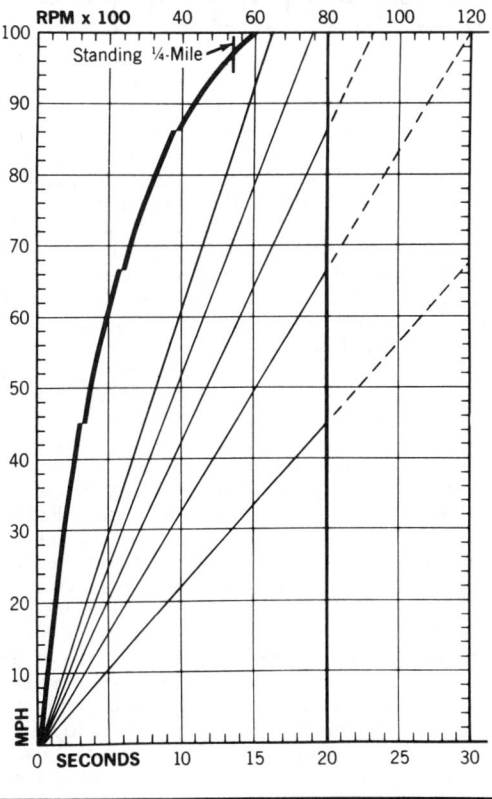

HONDA CB-750 K3

Price, suggested retail	West Coast, POE $1,822
Tire, front	3.25 in. x 19 in.
rear	4.00 in. x 18 in.
Brake, front	11.7 in. x 1.625 in. (x2)
rear	7.1 in. x 1.6 in.
Brake swept area	152.8 sq. in.
Specific brake loading	4.50 lb/sq. in., at test weight
Engine type	Four-cylinder, in-line, SOHC
Bore and stroke	2.40 in. x 2.48 in., 61mm x 63mm
Piston displacement	44.9 cu. in., 736cc
Compression ratio	9:1
Carburetion	4; 28mm; Keihin
Air filtration	Paper element
Ignition	Battery and Coil
Mph/1000 rpm, top gear	15.2
Fuel capacity	4.5 gal.
Oil capacity	7.4 pints
Lighting	12v, 210 watts
Battery	12v, 14 ah
Gear ratios, overall	(1) 13.29 (2) 9.08 (3) 7.08 (4) 5.83 (5) 4.99
Wheelbase	57.3 in.
Seat height	31.5 in., with rider
Ground clearance	5.5 in., with rider
Curb weight	526 lbs., with full tank of gas
Test weight	686 lbs., with rider
Instruments	Speedometer, Odometer, Tachometer
Sound level, Calif. Std.	80 d(B)A
Standing start ¼ mile	13.66 seconds 96.87 mph
Top speed	110 mph (est.)
Braking Force in Gs	0.84G

GOLDSMITH SAID of Garrick as a wit that he was "if not first, in the very first line". Rickman say the same of themselves as motorcycle manufacturers: they claim to be Britain's second largest. One might be forgiven for wondering whether that might amount to much nowadays, for without having seen the premises of Rickman, Dresda, Dunstall and a very few others it would be very easy to assume that NVT were the biggest and all the others were backyard affairs.

In fact I saw the Rickman factory about four years ago, shortly after they moved to their new location, deep in the Neville Goss country at New Milton in Hampshire. It was an impressive enough place then; it is a good deal bigger and more impressive now. When I had digested the fact that Rickman's export business earned them the Queen's Award for Industry in the course of building up a million pounds worth of business a year, it seemed fair to concede them the very first line.

The same Goldsmith dictum might apply to their latest product, the CR that appeared at the last Racing Motorcycle Show. When I spotted it there I thought it very handsome indeed, as compact and well proportioned a machine as ever housed a standard 750 Honda four. For what, though, did CR stand? It was not an established nor a self-explanatory suffix. Competition replica? Castrol R? Counter-revolutionary? *Cursor Rickmanis?* It was no good guessing; I would have to ask.

I was sorry when I did. Café racer, forsooth! Did they think it was just some kind of joke? Were they just cashing in on a new retrospective craze among people who were obsessed with the cosmetic aspects of a style of machine that would look suitably fashion-conscious as it stood in the Californian sunshine? What a pity that they were not taking the thing seriously; it looked so promising.

Months later, there came out of the blue an invitation to ride it. Down through the New Forest I went, there to discover that they were taking it very seriously indeed. Admittedly they had an unfortunate habit of pointing with pride to one scrambler after another as we went on a guided tour of the factory, so that I could sense their preoccupation with that kind of machinery, even if they failed to sense my distaste for off-highway motorcycles and all the muck and filth familiarly associated with them. It did not mean, however, that the CR was a mere side issue: they were already deeply absorbed in the manufacture and marketing of CR kits for Honda and Triumph engines, while a Kawasaki 900 lurked in the background ready for experimentation that would carry the principle even further.

Kits are the main part of the business. Honda engines cannot be bought from Honda so readily as to enable complete machines to be built even in respectable batches, let alone on the flow-line principle that has already been adopted in the Rickman factory for other bikes. People who already have Hondas, though, especially if

they are old or secondhand or crashed Hondas, need do no more to give their precious fours a new lease of a more hedonistic life than buy a Rickman chassis kit and transfer the appropriate parts from their original Honda frame.

The complete engine unit, along with its carburettors and air filter, the exhaust system, the prop and centre stands, the oil tank and pipes, all the instruments and electrics including the wiring harness and battery housing, and all the control levers and cables, can be installed in the Rickman chassis without any drilling or welding being necessary. Personally I always find that this sort of job calls not only for a full set of spanners but also for three hands and a trained octopus; yet I am told that a couple of Americans did the whole job, starting with a Rickman kit straight out of the crate (in which it travels fully assembled) and a complete 750 Honda, in $6\frac{1}{2}$ hours. In England, allowing for tea breaks and bad weather and the fact that the spanner shop is closed after noon on Saturday, it should be possible to effect the transformation in a weekend. The rolling chassis kit costs £498 with VAT.

What will the Rickman be like to ride when it is finished? That was all I cared to know. It was long ago established that Setright is the world's worst mechanic, who should never stray for creative purposes further from his desk than is necessary to reach the drawing board, and who never sees a Do-It-Yourself shop without looking for a nearby establishment saying Let Us Do It For You. Riding the finished product, even if it was called a café racer, was the real object of the exercise and the only part with any real appeal.

No, there was not much fuel in the tank. And no, the petrol taps did not embody a reserve setting. But the tyre pressures were

checked and the engine was by no means new and would stand plenty of thrashing, so the prospect of a few days on this low and lean percolator held oodles of promise that the crash of exhaust seemed to confirm as I thumbed the starter button.

The first few tentative miles, on the way to a filling station, seemed rather fumbly as I fidgeted around to get a good fit on a machine that was just a trifle too small for me, and acquired the habits that go with a left-foot gearshift that moves up for one and down for four. Then, as we began to move faster, the Rickman's genuine quality as a

RICKMAN'S COVETABLE ROADBURNER

road machine became more apparent. The ride was surprisingly good, for instance: less harsh than that of a Dresda, say, and suggestive of soft springs and firm dampers, which is theoretically the right way of doing it. The disc brakes had no vices, the rear Lockheed being especially welcome for its smoothness even though the single small one on the front wheel needed a little too much effort on the lever and lacked the power of a Laverda or Suzuki twin-disc apparatus.

The speed and acceleration could be taken for granted. With so little frontal area and so little weight — the CR weighs 439 lb, practically a hundredweight less than the original Honda 750 — and with standard Honda gearing modified only by the substitution of a 4.25/85H18 Dunlop TT100 for the original Japanese tyre, the bike went straight up to its red-lined 8500 rev/min in fifth gear as though Newton's laws had lost their validity. If the rev-counter were to be believed, that corresponded to 119.8 mph; if the speedometer, to 125. I am not persuaded that either instrument was credible, for the two were sometimes inconsistent in their agreement: at a given speed in top gear the rev-counter might from time to time indicate different figures, and vice versa, the

68

range of variation amounting to about six per cent. From watching the curious antics of the speedometer needle when accelerating really hard, I am more inclined to believe the rev-counter. Not that it really matters, for the Rickman is obviously a jolly quick machine, and the way it held over 100 mph (indicated) for literally scores of miles without a falter was adequate proof of its ability.

Proof of its efficiency as a windcheater and petrol-burner followed the measurement of a trifle over 39 miles per gallon of hard riding, including a lot of sustained three-figure work. That means that the Rickman can cruise at about 100 at the same cost as the standard Honda 750 cruising at about 80, which just goes to show how important is frontal area. It also means that the practical range of the CR is about 120 miles, and would be more if its 3½-gallon tank were graced with something better than a couple of miserable little plain lever taps. Detail scrimping of this sort always annoys me: it would have cost so little more to fit reserve taps, and to install them so that the levers could comfortably be reached instead of being so awkward that they were frequently left on even when the bike was parked on its propstand. It is facile to argue that the more particular owner could substitute something better; and as far as I am concerned it is futile so to argue, for if I were buying what amounts to a £1200 plus motorcycle I am not going to take kindly to having to rectify the manufacturer's errors, whether of commission or omission.

In particular I should be very annoyed at having to fiddle about with spanners and pairs of eccentric washers whenever the rear

" . . . As compact and well proportioned a machine as ever housed a standard Honda Four." But the well-tailored fairing that looks so neat severely restricts the steering lock. Notice the hydraulic cylinder for the operation of the rear disc brake.

chain needed adjusting. The Rickman system of compensation by incremental movements of 0.8 mm of the fork pivot axis is ingenious and positive and cheap, and it ensures the maintenance of rear wheel alignment; but I prefer some of the other (albeit more expensive) methods available, for they are less aggravating in their needs. I found it a little off-putting when I was handed a pack of hefty steel washers just before I set off from the factory; and I was doubly annoyed when I found that there was absolutely nowhere on or in the motorcycle where the pack could be stowed. That voluminous tailpiece or coda behind the seat is an unnecessarily and unjustifiably delusive piece of GRP (even if, like the rest of Rickman's home-made GRP, it is of exceptional finish and quality) for it serves to house nothing. As I said of the taps, so I say of the tail.

Likewise of the front fairing, which is of the fashionable narrow shape with long shallow lateral slots to clear the clip-on handlebars. Nearly all pseudo-sports fairings are like this today, and Rickman deserve no more blame than all the others

who put fashion before function. Somehow I had expected them to know better, though: one of the virtues of clip-on handlebars is the tremendous range of adjustment they allow, but this range was completely negated by the fairing, since there was only one position for the bars which avoided fouling. Even so, the fairing caused the steering lock to be severely constricted — a limitation that does not matter when riding at normal speeds but which, as I remarked of the similarly afflicted Dresda, is an abomination when turning round in a narrow road or manoeuvring past stationary vehicles.

It would not be so bad if there were aerodynamic advantages to be weighed in the opposite balance, but there are none: a full-width fairing would be cleaner and more comfortable and create less drag. This was proved years ago by a number of racers, including Dunstall; but even he now sells narrow skimped affairs on his bikes, so perhaps it is not the manufacturers we should blame but the crass obstinacy and ill-educated dogmatism of their fashion-crazed customers. It is not often that I offer bouquets to Norton, but their latest fairing for the Commando is far more sensible and deserves high praise.

Let us assume, however, that the performance of the Rickman Honda is sufficient, that its grips are all right where they are, and that you do not mind the buffeting of wind round the edges of the fairing. Let us remind ourselves (did you know?) that at speeds above 20 mph or thereabouts the handlebars are rarely turned more than 1½ degrees. At higher speeds, even much higher speeds, than this, how does the CR handle? Back we go to Goldsmith: if not first, in the very first line. The chassis is one of the few that can genuinely be called race-proven, and its beauty lies deeper than the skin of nickel plating that makes it look so attractive. There is nothing special about its design, but uncommonly good quality in its construction, with every joint of the tubing properly profiled, fitted and bronze welded by a master of the craft. The tubing is not your dreary En 2 stuff but Reynolds 531 manganese molybdenum steel, beloved of most bicycle makers since long before the Hitler war. It is not the absolute best (Goldsmith strikes again!) for I had a bicycle framed in Accles & Pollock nickel - chrome - molybdenum which was even better: manganese is present to some extent in almost all steels, whereas the NiCrMo steel has such resistance to fatigue and ease of manipulation as to make it the chosen stuff of Grand Prix car chassis by Mercedes-Benz, who are rather good at this sort of thing. Never mind: in their choice of material, and in their selection of large diameters and thin walls for stiffness and lightness (notably in their front forks) Rickman display a technological awareness that is superior to most other motorcycle manufacturers'.

It is their geometries, their spring rates and their kinematics that finish the job of making the CR handle well. It responds with alacrity to a shift of weight or pressure on seat or footpegs, less smartly to pressures

on the handlebars, but always accurately and predictably. On racing tyres it would surely be a humdinger; on 18-inch TT100s it is very good, with plenty of ground clearance that it can exploit — though I should be tempted to remove the bulky Honda centre stand after completing the assembly of the machine. Only in one respect does the CR cramp the rider's style: it does not like cornering on a closed throttle, especially on bumpy surfaces.

I learnt the reason for this when I returned the bike to New Milton. In the early days of the Rickman road-racing frame, when it was being developed in the hands of John Hartle and others, it was found that with the original phosphor bronze bushes locating the rear fork pivot the bike could be heeled over through tremendous angles without any warning of impending disaster as the limit of tyre adhesion was approached. The substitution of rubber bushes gave the rider some warning feel, but at the cost of some cornering instability in the power-off mode. For racing this was not a serious objection, for it is to be assumed that a racing rider knows where he is going and can plan to take all his corners under power. On the public highway the rider has no such guarantee of infallibility, but neither has he much need of the ultimate in cornering power such as might be exercised on a track.

The freedom to change one's mind, to close the throttles after committal to a corner, does wonders for one's confidence when riding hard (it was a particular feature of the Laverda) and is well worth the last few degrees of lean — which are still available, but to employ which might be a little more risky. I would recommend that the Silentbloc bushes be removed and metal ones fitted, so as to make good some of the present deficiency in the rear suspension's torsional stiffness; but to do so would probably invalidate the Rickman warranty, which is explicit in its refusal to accept any alteration or modification to standard specification.

Or perhaps it should be left alone. The basis of this Rickman Covetable Roadburner long ago lapped the Isle of Man TT circuit at over 100 mph, which is more than I am ever likely to do. ●

The fairing neatly wraps around the standard Honda motor, keeping the bike's width to a minimum. With small frontal area and a hundredweight less bulk the bike accelerates right up to the red line in top gear, and uses less juice than a stock Four. A touch of technical sophistication (below left) with a hydraulically operated rear disc brake — nice 'n smooth. Front disc is OK, but needs a good squeeze.

MORE MOTORCYCLE READING FROM BROOKLANDS

ROAD TEST
HONDA'S 750

UPDATED
NOISE ABATED
HIGHLY RATED

■ *There can be no argu-
ing with Honda's sales
record. From just about
every angle they seem to
have the entire motorcycle
market neatly stitched up
and in the big bike sector the
CB750 is no exception.*

The evidence is there to be
seen at any gathering of enthusiasts. At the last few race
meetings, I couldn't help notic-
ing that every other big bike
going through the gates seemed
to be a Honda four.

I find this mildly surprising,
because I remember the first
fours as big, heavy, admittedly
powerful but unwieldy, with
some unfortunate habits in the
handling department. But then I
hadn't ridden a CB750 since the
first ones appeared, so it would
be interesting to see how Honda
had rung the changes in the last
four or five years.

This year's model looks pretty
much the same as ever, but the
changes are there all right, just
waiting to be counted. After
commenting on the height of the
seat, which is one thing that
hasn't altered, my first reaction
was that I was on the wrong
bike. Passenger Cazalet and I
eased out into the West London
traffic and with a short, queue-
jumping squirt of throttle, we
were into the Chiswick round-
about. Balancing lean and throttle
while looking for a Honda-
shaped gap, I suddenly realised
that the 750 was *handling*.
Where were the wallows of
yesteryear? Certainly not on that
particular grand prix of a roun-
dabout, nor did they show up all
the way through the test.

This model is the K2, the most
up-to-date available for the UK,
while in America they've reached K4. Between the first KO and
here just about every single
component has been changed or
modified. It sounds typically
Honda, but none the less impressive for that, and has not, I
am assured, come about because the original parts weren't
up to the job.

The policy of constant updating is aimed at improving the
whole machine. Let's say that
the motor would run for 20,000
miles before it needed an overhaul and at this point it was
found that the pistons needed
renewing. Changing the piston

design then meant it could run
for 24,000 miles, when the
valves would give trouble so the
valves would be re-designed and
so on.

That's the theory, the way
they told me and the proof as far
as Honda are concerned is in
their overhaul mileages. They
claim that it isn't unusual for
CB750s to run 40,000 to
50,000 miles before having the
head off and quote a couple of
instances where machines have
reached 90,000-odd miles.

I was interested mainly in
chassis and suspension changes, expecting something fairly
drastic to explain the newly-
found handling qualitites. Sadly, from my point of view,
nothing dramatic has happened.

The frame is basically the
same and none of the major
dimensions, wheelbase, head
angle, etc., have been altered. It
is purely the result of five years of
development, with many subtle
changes adding up to the improved end product. When you
consider that that first 750, the
KO, was built in literally five-
and-a-half months and consequently had a lot of square
edges, the improvements aren't
that surprising.

The front forks incorporate
different rates and the damping
has been altered. They also have
a new oil seal to overcome the
problem of oil seepage,
although the seal on one leg of
the test bike went in less than
200 miles. Apparently they have
to be fitted very carefully.

The rear suspension has been
changed at least four times and
now they have it just about right
for a combination of comfort and
roadholding. One other significant change is that the disc brake
has been moved inboard and is
now some 6 mm closer to the
centre of the hub.

Engine development, like all
other Hondas, has been towards
a smoother silence and a com-
pliance with existing or project-
ed legislation. It doesn't seem to
have suffered too much though.
If the motor isn't as powerful as
the early ones, it is a lot quieter,
more flexible and generally less
fussy. The improved handling
and better ride also mean you
can use the power more of the
time, resulting in a machine
which isn't much slower from A

FIVE YEARS ON - HOW GOOD IS THE FOUR?

HONDA'S 750

to B than its predecessors.

One chassis change which makes a big difference to the long distance rider is the repositioning of footrest and handlebar. The footrests are further back and the handlebar is flatter, which makes for a much better riding position. The fact that the 750 is so generally tall still spoils riding comfort though, as the rider is forced up into the wind. The seat is amply big enough, but not quite comfortable enough and starts to get painful after a couple of hours. This isn't really acceptable for a machine on which you could expect to cover 300-odd miles at a stretch.

In all other respects, the Honda retains that character which made it the first of the superbikes. For the enthusiast it is a fast, powerful replica of the grand prix racers. For the tourer it is capable of hauling long distances and heavy loads with no more trouble than it takes to ride to work every day.

And high mileage doesn't have to mean high fuel bills. I thrashed the 750 quite unashamedly and got 44 miles to a gallon, 130-odd miles before needing reserve and as near as I could judge, about another 20 or so before running completely dry. I also got something over 55 mpg on a fairly gentle, out-of-town run. Not the most economical machine in the world, but reasonable enough considering what you're getting in other directions.

There's still enough power to break loose the back tyre and make smoke; and pulling a tall gear our model ran out of steam at about 112 mph. It's happiest crusing speed was more or less determined by the air speed and the shape of the rider, a sustained 90 mph soon produced aching arms.

Honda's brakes, particularly the hydraulics, have always been good and these, blending nicely with the handling, allowed very confident, relaxed riding. One thing about a big motor is that you don't have to bother about scratching to keep up speed. You can drop in behind slow traffic, potter around corners and as soon as the road opens up in front, you can let it go. This ability to get from

crawling-truck pace up to full cruising speed is worth much more than all the academic factors like maximum speed, standing quarter times and power figures which are usually quoted to let everyone know how good a machine is.

The Honda just does it efficiently — one minute you can be bogged down in traffic, the next will see you whistling along the open road.

This lack of fussiness shows up all the way through the Honda. Starting and warm-up, once a feat of delicate throttle control, is now more of a pure formality. You turn the key and press the button. In much the same way, the 750 responds to the controls in a nicely cut-and-dried manner. Open the throttle and it goes, put the brakes on and it stops. And yet it still manages to keep that slightly superior character. People, motorcyclists and non-believers, still stop and look at it, which, for a machine that's been around for five years, isn't bad.

From a passenger's point of view, apart from the footrests being so widely spaced, the ride was pretty comfortable even at high speeds. There was a slight, tingling vibration through the footrests and the mirrors got blurred over 70 mph. That and the moving scenery was about all there was to let you know the engine was still working.

If that is the general concept of the Honda, and obviously the reason people buy them, the detail points are no less important. There are lots of little things which can make the difference between a pleasant or a tiresome relationship between man and machine. In general the Honda is pretty good, and most things on it have been well thought-out.

But for a company who have bothered to set such standards in their developments and attention to detail, I find it hard to understand why they fall down on a few points and really take the edge off an otherwise fine machine. The lights are good, but the switches are hopelessly positioned for people whose thumbs grow next to their forefingers. The headlamp flasher is a miniscule button which is just as likely to sound the horn if fumbled in the wrong direction. The ignition switch still has to be groped for under the tank. There is a neat quadrant linkage to open the carburettors, but the twin-cable twistgrip still has to be turned too far, and is heavy in operation. And the gearshift is still notchy and clonks on occasion. Also, I hear that people still have trouble with ht leads.

These may be minor complaints, but as such it wouldn't be asking too much of Honda to clean them up.

Even so, the 750 lives right up to what it's expected to be and do and it's easy to see why the model is so popular. Five years of development haven't brought any startling transformations — in the light of the recently announced 1000cc flat four this isn't surprising either — but they have honed a finer edge to Honda's superbike.

To the question how good is the Honda after five years, the answer is quite good enough and better than I for one, had expected.

JOHN ROBINSON

ROAD TEST SPECIFICATION

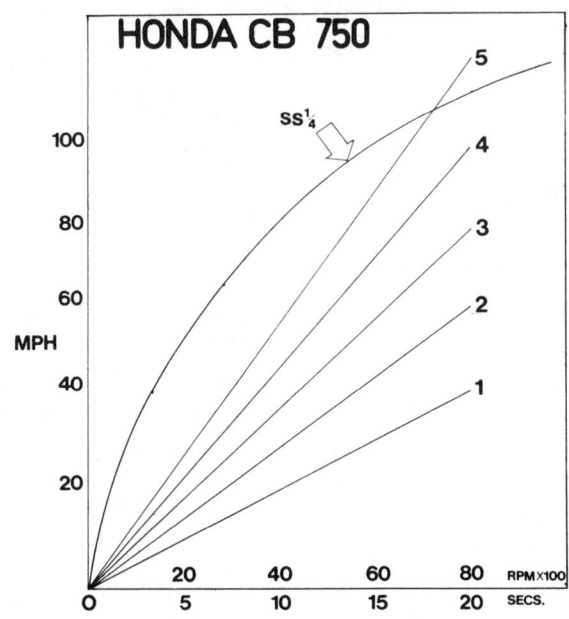

HONDA CB 750

lubrication	dry sump, pressure feed to engine and gearbox bearings
carburettor	four Keihin
ignition system	twin contact breaker and coil
lighting system	12Vac/dc from 210W alternator via
charging system	regulator to 14 a-h battery
clutch	multiplate coil spring
gear ratios, overall	11.4, 7.79, 6.08, 5.0, 4.27
primary drive	double chain, 1.708 reduction
secondary drive	chain, 2.667 reduction
gearbox sprockets	17,18T
wheel sprockets	45,48T
mph / 1000 rpm in top	14 mph
fuel tank capacity	3.7 gal, 1.1 gal reserve
oil tank capacity	6.2 pints
tyres, front	3.25 x 19 Bridgestone
tyres, rear	4.00 x 18 Bridgestone
brakes, front	hydraulically operated disc
brakes, rear	sls drum
wheelbase	57.3 inches
ground clearance	6.3 inches
seat height	32 inches
dry weight	480 lb
test weight	518 lb
suspension, front	telescopic fork
suspension, rear	swinging arm, 3-position dampers
castor	63 deg.
trail	3.74 inch
speedo error	8% fast
parts prices:	
front mudguard	£15.52 complete + VAT
handlebars	£5.27 + VAT
speedo cable	£1.42 + VAT
exhaust pipe (each)	£24.09 + VAT
set of points	£0.90 inc. VAT
set of pistons (complete)	£27.28 + VAT
list price	£979 inc VAT
concessionaire: Honda UK Ltd., Power Road, Chiswick, W4.	

braking distance from 30 mph	**29 feet**
fuel consumption, average	**49 mpg**
engine type	SOHC in-line four
displacement	736 ccm
bore x stroke	61 x 63 mm
compression ratio	9.0:1

Continued from Page 19

CB750 POWER PLANT

HONDA'S 750

The overhead camshaft driven by chain from the centre of crank

Primary transmission is by two single-row chains from centre of crankshaft to clutch 'in-rigger' sprockets

Gear selector mechanism has anti 'over-select' device. Note oil 'gallery' feed to centre of gearshaft for gearbox lubrication.!

■ **From drawing board to the production line in five months! That is the remarkable fact about the Honda CB750, the machine which stunned the motorcycle world when it was introduced some five years ago.**

Of course, there is nothing new in the production of a four-cylinder motorcycle, Henderson, Ariel and Brough all produced 'fours' long before the Second World War. But when the Honda appeared with its advanced specification of disc front brake, transverse, in-line, four-cylinder, overhead camshaft motor with five-speed gearbox, electric starter, etc., it started a new trend in motorcycling . . . the cult of the 'superbike'.

Surprisingly, in spite of its complicated looking appearance, the CB750 motor is in many ways quite conventional in design and reasonably easy to work on providing you have the necessary special tools.

For example: the overhead camshaft, which is chain driven direct from the crankshaft, runs in plain metal bearings with an oil pressure feed of approximately 60 lbs/sq/in. The valves, two per cylinder, are operated by rockers running direct on to the camshaft with tappet clearance set in the normal manner with a grub screw and locking nut set in the rocker above the valve stem.

Oil feed to the rockers and camshaft is cleverly accomplished by using the space between the cylinder retaining studs and the cylinder stud holes, which

does away with the need for any external piping. However, slight weeping of oil between the cylinder head and barrels brought about modification to seals and the cylinder head gasket on the later CB750 motors.

The flat top pistons have slight indentations for valve clearance and are fitted with two compression and one oil scraper rings. The plain metal small-end is 'splash' fed with oil, while the drop-forged conrods have split big-ends with white metal capped plain bearings.

Similar to the camshaft, the big-ends bearings are protected by a 60lbs/sq/in. oil pressure, which also applies to the crankshaft main bearings. There is not a single roller or needle bearing in sight. Therefore, it is obvious that regular oil changes and

maintenance of the lubrication system is vital.

The crankshaft is a one-piece casting with five plain main bearings. Such are the tolerances in manufacture of the crankshaft that Honda do not have oversize shells available to allow regrinding of shaft.

As may be seen in the photographs above, the drive to the camshaft and the primary drive are taken from the centre web of the crankshaft. Two single row chains run direct to a shock-absorber mounted sprockets which are set between the clutch and the gearbox on an 'in-rigger' bearing.

There has been a fallacy spread about uneven wear between the two primary drive chains. However, this apparent uneven wear is an illusion creat-

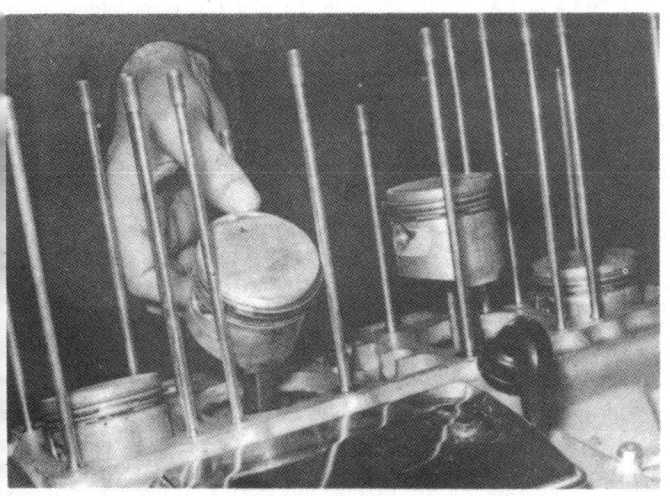

Flat top pistons have 'double' indentations at front allowing them to be fitted on any cylinder allowing for valve off-set

Multi-plate clutch runs in oil and due to low reduction gearing from engine, rotates at high-speed and has low torque

The gearbox showing final reduction pinion on shaft to final drive sprocket. Kickstart pinion also drives oil pump unit!

Crankshaft assembly showing five, plain main bearings and camshaft primary drive chains. Note split big-end con-rod

ed by the shock absorber sprockets, which are mounted independently and allow different tensions on the two separate chains depending upon the position or tension on the shock absorbers.

The shaft from the primary drive sprockets to the clutch also carries the kickstart pinion, which drives through the kickstart mechanism to the oil pump. This is a trocoidal unit providing both pressure feed and scavenge to both engine unit and the gearbox.

In fact, one of the unique features about the CB750 motor unit is that not only is the engine 'dry' sump, but so is the gearbox. For this reason, it is unwise to tow the Honda CB750 any distance without the motor running, or disconnecting the rear

chain. The reason is that without the motor running, the gearbox pinions are not receiving any lubrication and if the machine is being towed, without the chain being disconnected, the internals of the gearbox are still rotating but without oil!

Admittedly, the complete 'dry' sump system for engine and gearbox means all oil is constantly being filtered, but as mentioned previously, regular changes of oil and filter are absolutely necessary to safeguard the complete engine/gearbox unit, which relies heavily on perfect lubrication and oil pressure at all times when running.

Because of the fairly low reduction in gearing between the engine and gearbox, the speed of the gear pinions within the

gearbox is fairly high. This is one of the reasons for a tendency towards 'clunkiness' of the Honda 750 gearbox. However, because of the high-speed of rotation, the gearbox internals benefit from lower torque loadings.

At any set engine speed, this means that the gearbox is transmitting the power with far less stress on the pinions. Apart from this, the Honda box is a fairly straightforward 'crossover' design with only two shafts, input and output. But a further reduction in gearing is achieved by mounting the rear sprocket on a third shaft which carries a large pinion driven by the gearbox output shaft.

Electrics on the Honda 750 are straightforward, although the three-phase alternator pokes

out 210 watts, more than enough to cope with the electric starter and abundance of other items of electrical equipment fitted to the machine.

The electric starter drives direct, via reduction gearing, on to the crankshaft through a roller clutch pinion mounted behind the alternator.

At the opposite end of the crankshaft to the alternator is the contact breaker unit which incorporates an automatic advance and retard unit. Ignition is by normal contact breaker/coil system and similar to the rest of the design is straightforward in operation.

In fact, after having seen the Honda 750-four stripped in Honda's service training school, we were impressed by the entire simplicity of the unit.

HONDA 750-4
"Bread-and-butter" Superbike?

IN YEARS to come, when historians look back on the revival of motorcycling and the motorcycle in the 70s, one of the turning points will be seen as the day when Honda made one of the most sophisticated, supposedly complicated and certainly potent, motorcycles available to the general public at a price it could afford. Since then others have joined in the game. Now there are faster bikes, more expensive bikes, bikes with more cylinders but none have sold like the Honda 750. Thousands have poured into every motorcycle-importing country in the world and there have been very few disenchanted owners.

How did Honda succeed when others failed? Timing, of course, was all important. They made the glamorous four desirable with a string of racing successes and, judging the mood of the market to perfection, they then offered it to the motorcyclist at a price that was at least thinkable. The result was a boom in not only Honda sales but in those of every other manufacturer of big bikes. I think most sectors of the motorcycle industry recognise their debt to Honda for stimulating an ailing market.

That was long enough ago for the Honda "750-4" to be taken for granted on our roads today. It was also long enough ago for fashions to have changed (come to think of it yesterday was long enough ago for that!). Bikes have become more economy-minded, performance is no longer the only criterion a rider uses when buying a machine, and now he can choose from an array of like-capacity bikes. Yet, after all this time the Honda has hardly changed at all, at least to outward appearances. They are even still using at least one of the colour schemes they displayed some years back, a not particularly eye-catching gold.

Internally, we are assured, little of the original engine remains unaltered, a situation any dealer will readily endorse as he struggles to keep up with the spare parts lists. The basic concept of the setup is as before, with an air-cooled, chain-drive-overhead-camshaft, in line four-cylinder engine, differing from the Kawasaki tested last month in having one camshaft less, and a slight tilt forward. Bore is 61mm and stroke 63mm, giving a total cylinder capacity of 736 c.c. Compression ratio is 9 to 1. Still retained is the endless camshaft and primary drive chain running from the centre of the crankshaft, but our earlier fears of wreaking havoc and resulting in a complete engine strip down do not seem to have been justified for chain life, aided by running in dirt-free conditions, has apparently been good

and we have only heard of one primary chain breakage in the past five years, although we recognise that not every reader is going to write to us mentioning this. We were also bothered by the risk of damage to the protruding alternator on the right hand end of the crankshaft when we rode the bike all those years ago. This has, perhaps, given some riders unlucky enough to drop the bike on that side problems, but again few Honda 750 owners have complained.

Carburation is by four 28mm Keihin carburettors of the piston valve type. They are controlled by a double push-pull cable on a pulley with a bar activating the slides. Externally the engine differs from the original by having larger anti-vibration pillars on the cylinders and different plug caps. The curses as riders dried out the old ones must have been heard all the way to Tokio. Our machine, virtually brand new upon collection, had a handsome gleam to it with all the engine covers and cylinder fins looking pristine. Soon it was like most Honda 750s that we see around, with the engine block and exhaust system only clean where we could reach. Some riders manage to keep their bikes looking as though they have just left the factory but, frankly, we don't know how they do it. Particularly difficult to keep clean are the exhaust pipes and silencers. The "hidden" silencers are easy to neglect and tend to suffer somewhat. They are very expensive to replace, Honda exhaust systems, and we would like to see Honda, who have pioneered so much that is good in motorcycling, think about stainless steel as an alternative material. One thing about the pipes, they managed to keep their colour, an 8in double thickness from the exhaust flange effectively dissipating heat.

As always, the engine was reasonably oil-tight but a little oil *did* escape from the Triumph-style rocker caps. With such a massive alloy unit it was to be expected that some mechanical noise would be evident. It was what other Four owners described as "the good old Honda rattle"—nothing serious, just the sound of four pistons, eight valves and two chains working in unison! One sound that has left the bike is the loud screech as the starter-button was pressed. Now it is just a civilised whirr. Not for long, either, for the motor invariably fired instantly, the carburettor-mounted choke lever being used from cold. I *still* prefer a handlebar-mounted choke lever, even if it does mean an extra cable.

The gearbox, five-speed, has always been an area where Honda are just a little less than perfect. They are rarely bad, just . . . ordinary. Our 750 was always noisy when engaging bottom from neutral and one needed time and concentration to achieve quiet gear changes. Naturally our technique improved as the miles increased and clearly an owner would soon learn the trick. The clutch was surprisingly light and just about right for our taste.

The frame appears (which is the key word, Honda often appear to have remained unchanged when the reverse is the case) to have changed little. It is of duplex cradle type with twin tubes along the bottom of the tank and a large-section tube from the top of the steering-head to the rear. There is no gusseting at the front. The rear sub-frame has quite a robust triangular section either side to support the exhaust system and pillion rests. Little yellow blobs of paint are evident on various nuts (as they were on the 900 Kawasaki) to indicate that the nut has been torqued to the correct poundage.

The front footrests are spring-loaded and were, for our taste, a mite too easy to fold, often doing so unintentionally when we returned a foot to the rest upon starting. The dual seat, comfortable and ample, is hinged and lockable with helmet holders now fitted either side. All we have to do now is prevail upon helmet manufacturers to build special locking rings into safety helmets. Which, we will concede, is more difficult than it seems. No adjustment was required to the rear chain during the 500 miles of the test but we will agree that this in itself does not prove much. Chain life is still a major talking point wherever Honda 750 owners meet and we know of some who have transferred their affections to shaft-driven motorcycles although completely satisfied with the "Four" in every other respect.

The brakes. Disc front and drum rear. The rear was about right and, in the dry, the disc was superb. As on so many, if not all, disc brakes it is the wet that worries us. The situation seemed to be marginally worse with the Honda than with the big Kawasaki, but perhaps that is just because we had more rain while riding the 750. The plain fact is that on just about every disc brake that we have tried this year, British, Japanese, German and Italian, there has been a time-lag after applying the brake, in the wet, before getting results. Ride with it feathered all the time to keep the disc clear of water, some say. Ridiculous. They'll be wanting us to ride with our feet on the ground next in case we fall off. It seems to us to be an area of motorcycling that needs more work and, as things stand, makes the disc brake less of a good idea than it first appeared. Certainly this year the double-sided front disc brake, as fitted to the Morini and Benelli, has more to offer the touring rider. This is not, of course, a problem unique to Honda.

Electrically, the 750 compares well with most others in its class. The horn was pretty grim

but the lights were good, the control layout was fair and the instruments were superb, especially at night. One aspect which did annoy us was the engine kill-switch mounted on top of the right hand throttle assembly. It killed the engine all right but left the starter-motor in circuit, so if one overlooked that it was in the off position, or some passing children had let curiosity get the better of them or if one's glove

inadvertently moved it (this happened to us a couple of times) the engine stopped but the starter still worked. Might we suggest that Honda look at the arrangement on the Kawasaki where the same switch kills the starter too ?

Naturally the machine comes with just about every rider aid imaginable. Stop lights activated by both front and rear brakes, twin mirrors, centre and side stands (the side stand held the machine a shade too upright), reasonable 3½-gallon petrol tank, steering lock, an array of warning lights and even a document holder, under the seat. Less attractive was a front number-plate that could be used to peel potatoes with—or slice pedestrians—and powerful ammunition for those who are campaigning to get the front number-plate

abolished. As we have already indicated, we can take or leave the gold-finish on the Honda but, combined with black frame and chrome guards, it makes a pretty imposing package and, viewed overall, we would say that the bike is as handsome as they come.

It is not too difficult to criticise any bike, and when it has been around for five years, as the Honda 750 has, it is bound to have lagged behind in some areas. It has not done too badly in price, though, jumping from £680 to around £1,000 in the four-and-a-bit years since we first tried the machine. Is that too big a rise by today's standards ? We suspect not. The interesting thing is that, analysing the machine and discussing design features, there are some aspects that could be improved by

riding it. That is something to be cherished. I can recall quite clearly the moment, in February 1970, when I collected a privately-owned 750 from Leytonstone and cautiously made my way across an icy London. It was a milestone in my motorcycling career. Co-incidentally the Honda that we collected from Chiswick had done almost exactly the same number of miles, about 450, as had that first one we tried. In looks it had changed hardly at all. A little more chrome here, a little less there, identical exhaust system, petrol tank, and instruments pretty much the same. Enough to give the lie to all those stories we hear that Honda change their bike every Monday morning.

The real benefit of four years development came when we rode the bike. I well recall how *civilised* I thought the first Honda that I rode was and, indeed, it was then. But standards have changed, we now take the kind of performance and equipment that Honda, almost alone, offered in 1970 for granted. With the benefit of hindsight, and using today's standards, the Honda of old seems almost crude. The present machine is very much smoother, especially from low revs., it has more torque and pulls willingly from 2,000 r.p.m., it ticks over at an even 800 r.p.m. and altogether it felt as though the past five years have been really put to good use. Performance is no longer considered the be all and end all of the Honda 750. The first bikes to arrive here made a big thing of having a top speed of 125 m.p.h. The claimed power output remains unchanged at 67 b.h.p. at 8,000 but now the bike is content to settle for not much more than 110 m.p.h. It is a much better motorcycle for it.

Perhaps the one easily-identifiable characteristic of the Honda 750 is its deep but pleasant exhaust note. That has not changed—except that it's a bit quieter now—and we can well understand how Honda owners always enjoy winding it on, just to listen to the noise. The compulsory wearing of safety helmets has removed that old saying about being able to tell an enthusiastic motorcyclist by his dirty right ear, as he rides with his head cocked listening to his engine, from the vocabulary, but the principle still applies to the Honda owner. The Honda is still a big bike, weighing in at 503 lb with a gallon of fuel in the tank, but it sheds its weight with ease as the twistgrip is turned and the response is still as thrilling as ever. Little wonder that the bike has a reputation for wearing out chains. It is almost impossible to resist the temptation to wind it on at the slightest opportunity. That engine really is a dream, having power, flexibility and almost complete smoothness. It was not too uneconomical, either, averaging 46/49 m.p.g. during the test. If only we had been able to curb our enthusiasm it could well have been better.

Handling and comfort. They go together but are often in a different class. With the Honda they are about on a par, adequate without setting the world alight. The comfort is assisted by a 26½in-long, well-padded seat but, with a height of 33in and a wide tank to keep the legs apart, it was not perfect and stopping would be misery for a man with short legs. As it was we tended to rock from toe to toe. The footrests are also too far forward, for our taste, making the riding position more cramped than it need be. We did appreciate the handlebars, though, such a change from the sit up and beg type. They were as short as they should be while still leaving room for all the bits and pieces that have to be tacked on and were swept back to give the rider a good touring stance. Ideal for speeds up to 90 or so but uncomfortable much above. The handling has marginally improved over the years. Some of this may be due to the Bridgestone tyres, 4.00 × 18in rear, 3.25 × 19in front, which gave us not a moment of anxiety in the wet. It would not be reasonable to say that Honda have really solved the handling problems of their biggest bike, but now its only vice is a certain choppiness when cranked over at high speed, it is gentle and not too worrying. The suspension is hard, harder than of old, and this has stiffened the machine up at the expense of more road shocks being transmitted to the rider and (more so) to a pillion passenger.

Perhaps we have become too familiar with the Honda 750 over the years; we understand it too well and know what to look for. We might also mention in passing that for the past 12,000 miles the editor's staff bike has been a Honda 750 which, although it has a hard life, has never missed a beat in all that time, starts first time, leaks a little oil, and has generally endeared itself to him. It also means that we have had longer to learn its good and bad points and, as a result, we may be more critical of the Honda than of most other bikes. On balance, though, it comes out well. It is not the cheapest of the "superbikes" but it is also a long way from being the most expensive. There are also enough of them around for the chances of finding help, in the unlikely event of it being necessary, being good. It is reasonably economical, has more than enough performance and presents it in a thrilling and, more important, useable way. Spares are not cheap but they do not seem to be much worse than any other bike in its class. In short, one of the best balanced and most reliable bikes around.

HONDA CB750 K5

The 750 Four gets better and more refined every year, and loses a little of its personality in the process

It hasn't been so long since we last tested the Honda CB750 (We tested the K3 in July of last year.), but the 750 Fours are successful and popular enough that we decided to refresh our memory by testing the 1975 version, the K5.

It is interesting to note that the CB750, introduced in late 1968, is the only Honda of six years ago still surviving in the 1975 line-up, except for the indomitable Trail 90. (The 450 twin has become a 500.) And although the CB750 now stands in the shadows cast by the GL-1000 Four, it appears to have quite a few good years ahead of it. It has been accepted by the casual rider, the novice, the cafe racer, the commuter, and the veteran tourer, all with near-equal enthusiasm. Hordes of them fill the interstates during the warmer months and putter along downtown boulevards and rush along freeways during rush hours.

Six years have done nothing to make the CB750 any less modern; the design is as up-to-date now as it was at the moment of its introduction. Subtle changes have kept it abreast of the times while bikes introduced more recently have seen the first glimmerings of obsolescence in the concern about noise, air pollution, fuel economy, and some of the other horrors of civilization. The first CB750s were musclebikes, but small changes have made the later series quieter, milder, and more attractive to the rider whose prime consideration is not out-and-out performance. The refining process has reached the sixth generation in the CB750 K5.

THE BIKE: The Honda CB750 K5 still has the same 200-pound, four cylinder, single-overhead camshaft, four-stroke engine. Each cylinder has a bore of 61mm and a stroke of 63mm for a displacement of 184.1cc per cylinder, a total of 736.4cc. The crankshaft rides on five plain insert main bearings. A dry-sump lubrication system pumps oil to all vital clutch, transmission, and engine components, including the plain bearing inserts at the connecting rod big ends. Oil which collects at the bottom of the sump is pumped back to a 3.7-quart oil tank on the right side of the bike.

The overhead camshaft is driven by the traditional (for Honda) single-row chain, guided by a host of rollers and sprockets. The chain tension is taken up by an adjuster that uses a spring-loaded roller.

Dual primary chains run from the center of the crank to a jackshaft just ahead of the transmission. The jackshaft drives the wet clutch, which has seven drive and seven driven plates. The clutch is on the mainshaft of a five-speed gearbox.

Carburetion is provided by four 28mm Keihin slide/needle carburetors. The slides of all four carbs are linked to the same bar, which is operated by two throttle cables: One raises the bar and opens the throttles; the other pulls the bar back down and closes the throttles. There is nothing to stretch and require re-synchronization in the system, and the throttles can't stick open.

PHOTOGRAPHY BY ART FRIEDMAN

The Honda 750 pioneered the four-cylinder look. Each cylinder has its own one-piece exhaust pipe and muffler. The mufflers on each side are joined by a small balance tube near their ends.

Maybe Honda programmed *pride* into their automatic welding machines, because the welds on the 750's double-loop frame are neater than most other machine-welded frames we've seen. The frame still looks heavy, though, and no doubt contributes its share to the bike's 501-pound dry weight.

The front forks allow 5.6 inches of travel, and the fork tubes are protected by rubber gaiters. The forks have been given 27 degrees of rake and 3.7 inches of trail. The 3.25 x 19 Dunlop rib at the front of the bike is separated from the 4.00 x 18 Dunlop at the rear by a wheelbase that averages 58.6 inches. The rear shocks have five spring preload settings and allow 3.3 inches of wheel travel.

The original CB750 began the disc brake trend, and the current front brake is virtually the same. The 11.7-inch disc and its single-action hydraulic caliper are located on the left side of the front wheel. Later models have acquired a fender over the rear of the disc, which will throw off water just like a spinning tire. The single-leading shoe rear brake is a rod-operated affair.

The steel gas tank holds 4.5 gallons, and except for a different paint color, looks just like last year's tank. The gas cap doesn't lock, but the flip-up seat does. Beneath it are the battery, the tools, and a small compartment for an owner's manual and registration papers. Many of the electrical components, including a three-fuse box, rectifier, flasher, starter relay, and starter motor "safety unit" (interlock), can be reached by snapping off the left side panel.

The changes in the K5 include bigger turn signals, with a beeper included in the circuit to remind you that you are signaling. If it annoys you, the signal will work without the beeper if the switch isn't pushed all the way to its stop. The front turn signal bulbs also have a second filament that comes on when the headlight is turned on. It's a good idea, but why it isn't also employed in the rear signals, where it could go a long way in saving your life if the taillight bulb burns out, is a mystery.

A rubber tab has been added to the sidestand on all street Hondas for 1975. The tab hangs down below the foot of the sidestand and is designed to drag the ground if the rider forgets to fold the stand up when riding off. Theoretically, the rubber dragging on the ground will cause the stand to fold up slightly. We found that it would work if we leaned into a turn gradually with the stand down, but if we turned left quickly, the bike would bounce off the stand as if the rubber wasn't there.

Changes which didn't happen to the CB750 this year but will probably show up in the future include moving the ignition lock from beneath the front of the gas tank to a position between the 140-mph speedo and the 10,000-rpm tach. There are no smog-control concessions yet and the lights don't come on automatically when the key is turned on. There's no taillight or charging system failure indicators, either.

ENGINE AND GEARBOX: To start the bike when it's cold, you turn on the gas, flip up the choke lever (The Four has real chokes, not starting plungers.), turn the ignition on, and push the button. If the starter motor doesn't turn over, the bike is probably in gear, so either put it in neutral or pull in the clutch lever. That should do it if the battery isn't low. In that event, there is a kickstarter connected to the primary drive. If the engine turns over but doesn't fire, the kill switch above the starting button is probably off. (A lot of angry people with new bikes that wouldn't start have pushed them back to the dealer only to find the kill switch was off.)

The CB750 is very cold-blooded and won't idle until it warms up, which takes several minutes. It likes a minute or so

speed; the power just builds constantly as the engine speed increases. If you are in a particular hurry and the engine is below 5000 rpm, downshifting will give you a boost in acceleration. The power output is strong right up to, and past, the 8000-rpm redline. In fact, when we stopped our dyno run at 10,000 rpm, the 750 was still making good horsepower, although it had peaked at 8000. Maximum torque was produced at 7000 rpm. At the dragstrip the K5 didn't set any records and wasn't quite as quick as the early Honda 750s, but it did a respectable 13.64-second ET at 98.6 mph.

The engine revs up and returns to idle very quickly—almost instantly—because of

after a couple of fast, hard, slip-the-clutch starts.

The shift lever throw is light but long and requires a positive, deliberate movement of the foot to insure that the shift has been completed. A light, casual shift will usually work, but the transmission will occasionally either pop out of or fail to slip into gear after a too-easy shift.

Shifting into first from neutral produces a healthy clank from the transmission, and a shift that isn't well synchronized will also be marked by a similar noise. There is some transmission whine during acceleration, which probably accounts for a significant portion of the bike's 83.5-decibel sound level.

The gears are spaced fairly evenly; first gear isn't particularly low, but you can leave the clutch engaged at a creeping pace because of the smooth low-rpm power. And starting off requires very little throttle to get away smoothly.

HANDLING: The central factor in the CB750's handling is its high center of gravity. The engine weight is carried quite high in the frame for the sake of ground clearance, which raises the center of gravity. When the bike is leaned over past a certain point while cornering, the weight up near the top of the bike tries to drop and lean the bike further into the turn, making it take a line tighter than the one you've chosen. If the bike is closer to vertical, centrifugal force pulls this weight to the outside of the turn, thereby straightening up the bike and widening the line you're taking. At low speeds when there is less centrifugal force, the bike tends to fall inward more. At high speeds it tries to straighten up more.

The tendencies aren't extreme or dangerous, but they make it difficult to take and hold the precise line you have chosen. However, you improve with practice, and there are certain angles of lean for any cornering speed where the bike is stable. And by moving your body weight around on the motorcycle, you can compensate somewhat for the bike's center of gravity.

The high center of gravity also amplifies any sideways movement or any oscillation. If you hit a bump or ride into a sharp dip, the bike will tend to lean in the direction that it is bumped. If it starts to wobble, the high center of gravity can act like a pendulum and give the wobble the ability to continue. Under certain circumstances—like if the bike were to be used in a road race, for example—it will wobble. But the average street rider isn't likely to ever know about it because he won't ride it that hard or that fast.

The high center of gravity also makes it a bit difficult to throw the bike from side to side quickly in a tight S bend. And it is particularly difficult if you try to do so with real precision.

The ground clearance is adequate for most riders, but it's not exceptional. One rider climbed on the bike who had never before ridden a Honda 750, but he man-

of warm-up before you pull away, and it takes two or three miles of running before it responds to throttle changes.

Once warmed up, the 750 has an enormous powerband. It will run down below 1000 rpm in *fifth* gear and pull away smoothly and strongly if the throttle is opened gradually. If the throttle is opened wide quickly below 3000 rpm, the intake gas velocity drops off, and the engine will stumble and die. But it will run quite comfortably and smoothly at very low rpm with smaller throttle openings. The twist-grip has quite a large amount of travel, so whacking the throttle all the way open requires a bit of twisting—almost a second handful.

The engine pulls strongly from any

the Four's lack of flywheel effect. So, making a smooth shift requires that you synchronize the engine speed with the bike's ground speed. If you close the throttle too quickly as you shift, the revs drop sharply and the bike will slow down with a lurch as the clutch is engaged. If you blip the throttle and engage the clutch as the engine revs, the bike will jerk forward.

Smooth shifting is also made a little difficult by the clutch engagement, which is rather quick and unprogressive. It takes a little bit of getting used to—which at least is made easier by the very light clutch lever pull. That light clutch feel might lead you to believe the clutch will slip. It doesn't. What it does is heat up and drag

The guard on the sprocket keeps rocks, dirt, pant cuffs, and small frogs bent on suicide out of the sprocket and chain.

There are attachments on the manifold for vacuum gauges, almost a necessity for equalizing the carburetors.

Each ignition circuit handles a pair of cylinders. One circuit is for cylinders 1 and 4, the other for cylinders 2 and 3.

aged to scrape both the sidestand and centerstand in a left-hand turn before he'd ridden 100 yards. We could also scrape the footpeg and centerstand on the right side, depending on the suspension setting and the turn. If you are carrying a passenger, the ground clearance becomes more of a problem, and you find it possible to drag the passenger pegs.

The suspension works quite well in most situations. It is firm enough to avoid wallowing in corners and soft enough to keep the bike from being bounced around by bumps. The rear suspension is just slightly short on damping, causing the back of the bike to bounce up and down an extra time or two after a big bump.

The bike is very stable when traveling in a straight line. You aren't hassled by most crosswinds, and rain grooves will only occasionally wiggle the handlebars a little bit; generally, the grooves will go unnoticed. If you look over your shoulder or fall asleep or something else equally ridiculous, the bike won't wander off course right away.

COMFORT AND RIDE: The CB750 K5 is a very comfortable motorcycle, and only a few minor details prevent it from nearing perfection. One of our staffers took a 600-mile ride during the test, and it was over three hours before anything began to give him any discomfort. He got a slightly numb fanny, and his right hand and wrist grew sore from holding the throttle open. His hand was the first thing

to bother him. The four springs in the carbs are quite strong, and the friction lock that used to be found in the throttle drum housing is unfortunately gone this year. The locks used to wear out rather quickly if they were used frequently, but they were nonetheless a nice feature on a touring bike—especially one with four strong throttle springs.

The hand grips on the bike are new, bigger, and softer than the old ones; it's an improvement, but not quite good enough. The waffle pattern molded into the grips digs into your hands if you aren't wearing heavy gloves. This is especially true with your right hand, which has to maintain a fairly firm grip on the throttle twistgrip.

The vibration level is negligible. You notice just a little at odd rpm intervals above 4000 rpm (about 60 mph in fifth) mostly because the mirrors blur slightly. It's never annoying.

The seat is very comfortable for short rides, and only fairly comfortable for long ones. You'll have to go three or more hours before you start getting saddle sores, however. The seat height (33 inches) and width will make it a little difficult for shorter riders to get a firm stance while at a stop. Our shortest rider (5'10") wasn't bothered by it, but we've heard some negative comments from short-legged CB750 owners. The seat and seating position are well-designed to keep you from sliding around during braking and acceleration.

The rather high bars are something that may also annoy shorter riders who like bars they can lean on during high-speed riding. The 750 bars verged on being too tall for our 5'10" rider while he was riding the freeways, but our bigger riders liked them. The large instruments stick up into the windstream and act as a small spoiler to help cut down some of the wind pressure reaching your torso and chest.

The footpegs are placed fairly far apart, which you don't notice while you are riding. But when you are pushing the bike around by straddling the seat and paddling with your legs, your ankles bump the pegs. The passenger pegs, which mount outboard of the mufflers, are spaced even wider than the rider's pegs. In fact, when folded down, the passenger pegs are within an inch of being as wide as the handlebars.

The passenger is well provided for with a seat that is long, wide, level, and amply padded. The width of the pegs didn't bother any of our test passengers, and the fact that the pegs weren't up too high was a bonus, except when they scraped—which scared the hell out of some of our passengers.

The CB750's suspension offers a pleasant ride. It soaks up small bumps quite well, and only bigger bumps, especially sharp ones, will jar you a little bit through the rear end of the machine, even on the softest suspension setting.

BRAKING: Honda's designers seem to have taken a cautious approach with the brakes. The hydraulic front disc brake is capable of locking the wheel, but an enormous amount of lever pressure is required to do so. The feel at the lever is also just very slightly mushy, so bringing the wheel to the point of maximum stoppage takes a split second longer than normal. However, the Honda front brake isn't likely to get a novice rider in trouble if he instinctively grabs the lever. That split second required to build pressure may save him some skin, particularly if he has to brake quickly while heeled over in a corner. The lack of pin-point sensitivity will make it a little more difficult to get it stopped quickly, however. Unlike some

SPECIFICATIONS

Engine type	four-stroke
Cylinder arrangement	transverse parallel four
Valve arrangement	single overhead cam
Bore and stroke	61mm x 63mm
Displacement	736.4cc
Compression ratio	9.0:1
Ignition	battery/2 coils/2 points
Charging system	12-volt, AC generator, silenium rectifier
Carburetion	four 28mm Keihin slide/needle
Air filter	disposable paper element
Lubrication	dry sump, 3.7 qt. (3.5 L.) tank capacity
Primary drive	two single-row chains, 1.708:1 ratio
Clutch	wet, 7 drive plates, 7 driven plates
Starting system	electric, primary kick
Transmission	5-speed, left-foot shift
Overall drive ratios	(1) 11.38; (2) 7.78; (3) 6.07; (4) 4.99; (5) 4.27
Transmission sprocket	18-tooth
Rear wheel sprocket	48-tooth
Drive chain	⅝-in. pitch, ⅜-in. width (#530)
Front forks	5.6 in. (142mm) travel
Rear shocks	5-way adjustable, 3.3 in. (84mm) wheel travel
Front brake	11.7 in. (297mm) disc, single-action hydraulic caliper
Rear brake	drum, single-leading shoe, rod operated
Front tire	3.25 x 19 Dunlop rib
Rear tire	4.00 x 18 Dunlop block
Frame	tubular steel, double downtube
Steering head angle	27 degrees from vertical
Front wheel trail	3.7 in. (94mm)
Wheelbase	58 to 59.3 in. (147 to 151cm.)
Length	85.6 in. (217cm)
Weight	501 lb. (227 kg) dry
Weight distribution	46.8% front, 53.2% rear
Ground clearance	5.5 in. (140mm) at sidestand lug
Seat height	33 in. (838mm) unladen
Handlebar width	31.5 in. (800mm)
Handlebar grip height	44.5 in. (113cm)
Footpeg height	12.8 in. (325mm) right, 13.7 in. (348mm) left
Instrumentation	speedometer, tachometer, tripmeter resettable to zero
Speedometer error	30 mph indicated, 28 mph actual 60 mph indicated, 55 mph actual
Gas tank	steel, 4.5 gal. (17 liters) capacity
Gas consumption	42.6 mpg (18.1 km/L.)
Best ¼-mile acceleration	13.65 sec., 98.6 mph (158.6 kph)
Stopping distance from 30 mph	36 ft., 1 in. (11m)
Stopping distance from 60 mph	136 ft., 3 in. (41.5m)
Sound level as per SAE XJ 331a	83.5 db(A)
Suggested retail price	$2112 East Coast $2099 West Coast

HONDA CB750 K5

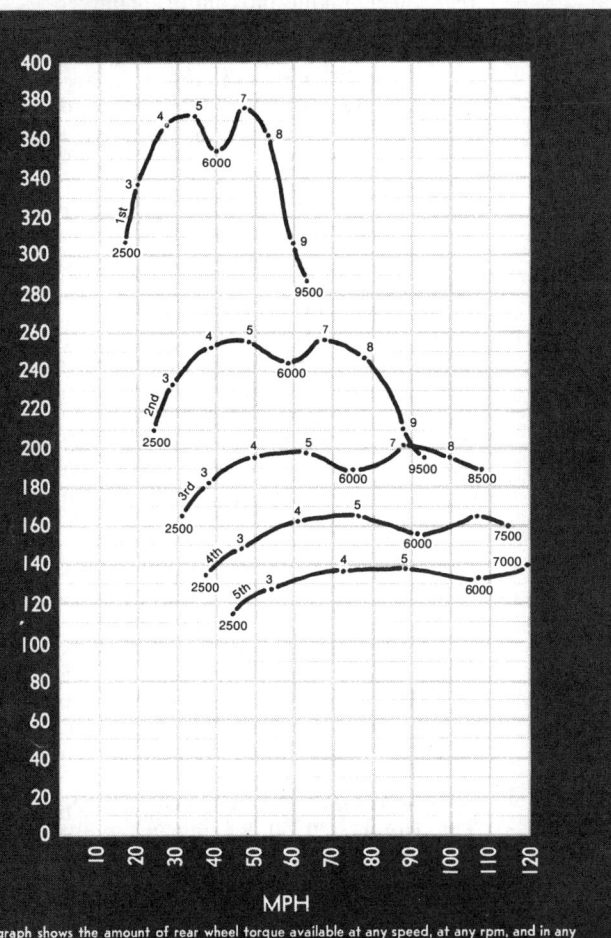

MPH

graph shows the amount of rear wheel torque available at any speed, at any rpm, and in any . Maximum acceleration will be obtained by shifting gears at the points where the consec- lines intersect.

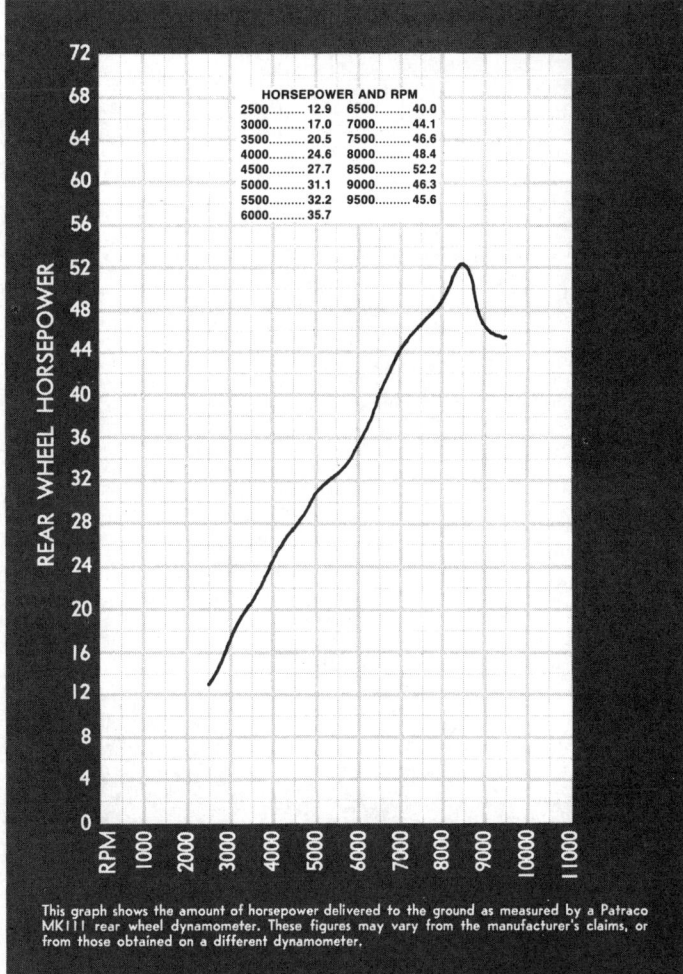

HORSEPOWER AND RPM	
2500.......... 12.9	6500.......... 40.0
3000.......... 17.0	7000.......... 44.1
3500.......... 20.5	7500.......... 46.6
4000.......... 24.6	8000.......... 48.4
4500.......... 27.7	8500.......... 52.2
5000.......... 31.1	9000.......... 46.3
5500.......... 32.2	9500.......... 45.6
6000.......... 35.7	

This graph shows the amount of horsepower delivered to the ground as measured by a Patraco MKIII rear wheel dynamometer. These figures may vary from the manufacturer's claims, or from those obtained on a different dynamometer.

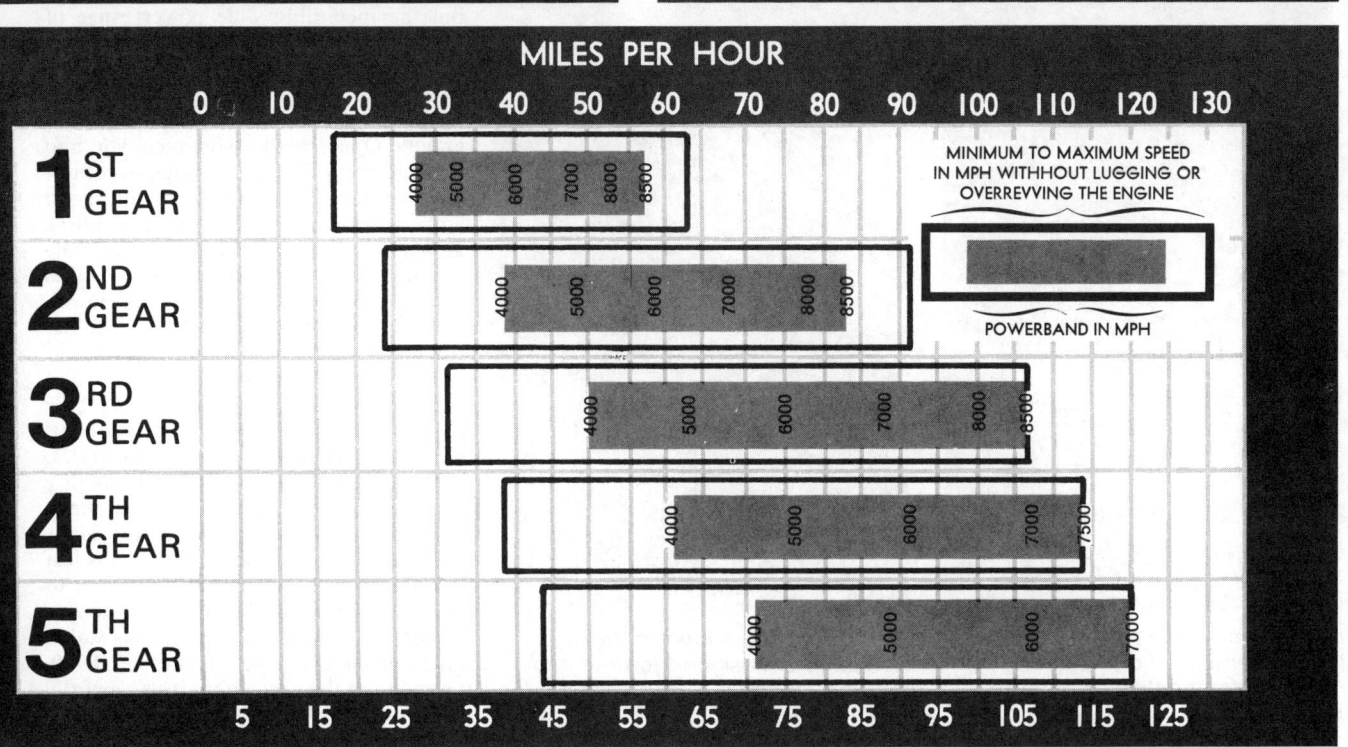

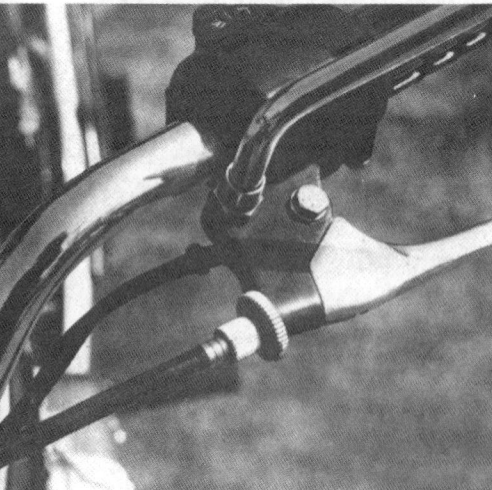

other manufacturers, Honda doesn't offer an optional second disc for the front end.

The rod-operated rear brake is very sensitive and progressive. But maximum rear wheel braking and control are limited by the hopping and chattering the rear wheel often goes through during hard braking, particularly over rough surfaces or if you downshift while braking hard. Neither brake ever faded perceptibly, but the front brake usually squeaked unless applied with a great deal of force. Rider control during hard panic stopping is aided by the firm front suspension, which keeps the front end from nosediving excessively.

RELIABILITY DURING TEST: The CB750 has earned a reputation for reliability since its beginning, and our K5 model upheld the tradition. Nothing broke or gave us any trouble whatsoever. We adjusted the chain once and lubed it. Otherwise, the engine was always clean enough to eat off because it didn't leak or ooze a bit of oil. The bike burned absolutely no oil and got 42.6 miles per gallon of gas. The CB750's apparent reliability makes spending $2100 on one easier to swallow.

With four carbs, four sets of tappets, and a battery-coil ignition with two sets of points, maintenance on the CB750 is a little more complicated than on some other big machines, but still relatively simple.

SUMMARY AND CONCLUSION: The Honda CB750 K5 remains pretty much the bike that it was in 1968, but a little tamer and more refined. The four-cylinder engine has a wealth of usable power and is smooth, quiet, and gets good gas mileage. Out-and-out horsepower isn't as great as some other 750s, but the incredibly wide power range of the engine makes up for it over and again.

The bike's handling requires some rider adaptation because of the high center of gravity. Once you have adapted, you find it stable, but still a little lacking in cornering precision. The suspension is quite good and contributes much to both handling and the very high level of comfort. The brakes are quite powerful, but it takes considerable effort to obtain that power. And our test bike was absolutely trouble-free.

The CB750 is a bike that's mild and refined enough for the novice big bike rider but sophisticated and powerful enough not to insult the experienced rider. If anything, it's almost *too* good. Its quality has made it popular; popularity has made it commonplace; and by being commonplace, and by being so refined, it has lost the ability to be exotic, to stand out, to display personality the way a Norton or Ducati or Benelli can. Success has stolen much of the excitement from the CB750, but none of the perfection. It's an awfully good motorcycle, perhaps too good to be exciting. **CG**

The electrical wiring running to the clutch lever is part of the starter interlock. You can't start the bike unless the clutch is pulled in or the gearbox is in neutral.

The rubber tab added to the sidestand is designed to drag and fold the stand up if you leave it down accidentally. It only worked about half the time.

Hidden away under the Honda CB-750 Four's fuel tank, flanked by its quadruple carburetors, you'll find the secret of this Superbike's success. Don't look in there expecting to find cabalistic symbols, mathematical formulae or a message for your Captain Midnight decoder ring. What you'll see is that part of the throttle return spring is now covered by a short neoprene sleeve, placed to protect a pair of rather unimportant carburetor vent hoses from pinching or chafing. Nothing of any great consequence would occur even if the return spring chaffed through both vent hoses. But the protective sleeve is there, just as a refinement, and it is typical of the kinds of refinements that make the Honda CB-750 what it is. Other Superbikes are faster and at least a couple handle better, but none are as slick, as steadfastly reliable, as the big Honda. None but the Sportster and the Norton have been in production as long but more important, none have had the incredible attention to detail typified by

HONDA CB-750

Meticulous sophistication and refinement characterize the most popular big-bore street bike in the world.

that little sleeve on the Honda's throttle return spring.

Now we have the latest CB-750, which is a slightly slower but more refined version of the original. Some of the CB-750's decline in absolute performance probably is attributable to subtle changes in its valve-lift specifications. There also has been a power loss incurred with the introduction of more efficient, and more restrictive, mufflers. With the new model the CB-750 becomes even quieter—and slower—due to a restricted inlet for the air-cleaner housing that more effectively silences intake roar. The net result is that there is little racket emerging from either the inlet or exhaust sides of the engine, and careful work inside has squelched what can be a lot of clatter from pistons and valve gear. The CB-750 is *quiet*!

Most of the other changes over earlier models found in the CB-750 have nothing to do with speed or lack of same. For example, there are the wear indicators on the

bike's disc brake pucks. Because the wear adjustments with hydraulic disc brakes are entirely automatic it is possible to scrub away the puck's friction material right down to the steel backing pieces before there is any indication of wear and impending trouble. This difficulty has been resolved very neatly with the addition of a little red tab to each brake pad. The tab marks the limit of the friction material; and indicates how much is left to anyone who takes the trouble to glance into the brake caliper. It's a service/safety measure, and a good one.

One of the CB-750 Honda's best features is its front disc brake, which it has had from the beginning. The only difference we can detect between then and now is the complete absence of brake squeal—a big source of aggravation with most discs, including those on other Hondas—and a splash guard wrapped over the disc itself to keep the thing from spitting rainwater in your eye. All the near-incredible stopping power of the modern motorcycle disc brake (another Honda first, introduced on the CB-750) is of course still there.

Ride, like handling, falls short of the CB-550's refined behavior but still puts the CB-750 right up there with the best. The bike feels like maybe its springs are a bit too stiff and the damping too limp by about the same amount. That doesn't keep it from being comfortable. Its seat is broad and soft, and there is enough distance from the seat down to the pegs to prevent your legs from getting cramped. This last may account for the CB-750 lending the impression that it is very tall, which it isn't. The difficulties those with short legs have in keeping the bike upright at a stop are due more to seat width than seat height, which is not much greater than the average for all motorcycles.

And would that all motorcycles were as basically refined as the Honda CB-750 Four, and as reliable. Our test bike had been thoroughly thrashed by a variety of test riders by the time we finished, and apart from developing a slight jangling in its clutch the Honda showed not the slightest distress at having been so harshly used. It wasn't puffing or leaking oil, didn't develop any tendencies toward hard starting or an uneven idle, and in general displayed a willingness to continue happily along in the face of our best (worst?) efforts.

Best of all, while the CB-750 is out there on the roads in numbers too large to give it any eye-appeal as a curiosity, it will boost the prestige of its road-rider owner at every coffee stop just because it is so incredibly well-finished. The Four sparkles and shines and gleams, and its every detail is just so tremendously tidy you can't help but admire the bike even if you're riding something else. You look at the CB-750 and you know that nothing in its broad layout, appearance, or smallest detail suggests anything except meticulous advanced planning. Or maybe what you get in the CB-750 is more nearly the result of meticulous afterthought. Either way it has produced in the Honda CB-750 an uncommon degree of refinement—and for the Honda company a hundred thousand pretty well satisfied customers. ◉

Road Test
HONDA CB750 K2
BARGAIN SUPERBIKE!

Honda's biggest and best is shortly to be upstaged by the GL1000. But does that mean that this legendary four-cylinder package is outmoded? Not on your life!

THEY CALL it the Harley of the '70s. Not because it's slow-revving and cumbersome. But because, in a world of built-in obsolence, the Honda 750 is an anachronism.

You see, the engine, that f o u r-cylinder behemoth that has been roundly criticised by performance freaks and aesthetes alike, is virtually indestructible. Oh sure, you hear that odd story about engine seizure (invariably caused by full-throttle acceleration on a cold engine). And the camshaft does wear out, but by then the bike's usually on its third owner. Yes, all things considered, in comparison to almost any other design you want to name, the 750 engine is trouble-free. How many sick Honda Fours have you seen recently?

In America, if we're to go by an ad appearing in PLAYBOY, they're already onto the revamped K4 model. But here in Sydney Bennett Honda is still selling the K2 model. At $1589 it's $10 less than it was three years ago, and in the six years since its release the 750's price has risen by little more than $100, although it has peaked at $1700-plus.

How's that for beating inflation?

The winds of change are blowing around B-H's squeaky-clean Alexandria factory, though: the next shipment of 750s (due to arrive in Australia this month) may cost over $2000. They could be K4s. On the other hand they may still be K2s. (No-one knows what happened to the K3).

But at the current price the K2 750 is the bargain Superbike of the year. Sure, it's been upstaged by the Kawasaki Z1, but then what hasn't? Anyway the Four is giving away 20 per cent. displacement to the Superfour. And an extra camshaft.

When all's said and done, it gives away precious little else. There's no way a Honda will beat a Kawasaki round a race-track, but that's not where most people ride them. And out on the

open road you don't really notice the difference. Both bikes are smooth, quiet, reliable, comfortable — and damn fast.

The number of detail changes Honda claims to have made to its top-of-the-liner since 1969 runs into the hundreds. It would take months to locate them, let alone list them, Suffice it so say that where something has not been quite right, Honda has fixed it. Usually.

Yet the K2 still looks the same as the first Four. Sure, the colours are different (our test bike, N.S.W. 1, was finished in a beautiful metalflake blue). But the tank and seat and wheels and 'guards are still the same.

Some call it bulky. In fact, we'd be the first to admit that it is not the prettiest-looking bike on the road. But beauty is only skin-deep, and the appeal of the Four goes beyond mere external appearance.

This was the bike that gave the world its first mass-production motorcycle disc brake. It's still amongst the best. One calliper is fixed, one floating. It's a firm, sure stopper, and transmits a surprising amount of feel back to the ·rider. These days it's also fitted with a plastic shield to keep off the water when it rains.

Complementing the disc is a 180 mm s.l.s. rod-operated drum, which also gives a good deal of feel, although it is possible to lock it up if you're too heavy with the right foot.

The Honda was also the first mass-production bike with four carburettors, four exhausts . . . four, in fact, of almost everything that matters.

The compact engine that is admired the world over is slightly undersquare at 61 x 63 mm bore and stroke, and pumps 50.3 kW (67 bhp) at 8000 rpm.

The first Fours were redlined at 8500 rpm, but over-enthusiastic owners were then tempted to push the needle way into the red zone, often with disastrous results!

A radical departure for motorcycling, if not for motoring, was the use of plain bearings throughout. Oil is pumped at high pressure through the five main bearings, reducing wear to a minimum. So long as your oil pump is in good shape (and Honda recommends regular pressure checks), the bottom end should last the life of the bike.

A large car-type oil filter slots into a bulbous cover on the front of the crankcases, and there's another filter immediately behind the sump plate. The dry sump motor holds a total of 3.5 1 (6 pt.) of 20/50 oil; the remote tank system undoubtedly contributes to the motor's cool running. A remarkable feature of the engine is that the rocker cover is not finned. Recommended interval between oil changes is 3000 km, although for maximum engine life this is often halved.

Actually, there's little remarkable about the engine beyond its four-cylinder design. Ignition is by dual points-and-coils; the condensers are mounted on the timing plate, under a cover on the right-hand side of the crankshaft. There are eight small flywheels on the latter, plus the alternator rotor. Valve timing is mild: inlet opens 5 degrees BTDC, closes 30 degrees ABCD; exhaust opens 35 degrees BBDC, closes 5 degrees ATDC.

Rocker clearance is adjusted via eight inspector caps on the head; the standard gaps of two and three thou are small enough to reduce noise from this area to a minimum. The only difficulty with adjusting the tappets, beyond their sheer number, lies in the closeness of the number two and three exhaust rockers to the frame down-tubes; it's a tight squeeze for hands, feeler gauges and spanners!

The whole unit, with its four 28 mm Keihin carburettors (feeding into an easy-access common paper air filter) slots into a stout double-cradle and massive triple backbone frame. The swinging-arm is made from rectangular, not round section tubing. Although the frame has been criticised for a number of alleged faults (amongst which are its sheer mass and the 'incorrect' positioning of the swinging-arm pivot), it does its job well. The CB750 is not the greatest handler in the world, but it can still get you round a corner damn fast!

The cam-chain, which threads up between the two centre cylinders, was

Stocky lines of 750 are not as pretty as they used to be.

originally fitted with an automatic spring-loaded slipper tensioners, but this placed excessive strain on the chain and a number of them snapped. With the K1 a locking device was introduced; nowadays at each service interval you release the lock, thereby allowing the slipper to take up the slack, then torque it up again.

The only real complaint we can make about the 87 kg (192 lb.) engine unit is its very size. Because of its positioning in the frame, it's impossible to remove the head without pulling the engine — a two-man job at the best of times! A most effective counter to this is, of course: how often do you **need** to remove the head?

Starting is almost always instantaneous, even after several weeks off the bike. The choke lever, which operates on all four carburettors simultaneously (as do the idle screw and the ingenious pulley-cable throttle system) is located on the left-hand side of the carburettor assembly. Snap it up (full choke is usually the norm, unless it's a very hot day), flick on the ignition key (still located under the left front of the tank) and press the starter button. Instant burble. The starter motor is located behind the crankshaft underneath a chromed inspection cover. In fact, once the engine is removed

from the frame, it's a simple matter to strip it down to the bare essentials.

The K2 is quieter than its predecessors and, we think, a little down on power. Still, the lack of noise won't disturb anyone and if you're really nuts about that four-cylinder howl it's still there, hovering just below the red-line.

One thing we also noticed about our test bike was that it seemed very high off the ground. Something that would partially account for that, when compared to the Editor's K1, were the tyres, two barely-worn Japanese Dunlops. These tyres, of different cross-sectional pattern than K81s, also exert an effect on the handling characteristics of the bike, as we shall see presently.

Be this as it may, only a six footer will be able to plant both his feet on the ground. The Four is a big machine.

Pulling in the clutch lever reveals another feature of the bike: its extremely light clutch pull. The conventional seven friction plate wet clutch is easy to use and is (usually) trouble-free. However, during our performance testing in 40 degrees Celsius heat, it began to slip quite badly, something we have never encountered before with this model. The worst that can be said of the clutch, though, is that it's not foolproof

The gearbox is another story. Not

Left: Engine pumps a claimed 50kW at 8000 rpm. It's the modern equivalent of the WLA Harley — almost indestructible.

Above: Plastic guard is useful addition to front brake.

only does it have the Honda 'clunk', but fourth gear is temperamental. We've struck it on other examples of the breed, and our test bike was no exception. Changing up to fifth you often strike a false neutral; changing back down again the cogs thud home with the precision of a .762 breech bolt.

Correct revs play a vital part in a smooth gear-changes; below 4000 rpm is the trouble zone. Keep the engine on the boil and you'll be unlikely to strike trouble.

There's not a great deal of torque down low but it's not necessary to slip the clutch round town, as some Honda-haters would have you believe. In fact, the 218 kg Four will move off almost at idle without any difficulty and throttle down to 30 km/h (19 mph) in top without chain snatch.

Where there is a problem is at the drag-strip. It's hard to draw the fine line between wheelspin and bogging down, In fact, despite our familiarity with the machine, we only managed it once; the result was a 13.45s/95.12 mph quarter.

In comparison, the editor's K1 (CA, Jan-Feb. '73) ran 14.24s/92.78. But moisture on the strip was dropping everyone's times by about a second, so that a more accurate e.t. would have been 13.24 — some 0.2s quicker than the K2.

This distinction is really academic, since these days no-one buys a (standard) CB750 expecting it to blow off Kawasakis. But the bike can very easily be made to run low 12s without reducing reliability to racing machine levels. An overbore, extractors and a hotter cam will do the job; Honda

hasn't already done it for you because they don't build their bikes that way.

No, the CB750 K2 is what Honda intended all the time: a reasonably fast, very reliable, all-purpose road-bike. There aren't very many motorcycles made that will keep up to a Four in full song on the open road! That engine will pull you between fuel stops at close to the ton and never even pant a little.

With this in mind, let's look more closely at the creature comforts. First, the instruments. Honda pioneered the swept-back look and the tacho and speedo are certainly easy to read, at least when the standard 'Western-style' bars are retained. Our test K2 had a well-calibrated Nippon Seiki Metric speedo and tripmeter (a zeroing type that picks up each digit as you rotate the knob). With this model, the 'idiot lights' were moved off the faces of the instruments and onto a small panel in between the handlebar clamps: they give you neutral, oil pressure, high beam and indicators at a glance. The glance unfortunately becomes more of a stare when wearing a full-cover helmet, since the chin-piece obscures the panel. Such is progress.

Switches are amongst the best on the market: compact, neat and functional. Left-hand is indicators and horn (which button also incorporates a headlight flasher); on the right are the easy-to-use kill switch and headlight dipper. A friction screw underneath the twist-grip is an effective item.

It's all simplicity itself: compare this arrangement with the hotch-potch of switches bolted, clamped and sometimes even taped to many Italian handlebars!

The tank is wide but you get used to straddling it with your legs; the seat is medium-hard and extremely comfortable on a trip. It's locking, too; the same lock also operates the Helmet Holder (sic). Electrics are superb; the 40-50W headlight is as good as you could expect on a motorcycle and even the horn is something more than pusillanimous. Only the tail-light detracts from the overall excellence; it's neat, but too small.

But there are a couple of minor points we're not so keen on: all the plastic bits should be reworked in light steel. (Honda did it with the chainguard, so why not with the headlight nacelle & c.?); the heavy twist-grip action can be tiring; and the endless rear chain can be annoying. You see, because people used to ride their 750s too hard and threw the chains through their crankcases, Honda decided to fit an endless chain (still ⅝"), thereby eliminating the master link. The only trouble is that if you want to remove the chain (and for long chain life you should do frequently, so as to boil it in grease) you have to break it. That's not the hard part: re-riveting is! A solution is to fit a Renolds chain conversion kit, which gives you a thicker ¾" chain and retains the master link.

There are no security bolts fitted to the front or back wheel — which we feel is a dangerous oversight.

Lack of vibration is one of the most noticeable traits of the Honda. It doesn't matter what revs the engine's at, you never get more than a slight tingle through the footpegs and handlebars. At 4100 rpm you're doing a cool 100 km/h (the legal speed limit in many places), and at these rpm there's no vibration whatsoever. The big Honda will purr along, gobbling up the kilometres and with enough torque to pull up any hill in top, yet still return better than 17.7 km/l (50 mpg). Adding a pillion passenger will make little difference, so if you like toting along a bird or mate, the 750's a natural for you.

Handling is good, although with the three-way (Showa) shocks jacked up to their hardest setting the rear end will bounce, and on their softest it will wallow. The middle ·setting is our recommendation, for all but the racetrack. The rounded profile tyres force you to throw your whole body over one side to get the bike round a corner **fast**; you lean over and the bike follows a discernible instant later. Fitting K81s, which have a triangular profile, will obviate this, since cocking a knee would

will be sufficient to throw the bike onto the tyres' side sections. The (folding) footpeg is the first thing to scrape in right-hand corners; the stands hit first in left-handers. Speaking of stands, the main-stand is pivoted incorrectly, since it's extremely difficult for the rider to lever the bike up onto it on the flat, and well-nigh impossible with the front pointing slightly downhill.

Our tested top speed was 181.8 km/h (113 mph), but you can add at least another three km/h to this for attainable top speed, since the Four takes a long time to wind up that last little bit. If that seems a little slow, remember that the bike will cruise at 161 km/h (100 mph) all day long — one or two-up. Does **anybody** tour faster than that?

Honda-haters claim that the bike is cumbersome round town. Granted, it's no Bials, but the 750 is still nimble enough in city traffic. Perhaps its worst feature is its width, which can make narrow gaps intraversible.

In summary, dollar for dollar, the Honda 750 Four is still about the best

buy in the Superbike market.

But it's been around for nearly six years now, and public taste has altered quite dramatically during that time. What was the **ne plus ultra** of motorcycling in 1969 is no longer exceptional in 1975.

What we'd like to see Honda do is to revamp the 750 into two models: one for touring, one for sports use.

The sports version could retain the four carburettors that can't be tuned without vacuum gauges and also have four-into-ones and a hotter cam. And the tourer could have two mufflers (lighter and cheaper to replace) and two carburettors, so that its owner could tune it anywhere, anytime — himself.

After all, the Honda people have already tarted up the CB350F. And the GL1000 super-tourer is soon to burst upon an expectant world. So the changes wouldn't be so radical.

Think about it, Honda. The 750 is a great product. But it can't be all things to all men ●

HONDA CB750 K2

engine

Type	sohc four-in-line four-stroke, points-and-coil ignition, five plain metal main bearings
Bore x stroke	61x 63 mm
Displacement	736 cm³
Compression ratio	9.0:1
Claimed max. power	50.3 kW (67 bhp) at 8000 rpm
Claimed max. torque	6.1 kg.m (44.1 ft. lb.) at 7000 rpm
Carburation	four 28 mm Keihin piston-valve

dimensions

Length	2160 mm (85.0 in.)
Wheelbase	1455 mm (57.3 in.)
Height	1155 mm (45.5 in.)
Ground clearance	140 mm (5.5 in.)
Width	885 mm (34.8 in.)
Weight (dry)	218 kg (480 lb.)
Fuel tank	17 1 (3.75 gal.)
Oil tank (dry sump)	2.2 1 (3.9 pt.)
Tyres (front)	Dunlop Gold Seal F9 3.25 x 19 ribbed tread
(rear)	Dunlop Gold Seal K87 4.00 x 18 block tread
Rake	27 deg.
Trail	95 mm (3.3 in.)
Colour	metalflake blue-gold

transmission

Clutch	wet, seven friction plates
Gear ratios	1st: 2.500:1
	2nd: 1.708:1
	3rd: 1.333:1
	4th: 1.097:1
	5th: 0.939:1
Primary reduction ratio	1.708:1
Final reduction ratio	2.667:1 (40:15)
Brakes (front)	296 mm (11.7 in.) disc
(rear)	180 mm (7.1 in.) s.l.s. drum

performance

ss ¼-mile	13.45s/95.12 mph
0-100 km/h	6.1 s
Top speed	181.8 km/h (113 mph)
Braking: 50 km/h — 0	9.7 m (31'9")
100 km/h — 0	39.3 m (128'10")
Fuel consumption (overall)	17.3 km/l (48.9 mpg)

distribution

Test bike suppliers	Bennett Honda P·L, 2 Ralph St., Alexandria 2015
Price as tested	$1588 excluding reg. and ins.
Options fitted	none
Warranty	six months/9600 km

summary

After six years' pounding the highways and by-ways, Honda's legendary 750 Four can still hold its head up in mixed company. A bargain at Bennett Honda's 'special' price, it does not look so attractive a proposition at $2000-plus. Yet it is unquestionably one of the finest long-distance motorcycles available.
*Performance figures adversely affected by 40.C temperatures.

Owner report
HONDA CB750

The K1's handling has always been first-rate.

CA Editor MICHAEL RICHARDSON has owned a Four since August, 1972. And it's been good to him, so much so in fact that he wanted to tell people about it. So we let him . . .

I BOUGHT my Honda 750 K1 because I had to. It encroached on my consciousness with awe-inspiring inevitability. I paid for it, $1599 cash on the knocker, in August 1972.

You see, I was a Norton Commando owner. And, much as I loved that bike, it just would not stay together. These days they make 'em better, but mine was a 1969 model and that was not a vintage year for Nortons. I calculated that during the two-and-a-half-years I had owned the bike I had spent an average of nearly $20 a week, or around $2,500, to keep it on the road. Mind you, that had included road racing, a lot of punishing interstate work, and more full-throttle acceleration than I care to remember, but it was still expensive motorcycling.

I can't honestly say that I was enraptured by the Four, in the same way one might be by a Ducati 750, for example. Its stocky, Japanese build has never appealed to me the way British and Italian (and even Kawasaki)

machines have. But I was eschewing aestheticism for pragmatism. I wanted a motorcycle for the road, not for the workshop.

Mine was one of the last of the K1 Hondas; the very next week, (almost) the first K2s rolled into the nation's showrooms. Perhaps I should have waited, since the model change has undoubtedly affected my machine's resale value. Then again, despite a couple of rather hesitant attempts to sell the Four, in inflationary 1975 I've decided to keep it. So its resale value is of academic interest only.

Bennett Honda super-salesman Rick Andrews threw in a set of crash-bars with the bike as compensation for a couple of minute chips in the tank. These are still the only marks on the tank, a red one.

Right from the beginning the Four settled into the pattern of dependability that has been its keynote ever since. Only three times has it refused to start at a touch of the starter button: once when the battery was flat (which I'll come to later on) and twice in abnormal weather conditions which made selection of the correct amount of choke well-nigh impossible.

This dependability has been the same whether I've been undertaking a 16-kilometre trip to work or a 600-kilometre Sunday drive. The chain has needed adjusting (although even that can be kept to a bare minimum by correct lubrication) and every now and again it's needed a tune-up. Otherwise, it's kept going.

One of my earliest 'incidents' on the bike occurred about three months after I bought it. It was summer, a beautiful, sunny Sunday afternoon. Just the sort of weather for a brief spin. So I spun down the road, spun around a few corners, and spun out in an unexpected oil patch at around 80 km/h.

Now, ordinarily I can control a rear wheel drift, but this one was so sudden and violent that I didn't have a chance. The bike did a complete 180 on the road, most of the impact being absorbed by the handlebars, the crash-bars and (or so it seemed) my hip, which for months afterwards was coloured by a multi-hued bruise the size of an omelette.

And the bike? well, all those stories I'd heard about holes in the engine cases and written-off exhaust pipes and bent frames came to nothing. It was a hard drop, of that there was no doubt, but the only damage was the odd scratch on the mufflers and crash-bars and a completely re-worked set of handlebars: right-hand side 'Western-style'; left-hand clip-on. I rode it home, ashamedly, skulking round the back-streets where no-one would see me, removed the handlebars from the bike (not an easy job, since the wiring goes inside, not outside the bars), and took them to my friendly Honda local dealer who just happened not to have a replacement set. However, a few minutes work with a rod and vice in the workshop and they ended up almost as good as new. It was two years before I got round to replacing them permanently with a new (and considerably flatter) set.

Let me say here and now that that is the only time I've dropped the Four (knock on wood). Granted, because for much of the time I ride O.P.B.s (other people's bikes) for test purposes, it has only covered 21,000 km. But It's still a pretty good safety record, for any motorcycle.

Warranty Work

Shortly before my unnecessary fall I had occasion to return the bike to BennettHonda for some warranty work. There was a slight amount of oil weeping from the number four cylinder head. To fix that you have to pull the head which means removing the engine from the frame which means a lot of hassle and a possible strained back. And, since the bike was under warranty, I couldn't see why I should have to do it myself. Besides, if I did (and here's the catch in all guarantees), it would have null and voided the warranty.

Well, Bennett Honda took it off my hands for two weeks during which time I did a lot of Shanksing because CYCLE had only just started and we were bi-monthly and I didn't have anything else to ride. Then they gave it back to me. I rode it for the next week, put up quite a few hundred kilometres on it, looked down at the right-hand side of the head and, sure enough, it was still weeping oil. I would have taken it back to them again but I thought: "What's the use?" It's still weeping.

I'd already fitted a chromed carrier rack to the bike but it was one of the type that bolt onto the number plate and won't support anything heavier that a can of bully beef. And, anyway, I was forever losing things off the back of it. So I decided to make the big purchase. John Galvin of Villawood was the supplier: one set of Craven panniers, with luggage rack and all the goodies. They took a while to fit, but suddenly motorcycling again became a practical, not simply an exotic, way of travelling.

I rode along quite happily for a few thousand more kilometres. Then a car hit me.

Ever collided with a Ford Falcon station wagon and **not** been knocked off? I have. The sheer mass of the bike must have helped me. The impact knocked me clear into the path of the oncoming traffic (which somehow or other I missed), but didn't put me down.

The Ford's driver wouldn't have stopped, but I did a very fast U-turn and pulled him over. He'd come through a stop sign on my left without looking. He dented a muffler and the rear mudguard. I screwed him for $15 and his 'phone number and told him I'd be back in touch, since repairs would almost certainly cost more than he'd given me. He plainly disbelieved me, but Bennett Honda quoted $37.50. I banged out the mudguard myself and decided to leave the muffler to fend for itself. It was just as well I did, because shortly afterwards it rusted through.

They tell me it's the fibreglass packing that does it; collects the water vapour from the engine combustion and offers it up to the vulnerable inside of the pipe. Whatever the reason, here I was with a 10-month-old bike and a muffler with a hole in it. And my warranty was good for only six months.

Since then Bennett Honda has changed its warranty on four-cylinder mufflers to 12 months. But at the time they hadn't done so. I still hit the roof, though, since the bike hadn't done more than 10,000 km and I'd looked after the mufflers (forewarned is forearmed) to the extent of religiously spraying them with WD40, once a week.

Rick Andrews advised me to hang on for an extra two months and see what happened to the others. It was a wise move. At the end of the year B-H replaced not one, but three mufflers. Cost of replacement not under warranty? Around $75!

The mufflers are certainly a weak link in the Honda's otherwise bullet-proof armour, but they are about the only one. Perhaps the only other thing that gets on my goat is tuning the carburettors.

One, or two, or even three carburettors you can tune by ear, But four are impossible to set up without vacuum gauges. They cost anything between $50 and $100, but they're still a worthwhile investment for anyone contemplating keeping his Honda for more than two years.

Apart from the carbs, tuning and servicing the Four is a snack. Two sets of points firing the Nos. 1, 4 and 2, 3 cylinders in pairs, lock-nut tappets, easy-detach air and oil filter elements ... what could be simpler? But those carburettors, which on the average

need setting once every 5000 km (or you risk having fuel economy drop by 10 per cent. and the engine may even start to miss under load) can't be set up as easily. And take the bike to a dealer, who's honour-bound to do the tappets and timing and oil for you as well, and it will cost you more than $20.

Anyway, enough griping. If you buy the gauges you can tune the bike yourself, and it's certainly hard to find much else to fault.

Honda recommends that engine oil should be changed every 3000 km, but I do it every 1500 km, partly because the unique sort of on-off riding I do plays havoc with even modern lubricants, and partly because I feel instinctively uneasy about the plain bearing mains etc. With rollers and balls, you know that if your lubricant isn't quite top-notch the bike will still keep going, but plain bearings will seize very quickly without proper lubrication.

I change the oil and air filter elements, however, at the recommended intervals: 6000 km and 10,000 km respectively.

These are not excessively short intervals and the 750 is still fairly cheap to run, if one discounts the absurdly high Third Party and Comprehensive insurance costs in N.S.W.

Tyre Change

The original Japanese Dunlops fitted front and back wore out at around 8000 km and I replaced them with Trigonic K81s 3.60 x 19 front and 4.10 x 18 rear. The chain wore out at about the same time and I fitted a Diamond (⅝" pitch). In all other respects the bike looked the same as when I had bought it.

The tyres made a noticeable difference to the bike's handling. Before it was a conscious physical effort to throw the bike fast around a corner. But now a knee cocked out does the job. The triangular profile of the K81s, as opposed to the rounded pattern of the original tyres, makes all the difference.

Some bikes become just a little bit too quick handling when shod with Trigonics, but because the Four is in essence a heavy, bulky machine, the two tend to cancel each other. The result is a good, safe handling road bike which if it's not exactly a racer can still scrape around a corner pretty rapidly!

Speaking of scraping, the stands on the left-hand side do hit the deck a little early and the pillion pegs could be higher up for passenger comfort. Otherwise, there's plenty of ground clearance and frame and suspension are up to the job. At low speeds, however, in city traffic, the Four is a bit of a handful; it's very wide, especially with panniers, and the front end becomes decidedly heavy.

Changing the tyres brought something else to my attention: the 750's tendency to twitch its front end with anything but new rubber on the rim.

I'd noticed, of course, that as the front tyre became progresively balder, the handlebars become less and less stable. Remove your hands from them and the wheel would shake from side to side. I'd already checked the wheel alignment and balance both front and rear and temporarily removed the panniers without solving the problem. But the new rubber did the trick — for a while.

Now that both tyres have done 13,000 km, this snaky business has started

again. Yet, although the rear tyre is near the end of its useful life, there's still plenty of wear left up front. I've tried tightening the steering head bearings and rechecking the wheel balance etc., all to no avail. Fortunately, the effect is not so strong as to wrench the handlebars from one's grip, so I'm prepared to live with it. It goes away over 80 km/h, anyway.

At Reynolds' invitation, I replaced both the Diamond chain and the ⅝" pitch sprockets at 12,500 km with a Transmar ¾" conversion kit. Since then it's done 8400 km and the chain shouldn't need replacing for a further 4,600 km. Regular lubrication is the keynote to prolonged chain life.

Spark plugs — I use Champion N4s; one set of NGKs I used lasted just 300 kilometres! — are good for around 12,000 km (7,500 miles), although I'm angling for 16,000 km out of my current set. Every now and again I pull them out, clean and re-gap them; the only hassle is getting a plug spanner into the number 2 and 3 takes.

I had to change the front disc pads at

18,000 km. One thing that appealed greatly to me was the ease of replacement. If you ever have to follow suit, remember to put a dab of grease on the back of each pad!

The rear shoes are still in situ but they'll be replaced along with the rear tyres Cost is around $4.70 for the pads and $4.10 for the shoes.

All of these replacement and maintenance intervals are within the limits of Superbiking, but the muffler rust rate is not. Just eight months after it had been replaced, the number one muffler again rusted through! It's getting worse by the day, with new holes appearing to complement old. Soon I'll only have the header pipe left...

I've thought, of course, of taking the whole lot off and buying a set of four-into-ones. But I know only too well that this action would attract the attention of the police, to say nothing of my neighbours on late nights.

So what I'm going to do is play a waiting game. If, by the time the

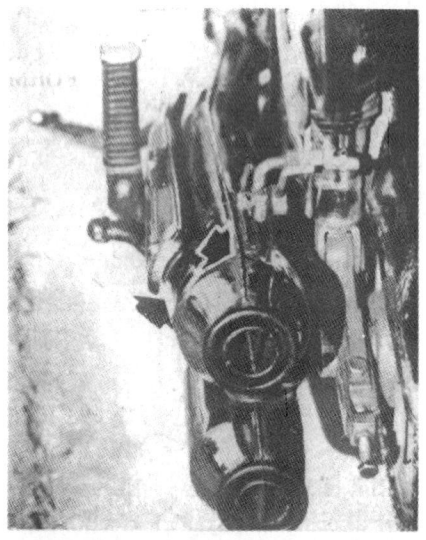

HONDA CB750

number one muffler drops away completely, no other holes have appeared in any of the other mufflers, I'll replace it (at a cost of $26). If, on the other hand, any other muffler has started to go, then it will be worth my while to buy the much more expensive ($60-$100) four-into-ones.

Another gripe about quality control concerns the plastic items fitted (fortunately, sparingly) to the bike. The red headlight nacelle, for example, is fading badly (the K2 model has a black nacelle). The red zone on the tacho is now a yellow zone (for chickening out, one wonders?). And the speedo face is as crazed as a car window that's played catcher for a high-flying rock. I'd like to see all these items reworked in metal.

Then there's the alloy used to cast the engine cases and fork legs. Ex-factory it's covered with a plastic film. But beware if this film should happen to wear off! Not only will the alloy oxidise virtually overnight, but you won't be able to clean it to leave a lasting shine. The result is that after a couple of years any Honda will start to look second-hand.

The bike is fitted with a Redlight burglar alarm that has functioned perfectly for more than two years. It really gives one peace of mind when leaving the Four parked away from home.

About the only problem with it is that if left unset it will flatten the Yuasa battery in very short order. Once I left the bike in a certain distributors' showroom while I gallivanted round the country-side on his shiny new 500 cm³ demonstrator, giving strict instructions to one of the 'boys' to reset the alarm if he should happen to turn on the ignition key and move the bike. He didn't — with the inevitable result that the battery had not a gram of spark left in it when I came to pick it up! I had to hotwire it from another bike, then do the same from a motor-car when leaving work, since the 750 won't start with a completely dead battery.

The surprising thing was, though, that within a week the battery was again fully charged and has never given a moment's trouble since!

Not a single bulb has blown in 2½ years and the horn is still at half-car strength. The seat has compressed slightly but is still very comfortable. I think that the Showa shocks will need

replacing in about another 18,000 km, and then I'll fit Konis.

At 19,000 km (12,000 miles), I gave the Four its first really big service. It took me most of a day . I cleaned the sump filter and changed the forks, oil and greased the swinging arm bushes and re-gapped the points and scrubbed the carburettor float bowls and generally got the bike in shape for its next 19,000 km.

Now, would anyone like to bet me that it won't gobble them up with as little trouble as it did the first 19,000? ●

Below: Crazed speedo face should not have happened.

Bottom: The machine is a superb tourer, able to gollop up thousands of kilometres at a stretch.

Japauto Honda 960 Cafe

Overkill is a 150-mph sprint or a 24-hour/100-mph junket. Unless, of course, you're into endurance racing.

By Steven Parker

AMERICANS generally consider themselves to be the best-informed people in the world. In the area of sporting events, the average American can tell you more than you want to know about everything from Formula 5000 racing to world league soccer stars. Ask an American about endurance racing, though, and he is likely to flash you a puzzled stare.

Le Mans and Bol D'Or are the places in Europe where they know about endurance racing on motorcycles. Grueling, man-and-machine-killing 24-hour marathons that can turn the strongest man and factory-based team into mewling babes. That's a long time to spend on a motorcycle, at speeds averaging 100 miles per hour (or more), and it is the type of sport that could be considered, well, foolish.

To some, though, it is the essence of man and machine combinations. Anybody, so it is said, can go fast for an hour or so. For a full day, though? That is the reason endurance racing may soon make a big-time appearance on the American scene.

Dick LaPlante is ready to corner the market. LaPlante is always ready to move in when he sees a good thing. A former executive with a computer firm, LaPlante caught wind of the cafe racing scene before most saw it coming, and

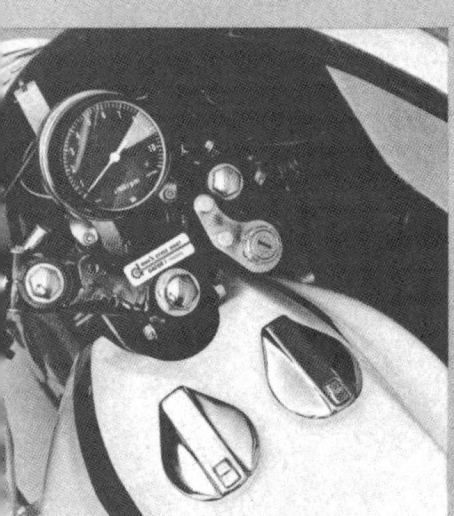

immediately went into business producing and distributing a line of products bearing the name "Racer 1." Though most will freely admit that the cafe racer "boom" never existed and never will, LaPlante has made enough money in the last two years to move to spacious offices, hire a pool of secretaries and workers and buy a new Alfa-Romeo. He is a success.

Successful enough that he is able to toy with new ideas. Other people do the dirty work in the shop now, so if LaPlante wants to build something exotic, he just goes ahead and does it.

LaPlante has always been intrigued with the idea of participating in—if only on the manufacturing level—endurance racing. He sees it coming to this country soon, and he hopes to be able to promote some amateur events of this sort at such Southern California tracks as Ontario, Riverside and Willow Springs.

Before you can race, you need a machine that will be capable of standing up to the rigors of endurance racing. LaPlante, with the able aid of Mike Johnson, has put together a machine from a stock 1973 Honda 750 that he feels will be competitive in such racing.

The K3 Honda that LaPlante has modified took close to a year of his time. He has invested enough money in

Japauto/Honda

it so that he "could buy an MV Agusta if I wanted". About six thousand bucks and a year of time. What came of all this?

A very impressive-looking machine. Striking in both engineering design and mechanical function, it is the only machine of its type in the United States. Painted in white, black and red with the "Dick's Cycle West" logo emblazoned on it, the machine looks all business. If an American wanted to design an endurance machine, this would probably be it.

The Honda's frame is stock, with some modification performed on the swinging arm. LaPlante, hoping to eventually market his "swinging arm secret," wouldn't tell us what the trick was.

Suspension on the machine consists of Koni rear shocks. They are, says LaPlante, "rebuildable, and will save us some money." For the front forks,

heavier-than-normal springs have been added and LaPlante has used a 40-weight ATF fluid and sealer to keep the springs moist. He is also tight-lipped about the suspension system, apparently wanting to wait until he can market the bike in kit form.

Some of the machine is available now from LaPlante as a kit. The seat and tank arrangement is available from "Cycle West" and will fit all 750 Hondas. The tank is unusually large and holds 5.5 gal. of fuel. The fuel tank is equipped with twin fuel caps to allow speedy fill-ups during racing. The seat is mounted on the Honda hinges and will open. There is also a storage area (lockable) in the rear of the seat. Fully one inch of foam padding gives the rider something comfortable to sit on, while the seat allows accessibility to electrics and air breather elements on the big machine.

The front fender is designated by LaPlante as "my funny fender." Its flared shape funnels cool air from the front of the machine directly into the oil cooler mounted in front of the engine. A Hurst-Lockhart cooler is utilized. Below the front fender LaPlante has added an extra Honda disc brake for added enormous stopping power. LaPlante likes to keep things stock when possible. Indeed, his large fuel tank fits right on the stock frame and uses the fuel petcocks found on the machine when you buy it.

The fairing, of course, is the most eye-catching feature of the bike. Manufactured in France by Japauto and then customized by LaPlante for the Honda, the fairing offers full wind protection for the rider when in race position, and also allows access to the oil filter, pipe collector and oil cooler.

The fairing is not available at this time for sale, and LaPlante refers to it as a "one-shot deal. I did this one and I don't plan on doing many more in the near future."

Hanging from the fairing are two Cibie H-4 quartz-iodine lighting instruments. These lamps can throw a beam powerful enough to provide visibility for up to two miles. They are, of course, illegal in this country and can be used only on race tracks or in off-road situations. They also draw enormous amounts of power, forcing LaPlante to rewire the Honda and set in special switching instruments for the lights.

The engine on the motorcycle has been punched out to 960cc with a kit from Japauto of France. Capable now of speeds in excess of 150 miles per hour, when properly geared, the engine sports new pistons, cylinders, valves, guides and other standard engine "performance increasers". The bike responds

Japauto/Honda

in kind. Reacting much like a race machine, the four-stroke has had added to it a new dimension of power and performance, making the first-time rider feel that if endurance racing is practiced in this country, LaPlante's machine will be a winner.

LaPlante has gone out of his way to keep things "stock" on this bike. Stock brakes (in front, with a disc in the rear), even stock passenger pegs. The original-equipment heat cover is used on the pipes, and engine supply systems are also factory items. Carburetion is normal for a 750 Honda, although the engine now uses 18mm spark plugs. The rear fender can also be saved, although LaPlante elected to cut his a bit short.

Problems? Mainly in starting the machine. The engine, with its increased size, has become a burden on the battery. This, added to the power-robbing headlights, serves to make the 750, or 960, if you will, a real electricity drainer.

Although it is now geared at 17:48, front to rear, LaPlante hopes to install 18:45, utilizing a rear sprocket from a 750 Suzuki. Cruising speed? Its creator estimates that the machine will be capable of 95-plus mph for 24 hours. And the machine will still be in one piece after that time.

While this Honda may not be the endurance bike to end all, it is a step in the right direction for a person interested in getting Americans interested in long-distance endurance racing. Certainly LaPlante has a stake in it all; but if his visions are as correct as they were in the cafe racing market, you'd better start building your very own endurance machine tomorrow.

BACK DISC FOR BIG 4

Model: Honda 750
Supplier: Hallcraft
Time: 2½ hours max.
Cost: 200 dollars
Place: Your pad

by DON GREEN

If you have a 750 Honda or late-model big bike, chances are you've fallen in love with the front brake—that big steel disc that can stop your multi-hundred-pound machine quicker than both drum brakes on most earlier bikes. To make the braking even more spectacular, nearly all bike manufacturers offer kits that add a second disc to the front wheel for ultimate braking. Yet, with few exceptions, the same manufacturers are continuing to install drum rear brakes on all but the newest, most expensive models.

Leave it to the aftermarket—the accessory builders dedicated to helping you make your bike exactly the way you'd like to have it. At least one company has heard the call for rear disc brakes.

Hallcraft, San Diego, California, custom wire wheel manufacturer, through affiliation with Hurst-Airheart, has developed a bolt-on disc conversion for the rear of all 750 Hondas. In 2-2½ hours, your Honda's stock drum brake rear wheel can be sporting a large, 11-inch disc brake so cleanly designed it's hard to believe the bike didn't come equipped with it.

The installation is an absolute bolt-on—no drilling, no welding, no hole-filling. The unit is everything a bolt-on kit should be; most of the tools you'll need are in your bike's stock tool kit, plus a couple of wrenches.

In use, the brake is again so right you'll think it's a stock Honda piece. Feel is positive and stops are sure. Far from over-sensitive, with brake lock-up requiring slightly more pressure than the stock drum. Like most discs when new, there is occasional brake squeal, but that disappears after the pads wear in. You won't believe how easy it is. ●

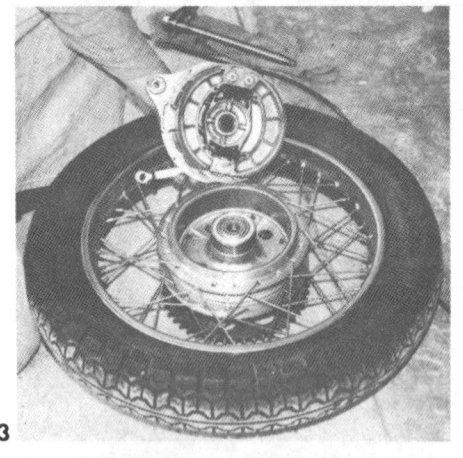

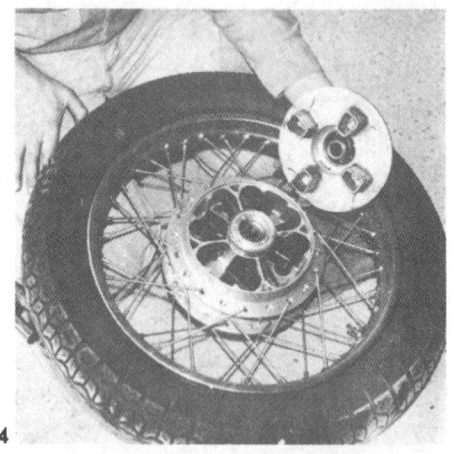

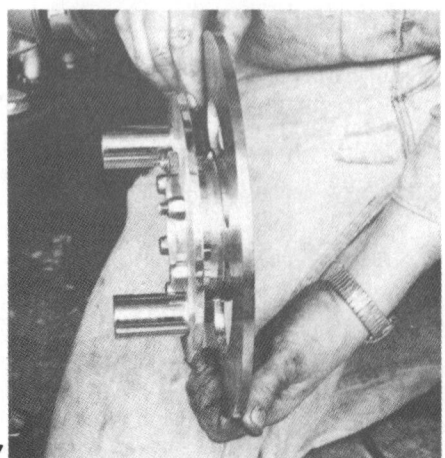

1 After placing bike on centerstand, disconnect rear brake actuating rod and locating strut from rear brake drum. Remove the cotter pin and loosen rear axle nut, sliding wheel/axle assembly forward in the swing arm so the chain can be removed from the sprocket. Loosen the chain adjuster bolts and remove the caps from the end of the swing arm, allowing the complete rear wheel assembly to be removed as a unit.

2 Rear wheel removal is also outlined in owner's manual for your bike.

3 Remove the nut from the end of the axle, then pull axle through brake drum, keeping as many parts as possible (chain adjuster, spacer, etc.) on left end of axle. These will be replaced later in their original positions. Then, with the rear wheel lying on the sprocket, lift off brake drum cover and shoes; this unit will not be reused in the installation. Clean the inside of the drum thoroughly. You may as well clean the entire rear wheel assembly while it is off the bike. You don't get many chances to do this.

4 Turn the wheel over and remove the sprocket and cast hub section as a unit (it is not necessary to unbolt the sprocket from the hub). If the sprocket assembly cannot be pulled easily, it may be necessary to tap it loose using a long punch and a hammer, tapping on the inside of the sprocket casting with the punch inserted through the axle hole from the opposite (brake drum) side. It won't take much force to get the casting loose, but be sure not to tap on the bearings.

5 With the sprocket removed, you will be able to pop out the four large rubber shock pads inside the hub. If the pads appear to be extremely dry and are starting to break apart, it would be a good idea to replace them.

6 Using parts from the Hallcraft kit, bolt the two chromed steel drive pins to the chromed aluminum drive plate using two of the self-locking Allen bolts supplied (be sure the deeply recessed end of the drive pins are away from the drive plate). Then bolt the 11-inch-diameter brake disc to the hub adapter and the aluminum drive plate using the six bolts and self-locking nuts supplied.

7 The disc assembly is now ready to install on the wheel.

8 Slip the stock axle into the hub to aid in positioning the parts. Slide the steel bearing spacer (arrow) onto the axle and against the stock bearing inside the brake drum. Place the disc assembly on the axle and seat the aluminum drive plate against the lip of the brake drum, turning the disc assembly to line up the drive pins with two of the four stock holes cast into the rear of the brake drum.

BACK DISC FOR BIG 4

9 Then, from sprocket side of wheel, bolt disc assembly in place using the two remaining Allen bolts and the two aluminum retainers with nylon washers placed through holes in the drum. Allen bolts should be tightened into the drive pins of the disc assembly using 35-40 ft./lbs. of torque.

10 Before reinstalling the wheel, remove the stock brake actuating rod completely by disconnecting it from the pedal linkage near the front of the swing arm, replacing the stock rod with the short piece of clevis linkage.

11 The compact master cylinder and its precut bracket fit inside the frame, bolting to passenger footpeg mount. Besides the clevis linkage being adjustable, the master cylinder mounting holes in the bracket are elongated so the cylinder can be moved slightly to adjust the brake pedal travel. Better invest in an angle-head screwdriver, though; the screws that hold the lid on the master cylinder are hard to reach once the cylinder is mounted in frame.

12 Back to the wheel, slip axle from sprocket side, add the two spacers, caliper bracket and adjuster on disc side.

13 The wheel is then ready to be reinstalled in the swing arm.

14 The stock Honda brake strut connects to the front bolt of the caliper bracket, locating bracket in a straight-down position. Install brass fittings in master cylinder and caliper, cut the brake line to desired length.

15 Fill the master cylinder with clean, heavy-duty brake fluid and bleed brake system as for the stock front wheel brake, checking system for leaks. Adjust the pedal travel with the clevis linkage and by moving the master cylinder on its bracket.

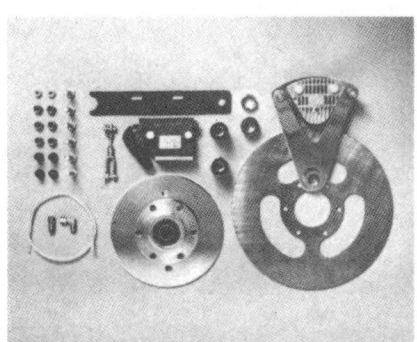

9

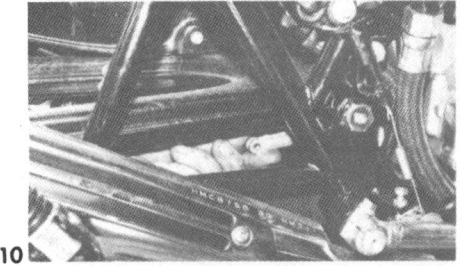

10

11

12

13

14

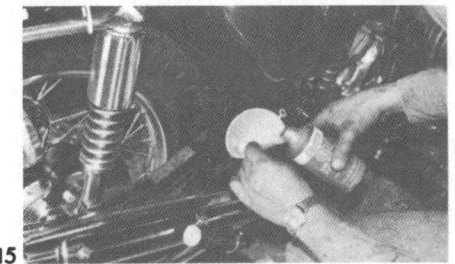

15

EASY RIDING *Continued from page* 25

Later I discovered that the traffic was stopped because the turnpike narrows down to one lane to go through a tunnel. During peak loads, the traffic gets jammed for five or ten miles back down the road, but the Turnpike Authority has not seen fit to place signs back where they would do some good, to warn people about sudden stops. Lots of carnage.

Tuesday was the last day of my journey. What a difference on the turnpike. There was almost no traffic. The Pennsylvania Turnpike crosses mountains and valleys, and it is the only superhighway with real character to it. I was enjoying the view from the saddle.

There were many innocent-looking cars parked by the side of the highway, with State Troopers sitting inside watching the goings-on, and maybe watching radar units too, so I held the Four to a careful, legal 65 mph.

After awhile the pike came to an end. I handed the booth attendant a crumpled-up punch card. He gave me a dirty look and tried to straighten out the card. His displeasure was surprising; the card had been neither punched, stapled, spindled nor mutilated.

The New Jersey Turnpike was as busy as ever, but I didn't care: they had let me on it, which meant that the crosswinds weren't too bad that day.

From Elizabeth to Newark (Newark looking like Manhattan after The Bomb) I breathed those industrial fumes so generously donated by local industry.

Up ahead, a thunderstorm was busy dumping rain on Manhattan and it looked as if I were going to get soaked at the last minute. But I fooled it; I took the Lincoln Tunnel and stayed dry. Crosstown traffic wasn't too bad for once, and soon I had the Four safely garaged.

Back at the office again, I didn't need my daily trip notes to write this story, because the memory of that ride echoes sharp and clear in my mind. It is one of two unforgettable rides. The

other one took place in 1964 on back-country roads in Georgia, when I broke most of the motor-vehicle laws as I put break-in miles on my first-ever production roadracer and discovered what it was like to ride a bike that would really handle. Maybe someday I'll luck into a third unforgettable ride.

The 4200 miles that I put on the Honda Four was my first experience aboard a street bike that is everything a street bike should be—what I'd call easy riding.

101

When Julian Grant ra on a bet, he didn't ga on his motorcycle.

ced around Australia
mble

Racing around the perimeter of Australia is no bed of roses. But that didn't stop English motorcycle racer Julian Grant from trying it. He was racing on a wager that he could not complete the 10,000-mile round-Australia run in less than 22 days. The bet was for $20,000.

For that kind of money, Grant wanted a motorcycle he could depend on. Not a bike that would skitter through the rough for a few days and then come unglued. So Grant chose a Honda 750.

The run for the money was fraught with spills. Two days out of Sydney, Grant and his Honda took to the air when they hit a railroad track unencumbered with a warning

sign. Somehow, both Grant and the bike came out unscathed.

On the twelfth day, near Pt. Hedland in Northwest Australia, Grant thrashed the 750's rear wheel and crankcase cover as he did an endo in a sand washout while hitting 80. When he came to, he wondered how he could get his 750 back in one piece again, out in the middle of nowhere. However, Honda motorcycles are found even in nowhere and that same day Grant found a man with a 750 willing to part with a few of its parts. Soon, he was off and running again.

The race continued with more spills to come, but both bike and man remained in reasonably good condition. Good enough to turn in an incredible performance—he re-entered Sydney just 19 days after his departure. It's a record that looks like it will stand for awhile.

We wouldn't expect you to try anything like a grueling number around a continent where you may run into water buffalo, sand, kangaroos, rocks, floods or cattle trucks that hog up the whole road. But we do expect you to appreciate a motorcycle that can stand such punishment. It's the Honda 750. And it's at your nearest Honda dealer's.

HONDA
Good things happen on a Honda.

Map labels: Darwin, Wyndham, Cairns, Dampier, P. Hedland, L. Woods, Normanton, Mt. Isa, Karratha, Brisbane, Perth, Esperance, Adelaide, Start Sydney, Melbourne

HONDA CB750F

In case you haven't noticed, the Honda CB750 has undergone a major personality change since it first appeared in late 1968. It has been gradually and subtly transformed from a superbike/tourer into a quieter, slower, more tractable, more reliable tourer. The ferocity of the first CB750s was sacrificed to make later models more reserved and nicer to ride. Honda seemed to feel that their buying public didn't care as much about eyeball-flattening acceleration as they did about increased convenience and comfort.

And Honda's feelings about what the buyer wanted were proven to be accurate in late 1974. In a period of severe economic depression, when almost everyone expected the sales of small, cheap, thrifty machines to pick up, the Honda CB750 sold better than any other motorcycle.

Honda reiterated their policy of providing the buyer with comfortable, reliable, tractable, less noisy, mildly-tuned motorcycles by introducing the GL-1000 Gold Wing. That machine wasn't nearly as fast as it *could* have been, but it was plush and easy to live with.

Knowing how Honda felt, we were surprised when we learned about the CB750F Super Sport. This model is engineered to be significantly faster than the most recent version of the "standard" CB750, the K5, which we tested in December of 1974. On top of that, the Super Sport's styling is more radical than that of any previous Honda 750. In addition, significant changes which affect the bike's handling have been made, and it has a disc brake at the rear wheel.

But the real shocker came when we learned the Super Sport isn't being offered as just an alternative to the standard 750, but that it is actually intended to replace it. That seemed strange because the Super Sport, if in no other way but image, is entirely different from what we have come to expect from Honda.

So our first look at the machine left us puzzled and intrigued. Could it really replace the K5? Is it a mild-mannered road machine, a potent performance package, or something in between? What kind of rider is it aimed at? These were the sort of questions that popped into our minds when we began testing the Honda 750 Super Sport.

THE BIKE: Basically the same Honda 750 familiar to so many American riders, the CB750F Super Sport incorporates changes ranging from the nearly inconsequential to those which affect the entire personality of the machine.

Some of the most obvious changes are

With its biggest face-lift ever, the CB750 is now closer to being what many buyers want, but quite different from what Honda has previously been building

external, and of these, the four-into-one exhaust system is the most prominent. The four header pipes sweep down and across the front of the engine to a collector under the right side of the crankcases. A large chrome muffler that looks, as one gawker commented, "like a cross between an expansion chamber and one of those big Harley pipes" is clamped onto the collector. The muffler is slightly upswept, and its rearward portion sticks out away from the motorcycle quite a bit. Honda claims the exhaust system adds power and makes the bike quieter than the four-pipe setup.

In the area of styling there are noticeable changes in the gas tank and seat. The steel tank is longer than the tanks found on previous CB750s and now holds 4.8 gallons, an increase of 0.3 gallons. The gas cap is recessed under a locking, hinged cover that folds down flush with the tank top. The thinking here is that a smooth surface on top of the tank is less likely to snag something vital on the rider's underside if he comes to a sudden stop—like against a truck. A chain attached to the gas cap insures that you won't forget it in a gas station, and there is a drain to get rid of any gas that spills over into the recessed area under the cover.

SUPER SPORT

PHOTOGRAPHY BY ART FRIEDMAN

The hinged, locking seat has a road-racing-style rear section like the type used on Kawasaki street bikes. Under the seat back is a waterproof plastic box for carrying spares, papers, and other odds and ends. The plastic seat back is painted to match the tank and a thin, painted strip runs along the bottom of the seat.

Another styling change is in the headlight area. The headlight brackets mount to the triple clamps instead of the fork tubes, giving the fork a much cleaner look. The headlight has been given a thinner profile, and rubber gaiters are no longer used on the fork tubes.

A final major external change is the switch to a hydraulically-actuated disc brake at the rear. The disc is the same size as the one found at the front, 11.7 inches in diameter. The rear caliper mounts on the right side of the wheel and is a double-action type; the front caliper is of the single-action variety. A large polished alloy bracket behind the right footpeg provides a mounting point for the master cylinder and the brake pedal.

Quite a few changes have been made in the four-cylinder, four-stroke, 736cc engine. The bore and stroke remain the same at 61 and 63mm respectively, but

the compression ratio has been upped two tenths of a point by using new pistons with slightly higher domes. The chain-driven, single overhead camshaft has been altered, primarily to make it more compatible with the new exhaust system. The intake and exhaust timing has been extended five degrees at both ends, and the valve lift has been very slightly increased. The cylinder head bears a new part number, but the changes in it are minor ones, like larger studs for the exhaust pipe header clamps. The four 28mm Keihim carburetors also have a new number, but they seem identical to those found on the K5—even down to the size of the main jets. The airbox has also been redesigned to be less restrictive.

As in previous CB750s, the F model's crankshaft rides in five plain insert bearings. Power is still delivered to the clutch through two single-row chains that drive a jackshaft, but two teeth have been added to the jackshaft sprockets; they now have 50 teeth each for a ratio of 1.985:1. The wet clutch has been modified to allow more oil to get at the plates, which is an effort to reduce the friction plate distortion and glazing that make the clutch grabby and noisy. The seven friction plates have also been altered slightly and the clutch center has been changed.

The first three ratios of the five-speed transmission are the same, but the fourth gear ratio has gone from 1.097:1 on the K5 to 1.133:1 on the F, and the fifth gear ratio has been changed from 0.939:1 to 0.969:1.

The transmission sprocket has also shortened the overall gear ratio by giving away one tooth for a new total of 17 teeth. It drives the same 48-tooth rear wheel sprocket through a new RK brand chain designed by Honda R and D. The chain has thicker side plates and is made of acid-resistant metals. (Previous chains often broke if battery acid was spilled on them.) All those gearing changes mean that the Super Sport's first three gears are 23 percent lower than the K5's, and fourth and fifth are 27 percent lower.

The lubrication for the engine, clutch, and transmission is provided by a dry-sump system, fed from a 3.7-quart tank mounted on the right side of the bike. You now have to remove the right side panel to get at the dipstick to check the oil.

The battery-coil ignition system uses two sets of points; one set fires cylinders one and four while the other sparks two and three. The ignition point cam attaches to the right end of the crankshaft and the alternator is on the left end. There is now

a crankcase breather which catches droplets of oil escaping from the engine and returns them to the system. The owner's manual recommends periodic cleaning of the foam element found in this basic smog control device.

The Super Sport uses the same basic tubular steel, double-loop chassis as previous models. However, the steering head has been raked out from 27 to 28 degrees. There is a corresponding amount of additional trail, which has gone from 3.7 inches to 4.5.

The front suspension now has 5.0 inches of travel rather than 5.6 inches, but no one at Honda knew what internal changes the factory made. The rear shocks have been redesigned and now allow more travel and more damping. A longer stroke allows 3.8 inches of wheel travel, a half inch more than before. Compression

damping has been increased from 25 kilograms per meter per second on the K5 to 30 kg/m/s on the F. Rebound damping has gone up from 100 to 120 kg/m/s.

The ignition lock has been moved up between the instruments, and it will also lock the fork when turned one notch past the normal "Off" position. This makes it easy to lock the fork because you only have to turn off the ignition to do so. It also means that you can't forget to unlock it before starting the engine. The electrical system helps you to avoid forgetting other things as well. The standard Honda electric starter interlock won't let you start the engine in gear unless the clutch is disengaged, and a beeper reminds you to turn off the turn signals. And the headlight, taillight, and running light filaments in the front turn signals come on automatically when the ignition is switched on.

There is a strange-looking box attached to the left downtube in front of the engine that contains the plug-in connectors previously found in the headlight. We wondered if you could hot-wire the bike here but found the ignition leads are routed elsewhere. The horn is loud enough for in-town situations, but a louder one is needed for freeway use.

At 503 pounds with the gas tank dry, the whole package weighs two pounds more than the K5 and costs between $2152 (West Coast) and $2165 (East Coast).

ENGINE AND GEARBOX: When the engine is cold, you must lift the choke lever on the left side of the carb bank to its fully-closed position to start the bike. After letting it run a few seconds, you can lower the lever to a partial opening. In less than a minute, the bike is ready to pull away—although it takes at least five minutes to lose its cold-blooded feeling and respond to changes in throttle opening without behaving sluggishly.

With a lower overall gearing (higher numerically) in every gear, the CB750 Super Sport gets away from a stop with less intentional clutch slippage than was required on earlier model CB750s. It is also capable of coming off the line harder and faster than its predecessors.

The lower gearing not only allows the bike to accelerate faster, but also to run at a higher rpm at the same speed in the same gear. This is helpful because the low-rpm throttle response is worse on the Super Sport than it was on the K5. Despite the lower gearing, some of the snap is missing when you turn the throttle wide open below 4000 rpm. Also, one of the inherent carburetion difficulties found on all past 750s is amplified on the Super Sport. The CB750 we tested in December stumbled and died when the throttle was snapped wide open below 3000 rpm. On the Super Sport, the range in which the engine can't handle full throttle has been extended up to between 3500 and 4000 rpm. This flaw was particularly annoying at the dragstrip, where we were trying to get away from a stop quickly. If we let the revs drop below 4000 rpm while the throttle was wide open, the engine would go from full charge to full stop. That almost threw the rider over the handlebars until he closed the throttle part way . . . at which time it would leap ahead again.

The lower gearing helps to keep the revs above the range where the throttle response lags. At 60 mph the Super Sport's engine is turning a little more than 4000 times per minute. The K5 model didn't hit 4000 rpm until about 72 mph. One by-product of the higher engine speed is easier high-speed passing. It is rarely necessary to downshift when you are nipping past a slower vehicle out on the highway. But if you do downshift, there is still more punch in the Super Sport's third or fourth gear than there is in the same gear on the old four-piper.

The power output of the 750 Four has

been raised from a maximum of 52.2 at 8500 rpm on the K5 to 53.9 horsepower at 8500 rpm on the Super Sport. The power increase combines with the lower overall gear ratios to make the Super Sport quite a bit quicker at the dragstrip. It ran through the standing-start quarter-mile in 13.10 seconds at 101.5 mph. The CB750 K5 we tested in December of 1974 logged quarter-mile figures of 13.65 seconds and 98.6 mph. The performance increase was obtained, however, in trade for a slight increase in gas consumption. The Honda CB750 K5 averaged 42.6 miles per gallon, but the Super Sport got only 38.3 mpg.

In other respects the Super Sport's engine is much like a standard 750's. It will idle just about forever once warmed up. You can run it down to 1000 rpm in fifth and accelerate cleanly if you open the throttle slowly and smoothly. There is very little flywheel effect, so if it's free of any load, the Four will accelerate or drop to idle almost instantly. This quick-revving

characteristic made it difficult for some riders to shift smoothly because they had trouble synchronizing the engine speed with the transmission speed.

Unlike the Honda CB400F Super Sport, which had its pegs moved rearward slightly, the 750 Super Sport has its pegs mounted in the same position, with no external linkage added to the shift lever. And shifting requires the same deliberate foot movement as with previous CB750s. A light or too-short shift will occasionally bring a false neutral or allow the transmission to pop out of gear. The gear ratios are spaced fairly evenly, but there is a bigger gap between first and second than between any other consecutive pair of cogs. Selecting first from neutral will elicit a healthy clank from the gearbox, and there are quieter clunks when the other gears are engaged. There is some transmission whine, a small amount of intake noise, and a little primary chain noise. But you can hear them only because the ex-

haust is so quiet. The machine showed only 78.6 decibels on our sound level meter.

A few fast takeoffs early in the test glazed the clutch friction plates. Consequently it would frequently groan and grab when engaged, especially if the engine was cold. Honda 750 clutches aren't very progressive anyway, and the grabbiness made it particularly difficult to use. Only the impressive low-end pulling power of the engine made everything tolerable when the clutch acted up while getting away from a stop in slow traffic. Clutch pull was light and we experienced no dragging or unwanted slipping. Even when it wasn't grabbing, the engagement span of the clutch was very short, requiring a rather careful release to make a smooth start.

HANDLING: The CB750F doesn't handle the way the numbers suggest it should. With more rake and trail, and an average wheelbase of a little more than

58 inches, you would expect it to be a slow and heavy-handling machine. But the additional rake and trail make the bike feel significantly more stable and precise while cornering at all speeds. And they don't make the steering feel heavy or clumsy, except at crawling speeds. For example, if you are trying to make a U-turn in an alley with your feet on the pegs, the bike feels a bit more clumsy than the K5.

However, at higher speeds, the Super Sport's handling is much more stable, precise, and confidence-inspiring. The tendency for the bike to fall inward when the throttle is closed slightly in a turn is gone. And, despite the fact the bike has more rake, more trail, more wheelbase, and

can be grounded during moderately hard cornering. Honda dropped the folding right footpeg down so it will drag before the exhaust system, which is solid and could lever a wheel off the road. The noise and movement of the dragging peg warn you that it is time to think about backing off. With softer spring settings, the first thing to drag after the peg will be the fat part of the muffler. With stiffer spring preloads, you'll get the exhaust collector. The peg is probably the only thing that will drag on the left.

Although he sacrificed some cornering clearance by doing so, our lightest staffer (160 pounds) preferred the rear suspension set on its softest spring preload setting and heavier staffers chose only slightly

ticularly over bumpy surfaces when the bars would twitch slightly. The demise of the rear shocks hurt the handling noticeably, but the improved steering geometry kept it from becoming unstable or unsteady. It was only slightly less pleasant during hard, but sensible cornering.

The front suspension felt a little stiffer than the rear but it tried to smooth out all bumps, no matter how large or small. Only large, sharp bumps jolted the front end hard enough to cause any concern from that quarter, and only during cornering. In all fairness, those same bumps would have undoubtedly affected any other machine we can think of.

The tires worked very well on all kinds of road surfaces, wet or dry. The Dunlop

more weight than the CB750 we last tested, it feels *lighter* when you lean it into a corner or steer it into a turn. Much of the top-heavy sensation has disappeared. It is a whole lot easier to make the bike start turning, or change its direction or line while turning, or flick it from side to side while negotiating an S bend. It also takes and holds the line you have chosen better than the previous chassis did.

There is a good deal more cornering clearance on the left side of the bike than on the right. Unless you're very heavy or are carrying a passenger and have the shocks backed off to minimum preload, the first things you'll ground on either side are the "warning balls" on the footpegs. It isn't too difficult to do on the right, since the peg is about half an inch lower than on the left. It's this way because the collector and muffler are out where they

stiffer settings. These softer-than-usual suspension positions were preferred because the bike tracked so well over bumps, and also because the resulting rearward weight transfer provided the best handling while exiting medium-speed turns (25 to 50 mph) under power. This handling trait seemed to come partially from the weight transferred onto the driving wheel, and partially from the increased rake and trail obtained when the rear end squatted down under power.

The rear shocks worked very well when they were new and added considerably to the road-holding qualities of the big bike. Unfortunately, they didn't stay new for very long. We noticed the rear suspension fading slightly before we put 500 miles on the machine, and within a couple of hundred additional miles, it became even more apparent. The loss of damping hurt the bike's precision during cornering, par-

K87 at the rear is the best Japanese-made road tire we've come across. It's unusual to find a street bike with two different brands of rubber, but the Bridgestone rib complements the Dunlop quite well.

The added stability plugged into the CB750F's steering geometry keeps the bike stable when buffeted by crosswinds or gusts from passing trucks. The bike will give off an occasional wiggle on rain-grooved road surfaces, but going down a straight road with both hands off the bars, it feels like it is on rails at any speed.

COMFORT AND RIDE: The only real comfort difference between the K5 and the Super Sport is a slight vibration increase in the latter. With the lower gearing and increased rpm, the vibration has picked up a little—mostly in the handlebars and very slightly in the footpegs. The vibration is most pronounced when the bike is accelerating. The biggest annoy-

The rear brake has an excellent feel and progression, although we experienced some rear wheel hop. The window at the top of the double-action caliper lets you monitor puck wear.

ance created by the additional vibes is blurry mirror images, although riders who are conscious of it may be bothered by the additional engine hum on long rides. Changing the countershaft sprocket and/ or rear wheel sprocket will allow the tourer to drop the engine speed and vibration level back down to where it was on the CB750 K5.

The handlebars have approximately the same shape as those on recent model CB750s. At 31.8 inches they are fairly wide, and they're also moderately high. They offer a lot of leverage, which is nice in tight turns or when maneuvering at slow speeds, but their height and width spread the rider out in the wind at high speed.

The seat is comfortable for the rider but less so for the passenger. The rider can go for quite a few hours before fanny fatigue sets in, but the passenger's portion is harder and will make his bottom sore in about an hour. The rear part of the seat must be higher than the front to clear the rear fender, yet contain enough foam padding to be acceptable for long distance touring. With this problem in mind, Honda made a small step in the seat just

The new muffler looks different than most Honda mufflers and makes the CB750 quieter than ever before. Honda credits the 4-into-1 design for some of the Super Sport's added power.

The headlight is smaller and lighter than those on previous CB750s because much of the wiring has been rerouted.

to the rear of the rider's section, then gave the passenger's saddle a slight upward slope. This way, the passenger has at least minimal padding beneath him, and he doesn't slide into the rider as much during stops.

The pegs are rather far apart for both the rider and passenger—although the passenger pegs aren't spread as widely as on the four-pipe models. We never found the width annoying or tiring.

The front suspension is just a tad stiff for maximum comfort. You never feel jolted or bounced by most road irregularities, but on a long ride your wrists become just a little tired from the mild

shaking they receive from small bumps. The rear suspension gave us an excellent ride for the entire test, even when the damping faded.

BRAKING: The front disc brake is the same unit used on previous CB750s. It requires a lot of pressure to lock the front wheel and is only moderately progressive.

The rear brake is very good. It's progressive and sensitive enough to allow you to lock the wheel but not so sensitive that you can do it accidently, even when downshifting. There was a lot of chattering and some wheel hop when the rear brake was applied hard on bumpy surfaces. The same symptom appeared if the clutch was snapped home in a lower gear during hard stopping with the rear brake. On smooth surfaces, the rear brake was just fine.

Our best stops were in 141 feet 8 inches from 60 mph and exactly 34 feet from 30 mph. (The K5 stopped in 136 feet 3 inches and 36 feet 4 inches.) The stop from 60 mph was worse with the Super Sport because the rear wheel had a tendency to step out to the left and get the bike sideways. To keep the bike straight and on its wheels, we had to back off the brakes a little.

Neither brake faded at any time during the test, at least when they were dry. Both brakes lost about 20 percent of their strength during their initial application when wet, although they returned to full strength almost immediately. They both squeaked when they got very hot and also made squealy noises for two or three days after the bike had been ridden in a rainstorm.

RELIABILITY DURING TEST: The clutch provided us with the biggest problem we had with the Super Sport. Early in the test, we made some fast starts with

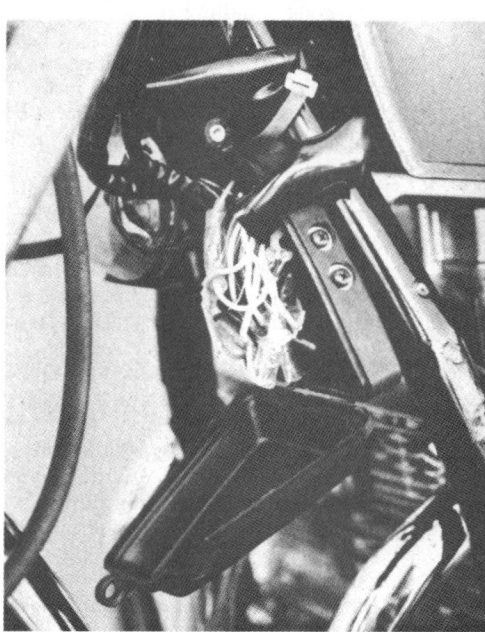

Most of the plug-in connectors formerly found in the headlight shell are now housed in this plastic box on the left front downtube.

the revs up and the clutch slipping. This overheated the friction plates, causing the clutch to grab badly and groan loudly when it was engaged. The fix prescribed by Honda was new clutch friction plates. There are seven plates, and each one retails for between $2.61 and $3.50. Those prices, incidentally, are for K5 plates. The CB750F has new style plates, precisely designed to remove the problem we encountered. At the time, there was no price established for them.

The speedometer on our bike also went South right after we received the machine. The needle wiggled around a lot and it read about 20 mph too fast much of the time. Since Honda instruments are not rebuildable, you would either have to live with it or replace it. The price of a new one ranged from $43.90 to $46.31 at the shops we checked.

A thousand miles or so of moderate use left some deposits on the plugs, so we had to replace them before getting a strong run at the dragstrip.

The bike required one chain adjustment every 500 to 900 miles, depending on how it was ridden. The disc at the rear removes entirely the need for brake adjustment. The dry-sump lubrication system never required the addition of any oil, and the bike never needed any attention except chain lubrication.

SUMMARY AND CONCLUSION:
The changes Honda made to the CB750 in creating the CB750F Super Sport have given it a new appearance, more power and more punch, and a sound level that is lower than ever. Some fuel economy and a small amount of bottom end power have been lost, however. The suspension changes have transformed the CB750 from an adequate handling machine into a really good handling one. Only the short-lived rear shocks hurt the handling at all. The comfort level is still high, although the vibration has increased just a little. We had several problems with our bike, ranging from a grabby clutch to an erratic speedometer.

The CB750F is better than earlier CB750s for some riders and worse for others. Providing the clutch problem is cleared up, commuters and in-town riders will find the machine easier to ride in traffic than previous models because of the Super Sport's lower gearing. Performance-conscious riders will enjoy the added power and acceleration which have brought the machine back to the fringes of the superbike category, with the added benefit of improved handling. Honda-loving tourers may appreciate its ability to pass more quickly in high gear, or they may be put off by the added vibration and fuel consumption—both of which can be changed with the external gearing. Or they may want to wait and see if Honda has a shaft-driven, automatic-transmissioned 750 for them. Those who don't wait will find the CB750F Super Sport to be a bit more frivolous, but a lot more fun. *CG*

SPECIFICATIONS

Engine type	four-stroke
Cylinder arrangement	transverse parallel four
Valve arrangement	single overhead camshaft
Bore and stroke	61mm x 63mm
Displacement	736.4cc
Compression ratio	9.2:1
Ignition	battery/dual coils/dual points
Charging system	12-volt, AC generator, voltage regulator, selenium rectifier
Carburetion	four 28mm Keihin slide/needle
Air filter	disposable paper element
Lubrication	dry sump, 3.7-qt. (3.5-L) tank capacity
Primary drive	two single-row chains, 1.985:1 ratio
Clutch	wet, 7 drive plates, 7 driven plates
Starting system	electric and primary kick
Transmission	5-speed, left-foot shift
Overall drive ratios	(1) 14.01; (2) 9.57; (3) 7.47; (4) 6.35; (5) 5.44
Transmission sprocket	17-tooth
Rear wheel sprocket	48-tooth
Drive chain	⅝ in. pitch, ⅜ in. width (#530)
Front fork	5.0 in. (127mm) travel
Rear shocks	5-way adjustable, 3.8 in. (96.5mm) rear wheel travel
Front brake	single-action hydraulic caliper, 11.7-in. (298mm) disc
Rear brake	double-action hydraulic caliper, 11.7-in. (298mm) disc
Front tire	3.25H19 Bridgestone rib
Rear tire	4.00H18 Dunlop K87
Frame	tubular steel, double downtube
Steering head angle	28 degrees from vertical
Front wheel trail	4.5 in. (115mm)
Wheelbase	58.0 to 59.3 in. (147.3 to 150.6cm)
Length	87.3 in. (221.7cm)
Weight	503 lb. (228.2kg)
Weight distribution	44.7% front, 55.3% rear
Ground clearance	5.6 in. (142.2mm), at exhaust collector
Seat height	32.6 in. (828mm), unladen
Handlebar width	31.8 in. (807.7mm)
Handlebar grip height	43 in. (109.2cm)
Footpeg height	13 in. (330.2mm) left, 12.4 in. (315mm) right
Instrumentation	speedometer, tachometer, tripmeter resettable to zero
Speedometer error	N.A., see text
Gas tank	steel, 4.8 gal. (18.2L)
Gas consumption	38.3 mpg (16.3km/L)
Best ¼-mile acceleration	13.10 sec., 101.5 mph (163.3kph)
Stopping distance from 30 mph	34 ft. (10.4m)
Stopping distance from 60 mph	141 ft. 8 in. (43.2m)
Sound level per SAE XJ 331a	78.6 db(A)
Suggested retail price	$2165 East Coast, $2152 West Coast

HONDA CB750F SUPER SPORT

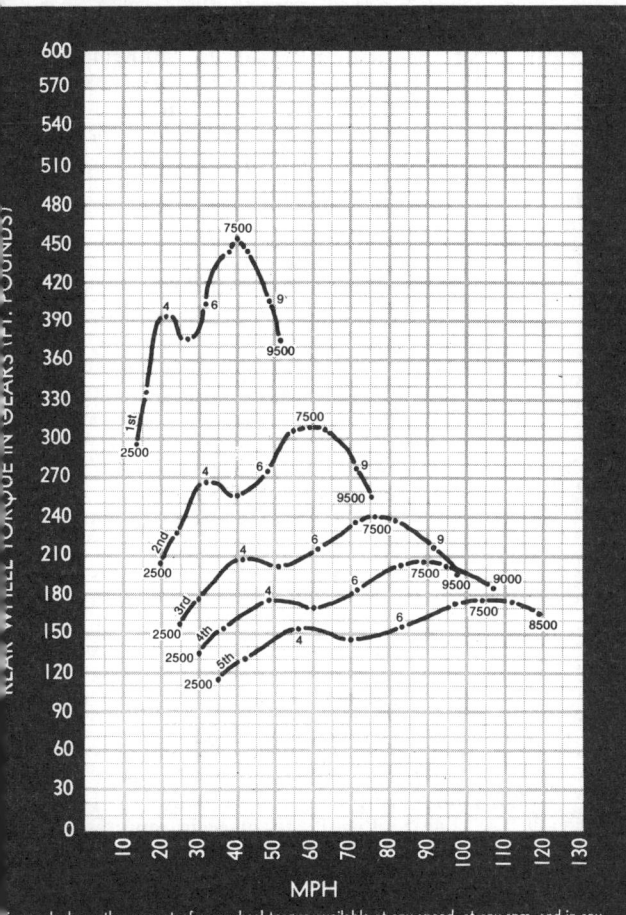

This graph shows the amount of rear wheel torque available at any speed, at any rpm, and in any gear. Maximum acceleration will be obtained by shifting gears at the points where the consecutive lines intersect.

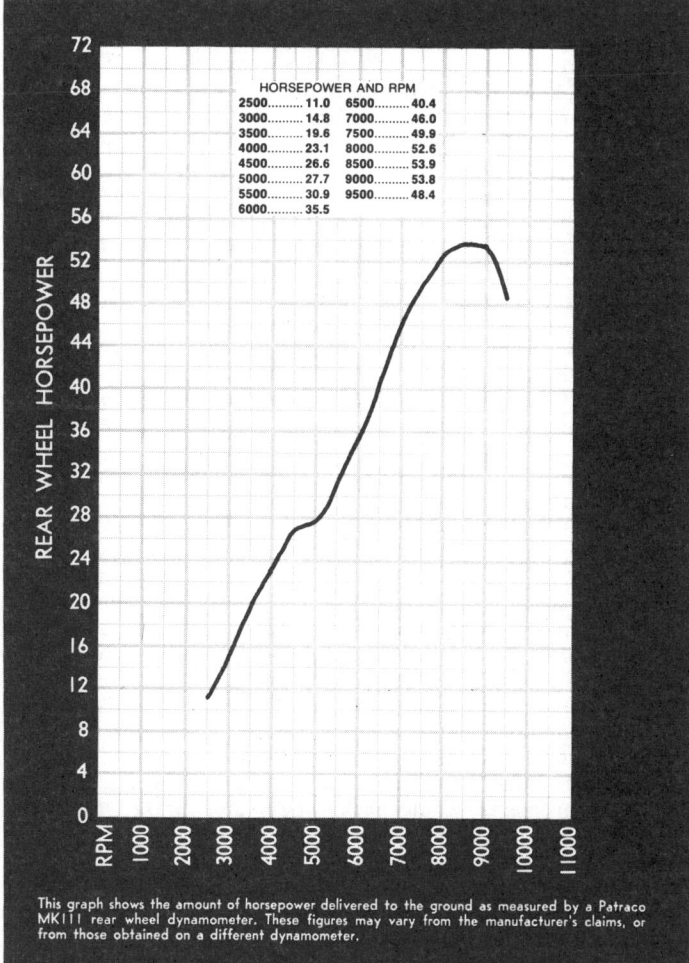

HORSEPOWER AND RPM			
2500	11.0	6500	40.4
3000	14.8	7000	46.0
3500	19.6	7500	49.9
4000	23.1	8000	52.6
4500	26.6	8500	53.9
5000	27.7	9000	53.8
5500	30.9	9500	48.4
6000	35.5		

This graph shows the amount of horsepower delivered to the ground as measured by a Patraco MKIII rear wheel dynamometer. These figures may vary from the manufacturer's claims, or from those obtained on a different dynamometer.

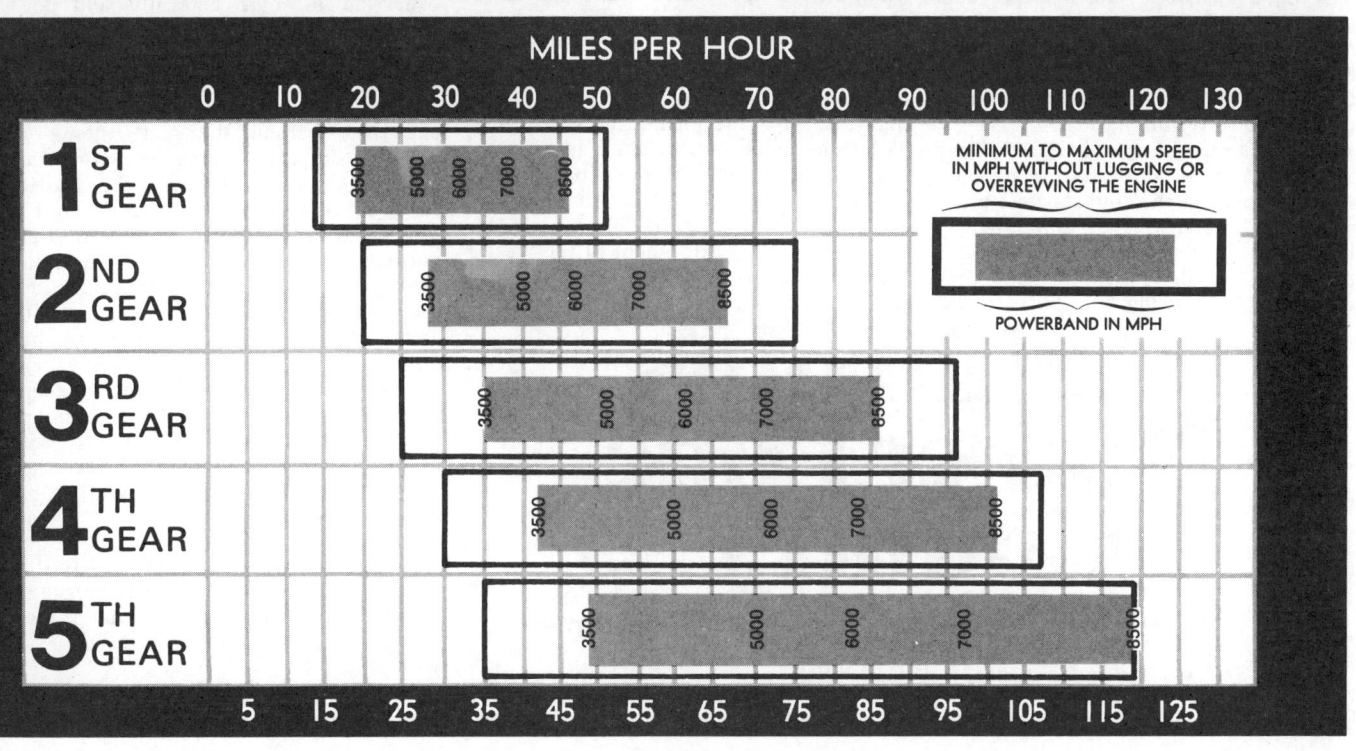

JUST PASSIN' THROUGH...

I GUESS I'M like a kid the night before Christmas whenever we're expecting a new road test machine at the CYCLE WORLD offices. There's always lots of expectation and excitement on my part, simply because I love motorcycles just about more than anything, and a glance in my garage would tell anyone that in a blink. But I was doubly curious about the new Honda CB750F Super Sport we were about to get, and when I spied it rolling into the parking lot by the CW shop on a big flatbed truck, I grabbed my helmet and headed out the door.

A lot of things were going through my mind just then about the metallic blue beauty sitting on the back of that truck. Because in the most recent years I've been touring on a motorcycle, there is no machine more prevalent out on the open highway than Honda's popular 750 Four. Well over 100,000 of the K series bikes have made their way into the hands and hearts of loyal owners all over the world, and many of these are used for strictly touring purposes. So when Honda introduced the new Super Sport version this spring, I was curious if the pseudo cafe racer motif would deter serious "long run" riders, or if the many improvements would make the machine a better one for crossing the country.

Let's face it. A change in the 750 was overdue. When the first big Four was introduced in late 1969, it was fresh and exciting, a major element in the then dawning "superbike" era. But the years took the sizzle out and sheer numbers made the 750 as common and humdrum as a VW Bus in Big Sur . . . the change the new Super Sport provides is welcomed and refreshing.

Honda's remolding of its famed Four includes a new four-into-one exhaust system replacing the four separate pipes and mufflers. The fuel tank appears longer and is slimmer looking. It uses a new recessed filler opening that's concealed by a locking lid, but the lid doesn't match the paint color, which cheapens the appearance. Accent striping is decaled . . . yellow and black to accent the metallic blue of our test machine. The blue finish also continues around the seat base and onto the tail section, both molded from plastic. Plastic is also used on the sidecovers that are painted a metallic gray and mounted in rubber grommets for easy on and off accessibility to electrical fuses and components and the oil tank and dipstick.

Like just about everything these days, the Honda appears to have suffered, if only slightly at this point, in the quality department. Workmanship seems to have slipped a notch and anywhere on the bike that a few cents could be saved by easing up on tolerances and what have you . . . they were saved. The seat hinge is a good example. K series bikes had two on which to pivot the seat, the F model has only one. So when you flip up the new seat it wiggles and shakes and feels as though it's going to come off in your hands.

Taking pretensions seriously, the Super Sports are supposed to bend around corners better . . . so Honda came up with a new frame with revised geometry for the F; there's now a rear disc brake, the clumsy looking fork gaiters are gone and the engine's been spiced up and quieted down considerably. No doubt about it, the 750 Super Sport is much more than "cosmetically new."

After the rest of the CW staff had its fling on the new machine and provided me with their comments, I was ready for mine, and I had a few ideas about where Miss Honda and I would be heading. It was a run I'd had in mind for months; up the majestic California coastline to Monterey, then across the state to the historic Mother Lode Country and famed Highway 49, running 300 miles through towns that played a leading role in the development of the West. I'd be as far north in the state as Sierra City, and I figured the mileage at trip's end to be roughly 1500. Time to prep the Super Sport.

Associate editor Fernando Belair had just made the run to the Laguna Seca National Road Race on the bike and turned it over to me with 2400 miles on the odometer. After a brief ride I knew three things had to go: the handgrips, the passenger assist strap across the seat and the turn signal warning beeper. With those in a proper circular file, I got down to more serious business. I called Des Bowman at Tru-Ride of Orange County, who fixed me up with some Tru-Ride for each of the Honda's tires. Tru-Ride is an amazing liquid tire balancer that also doubles as a puncture sealer. I use it in all my own motorcycles and it makes quite a difference. Any imbalance is taken care of and a bonus is the added insurance of puncture sealing. Many police departments are using Tru-Ride in their motorcycles with good results; I wouldn't be without it.

I then had to cope with some sort of a luggage carrier for my gear. Since the Super Sport is a new model, none of the existing racks on the market for the K series bikes fit. But my timing was perfect when I called Bob Hidiman at Amco. They'd just finished the first luggage racks for the CB750F; beautifully finished, high quality units that hold Amco's Tote Bag securely in place. The rack bolts in place in minutes and swings out of the way when the rider has to get under the flip up seat for tools or whatever. It made my entire trip far more convenient and comfortable.

The evening before departure I went over the machine carefully and performed a routine service, changing the oil and filter and generally seeing that I had a few little odds and ends to perform minor fix-ups. Under the faired extension behind the seat, there's a plastic storage compartment with a lid that has a built in hinge; the plastic material is polypropylene and can be flexed back and forth over and over without breaking . . . the lid is an interesting application of the material. Inside there's a clamp to hold owner's manual and documents to the underside of the lid, and the compartment itself is big enough to hold a set of metric sockets, assorted screwdrivers, a spare tube and a small roll of duct tape. The toolkit nestles in its own little shelf near the battery, and I had enough extra room next to it for a couple of my ISDT tire irons.

With the machine loaded and ready to go I headed out in the early morning coastal mist, onto a northbound Interstate, pointed for the magic of Monterey.

California's Mother Lode Country

Gold Nugget Lookin' On Honda's CB750F Super Sport

By D. Randy Riggs

Below Top: *Lightly traveled side roads off Hwy. 49 are the most interesting.* **Below Bottom:** *Lots of good features like strong disc brakes made the CB750F very worthwhile for a lengthy excursion.* **Above Far Right:** *Monterey has so much to see it's worth a good trip in itself.* **Below Far Right:** *Honda's Super Sport handles better than its predecessor but suffers some from a touring point of view.*

Photography: Walt Fulton, D. Randy Riggs

If the engine is cold on the SS, full choke is necessary for a couple of minutes; then it can be gradually eased off as the engine comes closer to operating temperature. The new fuel petcock is easier to figure out and the centrally located key ignition switch is a change that's been needed for ages. The switch also doubles as a very convenient fork lock when the ignition is switched off and the key is turned one notch farther counterclockwise and depressed. Now there's no excuse for leaving the machine unlocked.

My mind kept searching its memory banks for data on the older K series machines—on which I've probably logged 30,000 miles over the years—as I rolled down the freeway. I kept wanting to shift one more time even after I was in high gear; the engine was buzzing along fairly lively at 60 mph. The mirrors were vibrating images into enough of a blur that you couldn't tell a CHP car from a KW Semi, unless the throttle was slackened off to idle or you grabbed one of the mirrors to steady it . . . and that's a drag to have to contend with. K model 750s have a slight problem with vibration as well, part of the nature of the in-line Four, but the 750F has been geared lower by virtue of a 17-tooth primary sprocket and changes in 4th and 5th gear ratios, thereby magnifying the annoyance. But on the good side, the F accelerates harder, due in part to the new gearing. There's good and bad to everything I suppose.

I felt more comfortable in heavy traffic slow-going on the F than on any other 750K I've ever ridden, both handling and engine-wise; driveline snatch was annoying but expected, and response to throttle openings instant. The bike's silence never disturbed any of the early morning commuters' sleep. The new rear disc brake is also a big improvement over the previous 750's mediocre drum setup. But the disc on my particular machine was slightly warped and tended to grab and release, even with steady, constant drag on the pedal. Later, a visual inspection showed high and low spots on the disc itself, the reason for the disconcerting feeling.

Since the main part of my trip and main objective was to travel the full length of Highway 49 in the central portion of the state, some people would probably think it a bit odd to ride out of my way up the Coast Highway; there are many faster ways north from my home in Laguna Niguel. True, not the fastest or easiest way, but Highway 1 is one of those magic, two-lane curvy things that puts a smile on your face . . . kinda like a two-*legged* curvy thing. 'Course, the smile has to be put

there with the right kind of motorcycle for bending the bends. And I wasn't sure just how well the new Honda would cope. At San Luis Obispo I pointed the freeway cruising scooter toward the signs with the numeral "1," watching the Pacific melt into view once again for the first time since leaving home. The town was Morro Bay and the wind was chilling. I kept the bike at 60 mph and wished it had a throttle stop screw like the K series models so I could rest my now tired right arm and hand. Holding open those four 28mm Keihin carbs all day long turns out to be a hell of a chore. But don't castigate Honda for the lack of a stop screw; rather, put out to pasture the lawmaker who decided a throttle stop was unsafe. Never mind the fact that he may have never been on a motorcycle in his protected and far-removed life.

With the last of the four-lane rolling underneath my tires, I thought for a moment about the old "Bronson" T.V. show, and some of the spectacular footage they shot along this same highway. It brought back good feelings, because that weekly hour of television captured the free feeling of touring on a motorcycle. Sure, there were the usual Hollywood technical mistakes, the ones we used to laugh about in the garage as we polished our machines, but I've never forgotton the series and this road always reminds me of it.

And surprisingly, the Super Sport takes to this damn road, the one I can't stay away from for more than a few months at a time, like it's on rails. I can't believe the bike is a Honda 750 . . . it feels 100 pounds lighter than what the scales say, letting me throw the heft from side to side with minimal effort on the handlebars. On the bottom edge of the folding footpegs, Honda has bolted on a metal plate with "bumps" on the ends that work as "warners;" lean over steeper and you'll risk scraping that shiny but large muffler on the right . . . I did . . . and to the left . . . well, you've really got to be going some before you drag anything serious.

And cornering clearances aside, the Super Sport doesn't wiggle or wobble or do anything surprising . . . keeping in mind the slop in the drive train and the snatch that can be induced with an insensitive throttle hand. Tires are more than ample and are showing minimal wear on our test machine after 4500 miles. They perform adequately in the wet as well, as long as one keeps his head about him.

The ride on the challenging road had been fun, but the sun spent little time socializing. I was glad to arrive in Pacific Grove as daylight said "So long," eager

for a relaxing night in the comfort and friendliness of the Wilkie's Motel, a neat little place near Monterey and the heart of P.G. In this day and age it's hard to find people who truly care about their customers, but Wes and Joan Hodges do, and it really shows at Wilkie's.

In the morning I checked out and did an hour's worth of cruising around Cannery Row and the funky side streets that make up Monterey. Always worth a trip in itself, but I had to get along and head back inland. Through Hollister, I thought about pro racer Don Castro, who lives here, then got caught up in the truck traffic on Highway 152 across Pacheco Pass. You gotta wonder about those pro racers . . . how they drive themselves thousands of miles back and forth across the country . . . with all the pressure and all . . . year after year. What a contrast it is to the sedateness of many of their hometowns.

That's part of the thing I love about long-distance motorcycle riding. You get to be alone with your thoughts and you can mull over lots of things that may have never popped into your mind otherwise. I watched farmworkers bending over in the hot sun in the flat fields near Madera and wondered if they could ever straighten up at the end of the day. I watched a trucker driving an ancient Autocar and thought about how many engines the truck had outlasted and where it was headed on this particular trip. I wondered about an old gas station built in another era when times were different and cars were still fledglings, the broken neon and rusting pumps a memorial to what? And I was curious why, way out here in the countryside, a lady in a Ford was scowling and aggravated, with the face of a big city commuter. Lots of thoughts about nothing important . . . or were they?

Finally Highway 140 terminated at Highway 49 in Mariposa; the air was laden with moisture and thunderstorms threatened on the horizon. To the east lay the towering peaks of Yosemite, to the west the flatlands of the San Joaquin Valley. The 49er Highway bends its way through the Sierran foothills in two-lane splendor at its finest; and for many motorcyclists the road itself will be enough to satisfy. Most of the road is wide two-lane with an excellent surface; only occasionally are there spots worn to the shiny tar, slippery enough to dump the unwary who've lapsed into

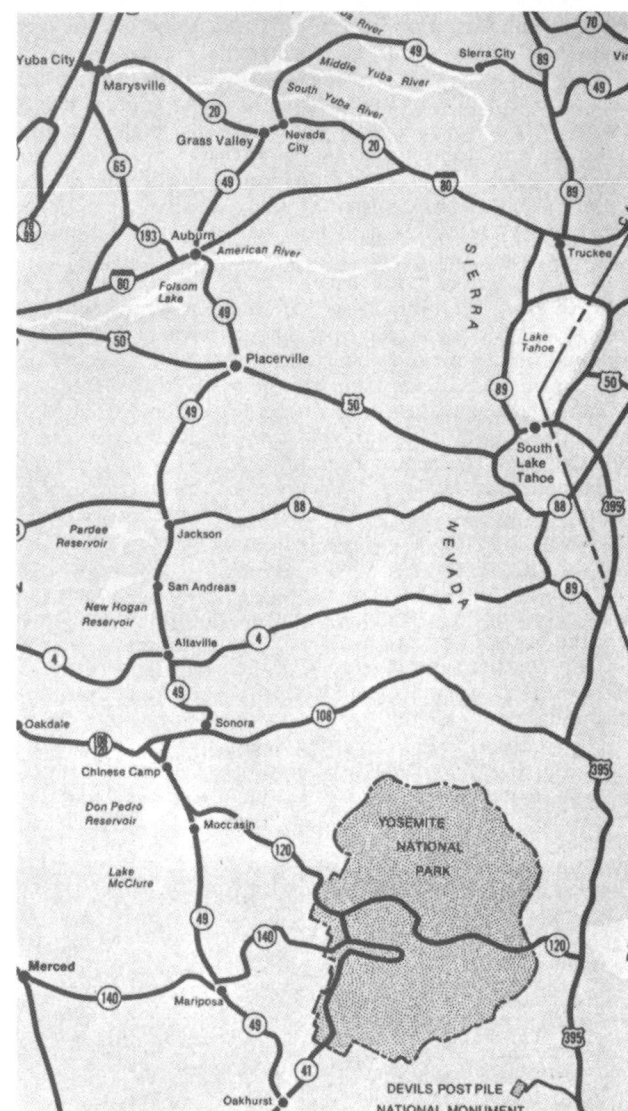

borderline concentration.

The hard thing about the highway boiling with history is to know how much time to allow yourself for a trip. Most often side roads lead to the more interesting and tourist-free spots, but the major towns with accommodations are along 49. Riders interested in really exploring the area thoroughly—or even one or two selected spots—should pick up on a softbound book called *Gold Rush Country* published by Sunset Books. The $3 guide has just about anything you'd want to know about the entire area, but don't take all their recommendations to heart. The book is simply a reference guide. If you're the type who prefers sleeping bags to motels, camping sights along the route are numerous. But prepare for any kind of weather, because the route's close proximity to the Sierra Mountains makes things quite unpredictable. I made my trip in mid-August, when it's supposed to be the hottest and driest time of the year. But the temperature stayed in the low 80s and there were thunderstorms all around me.

By now the Honda had settled itself into a fairly stable fuel consumption rate, but it was lower than I expected, in spite of my judicious use of the throttle. The 4.8-gal. tank was going on reserve at about 108 miles; the mpg figure was hovering between 31 and 38. At trip's end it averaged a disappointing 35 mpg, but used not one drop of oil in 1505 miles. Total fuel cost for the entire trip ran $27.35. I lubed the chain only when it began looking dry, and that was falling at about 250-300 mile intervals, with one adjustment required.

I made a stop at Columbia, a state park and restored town off the highway, where no vehicles are allowed. The buildings and artifacts are interesting, but the shops have the plastic atmosphere of your typical tourist trap. Of course you can pan for gold in a nearby spring, even ride a stagecoach with hordes of sticky-fingered kids. But I opted out and headed for some realness, of which there is lots to be had here.

There was plenty in Coulterville, where locals are obviously not that thrilled by the prospect of fat families stumbling around the settlement with loaded Brownies in hand and double-parked Country Squires blocking the entrance to the only gas station in town. A step into the Jeffery Hotel Bar puts one back just about a hundred years, it's *that* real and authentic. I truly felt like the stranger in all the cowboy movies who saunters into town and bellies up to the bar demanding a shot of whiskey. I didn't want to make any sudden moves while being eyed cautiously by the locals, and I damn near backed my way out of the swinging doors.

Just the names of the towns surrounding the route conjure up all kinds of vivid thoughts...Jenny Lind, Rough and Ready, Railroad Flat, Drytown, Sutter Creek, Volcano, Mokelumne Hill, Chili Gulch, Grizzly Flats...all are worth a trip and some time. And perhaps that's what makes the Highway 49 country so appealing. One can return year after year and not see it all...the appeal is everlasting. And if you happen to be the type who couldn't care less about history and that kind of thing...the road exists to enjoy in the best manner possible—on a motorcycle.

In Auburn I had spent the night and finished breakfast the next morning, only to walk out to the parking lot to find the Honda in a state of disarray. Some klutz had backed into it, knocking it over and breaking the turn signal lens and housing, and adding a couple of assorted dings. You really feel upset when something that stupid happens, but at least the culprit left a note and offered to pay for the damage. After a stop in a local Honda shop for the parts, I headed north to the end of 49 near Sierra City, knowing I'd return again to one of my favorite motorcycling haunts. I doubled back through Donner Pass, then went south on Highway 99 bound for the horrors of Los Angeles. In time I was home again, staring at the 750 in my garage, and thinking about the motorcycle and the trip.

The Super Sport is less comfortable in some ways and more comfortable in others than its predecessor. It handles better than any other standard large Japanese bike I know, which makes it more fun than Honda 750s have ever been. There are several other machines that make better straight-line tourers, but the CB750F does a variety of tasks well, which means it'll satisfy a variety of riders. In my case it made a 1500-mile trip a great way to clear the cobwebs, and I'd do it again tomorrow, without thinking twice. ◙

SPECIFICATIONS

List price	$2152
Suspension, front	telescopic fork
Suspension, rear	swinging arm
Tire, front	3.25-19
Tire, rear	4.00-18
Brake, front, eff. dia. x width, in.	11.5 x 3.3
Brake, rear, eff. dia x width, in.	11.5 x 3.3
Total brake swept area, sq. in.	203.7
Brake loading, lb./sq. in. (160-lb. rider)	3.4
Engine, type	sohc four-stroke Four
Bore x stroke, in., mm	2.40 x 2.48, 61.0 x 63.0
Piston displacement, cu. in., cc	44.9, 736
Compression ratio	9.2
Carburetion	(4) 28mm Keihin
Ignition	battery and coil
Oil system	dry sump
Oil capacity, pt.	7.4
Fuel capacity, U.S. gal.	4.8
Recommended fuel	premium
Starting system	electric; kick, folding crank
Lighting system	alternator
Air filtration	treated paper
Clutch	wet, multi-disc
Primary drive	single-row chain
Final drive	530 single-row chain

Gear ratios, overall:1

5th	5.43
4th	6.35
3rd	7.47
2nd	9.57
1st	14.01
Wheelbase, in.	59.5
Seat height, in.	33.0
Seat width, in.	9.75
Handlebar width, in.	31.5
Footpeg height, in.	14.5
Ground clearance, in.	6.75
Front fork rake angle, degrees	28
Trail, in.	4.5
Curb weight (w/half-tank fuel), lb.	525.5
Weight bias, front/rear, percent	46/54
Test weight (fuel and rider), lb.	698
Mileage at completion of test	4134

TEST CONDITIONS

Air temperature, degrees F	79
Humidity, percent	71
Barometric pressure, in. hg.	30.00
Altitude above mean sea level, ft.	351
Wind velocity, mph	3-5
Strip alignment, relative wind:	

start

wind

PERFORMANCE

Top speed (actual @ 8164 rpm), mph	114

Computed top speed in gears (@ 8450 rpm), mph

5th	118
4th	101
3rd	86
2nd	67
1st	46
Mph/1000 rpm, top gear	13.9
Engine revolutions/mile, top gear	4311
Piston speed (@ 8540 rpm), ft./min.	3492
Fuel consumption, mpg	35

Speedometer error:

50 mph indicated, actually	47
60 mph indicated, actually	56
70 mph indicated, actually	66

Braking distance:

from 30 mph, ft.	36.0
from 60 mph, ft.	130.0

Acceleration, zero to:

30 mph, sec.	4.7
40 mph, sec.	5.8
50 mph, sec.	7.0
60 mph, sec.	7.6
70 mph, sec.	8.7
80 mph, sec.	10.0
90 mph, sec.	12.0
100 mph, sec.	14.9
Standing one-eighth mile, sec.	8.23
terminal speed, mph	82.94
Standing one-quarter mile, sec.	13.52
terminal speed, mph	97.61

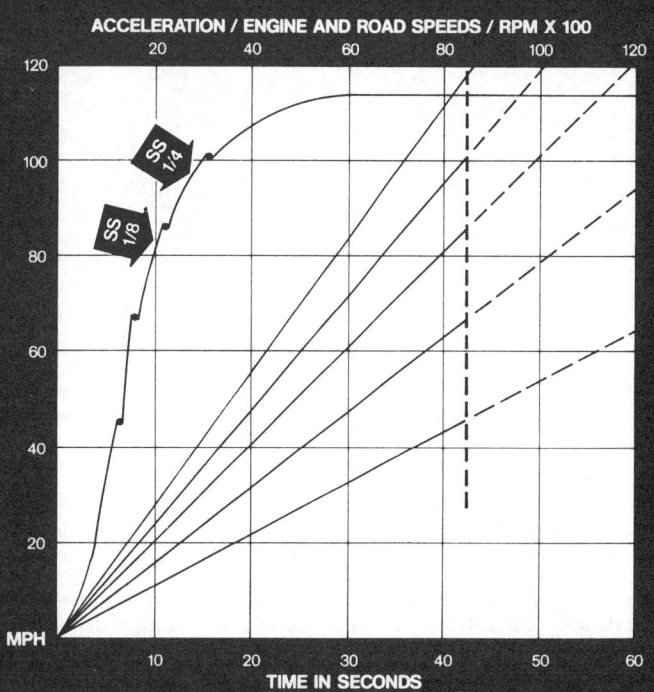

ACCELERATION / ENGINE AND ROAD SPEEDS / RPM X 100

The Four-Piper's Back!

Honda Ran Into A Storm When They Decided To Let The CB750 Wind Down And Eventually Step Aside For A Slab-Sided Four-Into-One Sport That Started A Revolution; Their Battle Cry: "Oh No, You Can't Take That Away From Me!"

HONDA CB750K6

BY JODY NICHOLAS
PHOTOGRAPHY: JODY NICHOLAS AND MIKE PARRIS

Honda had already captured the lion's share of the world market by 1969 with its line of small- and medium-displacement motorcycles. The name Honda had become a household word and virtually thousands of Americans had been introduced to the wonderful sport of motorcycling through the advertising and sales efforts of this huge company.

In Europe, Honda had become world champions in several road racing classes and their machinery, which included one-, two-, four-, five-

and six-cylinder engines, was second-to-none in engineering and reliability. Honda seemed to have everything going for it . . . except a large-displacement road-burner. The largest Honda in 1969 was the 450cc DOHC twin which was technically, if not esthetically, innovative. Twin chain-driven overhead camshafts and torsion bar valve springs set the CB450 apart from any motorcycle then available, but it didn't have the blazing acceleration, physical size and *machismo* necessary to make it immensely successful. Honda felt they needed a heavyweight, but not

an ordinary machine.

Until late 1969 and the CB750's introduction, the last four-cylinder machine to be manufactured in quantity was the 1000cc Ariel "Square Four" from England. Ariel stopped producing the "Square Four" in 1958 and shortly thereafter went out of business. Multi-cylinder motorcycle enthusiasts were simply out of luck.

Honda's experience with multi-cylinder engines was well known long before the CB750 appeared. The shriek of fours, fives and sixes had thrilled European road racing enthusiasts, and a few Americans on the West Coast were able to savor the sounds of the 250cc road racing fours that were brought over to contest amateur FIM road races in the early-1960s. But most knowledgeable motorcycle enthusiasts thought there would be little chance of ever seeing a racing-bred four-cylinder Honda outfitted for street use.

This writer was in attendance at the Tokyo Motor Show in December, 1968. After going to the Honda stand many times to get a look at the CB750, I finally pushed my way to

cess, the CB750 has been the mainstay of Honda's touring machines for six years. But then . . .

In 1975 Honda decided that since they were about to announce their new water-cooled 1000cc flat four that it would logically assume the role of the big road cruiser that the old CB750 had held, and that the 750 should receive sexy new styling and take on a pseudo-cafe air with extended wheelbase and blunt, squared-off, slab-sided metalwork. Production of the old CB750, mean-

changes to the engine. There have been at least three different cylinder heads, a couple of piston compression and physical shapes and there is a new camshaft this year. Previous changes include a longer chainguard, a single bar to raise the throttle slides instead of the one-into-four cable assembly, and both the exhaust and intake noise have been reduced, thanks to Uncle Sam.

Early CB750s had their handling quirks, but they too seem to have been ironed out over the years. Al-

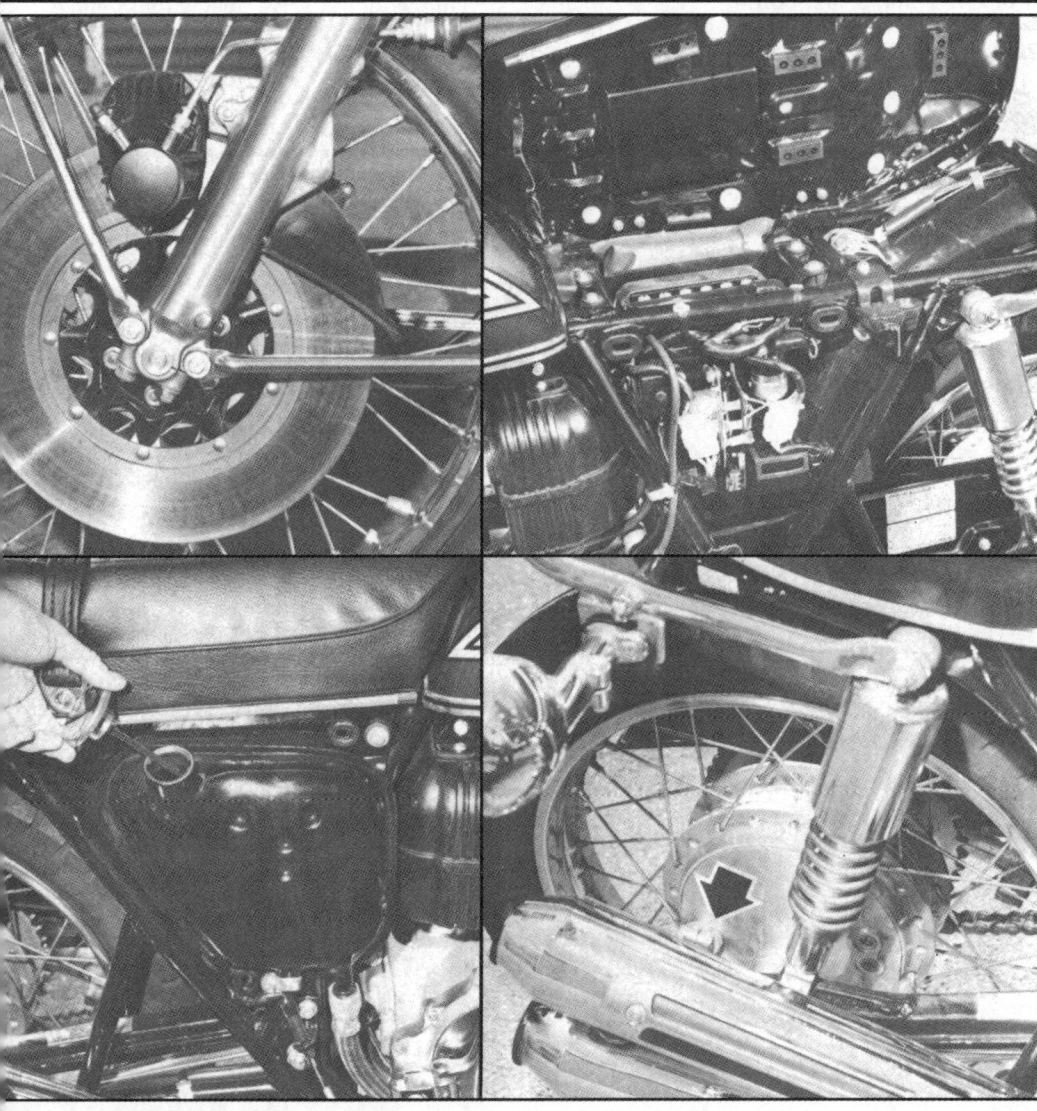

Far Left: Single acting front brake caliper is hinged at mounting point on fork leg. Plastic top cover keeps water spray out of rider's nose. Hydraulic disc works very well, doesn't squeak. Only noteworthy change in the CB750 from last year is automatic-on lights that come on with the ignition.

Left: Virtually all electrics are located beneath saddle and side covers. Wiring is neatly bundled but still vulnerable to abrasion by seat pan. Rear shocks are acceptable but still short of good aftermarket components. And Honda should attempt to lower saddle by couple inches.

Far Left: CB750 is one of few remaining big-bores with dry sump oil system. Oil consumption was negligible and entire power unit, as well as chassis, remained spotless throughout test that eventually crowded 2000 miles after Bob Greene took turn at bars. Work and back fuel mileage came to 37 mpg.

Left: DeCarbon shocks are mounted on square swing arm built from two hat-section stampings welded together. Arrow shows pointer that warns when it's brake lining time. But proximity of exhaust pipes to axle nut makes chain adjustment a pain in the you-know.

the edge of the display area and was astounded by what I saw: an absolute jewel, crafted with the precision that has become associated with Japanese machinery. It was big, beautiful and definitely brutish, a sight for a true enthusiast's eyes. I could hardly wait to rush out and buy one.

Dazzling acceleration, uncanny smoothness, electric starting, a disc front brake and a big motorcycle feel made the CB750 different from its brothers in the Honda line, and a more than reasonable price tag added icing to the cake. An instant suc-

while, almost came to a halt. But the Honda buyer wasn't having any, and while the new 750F Sport went begging, the cry went up from rider and dealer alike: "Bring back the CB750 with its voluptuous and rounded lines and four individual pipes!" And so Honda was literally forced to bring back their CB750, designated as the CB750K6 for '76.

The numeral 6 at the end of the 1976 model designation indicates this is Honda's sixth version of the CB750. Subtle alterations have appeared each year which range from paint and styling differences to minor

though Honda won't admit to having made any significant changes since the first CB750 regarding frame geometry and/or structure, the tendency of the early models to want to fall inward on themselves in very slow corners is gone. When new (1000 miles or so), the DeCarbon-pattern rear shock absorbers give a comfortable, well-controlled ride to the new four-piper, keeping the rear tire in contact with the ground on all but the roughest surfaces in corners. I think you'll like the front forks; they're a little on the firm side but still feel to respond pretty well on mi-

"A Friend Of Ours Has His Early CB750 Attached To A Sidecar And His Speedo Has Gone Past The 100,000-Mile Mark…"

nor irregularities without bottoming on the big ones, such as fast driveway entrances. And they are covered by rubber gaiters to keep crud out.

Some of the credit for nice handling traits can undoubtedly be given to the Dunlop Gold Seal tires, a rib pattern on the front and a block pattern on the rear. Excellent traction

was provided and it was possible to feel the rear wheel step out gradually only when really burying the machine into a fast corner.

Comfort rating of the CB750K6 is excellent for medium-to-tall riders, but the short stuff will have to stretch for terra firma. The saddle is thicker than before and is 33.3 inches off

the deck. Padding is somewhat firmer, very similar to the BMW Sport, and offers equal untiring support that doesn't try to get too friendly with your posterior before day's end. Ditto for the passenger area. Relationship between saddle, bars and pegs is about right for all, positioning the rider in an upright attitude. But why they made the footrests so damn long is beyond me; they deserve to have at least an inch or so cut off each end to stop them from banging your ankles upon each touchdown.

Even though the K6 is the sixth offering of this model, there are several annoying traits we feel should have been rectified by now. The first is the clutch. Driven like it is from the crankshaft by a twin-row chain at a low reduction ratio, only four springs are necessary to squeeze the plates

Above: CB and JN cool it among the pines after a hard day's work (play?). Might have topped the mountain a few seconds sooner on one of the F-Sport versions of the Honda Four with its bigger air box and muffler and longer duration cam but we, like you, still prefer the ol' CB with its fat little sides and curvaceous sheetmetal.
Right, Top To Bottom: Arrows call out safety sidestand that flips up should you forget; turn signal beeper and knurled thumbscrew on single rod that adjusts idle speed on all four carbs. We found out you can't buy more motorcycle for the money, and there are many who feel you can't buy more motorcycle period. Could be.

together hard enough to prevent slippage, even under drag race starts. But the oil seems to flow off the plates rapidly, and after the engine has cooled for a couple hours the clutch plates shriek like a banshee upon initial engagement in low gear. Honda Tech School teacher Howard Jones states that the fix is to remove the clutch plates, soak them in motor oil for a half-hour or so and reinstall them dripping wet. Seems like they are not sufficiently saturated at the factory and won't stop complaining until once properly soused. Ed Kretz Honda in Monterey Park, California, says that the cold shrieks go away after 2500 miles, so you can take your choice. Either way, the malady is covered by warranty so is a moot point for all but the professional road tester. Usually you'll experience the noise for only the first couple of starts from cold when pulling away in low, for as soon as the temp comes up it disappears completely until parked again.

The heavy gear clunk, when engaging low at a stop, and again occasionally when moving into a higher gear—most of the time the upper gears are silent—is basically a result of Honda's three-shaft box: mainshaft, countershaft and final drive shaft. There is no fix for this, just keep excess slack out of the final drive chain and try to improve your technique. The drivetrain snatch, however, that was so noticeable on CB750 Fours of yore, has virtually disappeared, or is at least so minor as to no longer be an annoyance.

While on the subject of audio affects, might as well mention the turn indicator buzzer that reminds the rider his blinker is working. Kinda neat since it also reminds car drivers that you are in the area when waiting for a turn. It can be pushed into a detent, where it will remain on indefinitely, or just leaned on for a second or two, after which it will pop back to off automatically when pressure is released. A neat idea in itself but not so neat is the placement of the turn signal switch. As it is, it is necessary to stretch across, over the top of the horn button, to thumb the switch, and invariably the gloved thumb will bang the horn en route. Now since the turn signal is probably used a hundred times to the horn's once, wouldn't it make sense to transpose the two switches and put the most frequently used one closest to hand?

Otherwise the instruments and controls are thoughtfully planned. Speedo and tach faces are huge 3½-inchers with soft green backgrounds and ¼-inch-high numerals adequately lighted for positive nighttime identity. But the ignition switch is still down under the gas tank (I notice this has been remedied on the new Model F Sport version which features a centrally mounted key).

Although maximum performance has taken a slight dip because of more restrictive intake and exhaust systems, the braking power has remained unchanged. A powerful disc at the front and a smooth, progressive drum brake at the rear provide more than adequate stopping power, even when packing double. Under hard application, the front forks twist slightly to the right, and when riding well over the speed limit, two-up, on the downhill side of a mountain road, the rear brake will begin to lose its effectiveness. But under normal braking, capabilities are ample.

The automatic rear chain oiler which oiled the rear of the motorcycle more than it oiled the chain has been dropped and an endless rear chain has been fitted. A larger countershaft sprocket tends to make life easier on the rear chain, but the owner is cautioned in the instruction manual to carefully lubricate the chain by hand every 300 miles to ensure long life.

If you've ever wondered why you see so many CB750s on the road (100,000 sold since 1969) you might consider that it's been one of the most reliable motorcycles to appear in recent years. Mileages approaching six figures have been recorded. A friend of ours has his early CB750 attached to a sidecar and his speedo has gone past the 100,000-mile mark. Virtually the only things needing replacement besides plugs, points and oil are tires and chains for many thousands of miles. What was originally conceived as a "Superbike" has mellowed into one of the most respected and sought-after touring machines this country has ever seen. This fabulous motorbike for only $2124 retail? No wonder ol' four piper's still the king.

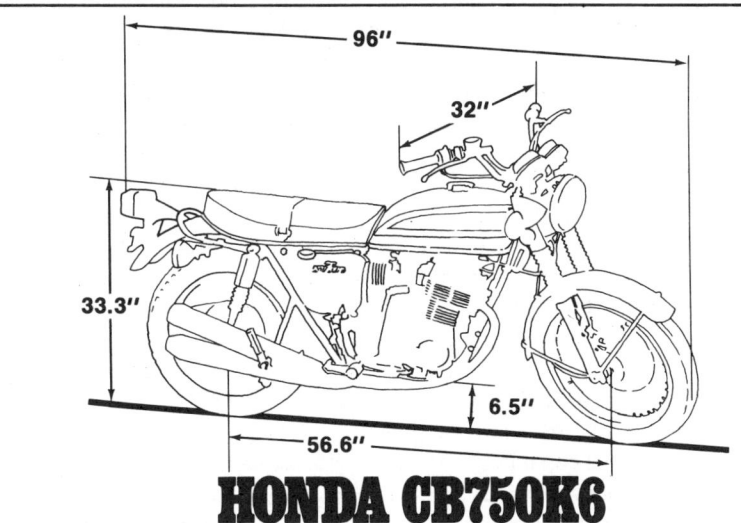

HONDA CB750K6

TEST BIKE: CB 750 K6
Sugg. List Price.....................$2124
West Coast
Engine Serial.......CB750E 2430669
Factory Warranty...............Six mo./
6000 mi.

ENGINE
Type....................SOHC inline four
Bore x Stroke....................61x63mm
(2.402x2.480 in.)
Piston Displacement............736cc
(44.9 cu. in.)
Compression Ratio..................9.0:1
Carburetion...........(4) Keihin 28mm
Air Filtration.......Dry paper element
Ignition..................Coil and battery
Claimed hp @ rpm.............N.A.
Claimed torque @ rpm...........N.A.
Piston speed @ redline rpm...3306
ft./min. @ 8000
Electrical System.....12V alternator,
14-AH battery
Oil System........................Dry sump,
trochoid pump
Starting System.........Electric; kick,
folding crank

DRIVETRAIN
Primary Drive..........Twin-row chain
(1.708:1)
Secondary Drive............Single-row
chain, ⅝x⅜ (2.667:1)

Clutch.............................Multi disc
Gear Ratios....................1st 11.388;
2nd 7.779; 3rd 6.071;
4th 4.996; 5th 4.418

CHASSIS AND SUSPENSION
Suspension,
Front.......................Telescopic fork
Rear.......................Swinging arm
Frame type..............Double cradle
Wheelbase....................56.6 inches
Rake/Trail............27/3.74 inches
Brakes,
Front.............Single hydraulic disc
(11.7x1.625x2)
Rear.................................SLS drum
Brake Swept Area.......152.8 sq. in.
Tires,
Front......................3.25x19 Dunlop
Gold Seal F6
Rear......................4.00x18 Dunlop
Gold Seal K87
Instruments........................150-mph
speedometer, reset odometer,
11,000-rpm tachometer

WEIGHTS AND CAPACITIES
Curb Weight.................529 pounds
Fuel Capacity.........4.5 U.S. gallons
(17 liters)
Engine Oil Capacity..........3.7 U.S.
quarts (3.5 liters)
Average Fuel Consumption........37
mi/gal.

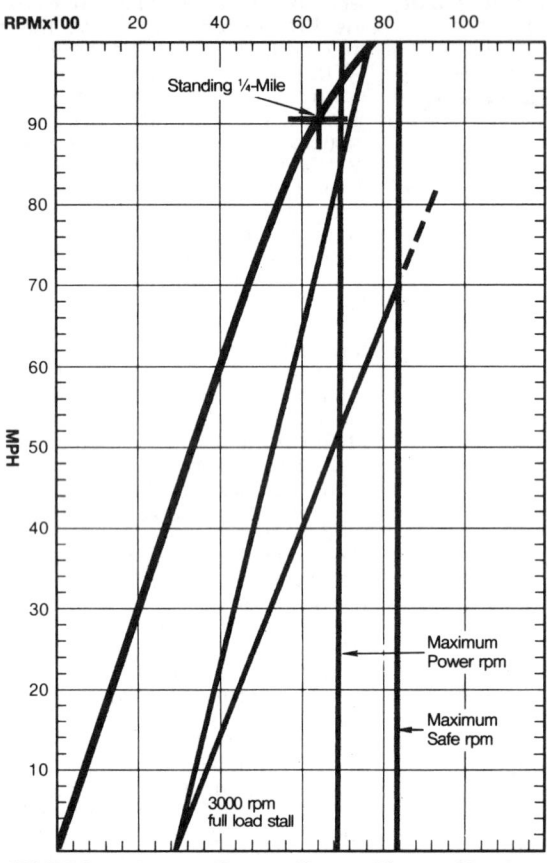

RPMx100 20 40 60 80 100

Standing ¼-Mile

Maximum Power rpm

Maximum Safe rpm

3000 rpm full load stall

MPH

SECONDS 5 10 15 20 25

HONDA CB-750A

Price, suggested retail	$2194 West Coast
Tire, front	3.50 x 19 Dunlop F6
rear	4.50 x 17 Dunlop K87
Brake, front	Disc, 11.7 x 1.625 in. (29.7 x 4.12 cm)
rear	Drum, 7.1 x 1.6 in. (18 x 4 cm)
Brake swept area	152.8 sq. in. (986 sq. cm)
Specific brake loading	4.74 lbs./sq. in.
	(0.33 kg/sq. cm)
Engine type	Four-stroke SOHC four
Bore and stroke	61 x 63mm (2.402 x 2.480 in.)
Piston displacement	736cc (44.9 cu. in.)
Compression ratio 8.6:1
Carburetion	4; 24mm Keihin
Air filtration . . . . Dry paper
Ignition	Battery and coil
Rake/Trail	28°/4.5 in. (115mm)
Mph/1000 rpm, top gear	13 (approximate)
Fuel capacity	5.1 gal. (19.3 liters)
Oil capacity	5.8 qts. (5.5 liters)
Electrical power	290 watt alternator
Battery	12V, 20AH
Primary transmission	Hy-Vo chain (1.35:1 ratio)
Secondary transmission	5/16 x 5/8 in.
	#530 roller chain
Gear ratios, overall	Low 8.63:1, high 5.80:1
Wheelbase	58.3 in. (148 cm)
Seat height	32.5 in. (82.5 cm)
Ground clearance	7.5 in. (19.05 cm)
Curb weight	565 lbs. (256.3 kg)
Test weight	725 lbs. (328.9 kg)
Instruments	Speedometer, odometer,
	fuel gauge
Standing start ¼-mile	15.86 sec.; 90.72 mph
Average fuel consumption	51 mpg (21.69 km/liter)
Speedometer error	30 mph actual 32.52
	60 mph actual 57.17

HONDA CB-750A

Less public notice and more concentration for the rider who has nothing to prove and places to go.

● When the Honda R&D types began to ask what we thought of automatic-transmissioned bikes just over a year ago, our response was one of reserved curiosity. Such a machine could range in nature from being the equivalent of Jim Hall's brilliant Chevy-powered two-speed/torque converter racer to the mid-fifties Powerglide. Knowing Honda as we do, something between these extremes seemed probable.

The result of the questioning, which occured when the still-secret Honda automatic was at the mid-prototype stage, is our CB750A-76 test bike. This new machine is a thoroughly worked-over version of previous CB750 models. The chassis is essentially a CB750F unit with 10mm more wheelbase, and the engine is retuned (for less top-end power and more torque at low rpm) in the same manner as automotive automatic-transmission powerplants. But the engine is no quick lash-up for a marketing test: a completely new set of crankcases and side-covers house the gearbox and fluid coupling components of the Hondamatic system.

The engine breathing changes begin with four 24mm carburetors (4mm smaller than the other CB750s) feeding cylinders with lower compression ratios (8.6:1 vs. 9.0:1 for the CB750-76 and 9.2:1 for the harder-running CB750F). And the camshaft gives less valve-open duration to provide maximum cylinder filling at low rpm. We suspect that the reason for using the four-into-one exhaust had more to do with its easily-tunable scavenging effect than for appearance.

Changing the engine to a wet-sump oiling

PHOTOGRAPHY: DAVE HOLEMAN (COLOR), PAUL R. HALESWORTH

system, in which the lower crankcase-half holds a common 5.8 quarts for the engine, transmission, and torque converter, allows the installation of a much larger 20 amp-hour battery in the space previously occupied by the remote oil tank. The bigger battery will give much better cold-weather starting and deal easily with multi-stop urban commuting where there are no sustained periods of cruising to allow for re-charging time. Feeding the battery is an alternator, with an output increased from 210 to 290 watts.

Any similarity to previous CB750 power/transmission packages ends at the crank-

shaft. Even the triplex-roller primary drive chain has been changed to one of the Hy-Vo type to decrease mechanical noise. This chain connects the crank to a jackshaft mounted between the engine and transmission components. The left end of the jackshaft drives tandem engine and transmission oil pumps, and the right end is geared to a mating pinion which drives the torque converter. Actually, the coupling drive is the outermost of three concentric shafts: the one in the middle connects the torque converter stator to a pressure regulating valve, and the innermost is the gearbox mainshaft—which is splined to the converter's driven half.

There are two pair of gears on the mainshaft and layshaft, and the rear chain drive sprocket is on the left end of the layshaft. This would constitute a straightforward two-speed gearbox, except that in place of conventional sliding dogs to engage the free-spinning pinions to their shafts there are hydraulically-operated multi-plate clutches. The Low clutch and pinion are on the mainshaft and the Drive pair are on the layshaft. The foot-pedal lever operates a hydraulic valve, which directs pressure from the pump to the appropriate clutch, where it works against a piston to force a small stack of metallic plates together to make the gear engagement. Under full throttle at low rpm, where torque multiplication is greatest, the torque converter's stator operates a linkage to direct additional pressure to the shifting clutch so that it can't slip. Drilled passageways in the case lead to sealed slip-ring

Linkage above new 24mm carbs is electric-solenoid-controlled idle speed governor for Hondamatic.

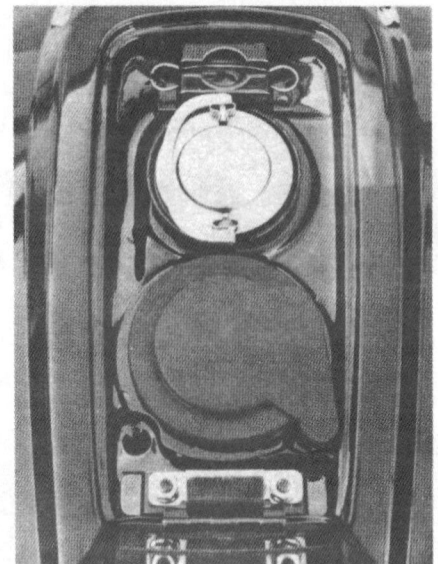

Panel in top of fuel tank hinges backward for safety and opens with ignition key for filling 5-gal. tank.

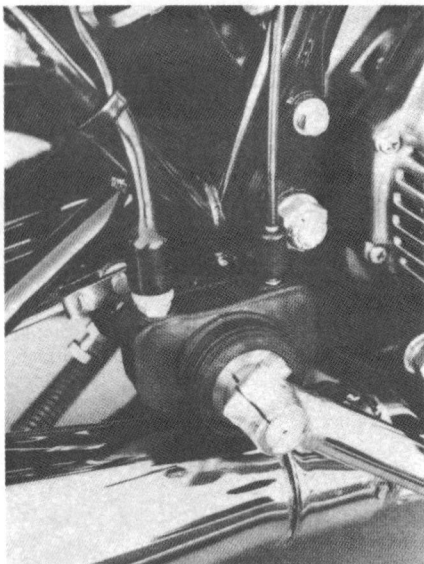

Rubber boot on rear brake lever pivot covers stop switch and cable-controlled ratchet on park brake.

carriers on the shifting clutches to transmit the engaging pressure. Petal valves in the shifting pistons allow complete dumping of oil by centrifugal force when system pressure is removed. Were it not for this hydraulic gear-engagement system, a complete conventional clutch would have to be placed in the drive train in order to shift gears, as it has in the Guzzi system.

The rear drive sprocket, chain and rear hub are the same items used on the CB750-76 (this year's version of the regular four-pipe CB750). In order to get higher load capacity and better tire life, Honda has chosen to fit the larger-profile 4.50H17 tire and rim from the GL1000 on the CB750A's hub. Although the rim size is an inch smaller in diameter than the other two Honda 750s, the fatter tire gives a greater rolling circumference than a 4.00 x 18. And the added section also gives a bigger footprint for added traction. The tire fitted is a Dunlop K-87. The new style GL1000 alloy rim is also fitted on the front wheel, and it is shod with

the tried and proven Dunlop F-6 3.50H19 rib-pattern tire. The rest of the fork and wheel assembly is virtually unchanged from the CB750F components. Both fenders are new chromium-plated steel items that are quite wide and flared at their lower extremity to shield the rider from road spray.

One must become accustomed to much change in the instrument cluster. Both the ignition key and choke control knob are exactly where they should be: right up there between the handlebar clamps where you can see them. No more dark-of-night fiddles to find the key hole or fumbling around to find a choke lever to push off after you are doing the speed limit and the engine is warm. Another convenience is that the key fits the switch either way, and with the handlebars turned against one of the stops a push and counter-clockwise twist of the key locks the fork in that position for parking.

In the speedometer dial, there are two bands to tell you when the engine is at its maximum permissible rpm, which occurs at

60 mph in low range and 105 mph in high. And that's all there is to tell you of engine revs: no tachometer is provided. In the round housing that looks exactly like a tach, there are a series of warning lights and an electric fuel gauge. Across the top, the three small lights tell when the high beam of the headlight is on, when the oil pressure is dangerously low, and when the parking brake is engaged. Three more lights indicate whether the gearbox is in neutral, low, or drive. The turn signal lights are on the right and left under that, and the fuel gauge is at bottom. All are easy to read, even at night, and there is no mistaking their message.

The parking brake is a little ratcheting devise that locks the rear-wheel brake when a two-part knob is pulled out near the fuel valve on the left side of the bike. This feature is necessary because the gearbox automatically returns to neutral anytime the sidestand is lowered. And the fluid coupling would allow the bike to roll even if the transmission could stay in gear. As it is, the

HONDA CB-750A

Linkage is for automatic neutral device when side stand is down. Emergency start lever fits on stub.

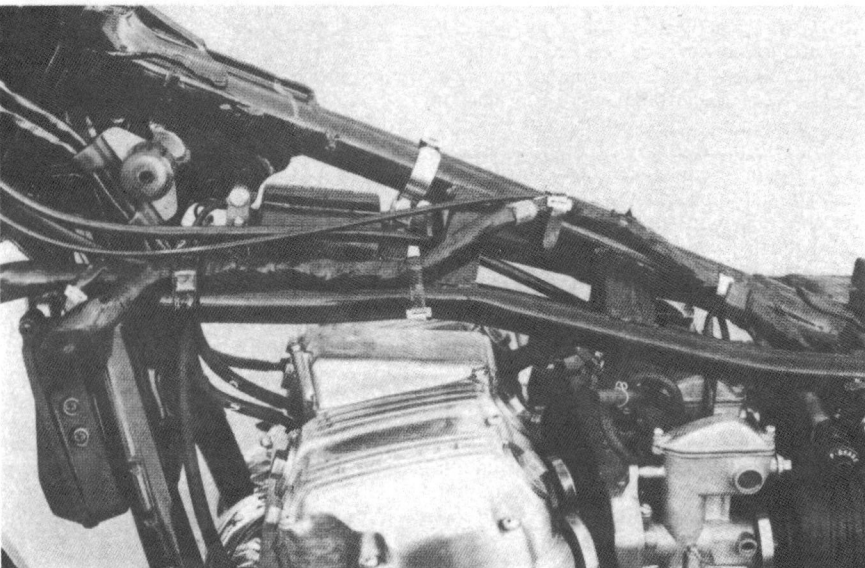

Plastic box on frame downtube holds the wiring connectors so electrical problems can be found fast.

The exhaust system is similar to that of the CB750F, but has been modified for max torque at 6000 rpm.

Beautiful shoulderless rims from the GL1000, and fork sliders that move easier over little bumps, are new.

machine will stay stationary, held by the rear brake, with either end pointing downhill. Pushing the center button releases the knob, and then a dab with your toe on the brake pedal releases the brake ratchet. The parking-brake warning light is there so you won't ride off with the knob pulled out and then unexpectedly find yourself being pulled down to a full stop the first time the rear brake is applied.

An additional safeguard connected to the sidestand linkage is one that allows the engine to be started with the sidestand down, but locks the gear control lever so it cannot be moved from its neutral position until the stand is raised. This prevents novice riders from crashing in the first left corner they reach after taking off with the stand down. Additionally, an interlock-switch prevents the starter from being actuated unless the gearbox is in the neutral position.

All Hondas have cold-natured engines, but this one is particularly so. Even on warm days full choke is required when the engine is completely cool. And on brisk mornings, several twists of the throttle to actuate the accelerator pump are required before the engine will fire up. The engine usually sputters and dies a few times before it catches and groans to life. After a couple of minutes the engine will respond to the throttle on about half-choke and low range can be selected without killing the engine. After a mile the engine will run cleanly with the choke fully returned, but a sluggish feel from the engine and buzzing vibration in the seat and footrests indicate there's still a lot of thick-oil resistance for the engine to fight. After about ten miles on a 40-degree morning, the oil thins out and the CB750A begins to run normally.

The transmission is not an automatic. If you take off in low, the transmission stays in low until you shift. If the lever is left in high, the bike takes off in high and stays there. The automatic part is the change in ratio provided by the torque converter, which gives the equivalent of an approximately 2:1 reduction ratio at stall, but eases toward a 1:1 straight-through drive as its speed rises. This assists the two transmission ratios so that acceptable acceleration and a broad speed range can be squeezed out of them.

Actually, more-than-decent acceleration is only a part of the Hondamatic's traffic capabilities. Freed of the attention required for the usual clutch and gearshift operation, a rider can concentrate on the ever-changing traffic pattern around him and make the most of its opportunities. Our initial prejudice against automatics (they didn't seem sporting) was quickly overcome during our first encounter with an automatic, the Rokon dirt bike. Riding an off-road bike fast and guiding a street machine through dense traffic present similar concentration problems. Your eyes are constantly scanning near and far to judge immediate and future problems. A mistake in deciding the trajectory of your machine can be disastrous in either situation. There's a definite gain in one's ability to concentrate, and less disturbance of the vehicle's balance, with both the Rokon Automatic and the Hondamatic.

Two other very attractive characteristics of the CB750A contribute greatly to its dense-traffic capabilities. First, there's absolutely no lash in the drive components: when the throttle is opened and closed, the bike's reaction is always fluid and very smooth. One of our on-going complaints about many Hondas (and other makes) is the decided lurch that occurs when the total driveline slack is abruptly banged against the engine or rear wheel resistance. This trait can be enormously annoying in a line of stop-and-go traffic. Second, the Hondamatic provides very strong engine braking in low range. With a maximum speed of 60 mph available in low, the system gives fantastically smooth and responsive control when you need it.

The turn-signal switch is made so that it can be pushed part-way to either side to produce a few flashes for a lane change, or pushed all the way over to a self-held position for longer periods. When in the self-held position, each flash of a signal is accompanied by a loud beep from the reminder device mounted behind the headlight.

By sporting-motorcycle standards, the Hondamatic 750's acceleration from a dead stop is poor. Even with the engine's design compromises, which increase low rpm torque, and with the converter's maximum multiplication ratio of about 2:1, there simply isn't enough force available at the wheel to accelerate at a brisk rate. But acceleration performance in the real world of traffic is not as bad as the dragstrip figures might suggest. Once the engine is revving within its efficient range, acceleration is actually quite good. The 30- to 70-mph times for the CB750A and the CB750-76 are much closer than the quarter-mile times indicate.

Looking at the performance of even the fastest new cars puts the CB750A in an entirely different perspective. This year's stock Corvettes with four-speed manual gearboxes run the quarter-mile in the mid-to-low 15s at just over 90 mph. The CB750A (15.86 seconds at 90.72 mph) is quick enough from a dead stop to zap the four-wheeled herd and allow several lane changes within a block, if necessary. And when rolling along with a stream of cars, the Honda can accelerate hard enough to do

The Hondamatic Torque Convertor

● The Hondamatic hydrokinetic torque converting device has the same basic design as those found in many standard automobiles, and is practically identical to the one in the Moto-Guzzi V-1000 described in *Cycle*, March '76. Actually, the motorcycle torque converter is the same as was fitted to Honda's domestic-model N600 cars, and very similar to the one on the present Civic automatic.

The converter is a three element assembly in a single toroidal housing. The part driven by the engine is a centrifugal hydraulic pump, which throws oil at the turbine wheel, which drives the gearbox shaft. This works the same way as when you have a stream of water hitting the vanes of a mill wheel. But the many streams of oil from the vanes of the pump hit all the vanes of the turbine at the same time. After imparting the bulk of its energy to the turbine vanes, the oil is forced by the curved housing wall back down to the center of the turbine. There the oil encounters a third wheel, whose function is to catch streams of oil returning from the turbine in its cup-shaped vanes and deflect them back toward the pump's hub at the right attack angle and with minimum energy loss. This third wheel is called the stator.

The amount of torque multiplication is governed by the maximum speed differential allowed to exist by the angle of the vanes in the turbine and the kinetics of fluid flow. The maximum torque multiplication of this system is about 2:1 and occurs at "stall", when the engine is straining against the load of the pump but the turbine has not yet begun to turn.

As the pump rotor drags the turbine along in its wake, the torque multiplication decreases in proportion to the increase in speed of the turbine. When the turbine speed rises to 95-percent of the pump speed, the torque multiplication is zero.

Were it not for the necessity of cooling the oil in the converter, it would operate perfectly well as a sealed oil-filled unit. Since hydraulically-controlled shifting was chosen, Honda's engineers neatly combined the engine lubrication oil, hydraulic shifting oil, and converter cooling oil together in a common pool. The engine has enough cooling area to dissipate what heat the finned aluminum converter housing can't get rid of for itself.

The oil pump which supplies pressure to the shifting circuit has its output controlled by a spring-loaded regulator valve. A unique feature of the Hondamatic system is that it has an arm attached to the converter stator to override the relief valve at stall and supply extra pressure to the shifting clutches to prevent slipping. Cooling oil circulated through the converter is that which is the excess valved away from the shifting circuit by the system's pressure regulator.

When an upshift is made, the feel to the rider is extremely smooth. Even at full throttle, there are no jerks or lurches. But the blend in speed change is tight: the engine does not rev for an indecisive moment as many automotive units do. There are no overrides in the system. When the lever is pushed down, the gearbox is going to shift. And if the bike is above the low-range rpm limit when the downshift is made, the rear wheel is going to hop up and down or slide in protest. One wouldn't want to downshift while negotiating a fast curve at high speed.

A regular whirring sound can be heard from the converter when the bike is at rest, particularly if the oil is cold. On the highway, the only sounds come from the exhaust pipe and the rear chain. There is decidedly less noise than comes from the standard five-speed transmission.

—Jess Thomas

Removed bottom case reveals Hy-Vo primary chain and hydraulic shifting clutches on gearbox shafts.

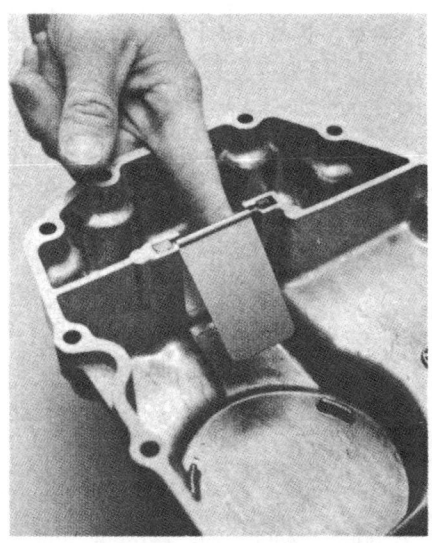

This one-way valve in the oil sump prevents surges from robbing oil pickup at the pump during braking.

Under sump and pressure-control covers are passages from pumps to clutches and engine galleries.

Distribution cover houses strainer for pump pickup, engine pressure relief valve, and gearbox relief.

The converter cover is removed to show toroidal turbine housing. Cooling oil passes through shaft.

Gearbox mainshaft shows detail on shifting clutch, stator reaction arm, and sprung converter gear.

Outer turbine, with torque-multiplying stator lying in place, is driven half of Hondamatic converter.

Dual-chamber trochoid pump with flow-control panel supplies pressure for engine and Hondamatic.

Gear shift control lever actuates a simple, three-position hydraulic control valve for shift clutches.

any kind of manuever desired within the bounds of legality and rider experience.

Both the rear shocks and front fork have spring compression rates and rebound damping that are set to the stiff side of just right. The settings give extremely accurate steering and oscillation-free ride stability, even during hard cornering at moderately high speeds. Ordinarily, firm springing and damping are synonymous with very uncomfortable riding on highways that are laced with expansion seams. The slight bumps caused by the seams aren't emphatic enough to overcome the initial friction between the fork tubes and sliders. Marked improvement in slider bearing material on the CB750A allows them to react sufficiently to small bumps, and as a result, the Automatic's ride is firm but comfortable.

With steering geometry almost identical to the CB750F's, the A has about an inch more trail than the older CBs. The result is more positive self-alignment, as opposed to the quick-turn oversteer feeling common to earlier 750s. This extra trail contributes greatly to the high-speed stability we noticed, and allows the bike to ride across a row of lane divider mounds on the freeway without attempting to dive quickly to either side.

The CB750A has really great cornering clearance. A concerted effort to raise the brake lever, side stand, footrests, and exhaust collector has resulted in greater maximum lean angles than even the cafe-racer CB750F. Metal feelers on the ends of the footrests are designed to touch the pavement first during hard cornering to warn the rider that he is getting close to hanging up something immovable. Even with the rear shocks set at their full-down spring load position, the A must be leaned over an amazing amount before the footrests drag.

With the pegs mounted high for maximum clearance and the seat height left at 32.5 inches, the seat-to-footrest distance is on the cramped side for taller riders. It's fine for fast, spirited blasts, but can cause leg cramps during extended touring rides.

A good compromise between firmness and conformability was made in the choice of seat padding, and the rider's portion of the saddle is nicely rounded for the proper thigh clearance. The seat is moderately comfortable for long trips, but nothing extraordinary. One extremely nice feature of the seat is the thickly padded grab rail which surrounds the passenger portion.

We would have predicted that fuel economy would be poor with the Hondamatic, but the reigning geniuses of engine-building have pulled off another hat trick: the worst mileage we got was 46.8 mpg. And freeway cruising produced a sparkling 55.7 mpg.

The CB750A is a long first step toward a motorcycle that appeals to people who perhaps would never have otherwise been drawn to the sport. These people just might not have any interest in conquering a truculent machine or leaving a great deal of public notice in their wake. Where conventional motorcycles are still characterized by rough transitions of all kinds, the Hondamatic glides and blends and whirs—without ever, for a second, letting its rider forget that it is indeed a motorcycle. ◉

128

Not that long ago a four-cylinder, overhead camshaft road bike was a machine dreams were made of. It took the technology, marketing know-how and mass production techniques of Honda to bring the smooth power and glamour of four-cylinder motorcycling within the price bracket of the average enthusiast. The bike they did it with was, of course, their remarkable CB750-4.

Even now, seven years and a staggering million plus sales later, the big Honda is still a bike to be reckoned with and the latest re-styled F version could well restore some of the sales recently lost to Suzuki and Kawasaki and, to a lesser degree, the Italian manufacturers.

One of the charms of the CB750 is that for all its size and apparent complexity it is an easy bike for the owner with average mechanical ability to service. Apart from a couple of jobs needing special equipment, a complete service is straight-forward and quickly done with a standard tool kit and grease gun. For the jobs you can't do yourself a visit to a Honda Five Star service centre is the only answer.

First task is to drain out the old engine oil. The 750 has a dry sump engine with the bulk of the engine oil kept in a right-hand side mounted tank and a small amount trapped in the sump. With the oil hot, remove the tank drain bolt and the sump bolt and leave the bike to stand for half an hour or so until all the old oil is in the drain tray. After cleaning and refitting the drain plugs remove the sump plate, it will come out with the engine in the frame, even though it looks a tight fit, and pull the wire gauze strainer out of its recess at the bottom of the engine. Any large particles get trapped on the screen and if it isn't cleaned every 6000 miles there is a chance of restriction in the oil return to the tank. Washing the filter off in paraffin and then blowing it dry should do the trick.

The main engine oil filter is at the front of the engine and is removed after unscrewing the large centre bolt. Be careful how you pull the filter and its housing away from the engine because there is a flat washer which sits between the filter element and the large spring which keeps the filter in place. Sometimes this washer sticks to the filter and could get thrown away with the old element. There is still some controversy about genuine and pattern filters. Quite possibly some pattern filters will do the job, but can you afford to take a chance? With genuine Honda spares there is a three month guarantee, so if you buy a genuine filter and for some reason there is something wrong with it at least you'd be covered. Not only that, genuine filters now aren't very much more expensive than pattern.

HONDA CB750
SIMPLE SERVICE

HONDA CB750
SIMPLE SERVICE

1 Don't be tempted to over-tighten the oil tank drain plug. If the bolt is clean and dry light pressure will suffice.

After replacing the drain plugs and the filters put about five pints of oil in the tank and run the bike slowly for about ten minutes. This is done to check for leaks and secondly to allow the level in the tank to drop before finally topping the tank up. The oil level is checked with the cap mounted dipstick, but remember that the tank cap isn't screwed in when the oil level is being checked.

Next, on to the plugs. There has recently been a change in the recommended spark plugs. CB750s used to use NGK D8ES plugs but the current recommendation is the D8ES-L which has a slightly wider heat range with the ability to withstand more cold running without fouling. If the plugs are not due for a change then all that is required is to check the plug gap. The correct gap is between 0.6 and 0.7mm, and the right way to check the gap is to use your feeler gauges as a go/no-go gauge. All that means is that the 0.6mm feeler should slide between the plug electrodes but the 0.7mm shouldn't.

While the points gap is easy enough to check and adjust, ignition timing isn't, unless you have a strobe. The points gap is set at between 0.3 and 0.4mm and once again the right way to use the feeler gauge is as a go/no-go gauge. If you have a strobe or can borrow one then ignition timing is straightforward. On the auto-advance plate which you can see through a small hole in the points plate there is an "F" 1/4 mark which is the tickover timing mark for the two outside cylinders. At 180 degrees to this point there is another "F" mark which is for the centre cylinders numbers 2 and 3. The tickover timing has to be set with the engine running at less than 1200 rpm. Just forward of the "F" marks there is another scribed line which is the fully advanced timing position. The ignition should reach full advance by 2500 rpm.

Before replacing the contact breaker points cover plate there are two other adjustments where you have to use the auto advance plate as a reference point. The tappet setting reference point is T 1/4 and when the engine is in this position four of the valves should have clearance between the top of the valve stem and the screw adjuster. After setting the four valve clearances turn the engine through 360 degrees until the T 1/4 mark aligns again, in this position the other four valves should have clearance and can be adjusted. The correct setting is 0.08mm exhaust and 0.05mm inlet. After watching Bryan O'Reilly at work I think some owners could have trouble get-

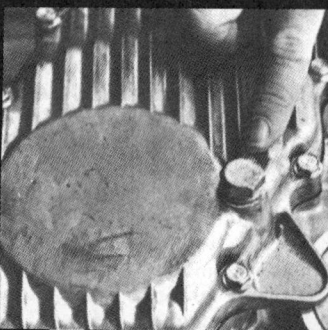

2 The finger is pointing to the sump drain plug. For clarity this photograph is of an engine out of the frame, but there is room to drop the sump.

7 Spark plug life can be shortened considerably by using too high an octane fuel. Low lead fuel doesn't foul the plugs as quickly.

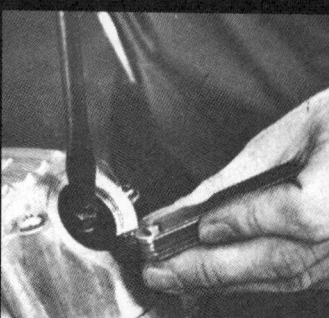

12 Tappet inspection hole is rather small, but there is just enough room to get a thin feeler gauge in. It would be easier to use wire gauges here.

17 Before adjusting the clutch push rod, slacken off both the cable adjusters, one on the handlebar lever and the other one on the gearbox end.

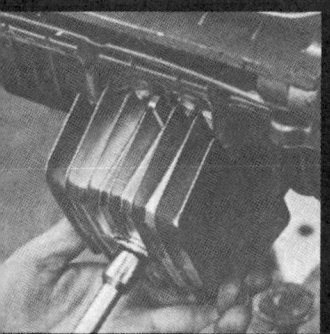

3 The oil filter housing has a pip at the top to ensure that it is replaced the right way up. Don't overtighten the retaining bolt.

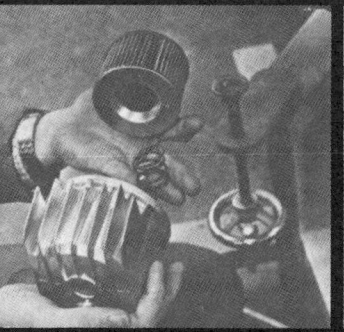

4 Between the oil filter element and the housing there is a flat washer and a coil spring with the washer towards the filter element.

5 With the sump cover plate removed, the wire mesh oil strainer can be seen. The mesh catches any large particles before they get to the main filter.

6 The mesh screen is a push fit in its housing. Careful leverage with a thin screwdriver should get the screen free without damaging it.

8 Accurate ignition timing is essential. First stage is to set the contact breaker points between 0.3 and 0.4mm. Clean the points off with contact spray.

9 With the points' plate removed for clarity you can see the T 1/4 mark which is the ignition point when the engine is ticking over.

10 When the engine is fully advanced, by 2500rpm, the timing mark moves to the right and should align with the static mark as shown here.

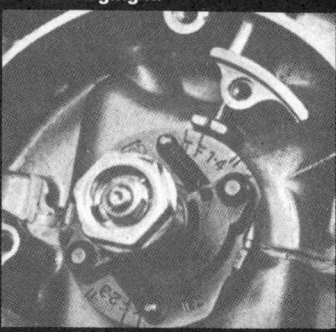

11 After checking the ignition timing, stop the engine and turn it over till T 1/4 is aligned again. In this position the tappets are set.

13 The cam chain tension is reset when the engine is in this position. Note the spring post to the right of the timing mark on the rotor.

14 Below the chain tensioner is the locking bolt and lock nut. Both are slackened off and the chain then tensions automatically.

15 The air filter mounting is different on the earlier models. Important point here is that the element must be perfectly clean and dry.

16 Carb synchronisation is really a job for the dealer since it involves the use of the complex vacuum gauge assembly shown here.

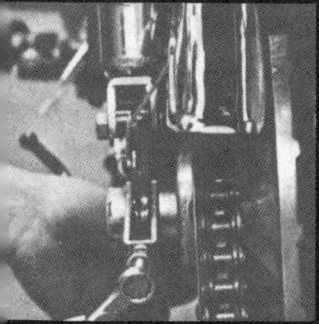

18 Chain tension is made easy by having marks on the ends of the swinging arm. After tensioning chain recheck wheel alignment.

19 Below the master cylinder cap there is a synthetic rubber bellows which keeps water and dirt out and stops fluid swilling out.

20 The same sort of seal is used on the rear master cylinder on the latest CB750F. It's important to clean it carefully before refitting.

21 A quick visual check on disc brake pad wear can be made through this plastic window in the rear caliper. Inspect every 3000 miles.

HONDA CB750
SPECIFICATION

Specifications change from model to model and it would be advisable to check with your workshop manual or local Honda service centre if in doubt.

Engine oil	10W/40 API classification to SE quality
FRONT FORK OIL	ATF (automatic transmission fluid). Early models use 220 - 230cc in each leg: CB750F uses 145 - 155cc in each leg
BRAKE FLUID	Any fluid to J1703 or DOT3 specification
SPARK PLUGS	N.G.K. D8ES-L
SPARK PLUG GAPS	0.6 - 0.7mm
POINTS GAP	0.3 - 0.4mm
BATTERY	12V 14a/h
TYRE PRESSURES	front 28psi rear 30psi CB750F ONLY 32psi front 40psi rear
CARB PILOT AIR SCREW SETTING	One turn out $\pm \frac{1}{8}$
TAPPET SETTINGS	exhaust 0.08mm inlet 0.05mm
SWINGING ARM BOLT TORQUE SETTING	32.5 - 50.6 lb. ft.

SERVICE TASK — MILEAGE INTERVALS

SERVICE TASK	1500	3000	4500	6000	7500	9000	10500	12000
ENGINE OIL	R	R	R	R	R	R	R	
OIL FILTER					R			
OIL FILTER SCREEN					C			
SPARK PLUGS	I	I	I	I	I	I	I	
CONTACTS IGNITION TIMING	I	I	I	I	I	I	I	
TAPPET SETTINGS	A	A	A	A	A	A	A	
CAM CHAIN TENSION	A	A	A	A	A	A	A	
AIR FILTER ELEMENT	I or R	I or R	I or R	I or R	I or R	I or R	I or R	I or R
CARBURETTORS	A	A	A	A	A	A	A	A
THROTTLE OPERATION	A	A	A	A	A	A	A	A
FUEL FILTER	C	C	C	C	C	C	C	C
FUEL LINES	I	I	I	I	I	I	I	I
CLUTCH	A	A	A	A	A	A	A	A
DRIVE CHAIN	I	L	I	A	I	L	L	A
BRAKE FLUID LEVEL	I	I		I		I		I
BRAKE SHOES OR PADS		I		I		I		I
BRAKE CONTROL LINKAGE		I and A		I and A		I and A		I and A
RIMS & SPOKES		I and A		I and A		I and A		I and A
TYRES & PRESSURES	I and A	I and A	I and A	I and A	I and A	I and A	I and A	I and A
FRONT FORK OIL				R				R
FRONT & REAR SUSPENSION		C		C		C		C
REAR FORK BUSHES		G		G		G		G
STEERING HEAD BEARINGS				A				A
BATTERY	C	C	C	C	C	C	C	C
LIGHTING	C and I	C and I	C and I	C and I	C and I	C and I	C and I	C and I
NUTS & BOLTS	I	I	I	I	I	I	I	I

code: A—adjust   C—clean   G—grease   I—inspect   L—lubricate   R—replace

ting ordinary feeler gauges through the small rocker box inspection hole so the extra cost of wire type feeler gauges could be well worthwhile.

The last job before replacing the points cover is to set the cam chain tension and here, once again, the engine must be in the T 1/4 position. Then turn the engine forward 15 degrees till the auto advance spring mounting aligns with the fixed index mark. The engine should be on compression on number 1 cylinder. At the bottom of the alloy casting carrying the chain tensioner there is a small bolt and lock nut and to set cam chain tension correctly slacken the locking bolt by about two or three complete turns and then tighten it up again. Finally lock up the clamp bolt with the lock nut.

Like most manufacturers and importers Honda don't specify a life for the air cleaner element. How long it lasts depends upon the conditions the bike is used in. When the filter starts to look dirty it is due for replacement and even if it looks alright it isn't a bad idea to give it a blow through in the reverse direction.

The secret to smooth running in any multi-cylinder engine is in getting all the cylinders to pull equally. On the Honda this means setting the ignition timing exactly right and getting the same volume of air passing through each carburettor. The only satisfactory way to set the carbs is with a vacuum gauge and this is an expensive piece of equipment the average owner won't have. The simple solution is to take the bike to a Honda Five Star Service dealer and get him to adjust the carbs.

The early Honda 750-4 was fitted with a fuel filter just below the fuel tap but on later models there isn't as much room below the tank and the filter is back in the fuel tank. Cleaning the early model fuel filter is just a case of dropping it off the bottom of the tank tap, blowing it out and refitting. With later models the tank will have to be drained.

In the service schedule there is a note that the fuel lines have to be inspected every time the bike is serviced. This is just a visual examination to ensure that the wire clips holding the pipes in position are fitted.

There are three adjusters for the clutch, two for the cable fixed at either end of the cable and a screw and lock nut adjuster on the gearbox. The thing to remember is not to confuse the cable adjusters with the clutch adjusters. The correct way to set the clutch up is first of all to back off both the cable adjusters and then set the clutch adjuster. The lock nut is loosened off and the adjuster screwed in until it is butting against the clutch push rod. At this stage carefully turn the adjusting screw back by $\frac{1}{8}$th of a turn and lock the adjuster up with the lock nut. It's better to take up slack in the cable with the bottom adjuster leaving the full length of the handlebar adjuster to compensate for stretch in the cable.

Because of weight and performance the Honda, like any big bike, is hard on chains and for maximum life it needs a lot of attention. Keep it well lubricated and properly adjusted so there is the minimum of slack. Modern aerosol cleaners and lubricants take the hard work out of chain care but don't be tempted to put adjustment off until you have more time. If the chain runs slack, jerk and snatch can double the loading, thus accelerating wear and increasing the risk of a complete break. The rear swinging arm is marked with notches to make wheel alignment easier, but even though the notches are accurately cut it is still worth the effort to check the wheel alignment with a plank of wood or piece of string between the wheel rims. Don't forget to turn the wheel slowly and find the tightest point in the chain run before taking up any slack.

The hydraulic disc brakes use any fluid which conforms to DOT3 or J1703 specification. If there is a big drop in fluid level then urgently check the pipes and junctions for leaks.

Current American legislation demands that a visual examination of brake lining or pad condition can be made at a glance so older models with a drum rear brake have an indicator cast into the hub with a pointer on the cam and the later disc models have a red line moulded into the pads. When the pads wear down to the red line they are due for renewal. Apart from adjustment the only other brake service job is to put a drop of oil on the rear brake pedal linkage. Duck oil or a similar aerosol lubricant is the best way to make sure that all parts are lubricated.

An important job is to check both wheels for buckles, a buckle in the wheel rim of a big bike like the CB750 can upset handling in a big way. Spoke tension is important too. It can be checked by tapping each spoke in turn with a small spanner, if any are loose the note will be flat. If there are more than three loose spokes leave retensioning to an expert wheel builder.

The legal minimum for tyre tread depth is 1mm, but don't let the tyres on a CB750 run down to this level because the bike will be almost unrideable. The minimum safe tread depth is 2mm on the front tyre and $1\frac{1}{2}$mm on

22 If the metal top cap is removed both the pads can be removed without taking the caliper off the swinging arm mounting bracket.

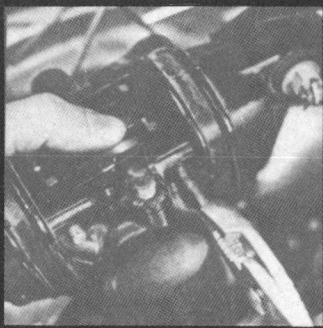

23 If the pads have to come out push the flat metal spring down with one hand and pull the securing bars out with a pair of pliers.

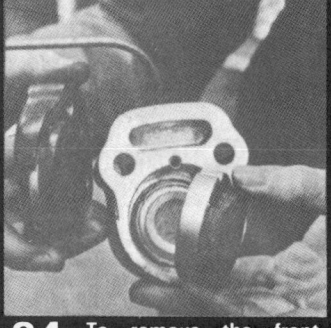

24 To remove the front pads it is necessary to pull the caliper off the fork tube. It isn't necessary to disconnect the hydraulic pipe.

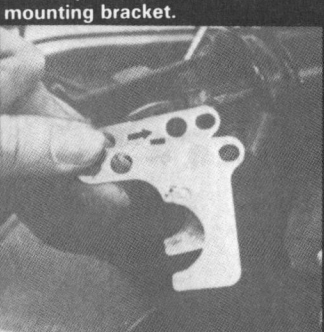

25 If the pads are removed for any reason check the order the parts go back. This rear brake has shims which are handed and arrowed.

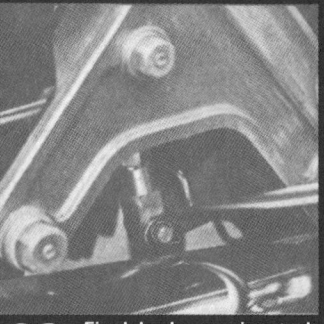

26 Final brake service task it to lubricate all linkages. An aerosol lubrication spray is the best way to do the job quickly.

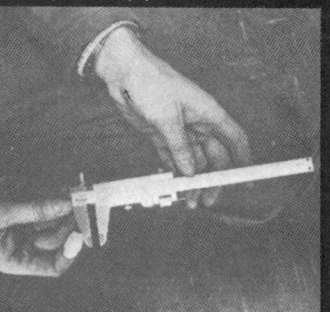

27 With any big, fast, heavy bike, tyre tread depth is important, not only for wet road holding but also steering control in the dry.

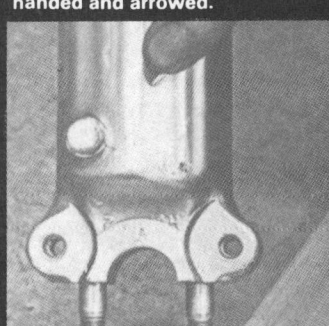

28 Front fork drain bolt is set in the outside at the bottom of the fork legs. Front forks are filled with automatic transmission fluid.

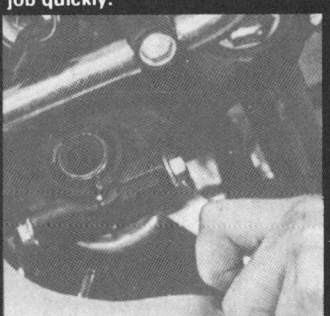

29 To tighten the steering head crown nut it is necessary to lift the top yoke and use a thin "C" spanner which will be a close fit under the yoke.

30 These are the special locking nuts which Honda now use. Called uniform bearing stress nuts they are guaranteed not to come undone.

the rear.

Some time ago Honda had second thoughts about the specification of front fork oil and they now recommend using automatic transmission fluid, primarily because it doesn't froth when it is aerated. To change fork oil drain the old oil out of one fork leg at a time through the drain screw at the bottom of each leg. Refill with 220-230cc of ATF oil for the earlier Hondas or 145-155cc of ATF for the later CB750F.

The swinging arm on the CB750 pivots on a fibre bush and on the earlier models there was no provision to lubricate it. On the later models there are two grease nipples underneath

the swinging arm and both need a few pumps with a grease gun filled with ordinary multi-purpose grease.

Adjusting the steering head bearings needs a special "C" spanner and a certain amount of dismantling. If the top fork bolts and the bolt and nut which hold the top yoke in position are slackened off there is just about enough room to get a very thin "C" spanner in between the top yoke and the steering head. The top yoke when pulled back down again stops the bearing adjuster ring from coming undone.

The battery should be checked to ensure that the leads are properly attached, there is no corrosion around the terminals

and the battery fluid level is up to the mark. Honda say that it is worthwhile to occasionally have a dealer check the voltage from the battery and also the charge rate into the battery. Fortunately the electrics on the CB750 are so reliable that a check on the electrical circuits is only really necessary once a year.

Finally, run over all the important nuts and bolts and make sure that none are loose. On later models there are special nuts with built-in washers which hold the front disc in position. Although there doesn't appear to be anything to stop the nuts from coming undone they are designed to lock themselves to the disc mounting studs.

Honda's CB750F Stick

We know what the automatic transmission did to Detroit.... Will it have the same effect on motorcycles?

DIF·FER·ENT/ dif-ərnt, dif-(ə-) rənt/ adj **1:** partly or totally unlike in nature, form, or quality: DISSIMILAR **2:** not the same: as **a:** DISTINCT **b:** VARIOUS **c:** ANOTHER **3:** UNUSUAL, SPECIAL.

Honda's most recent entry into the street bike melange not only fits Webster's definition, but is destined to gain rank among the world's motorcyclists in a rather short period of time. The reasons why are simple.

The CB750A is based on one of the most successful motorcycles of all time, the CB750 Four. Yet it also sets itself apart from that model by virtue of a feature that will guarantee its appeal among a whole new breed of riders. The "A" following the CB750 designation, if you haven't already guessed, stands for "Automatic," and for most people this is going to conjure up thoughts of an automatic transmission. And, they're basically correct (although the Hondamatic, as it is called, *does not* shift itself).

The 750A is a curious new piece of equipment for people to ponder and it puts an entirely different slant on riding. Like most, we found ourselves staring in wonderment at it and thinking especially about how it would compare to its parallel in the Honda model lineup, the CB750F. Unlike the CB750K four-pipe version, the F shares many of its basics with the A. So we obtained both the Automatic and Super Sport 750s from American Honda, the U.S. distributor, and put them to the test.

No one will have any trouble telling the two bikes apart. The A uses different fenders, seat, fuel tank, wheels, sidecovers and assorted components, so there's no reason for any confusion. Unmistakably Hondas both, but with *very* individual personalities.

Both machines start off with basically identical chassis, although the A has a fractionally longer wheelbase. The F and the A are once again set apart from the K in this category because of the trail portion of its steering geometry, which causes some handling irregularities. With a full inch more of trail, both the A and F steer considerably better than the K in slow, tight turns and show a higher degree of stability at freeway and faster speeds.

In terms of ride characteristics and quality, we would've expected nearly identical performances from the Automatic and the Super Sport, since they share the same suspension components. Out on the road, though, the A rode harsher and stiffer than the F, and even the F was nothing to write home about. When we got to the suspension dyno and explored the innards of shocks and forks, we found out the reasons for the poor-to-fair ride quality and why each machine performed differently.

The rear shocks *look* different on each machine, but in reality are quite similar. The exception is a chrome decorative cover that slips over the top half of the spring on the Automatic. As is common practice with OEM dampers these days, the units have limited oil capacity and are built with low cost as the foremost factor.

Shocks on both have 8 to 10 pounds of compression damping and 110 lb. of rebound damping, about right considering the weight factors involved. The slight damping variance we discovered between shocks was primarily a result of manufacturing tolerances, not a difference in the shocks themselves. Although each shock spring has the same 100-lb. rate, the Automatic's spring has about twice the amount of preload, which may be an overreaction on the part of Honda engineers to the additional 40 pounds of weight the 750A carries.

As a result of the extra preload, the 750A rides terribly rough with one person aboard and barely reaches acceptable levels with a passenger added. In the meantime, the "stick" version can share the same lane and deliver a far more enjoyable ride with the identical shocks and springs. The preload we're discussing is measured with the adjusting ring spun to the "soft" setting.

Our suggestion for improvement would be to go to a slightly heavier spring (110 lb.) with a minimal amount of preload. This would allow good carrying capacity (as with a passenger and/or luggage), yet would provide less resistance at the beginning of the stroke movement. For an example, it takes 110 lb. of force to move the shock 1 in. with the 110-lb. spring and no preload. With the A's standard 100-lb. spring and 1½ in. of preload, it takes 250 lb. to move the shock that same inch. Let's take a look at the 750F shock for a moment to see the difference its factory preload setting makes with the same shock and spring.

To move that first inch of travel, 175 lb. of force is necessary as compared to the 250 lb. for the 750A. To move the full travel of the shock, which is 3 in., 375 lb. is needed, as compared to 450 lb. for the A. One staffer said he resorted to wearing his contact lenses when riding the Automatic because the ride was so rough it made his glasses jump up and down! But the rear shocks aren't the only culprits.

The forks aren't performing to their ability, either. Both the A and the F forks have 10 lb. of compression and 20 lb. of rebound damping. But rebound damping is too light for the spring (see accompanying suspension dyno chart). Standard spring rates are 40−42 lb., but, like the shocks, they are preloaded excessively, particularly on the 750A. A 30/40-lb. progressive spring with 1 in. of preload makes the forks perform far better. The ride is still firm for work at higher speeds, but at least won't dislodge eyeballs from their sockets.

We were surprised to learn that ground clearance was slightly better on the Automatic. There's obviously been a concerted effort to tuck things up and in to gain that additional lean angle. For one thing the footpegs have been mounted higher up, which accounted for the cramped feeling in the knees our taller staffers experienced after long periods in the saddle. Also, the pegs seem to fall in position right where it is normal to place your legs during a stop to hold the machine upright. We never quite got used to their positioning, but relished the additional ground clearance provided. The 750F grounded the pegs more often in the same turns—particularly on the right side—and banged the exhaust pipe soundly to boot.

The Automatic's seat is far superior to that of the 750F; in fact, we think it's the best seat Honda has come up with on any of its models to date. Prolonged periods of distance riding will not be objectionable to average posteriors. That's a switch from the F, whose seat is not only hard, but has one of those passenger assist straps that serve no purpose other than annoying the rider.

The Automatic has a much better solution for the passenger hold. Attached to the rear portion of the seat is a heavily-padded, wrap-around grab rail. It provides a firm hold for the person along for the ride and is especially useful during braking, when the passenger often has nothing more to lean against than the rider.

Seats on both machines lock in place and flip up to reveal other items. On the Automatic there's a giant 20-amp-hour battery taking up most of the space and a removable kickstart lever that can be used when that huge battery decides to stick its tongue out. Space for the toolkit is found in a metal receptacle on the bottom of the seat base; a thumbscrew undoes the lid.

The 750F provides a nicer under-seat arrangement. The battery is smaller (14 amp

hours), and so the toolkit can nestle beside it in a plastic bin. Toward the rear, a very handy storage compartment sealed from the elements allows space for small items like additional tools, chain lube or bungie cords. The cafe-type tail section provides extra storage space that Honda has wisely made good use of.

Pop-off plastic sidecovers on the 750F hide an oil tank on the right side and electrical components on the left. With the 750A's wet-sump engine no oil tank is necessary, so the covers hide only battery and electrics and hold the emblems that say ''Hondamatic.''

Each machine has a recessed fuel tank cap with a hinged, locking lid atop. The caps themselves are attached to the tank with small chains to preclude loss. If you're perplexed by a queer rattling, chances are it's the chain shaking around in the tank. Drain holes are fitted in the recess just in case fuel is spilled; and a rubber tube directs spillage to the ground.

A convenient ignition switch location is a welcome feature of both bikes. The key is double-sided and also operates the lock mechanism on the seat and fuel tank lid. There is also a steering lock integrated into the ignition switch. Once the lock is turned to ''off,'' the key can be depressed and turned to the left, which will lock the steering if the forks are in either the full-right or full-left position. A welcome safety feature that more manufacturers should adopt.

It is at this point that the two Hondas begin to go their separate ways. While the 750F features conventional Honda instruments, easily readable day and night, the Hondamatic's different requirements make different instruments necessary. A 140-mph speedometer face is found on the 750F, along with a resettable trip meter. On the other hand, the Automatic has a more realistic 120-mph face, with marks for the semi-Automatic's shift points: 60 mph for ''low'' range and 108 mph for ''high.''

Color Photography: Scott Malcolm

CYCLE WORLD COMPARISON TEST

Honda Stick versus Automatic

Warning lights have a separate panel on the 750F and include oil pressure, turn indicators, high beam and neutral. The Automatic houses its lights in the face of what would normally be (and is on the 750F) the tachometer. At the top are included high beam and oil pressure, as well as a parking brake lamp. Yes, Virginia, this one's got a parking brake! Below those is a broader band of lights indicating gear selection: neutral in green and low and drive in blue. Amber turn indicators are below that, with a fuel gauge topping off the group.

Handlebar switches, the same on both machines, are up for heavy criticism. There is no on/off switch, which no doubt sells Honda a lot of batteries in the course of a year, and the high/low-beam switch placement is extremely awkward. The turn signal rocker switch features a lane-change detent, but the Yamaha self-canceling signals have us spoiled. We didn't care for the bars on either bike, particularly the Automatic's, nor did we like the waffle-pattern grips that are out of the dark ages. And that turn signal warning beeper should be unplugged before the machine ever leaves the showroom floor.

CATEGORY ONE
MANUFACTURER'S
SUGGESTED RETAIL PRICE
Hondamatic $2194
Super Sport $2186

Super Sport

Hondamatic

Photography: D. Randy Riggs

CATEGORY TWO
FACTORY WARRANTY
Hondamatic . . . . .6 mo./6000 mi.
Super Sport . . . . .6 mo./6000 mi.

Expecting similarity in the wheel and tire departments, we soon learned otherwise. The 750 Auto has some gorgeous aluminum rims that are GL1000 style right down to the 17-in. rear wheel diameter. In fact, the Automatic pirated a rear hub drive sprocket and chain directly from the K model CB, while the 750F uses a disc brake arrangement. Wheel rims on the shift-it-yourself model are steel.

Honda uses a large-profile 4.50-17 Dunlop K-87 tire on the rear of the A. The smaller rim diameter doesn't lower the seat height any; in fact, the large rear tire has a greater rolling circumference than a normal 4.00-18 size. Up front, the Automatic rolls a 3.50 Dunlop K6 on a 19-in. wheel; the ''stick-shift'' does the same, but in a smaller 3.25 size. On the backside the 750F has a Bridgestone Super Speed, 4.00-18. All in all, the tires on both motorcycles work well under most riding conditions. Even faster riders won't feel an immediate need to swap rubber for safety reasons, since the stock tires on

both bikes stick pretty well.

The staff of CYCLE WORLD is comprised primarily of sporting riders and we'll be the first to admit that we had mixed emotions and a lot of reservations about the Honda Automatic. Even when it comes to our automobiles, the largest percentage of us opts for shifting gears. Prejudice against automatics runs fairly rampant here. So what kinds of feelings and thoughts did the Automatic evoke from us, particularly since we had the ''stick'' version as a partner throughout the test?

Surprisingly, we didn't go away laughing or snickering about the ''slushbucket out back'' or ''that thing they call a motorcycle.'' Without a doubt, Honda's CB750A is every bit a real motorcycle, delivering all of the same pleasures, though in a slightly different manner. As a result, it demanded and got all of our respect. Disregarding all of the likes and dislikes other than those transmission-related, we like Hondamatic.

Super Sport

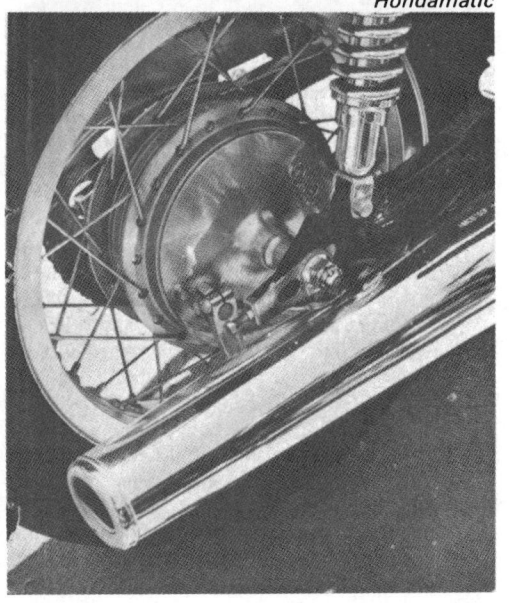

Hondamatic

FRONT FORKS

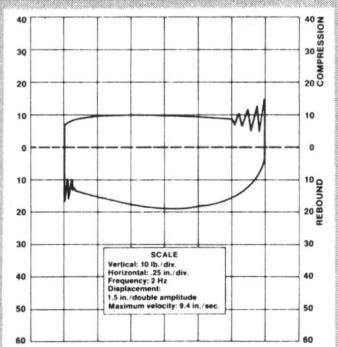

SCALE
Vertical: 10 lb./div.
Horizontal: .25 in./div.
Frequency: 2 Hz
Displacement:
1.5 in./double amplitude
Maximum velocity: 9.4 in./sec.

Description: Showa fork, HD-315 oil
Fork travel, in.: 5.25
Spring rate, lb./in.: 40
Compression damping force, lb.: 10
Rebound damping force, lb.: 20
Static seal friction, lb.: 16

Remarks (CB750F): Unlike earlier 750s, the F uses a conventional damper rod assembly to control compression and rebound damping. Compression damping is excellent. Rebound is too light for the 40-lb. spring. The ride is very harsh for two reasons: 1. The stiff spring, which is preloaded .75 in. 2. Excessive static seal friction. Spring replacement and some Yamaha fork seals would work wonders. Both S&W and Number One Products make appropriate springs. Yamaha 500 or 750 seals should work.

Remarks (CB750A): Specifications on the Automatic are identical to the F version's, so rebound damping is again light. In order to compensate for additional machine weight, however, a longer 40-lb. spring was installed to increase preload. The net result is that it takes a 100-lb. force to make this fork react vs. a 70-lb. force for the F. Needless to say, this bike needs a spring change even worse than the F. A seal change will also help considerably. The same units suggested for the F will work here.

REAR SHOCKS

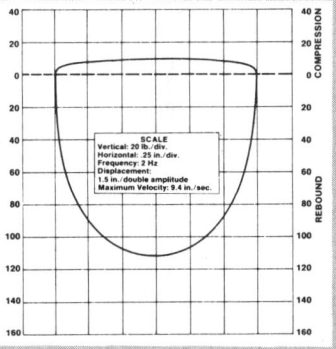

SCALE
Vertical: 20 lb./div.
Horizontal: .25 in./div.
Frequency: 2 Hz
Displacement:
1.5 in./double amplitude
Maximum Velocity: 9.4 in./sec.

Description: Honda 750 shock, non-rebuidable
Shock travel, in.: 3.25
Wheel travel, in.: 4.0
Spring rate, lb./in.: 100
Compression damping force, lb.: 8
Rebound damping force, lb.: 112

Remarks (CB750F): Compression and rebound damping are excellent, but these are not good shocks for fast riding because of their limited oil capacity and high rate of fade. Ride is harsh for solo riding because the spring is preloaded .75 in. For riding two-up or with luggage, this combination of spring and preload is perfect. Better would be a 110-lb. spring with just enough preload to put pressure on the spring clip. This would allow a softer initial ride, as it would require only 110 lb. to move the unit the first inch, as opposed to 175 lb. for the preloaded stock spring. With this setup solo riders will not have to suffer.

Remarks (CB750A): Shocks on the Automatic differ cosmetically from those on the F (they have a chrome spring cover), but are the same internally. Spring rate is also identical, but the Automatic's springs are preloaded twice as much. The result is an exceptionally rough ride, especially on concrete surface streets or freeways. Spring replacement like that suggested for the F is the single best thing you can do.

Tests performed at Number One Products

Honda Stick versus Automatic
CB750F

The starting procedure is the same as for any other Honda, with some slight differences. For one, there is that parking brake we mentioned earlier. To operate it, one must pull out a two-piece knob mounted under the left rear portion of the fuel tank behind the on/off/reserve fuel petcock. It snaps in place and if your foot is depressing the brake pedal, a ratcheting device will hold the rear brake shoes in a locked position. This enables the machine to be parked on an incline without rolling away, because, as you remember, this one can't be clicked into a gear that will keep it from moving. One reason is that there is a safety device built into the sidestand in the form of linkage that slips the transmission into neutral any time the stand is lowered. And the other reason is that the fluid coupling of the transmission won't prevent the bike from moving. To release the brake, a push on the center button of the knob and a step on the brake pedal will do the deed. The parking brake warning light lets you know when the unit is operating.

Once the engine is started (and it will take some fiddling with the throttle and choke because this is the coldest-blooded Honda ever), there is no way anyone can come along and move the lever into gear while the bike is on the sidestand and have it take off and wind up in a heap. The linkage device built into the stand prevents such accidents. It also keeps the rider from taking off with

List price $2186	Front fork rake angle, degrees 28
Suspension, front . . . . .telescopic fork	Trail, in. 4.5
Suspension, rear . . . . . .swinging arm	Curb weight (w/half-tank fuel), lb.
Tire, front 3.25-19	. . . . .525.5
Tire, rear 4.00-18	Weight bias, front/rear, percent .46/54
Brake, front, eff. dia. x width, in.	Test weight (fuel and rider), lb. . . .685
. . . . .10.71 x 1.625	Mileage at completion of test . . .3138
Brake, rear, eff. dia. x width, in.	Engine rpm @ 60 mph 4305
. . . . .10.71 x 1.625	Piston speed (@ 8500 rpm), ft./min.
Total brake swept area, sq. in. .109.13	3513
Brake loading, lb./sq. in. (160-lb. rider)	Lb./hp (160-lb. rider) . . . . .N.A.
. . . . .6.23	Fuel consumption, mpg 39
Engine, type . . .sohc four-stroke Four	Speedometer error:
Bore x stroke, in., mm	50 mph indicated, actually 48
. . . . .2.40 x 2.48; 61.0 x 63.0	60 mph indicated, actually 57
Piston displacement, cu. in., cc	70 mph indicated, actually 67
. . . . .44.9; 736	Braking distance:
Compression ratio 9.2:1	from 30 mph, ft. 32
Claimed bhp @ rpm . . . . .N.A.	from 60 mph, ft. 129
Claimed torque @ rpm, 1 lb.-ft. . .N.A.	Acceleration, zero to:
Carburetion . . . .(4) 28mm Keihin	60 mph, sec. 7.6
Ignition* . . . . .battery and coil	Standing one-quarter mile, sec. .13.52
Oil system . . . . .dry sump	terminal speed, mph 97.61
Oil capacity, pt. 7.4	Top speed (actual @ 7923 rpm) mph
Fuel capacity, U.S. gal. 4.8	110
Recommended fuel . . . . . . .premium	
Starting system	
. . . . .electric; kick, folding crank	
Lighting system . . . . .alternator	
Air filtration . . . . .treated paper	
Clutch . . . . .wet, multi-disc	
Primary drive . . . . . . .single-row chain	
Final drive . . . .#530 single-row chain	
Gear ratios, overall:1	
5th 5.43	
4th 6.35	
3rd 7.47	
2nd 9.57	
1st 14.01	
Wheelbase, in. 59.5	
Seat height, in. 33.0	
Seat width, in. 9.75	
Handlebar width, in. 31.5	
Footpeg height, in. 12.5	
Ground clearance, in. 5.0	

ACCELERATION / ENGINE AND ROAD SPEEDS / RPM X 100

Super Sport

the sidestand in the down position. Moreover, there is an interlock switch that prevents the starter from turning over unless the machine is in neutral.

First-timers on the Automatic will instinctively step down on the gear change lever to engage the transmission, since that's where first gear is on the majority of conventional motorcycles. But on this one that's where neutral is. Low is one notch up, drive one notch farther. We stated earlier that the transmission is not a true automatic . . . and it isn't. Start out in low and the bike will remain in low until the engine runs out of revs, or until the rider shifts to drive. Start out in drive and it will remain in drive, while an internal change in ratio is taking place with the torque converter. (See the accompanying technical sidebar for an explanation of how the Hondamatic works).

CB750A

List Price	$2194
Suspension, front	telescopic fork
Suspension, rear	swinging arm
Tire, front	3.50-19
Tire, rear	4.50-17
Brake, front, eff. dia. x width, in.	10.71 x 1.625
Brake, rear, eff. dia. x width, in.	7.1 x 1.6
Total brake swept area, sq. in.	90.24
Brake loading, lb./sq. in. (160-lb. rider)	7.94
Engine, type	sohc four-stroke Four
Bore x stroke, in., mm	2.40 x 2.48; 61.0 x 63.0
Piston displacement, cu. in., cc	44.9; 736
Compression ratio	8.6:1
Claimed bhp @ rpm	N.A.
Claimed torque @ rpm, lb.-ft.	N.A.
Carburetion	(4) 24mm Keihin
Ignition	battery and coil
Oil system	wet sump
Oil Capacity, pt.	11.6
Fuel capacity, U.S. gal.	5.1
Recommended fuel	premium
Starting system	electric; emergency kick
Lighting system	alternator
Air filtration	treated paper
Clutch	none, hydraulic torque convertor
Primary drive	Morse Hy-Vol chain
Final drive	#530 Single-row chain
Gear ratios, overall:1	
High	5.80
Low	8.63
Wheelbase, in.	58.0
Seat height, in.	33.0
Seat width, in.	10.5
Handlebar width, in.	31.5
Footpeg height, in.	13.0
Ground clearance, in.	6.0
Front fork rake angle, degrees	28
Trail, in.	4.5
Curb weight (w/half-tank fuel), lb	557

Weight bias, front/rear, percent	45.4/54.6
Test weight (fuel and rider), lb.	717
Mileage at completion of test	4237

PERFORMANCE

Engine rpm @ 60 mph	4560
Piston speed (@ 8500 rpm), ft./min.	3513
Fuel consumption, mpg	43
Speedometer error:	
50 mph indicated, actually	47
60 mph indicated, actually	58
70 mph indicated, actually	67
Braking distance:	
from 30 mph, ft.	31
from 60 mph, ft.	129
Acceleration, zero to:	
60 mph, sec.	10.0
Standing one-quarter mile, sec.	15.90
terminal speed, mph	86.34
Top speed (actual @ 7361 rpm) mph	97

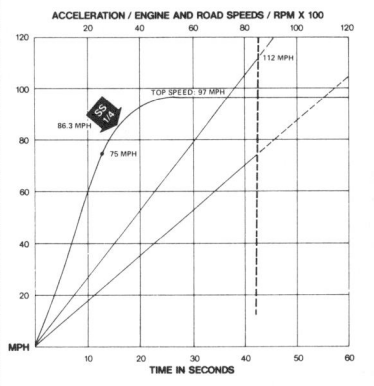

Hondamatic

CATEGORY SIX
QUARTER-MILE
Hondamatic	15.90 sec./86.34 mph
Super Sport	13.52 sec./97.61 mph

In essence, what this automation does is free the rider from thinking about and worrying about the gears. He can now concentrate on the traffic and surroundings. This can benefit an experienced rider as well as a green one who has his hands full enough without worrying about the gears.

We mentioned the cold-blooded nature of the beast, which requires longer than normal warmup and lots of choke before the engine will stay alive. Part of the reason is the change to a wet-sump engine, which means there's quite a lot of oil in the lower end to be churned and warmed. One can almost sense when the engine is finally at normal operating temperature, because it suddenly seems to *want* to run.

Carburetion is radically different from that of the 750F. Instead of the 28mm Keihin slide/needle carbs found on the F, Honda has equipped the A with 24mm units. With the 28s there is a rather pronounced flat spot just off of idle when the throttle is opened a significant degree. On a clutch bike it makes no difference because the clutch is slipped when starting off and the peculiarity doesn't make itself known. On the Automatic, however, it would be a definite aggravation, so an accelerator pump system has been designed in to fill up the flat spot.

There's only one pump—on the number two carb—which connects up to the others with hoses and passages. When the throttle is opened up at any point, each carburetor gets an extra dose of fuel to wipe out the flat spot. It works, but that doesn't mean that the carbs are completely dialed in.

We discovered that while cruising at a steady speed at which there is little or no throttle load, the engine surges and stumbles

CATEGORY SEVEN
TOP SPEED

Hondamatic	97 mph
Super Sport	110 mph

Hondamatic

Honda Stick versus Automatic

enough to be disconcerting. It almost feels as though the bike is running out of fuel and the time has come to switch to reserve. Upon returning our machine to Honda for a remedy, it was discovered that the problem is caused by an overly lean condition in jetting that can't really be corrected completely. Some machines have the problem and some don't, but Honda has yet to eliminate the trouble spot entirely. At another point our machine quit completely. This time the problem was traced to a faulty fuel petcock that would only flow fuel when the bike was leaned to one side or the other.

The only other annoyance that occurred was squealing front brakes on both bikes, the 750F in particular. Since we've never before experienced Honda discs that squealed so badly, we suspect that brake pad composition may have been altered this year. Whatever the cause, it was most irritating.

The choice between the 750F and the 750A is going to be a difficult one for most people. Though they have many traits in common, they are really very different motorcycles. The Automatic allows a rider new freedom and has distinct advantages for the motorcyclist who spends a lot of time in heavy traffic or wet weather. Performance suffers, but the Honda 750A won't have to take a back seat to many four-wheelers. And once both machines are underway at highway speeds, differences in acceleration are not nearly so pronounced.

A rider who enjoys snaking through the

CATEGORY EIGHT BRAKING

60-0 mph	
Hondamatic	129 ft.
Super Sport	129 ft.

30-0 mph	
Hondamatic	31 ft.
Super Sport	32 ft.

mountains or back roads will find the Hondamatic somewhat limiting, but the situation reverses itself when towns approach and traffic becomes a big part of the scene. We absolutely loved the 750A in Los Angeles' rush-hour freeway traffic; its low-speed handling ease and lack of clutch really shone through in this application.

There are theories popping about that the Hondamatic will bring into motorcycling a lot of people who never would have trespassed otherwise. We think that will be true only to a very limited degree. It is more likely that newcomers will be put off by a 750cc motorcycle that weighs nearly 550 pounds, and continue to learn to ride on something smaller, lighter and less intimidating. On the other hand, those who have spent considerable time on two wheels will look forward to the automation part of it and not be bothered by the bulk.

We know the 750A will be a tremendous success and feel that the foundation of that success will be based on sales to older, more

Hondamatic:

By Fernando Belair

HONDA'S AUTOMATIC is not, in the true sense of the word, an automatic. Rather, it is a semi-automatic, very similar in performance to that of the first Volkswagen Automatic. The rider selects either a low or a high ratio and the torque converter takes care of the power delivery in the manner that provides the best possible acceleration. Still, the Hondamatic is a very intriguing animal. We thus decided to take a look inside one to see exactly how it works.

The Automatic's shift-mechanism is merely a three-position hydraulic valve. The left splined shaft is for the automatic neutral locater that is operated by an arm attached to the descending sidestand. The central splined shaft is the actual shift shaft. The splined shaft at the lower right is for the emergency kickstart pedal that is stored beneath the seat.

Beneath the shift mechanism are two trochoidal pumps. Both of them draw through the filtered scavenger from the wet sump. One pump is used to feed the engine and lubricate the mainshaft

and output shaft bearings. The other pump is slightly wider and is purely a pressure pump whose job it is to fill the torque converter and the particular pressure-activated clutch selected through the shift mechanism. Engine pressure is normally about 70 psi, while the pressure in the torque converter and clutches can be as high as 180 psi.

(Note: In this photo the bottom and left sides of the engine are in view).

With the shifter mechanism and oil pumps out of the way, the oil passages can be seen near the protruding kickstart shaft. Oil is drawn through one of these tube-like passages and then pressure-fed back through the others to the maze-like galleys at the bottom of the engine. The galley-filled plate opposing the galleys cast into the crankcase directs the oil to either the engine or the torque converter and clutches, depending upon the galley. Before reaching the torque converter, the high-pressure oil passes a relief valve. The valve also contains a relief override, the spring for which is partially visible in the photo.

The high-pressure oil travels through cast-in passageways until it arrives at the exposed outer plate. As can be seen, five of the seven holes are cut all the way through and are used for bolts that secure the plate. The other holes are oil passageways. The top one receives the oil and directs it to the center of the hollow shaft from which the torque converter gets filled. The left hole is a return hole that is blocked by a lightly sprung dowel in order to prevent the torque converter from draining when the engine is in neutral and no transmission pressure is being created. When low gear is selected, the oil pressure forces circulation in the torque converter for the purpose of cooling. As fresher oil is fed in, the existing oil drains past minute semi-circular cutouts on the inner surface of the bushing that rides over the visible splined shaft. This pressurized oil causes the dowel to recede and allow the oil to pass back into the sump.

Photography: Fernando Belair

CB750A PARTS PRICING

Warranty	N.A.
Major Tuneup	N.A.
Air Filter Element	$9.90
Rear Tire (standard)	24.40
Drive Chain (standard)	45.20
Headlight Bulb or Sealed Beam	9.50
Taillight Bulb	74
Turn Indicator Bulbs	74
Battery	55.30
Throttle Cables, ea.	6.60
Ignition Parts	
Points	3.10
Condenser	4.30
High Tension Coil	32.60

CB750F PARTS PRICING

Warranty	N.A.
Major Tuneup	N.A.
Air Filter Element	$9.90
Rear Tire (standard)	24.40
Drive Chain (standard)	43.20
Headlight Bulb or Sealed Beam	9.50
Taillight Bulb	74
Turn Indicator Bulbs	74
Battery	39.30
Clutch Cables	3.70
Throttle Cables, ea.	7.10
Ignition Parts	
Points	3.10
Condenser	4.30
High Tension Coil	32.60

experienced riders. The Super Sport, meanwhile, will continue to appeal to riders who like snappy performance and the image the 750F carries. It is a distinct possibility that in the future Honda will broaden its Hondamatic's horizons by coupling up the torque converter to mid-sized machines, thereby grabbing the people who don't feel like contending with a large motorcycle. There is quite a difference between the 750A and the 750F, and anyone at all interested in motorcycles owes it to himself to approach the 750 Automatic with an open mind. It deserves all the attention it will get. ◨

CATEGORY NINE
PASSING
40-60 mph

Hondamatic	3.8 sec.
Super Sport	3.0 sec.

60-80 mph

Hondamatic	5.4 sec.
Super Sport	3.7 sec.

How it works

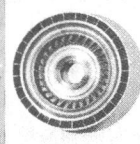  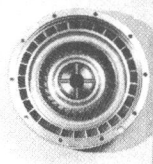

Honda's torque converter consists of three basic parts and is very much like torque converters on automatic automobile transmissions. The three parts are the pump (left) the stator (center) and the turbine (right). As you can see by the varying sizes of the individual center holes, each rides on a different concentric shaft. The pump is the only part of the engine that is directly driven by the engine. As the engine is revved, the pump's vanes throw oil at the turbine's vanes, rotating the turbine and the center shaft of the concentric shafts. It is on this shaft that the low-gear clutch rides. The turbine's vanes receive the high-speed oil and send it, through its central vanes, back at the pump. Unfortunately, at this point the returning oil is exerting force in the opposite direction of the pump's revolutions. This is where the stator comes in.

The stator is the smaller vaned device that rides on the mid-sized concentric shaft. It is equipped with a one-way clutch that allows it to spin only in the same direction as the pump and turbine. As long as the differences in speed between the engine-driven pump and the gear-driving turbine are great enough to keep the stator pressed back against the clutch's lock, the turbine just sits there, its vanes altering the direction of the turbine's returning oil so that it can be picked up once again by the pump and reused.

Since oil that has passed through the stator is now traveling in a direction favoring the pump, the oil's forces act to increase the torque force exerted by the pump on the turbine. Therefore the stator acts as a torque multiplier.

In addition, the stator's shaft is fitted with an arm that rides directly above the transmission relief override. When the oil pressure against the stator is great enough, such as under hard acceleration, the arm activates the relief valve override and pressure in the torque converter increases, improving oil flow for better cooling.

As the speed of the gear-driving turbine begins to match that of the engine-driven pump, a simple fluid coupling takes place with the stator now spinning merrily along.

Now that we have power to the mainshaft, we have to get it to the gears. This is controlled by the shift mechanism. It opens valves that direct the high-pressure oil to the clutches. This oil presses against steel pistons that in turn press against the clutch plates, thus transmitting the power to the gears, then to the output shaft and summarily to the rear wheel. Select the high ratio and the oil is then fed to the second or rearmost clutch, engaging the taller drive ratio. As can be seen in the photo, there are no sliding gears in this transmission, no shift plate, shift forks or dogged gears. Everything operates hydraulically. The O-ringed hole on each clutch collar is where the clutch actuating oil enters.

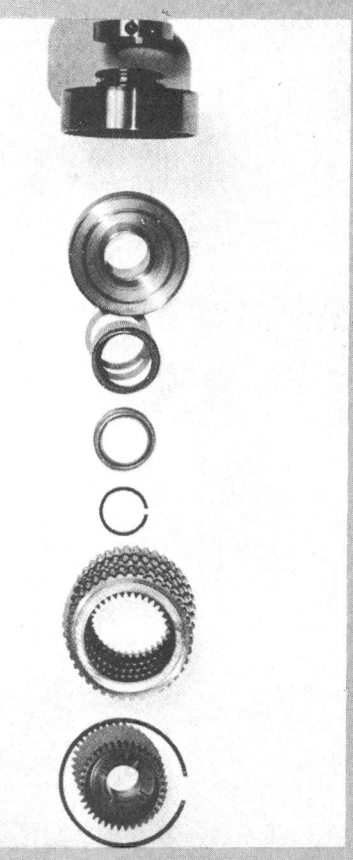

A disassembled clutch reveals all of the internal working parts. From top to bottom they are the hub's bearing/collar, the clutch hub, piston, piston return spring, retaining collar, snap ring, clutch plates, the gear and drive hub and the plate-retaining snap ring.

OLD SOLDIERS NEVER DIE

THERE WAS a bit of doubt about this road test; after all, *everyone* has ridden a Honda 750 Four haven't they? Bennett Honda still wanted us to test it. But the design's eight years old and practically untouched!

"True," the man said, "but time hasn't hurt it and the price has gone down while everything else has gone up. Test it. See if you reckon the low price outweighs the age."

Okay. They still make Royal Enfield Bullets in India, and now they're exported to Britain where they're selling like hot cakes because they're so cheap. If a bike that began life in 1936 can sell well in 1977, why can't a bike that knocked the world on its ear eight years ago do a similar trick?

So we test the K6, straight after three weeks on a Z1000. The first ride didn't give favorable impressions; it didn't even bring back any fond memories! Felt small after the Z1000 — nothing up ahead of the rider. The headlight and gear were down out of sight like a "small" bike. And the design's age showed too. Nothing concrete, it just lacked the feeling of rigidity and solidness which the best Japanese bikes, the Z1000, GS750 Suzuki, Yamaha RD 400 and CB400 Honda, give on the first ride.

But the engine felt — and looked — magnificent. The brakes felt pitiful after the Z1000's. The ignition switch is still under the left front side of the tank . . . Nothing has changed. When facing the usual cross-examination in the office there was nothing to do but shrug, wait a bit and say "beautiful engine".

And there's no arguing with that. The engine is beautifully put together and is a lot better protected against corrosion than most Japanese bikes. And it delivers the power smoothly and progressively. We've heard it called peaky, but that just ain't right. It's not the most powerful, but it does deliver progressively and has an almost turbine feel as it spins over 4000rpm, accelerating hard.

An advantage of not having tyre-shredding power is smoothness — the K6 doesn't suffer from driveline snatch as much as the big Kawas and a couple of pillion passengers commented that this was a big plus after the Z1000.

With the Z, when moving from rest and changing gears the rider notices a slight lurch as the power takes up; apparently to a pillion this feels like a heavy push in the chest, for that I'm-going-over-the-back-omigawd feeling. The K6 scored much better here.

Then as the first week passed and the K6 was ridden into and around the city,

with a few trips to the outer suburbs, the reasons for the first pre-K1 model's success became more and more apparent, and also explained why the K6 was still selling well — if not spectacularly — alongside the model which was to have replaced it, the 750 F1.

Let's face it, the F1 was a better motorcycle; it had more power, more suitable gearing, better handling and suspension. The styling wasn't a hit (we reckon because of the seat tail-piece which had too much overhang, making the seat look elongated and high) and the four-into-one exhaust, which was not only bulky and ugly, it limited cornering clearance on right handers. The bike bombed badly in the US and dealers started screaming for "the good ole Four", so Honda simply put the K6 back into production.

In Australia the F1 fared a bit better, even though it sold side-by-side with the K6 from its release (after the experience in the US, it was no longer labelled as a replacement model). But as people

Differences between the original 1969 Honda (right) and the latest K6 are minimal; chromed headlight bracket and bigger reflectors, sidecovers and airbox, tail light, seat and disc caliper. The K6 is a little quieter and is also down slightly on power.

The Honda Four has been battling on for eight years with no significant updates to the mechanicals, or even styling. Gradually the market has overtaken it, yet the Four is still being produced and is selling at bargain prices. Here's how it shapes up in 1977.

road test

realised the F1 was actually a better bike which missed out in a couple of areas, sales picked up, right until the release of the bike the F1 should have been in the first place, the F2 which comes complete with a decent exhaust, trick wheels and '77 styling.

But we digress. We're testing the bike that all these things developed from. And that's one of the Four's big strong points; it doesn't have any tricks — it's solid, functional, no tinsel. It also has the muted growl exhaust note which sold so many in the early days. There's also the Four's reputation for reliability and toughness . . .

In the early days of our test the Four impressed with its city manners; the steering is light and manageable at speeds up to about 80km/h, and at trickle speeds is more nimble than a lot of lighter bikes because the steep forks (27 degrees rake, 95mm trail) compensate so well for the bike's 218kg dry weight. It makes the Four easy to ride, particularly for novices, and for experienced hands the bike can be flicked about with confidence from the first ride.

After the city running the K6 was taken for a few one-day rides — to Bathurst and back to Sydney, up the coast to the Entrance, and down to Kiama. That's where the real riding started.

First the bad bits: Like the first Four, the stability drops off as speed rises. Running at 150km/h plus for long stretches gave a lot of wobbles, particularly when the rider shifted position or eased off the throttle.

The K6 is also sensitive to road surfaces — a bad thing on NSW roads! — and this leads to snaking and the occasional heavy weave at high speeds.

Suspension might have been uprated since the first Four, but not so you'd notice these days; the rear units are dreadful — under-damped and nowhere near stiff enough. They show how much the real 1977 Japanese bikes' rear units have improved. Into a typical NSW country road 80km/h corner at about 120km/h the K6 was a handful when you hit the bumps. Because of the soft rear end the bike doesn't so much scrape the centre stand as bash it, leading to sudden, hairy hops across the road. The K6 is great in the suburban streets and a good medium speed cruiser but it isn't in the same league as the 1977 Japanese big bores, let alone the Europeans, for suspension and high speed manners.

The front forks were better than we remembered on the first Four, with good damping for all but small high frequency ripples and expansion strips on concrete roads, which gave a thump and a mild jar to the rider's arms.

Comfort for solo riding is good up to 100km/h but over that the high handlebars force the rider to move back on the seat to give himself a chance of hanging on and this places the feet too far forward for comfort. BMW touring bars or flat bars cure this, though the footpegs could still be moved rearward about 30mm. Gear changes were smooth, particularly if the engine was on the boil, but the long shift lever gave a few false neutrals unless it was given a firm prod.

The brakes on the K6 are unchanged from the early models', apart from the addition of a water guard which supposedly stops water running down the fork leg onto the disc. Didn't seem to make much difference; when it rained the disc got wet and didn't work initially just like any Japanese disc.

The front disc also lacked feel and power compared to the Kawasaki Z1000's dual set-up, but the good thing for less experienced riders is that it's impossible to lock on dry, hard surfaces. Braking distances were average at 39 metres from 100km/h, but were surprisingly good considering the impression the brakes gave during the stopping; we expected maybe another five metres on that because of the complete lack of drama. It's a similar deal to the suspension and stability — great at low speed and for the average rider because of the ease of operation, but lacking during hard charging for the speed freaks.

The rear brake is good for a 180mm single leading shoe unit, with a lot of feel and 'no vices for the unwary. But the non-floating backing plate still transmits suspension movement through the brake pedal — a weird feeling.

On the auxiliaries side, the audible blinkers are just like all the rest — a pain in the ear which we're sure causes owners who haven't disconnected them to use the blinkers less than they should in traffic. Instruments are unchanged — excellent.

And the headlight ... what headlight? Let us tell you about Editor Brown's midnight run along the Bell Line of Road from Lithgow to Sydney, chasing photographer Bill Forsyth's hot Civic wagon towing three trail bikes.

The Civic was pulling a consistent 140km/h, though it died a bit on hills, and there was no way Brown could keep up when the Civic got out of eyesight.

It got away from the Four a few times when the bike was stuck behind traffic on some of the twisty bits, and once when Brown hit a largish oil slick at Kurrajong Heights and after a quick slip across the road to the shoulder, the speed was held down for a while. Y'see

the thing is, you can't see! Both high and low beam are 45W, and are pathetic for anything but night city riding, and then with one hand on the high beam flasher. On the run from Lithgow the bike could have given the speed and usual buzz the road produces, but not when the lights don't let you see dark patches of oil — or anything else for that matter — until it's too late.

While the Australian Design Regulations are doing a wonderful job of ensuring we don't buy bikes with plastic brake hoses, and that bikes don't make noise, a lot more lives would be saved if they demanded that headlights match a bike's performance. 'Nuff said.

For performance, the K6 is still the Four the bike world has come to know and ... er, see so many of (which is at least popularity, if not love). The clutch is typical Honda; light with quick take-up which requires a delicate left hand for fast standing starts. But the acceleration runs were still no sweat, with the K6 returning consistent times in the low 13s. First run gave a 13.8 second and by the third it was 13.3, which held for the next three passes. Maximum speed was spot on 190km/h, which the speedo indicated as a shade under 200.

On the trips the engine was perfectly

smooth below 6000rpm, but buzzed slightly above that; we couldn't comment on whether it affected comfort, because anywhere near 6000rpm in fifth the rider was flapping like a sail off the high handlebars — comfort was just a memory over 120km/h. Another comfort point was the handgrips, which can only be called rotten. They left more callusses and blisters after one day of riding than a week of full-on bush riding! The throttle was also too stiff (see, nothing's changed) because of the two cable system.

So the Four is still very much the Four; it's solid as a rock, reliable and easy to ride — if you don't push it reasonably hard. For a 120km/h interstate cruiser-cum-outer suburbs commuter, it's fine.

And then there's the $1959 pricetag, which like the man from Bennett Honda said, makes it bloody good value in 1977 because even though the bike doesn't operate with the finesse and poise of the best of the new blasters, it operates well enough for sane riding under most Australian conditions, and the engine is still superb. That's one area where it does match the newies for quality of performance, if not outright muscle.

*

SPECIFICATIONS

MAKE	HONDA
MODEL	CB750 K6
PRICE	$1959
WARRANTY	6 mths/10,000 km

ENGINE: Air-cooled, transversely mounted four-cylinder four-stroke. Chain driven single overhead cam. One piece crank riding on plain bearings.

Bore x stroke	61 x 63 mm
Capacity	736 cm^3
Compression ratio	9.0:1
Lubrication	Dry sump, high pressure system
Carburetion	Mikuni 28 mm (x4)
Air filter	Dry pleated paper
Ignition	Battery/coil
Starting system	Electric or kick

TRANSMISSION: Double row chain primary drive. Wet multi-plate clutch, five speed constant mesh gearbox. Left side change one down four up. Final drive; spur gear, output shaft and chain.

RATIOS: (Overall:1)

1st	13.29
2nd	9.08
3rd	7.09
4th	5.83
5th	4.99
Primary reduction	1.708:1
Secondary reduction	2.667:1

FRAME: Welded tubular steel full duplex cradle.

SUSPENSION:

Front: Telescopic forks, oil damped coil springs. 100 mm travel, 27 degrees rake, 95 mm trail.

Rear: Pivoted fork, twin spring/damper units with five preload positions. 75 mm travel.

WHEELS, TYRES AND BRAKES:

Front: Spoked steel rim, 3.25H x 19 tyre, 295 mm steel disc, single piston pivoted hydraulic caliper.

Rear: Spoked steel rim, 4.00H x 18 tyre, 180 mm sls drum brake.

CAPACITIES:

Fuel tank	17 litres (inc 5 litre reserve)
Engine oil	3.5 litres

DIMENSIONS:

Dry weight	218 kg
Wheelbase	1455 mm
Overall length	2175 mm
Overall width	870 mm
Seat height	800 mm
Ground clearance	135 mm

PERFORMANCE

STANDING 400 METRES	13.3 seconds
MAXIMUM SPEED	190 km/h

FUEL CONSUMPTION:

Overall	15.3 km/l (43 mpg)
High speed	14.6 km/l (41 mpg)
Cruising	17.65 km/l (49.7 mpg)

BRAKING:

From 50 km/h	8.6 m
From 100 km/h	39 m

HOW DO THE FINER POINTS SCORE
(Out of 10)

Instrumentation	9
Comfort	8
Tool kit	6
Quality of finish	8
Vibration	8
Lighting	6
Positioning of controls	7
Suspension	6
Stability (100 km/h plus)	7
Stability (to 80 km/h)	9
Engine performance	9

TEST BIKE SUPPLIED BY: Bennett Honda Pty Ltd, Ralph St, Alexandria, NSW.

1. With the cam-cover off, turn engine to close all valves on one side, then undo rocker shaft . . .

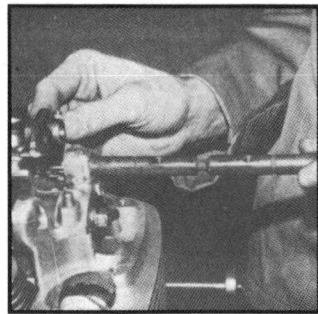

2. . . . bolts and don't get them muddled up. Shafts then push out. Check for wear as usual.

3. Camshaft bearing caps and carriers are already marked: not a common wear-point.

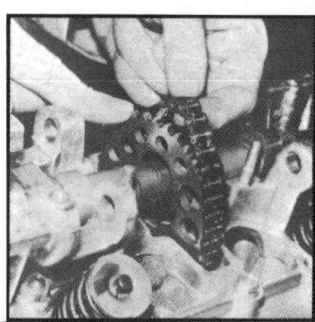

4. With all the rockers out, release cam sprocket and chain, and pull camshaft out through sprocket.

Engine Rebuild series

HONDA 750-FOUR

WHEN people ask us whether a Honda 750 four is a practical proposition for a kitchen-table stripdown, we never know quite what to say. It sounds silly to come back with: "Yes, if you're Goddamn careful" — but that, quite simply, is the case. On one hand the device is exquisitely designed and comes apart like a Meccano set — but on the other, it is also a fact that there is an awful lot of it, and that awful lot includes a great many small details which the fumble-fingered could make a nasty mess of.

So perhaps we should put it this way: if you're the type who always has a nut and two washers left over after a rebuild, then forget it — but if you're one stage better than that, then go ahead but be careful. And above all, as you dismantle it, label everything . . .

The importance of labelling rears it's head right at the start, as soon as you have the cam-cover off. You turn the crank-shaft until all four valves on one side of the engine are closed (very important, that, to relieve the stresses) and then set about undoing the bolts securing the rocker shafts on that side. Each shaft will have one or three bolts, depending on the age of the engine — and it is important not to muddle up these bolts or their washers with others in the vicinity, because some of them

will be high-tensile and some of them not. In fact, all Honda bolts are stamped with either a 9, which means high-tensile, an 11, which means high shear-resistance, or an 8, which is the ordinary common or garden bolt-strength bolt: the golden rule, obviously, is not to put 'em back in the wrong 'oles.

Anyway, with the bolts out, the rockers should be marked to show their positions, and then the shafts pushed out. Check the shafts for wear ridges and the rockers themselves for pad and bearing wear in the usual way. If you need to replace a set of early-type rocker shafts (single bolt fixing) you'll probably find you can't get them: in that case you get the later shafts along with a new pair of cam-carriers

to match.

With the rocker gear removed on both sides, the next step is to remove the cam bearing caps. These already have their positions marked (see pic). The cam chain tensioner is removed next, and then the two camshaft sprocket bolts can be undone, the chain picked off the sprocket, and the camshaft wiggled out. Make the usual checks for scoring on both cam lobes and bearing surfaces.

Next items off are the cam carriers — and here, take careful note of the position of the little oil metering valves (see pic), the various rubber seals, and the locating dowels. (Honda locating dowels, as a rule, are **not** fixed into their various casings, as they are in most engines: it is

more than possible to lose them.)

Next thing is to get the head off. Slacken the bolts progressively, from the outside inwards in the usual way, and again take note of all the little dowels and seals 'twixt head and barrels. Valve gear overhaul is conventional except that you **don't** reface Honda valves — if a little lapping-in with paste doesn't do the trick, you need a new valve — and you want to take care to ensure that the valve seats are the correct widths and no wider (see chart). Over-wide seatings in the head lead to incorrect seat-pressures and premature leaky valves — and the usual cause of over-wide seatings is some zealous soul persevering with the coarse grinding paste

5. Cam carriers lift off next. Note rubber bungs and the oil feed metering jet.

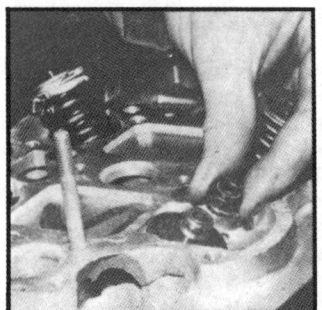

6. With head off, remove valves as usual. Seals (if any) only need replacing if they're brittle.

7. Valve seat width is important. (See text and chart.) Seats can be ground, but valves just lapped.

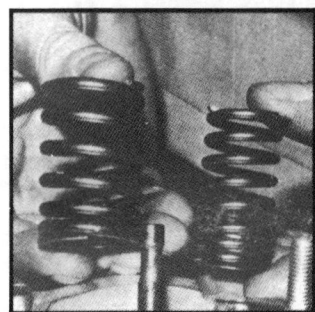

8. On re-assembly, fit the (new) valve springs with their tightest coils towards the head.

9. Number pistons. They may be arrowed for front, but anyway the front has 'double' valve pocket.

10. Remove engine-turning nut, points-plate complete, and then the auto-advance unit.

11. Undo the clutch spring bolts progressively to avoid distorting the lifting-plate.

12. Knock down lock-tab and undo centre-bolt with special spanner. Note order of clutch thrust washers.

when he really ought to be replacing the valve instead of trying to rescue it. If you *do* find you've got an over-wide seat, (beg pardon, madam), then take the head along to a switched-on Honda dealer: he should have valve seat top-and-interior cutters which will rectify the situation. You also ought to take the head to him if your valves have more than the permitted sideplay in the guides (see chart), since changing the guides calls for some very accurate reaming of the new ones.

The little rubber seals which you may or may not find on top of all or some of the guides (depending on the age of the engine) need only be replaced if they've gone hard and brittle. We would fit new valve springs as a matter of course: they go in with the closer-pitched coils towards the head.

With the tensioners out, the barrels can be lifted off — again, making a note of all the little dowels, etc. The bores must be checked with a micrometer, since Honda bores don't generally have the conventional telltale wear lip round their tops.

Next things to come out are the cam chain tensioners, both the strip-tensioner at the front and the jockey-wheel job. The chain itself should be replaced automatically at overhaul time

(along with the primary chains) but the tensioners practically never need renewing. Don't worry about the two grooves you'll find worn in the composition tensioner material: they get cut in the first few miles, and they don't mean a thing.

After that, you number and remove the pistons. If you're not planning a re-bore, don't forget to check the piston ring side-clearances in their grooves (see chart) — and whether you're having a re-bore or not, all new rings ought to have their end-gaps checked in the bores (see chart again). When you're fitting rings to pistons, note that the top ring is chrome, and both top and second rings have a tiny letter engraved on their top sides. The three-piece oil rings should be fitted with the gaps of each section staggered. And finally, always renew any gudgeon pin circlips which have been disturbed.

Turning now to the bottom end, the first things off are the points-plate and the ignition cam. If you have occasion to pull the cam out of the auto-advance, make sure it goes back in the correct way round. (See pic).

Next is the clutch. With the cover plate removed, undo the four lifting-plate screws progressively to avoid distorting the plate, then use the special cas-

tellated spanner to undo the centre nut. Take careful note of the spacer washers as you pull the clutch bits out: they not only have to go back in the right order when you come to the rebuild, but also the right way round. The exact details of them vary according to the age of the engine (the ones illustrated are the later pattern) but the right-way-round bit is important whatever pattern they are. The friction plates are measured for thickness and warpage in the usual way (chart again), and the springs should also be measured.

Turning to the underside of the engine now, the next thing off is the sump. Do not touch the round blanking-plug thing alongside same, because it doesn't do anything, and you can't get new seals for it.

Underneath the sump is the oil pump. This is removed — noting the dowels and rubber O rings — and can be dismantled for inspection. When you pull it apart, note the position of the dimples which you'll find on one face of each rotor element. They should all face the outer covers: The important thing is to put them back the same way round as they came out. The rotor lobe clearance and the outer rotor-to-casing clearance can be measured with feeler gauges — but more important than that,

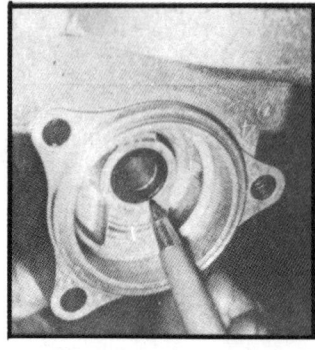

17. . . . . clearances, but you're mainly looking for obvious scoring. Renew rubber O rings and seals.

19. Next off is the positive-stop mechanism. Take careful note of the order of things here. Our late . . .

21. Next, remove the layshaft bearing housing plus bearing. Note rubber O ring (arrowed).

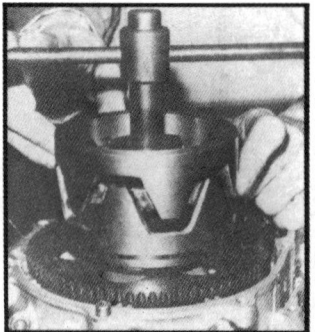

22. The alternator rotor needs a puller to free it, but leave it on unless you're renewing the crank.

23. Starter sprag clutch is in rotor. Slipping or screeching usually means just new springs.

24. With crankcase separated, lift out final drive unit. Later motors have bigger bearing. (See text.)

13. Next off after clutch is the sump-plate. Don't remove this bung: seals for it aren't obtainable.

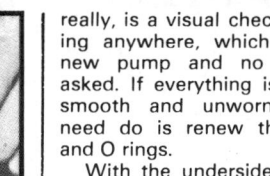

18. Remove circlip from gearlever shaft, disengage gearshift linkage, and slide shaft and linkage out.

20. ... model had the bits in this order (parts on the left at the bottom) but the details do vary.

14. This is how you measure primary chain wear, with depth gauge. We'd renew chains anyway at overhaul.

really, is a visual check for scoring anywhere, which means a new pump and no questions asked. If everything is nice and smooth and unworn, all you need do is renew the oilseals and O rings.

With the underside work out of the way, we can turn to the left hand side of the engine. With the rear side-plate removed, the first thing out is the gear shift arm and shaft, as a unit. Next is the selector drum stopper and all the other little gubbins which pivots on the same stud. The detail of this assembly varies according to the age of the unit, so the best thing we can say is take a very careful note of the order of things so you can put it all back the same way: our 'exploded' picture in the strip shows the order of things on the current models.

Anyway, the next step is to remove the layshaft bearing cover complete with layshaft end bearing, taking note of the wee rubber O ring 'twixt cover and casing.

After that, the generator cover can be taken off, complete with stator. If you want to get the rotor off the crankshaft you'll need a special puller (see pic) — but when it comes down to it, you don't actually have to get the rotor off in order to get the crankshaft out. The whole thing

15. Unbolt the oil pump, and note where all the little seals, etc, go. Dismantle pump and check for ...

— rotor and starter gear — can be left attached to the crankshaft unless you're going to have a new crank or you're having starter-engagement trouble. If you have got engagement trouble — either a screaming noise as the starter works or no connection between starter and engine at all — then the trouble will be in the three-roller sprag clutch on the inside of the rotor. Buy it a new set of springs (which ought to cost all of 5p) and perhaps a new roller or two if you're feeling generous, and all will be hunky-dory again.

With the generator thus dealt with — or not dealt with, as the case may be — the two halves of the crankcase can be split. This is achieved by undoing the eleven bolts on the top of the crankcase (working progressively from the outside inwards, of course), and then turning the engine downside up and doing likewise with the other 22 on the underside. The bottom crankcase half is then lifted away, leaving the clockwork in the top half.

Next, when you've finished staring in awe at all the cogs and things, is to lift away the final drive shaft as a unit (see pic). The final drive bearing — which, like all the other gearbox bearings in the main case, is located by a half-round circlip — was a bit prone to handing in it's dinner

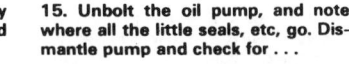

16. ... scoring and wear. Note pips (arrowed) which should be on outer lobe-faces. See chart for pump ...

pail on early 750's. It was later superseded by a larger bearing, (without a locator-ring), which solved the trouble — but reasonably enough, the larger bearing won't fit the earlier cases. So if your bike has the smaller bearing (like the one in the pic), we'd recommend replacing it almost as a matter of course during a high-mileage overhaul. (The rest of the cogbox bearings will very likely go on for ever: just make the usual check for roughness).

Next item out is the gearbox mainshaft, complete. Merely lift the whole thing, clutch, primary chain sprockets and all, and then pull the shaft out as per the pic. Make the usual check for chipped gear teeth, etc., but don't worry about the gears having a bit of rocking play on the shaft: they're meant to have a litle bit, so just look for any one gear having more rock than the others. The same applies to the layshaft gears. The fingers of the selector forks can be measured for wear (see chart) but they're not usually prone to it.

Which brings us to the crankshaft.

With the primary drive gubbins removed from the primary chains, the crank can be lifted out as a unit. Do not drop the thing on the deck as you will bend it. The rods can then be removed in the usual way, after

25. Lift clutch and final drive sprockets and withdraw the gearbox mainshaft. Unhitch final drive ...

26. ... from primary chains, and crankshaft can be lifted out. Renew chains at overhaul time.

27. Use a bolt to pull out selector fork shaft. Fork thickness should be checked: wear is unusual, though.

28. The selector drum can be removed after the neutral light switch has been taken out.

29. Pull out top gear dog, then layshaft set. Slight gearwheel rock on shafts is normal.

30. Main bearing housing grades are stamped on top crankcase. See text for details.

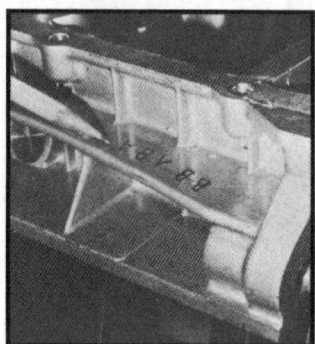

31. Crank journal grade codes are on centre crankweb, and rods are stamped with grades and weight.

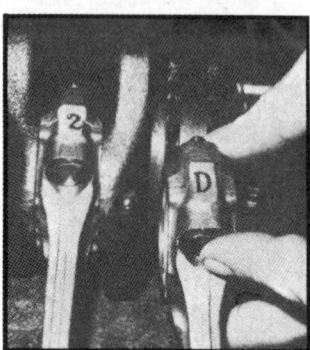

32. Rods are fitted with bearing-splits forward. You don't need new big end bolts.

you've marked them one to four. Honda do not approve of their crankshafts being re-ground — and accordingly, they do not provide undersized bearing shells. What they **do** provide is a very finely graded selection of colour-coded bearing shells (accurate to within .0004 of a millimetre!), which must be matched according to the crank journal size and also to the crankcase/conrod eye size. The latter two dimensions obviously don't change, and are to be found as code-stamps on the rods themselves and on the upper crankcase half (see pic). The journal diameters, equally obviously, **do** change as the crank wears, and therefore have to be measured. So what you need to do is have someone who's real good with a micrometer check all the journals, make a note of all the sizes — all nine of them — and then make a note of the crankcase and conrod stampings and take the whole lot along to a large and concientious Honda dealer. He will mutter into his beard, study his size-code tables, and produce the correct bearings. The rods and crank are then put back as per usual — with new chains, of course — making sure the big end bearing cut-outs are to the fornt.

Re-assembly is basically the reverse of the dismantling procedure. The crank, gears, etc go

back in, you check that the two locating dowels and the oilway ring (see pic) are in place, and then the two halves of the case are put up with a light smear of some thin non-setting jointing compound on the mating surfaces. (The rest of the joints have gaskets, and do not need compound.) Once you've got the two halves of the case bolted up — tightening gradually from the centre outwards, of course — check the gear selection by revolving the selector drum by hand while turning the output shaft to allow the gears to mesh. If you've screwed anything up, it's better to find out now than later ...

The next area requiring a word is replacing the rotor on the starter gear. You will find that as you lower the rotor, it seems reluctant to fit down on the inner clutch track. The answer to this is to revolve it clockwise: this pushes the sprag clutch rollers into the disengaged position, and the rotor drops down into place.

On the other side of the engine, the clutch has a few points to watch. The first is to make sure that you oil the plates copiously as they go in, otherwise they suffer a couple of years' worth of wear the first few times you engage them. The next is to note that on

later engines the outer-most friction plate has slightly different ears to all the rest. And thirdly, when you start bolting down the pressure plate, lift it up and jiggle it to make sure all the clutch centre splines are engaged as you wind the screws down (see pic). If you don't do this, it's possible for the splines to be end-on instead of properly engaged in the backplate. Finally, with the cover on, adjust the clutch by nipping up the adjusting screw, backing it off a quarter turn, and tightening the locknut.

Putting the top end up has no problems. If the pistons aren't arrowed to show the front, then the front is the edge with the double valve-pockets in it. The big rubber O rings round the base of each barrel don't need renewing unless they're dry and brittle, but you do have to remember the two locating dowels on the front outside studs and the two oilway rubber O rings on the inside rear ditto. (The oilways come up the stud holes in barrel and head, you'll understand.) The same dowels and O rings are repeated on the barrel-to-head joint, and then there's the metering valves and all the rubber grumminks that go in under the cam carriers. You know — the ones you carefully labelled like we said ...

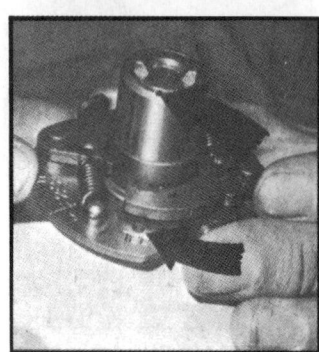

37. Ensure that these dimples (arrowed) line up if you disturb the auto-advance unit.

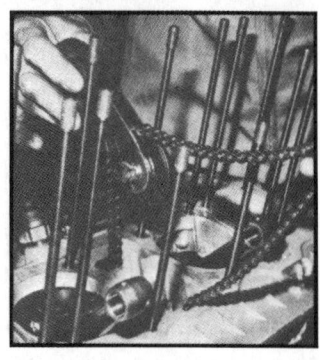

39. Lower tensioner into the block, and lean it rearwards while you lower the barrels on.

41. To set valve timing, turn engine to T (TDC) 1-4 position, then rotate cam (without rockers) ...

42. ... so that these marks are thus, with the cutaway in the end of the camshaft at the top.

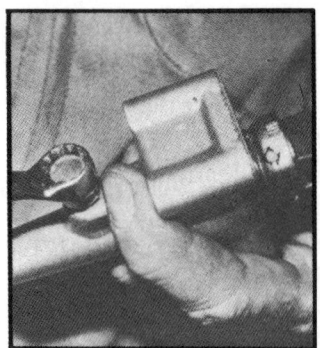

43. With valves timed, nip up cam chain tensioner spring fully compressed, then ...

44. ... bolt the unit in place, slacken the lockbolt for a moment, then re-tighten it and lock.

33. Re-assembly is reverse of dismantling. Use thin non-setting gasket goo on joint, and don't . . .

38. Putting back the cam chain tensioner is straightforward, but ensure shaft is this way up.

40. Don't forget the dowels and the oilway O rings before replacing barrels. Ditto on top of barrels.

34. . . . forget the oilway insert at the front of the case. Oil all parts liberally.

The valve timing is dead easy. You merely pop the auto advance unit into place, turn the engine so that the T 1-4 mark (top dead centre, cylinders one and four) lines up with the static point, and then turn the camshaft (sans rockers at this stage, of course) until the marks at the starboard end line .up as per the pic, with the notch at the top. You then fiddle around with the cam sprocket until you find the position for it where the chain is engaged and the bolt holes line up. After that you turn the engine so that one end of the camshaft has all the cams off-lift, replace the rocker gear and tighten all the bolts down on that side, and then repeat the performance on the other side. The cam chain is tensioned by the simple procedure of slackening the tensioner locking-bolt, pushing the plunger fully in by hand, re-tightening the lockbolt to hold it there, and then fitting the tensioner into place on the rear of the barrels: then rotate the engine past T 1/4, until the spring post on the advance plate passes the static mark. Slacken bolt, let the plunger spring out and re-tighten it in the usual way. All that's left is the ignition timing (see pics) and to set the valve clearance to .002 in (.05 mm) intake and .003 (.08) exhaust.

35. When putting up the clutch, get the top thrustwasher the right way round, belling outwards.

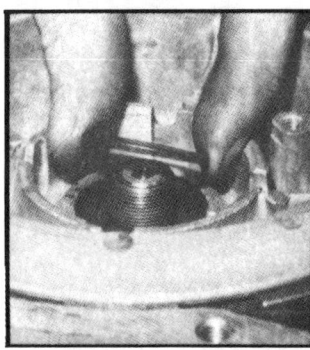

36. Lift the clutch centre to ensure the splines are engaged while progressively tightening bolts.

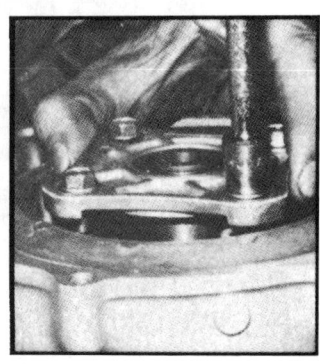

DATA

LIMITS	IN	MM.
Valve springs min. free length: outer	1.475	40.00
inner	1.457	37.00
Valve side-play, max: inlet	.003	.08
exhaust	.004	.10
Valve seat widths, inlet & exhaust	.040-.050	1.00-1.3
New valve guides reamed to:	.260	6.60
Standard bore size:	2.402	61.01
Max wear:	2.406	61.10
Max ovality:	.002	.05
1st re-bore:		+.25
2nd re-bore:		+.50
3rd re-bore:		+.75
4th re-bore:		+1.00
Min. ring gap; top and second	.008	.20
oil control ring	.001	.30
Max ring side clearance: top	.007	.18
second	.006	.16
oil	.005	.14
Crank journals max wear: mains & big ends:	1.415	35.94
Crank max out of true at centre:	.002	.05
(Can be straightened with press)		
Oil pump lobe clearance, max:	.014	.35
Oil pump outer rotors body clearance, max:	.014	.35
Min clutch friction plate thickness:	.122	3.10
Max clutch plate warpage:	.012	.30
Min clutch spring length:	1.200	30.50
Selector fork bearing area thickness, min:	.240	6.10
Primary chains wear limit, (see pic)	2.756	70.00

TORQUES	LBS-FT	KG-M
Cylinder head nuts:	18.0	2.5
Cam carrier & caps:	9.0	1.0
Generator rotor bolt:	65.0	9.0
Big end nuts:	15.5	2.2
Drive sprocket net:	10.5	1.5
8mm crankcase bolts:	18.0	2.5

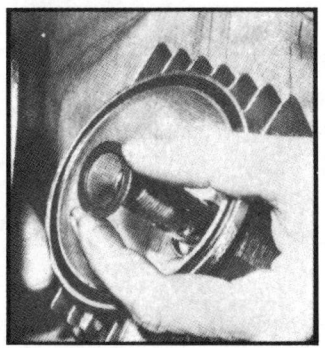

45. When replacing oil filter, don't chuck this washer away with the old one.

46. Set the points by slackening static point screws and moving static points-plates.

47. Time pots 1-4 by rotating base plate until points are just opening at F point, (arrowed).

48. Centre pots are timed by moving the points mounting plate radially on base plate.

TEN YEARS ON Honda's 750K7

Test: Martin Christie
Photography: John L. Robinson

I CAN still remember very clearly my first reactions on seeing photographs in the press of the original seven-fifty Honda. I, and a generation like me who'd been brought up to think of the Bonneville and the Norton 99 as the be all and end all of big bike technology, were dumbfounded. The Japanese had already taken over the small bike market, to be sure, but until then the biggest they'd gone was only 450cc. I suppose nobody thought they could really make a big bike. Especially not Triumph and Norton.

But one day in 1968, the covers slid back, and there it was in all its chromium plated glory. And even those to whom there's normally nothing new under the sun had to admit they'd never seen anything quite like it before. But of course, they'd add, it's just a car on two wheels: not a real motorcycle. It'll never catch on.

Feelings were very definitely mixed; a combination of excitement and apprehension. And after several years, when the exotic machines had become a more familiar sight on English roads, the novelty was still there. That and the nagging disbelief that anything so big and so complex could really work in a motorcycle frame.

I was an impressionable teenager then. Now, nearly ten years on, when multi cylinders are the order of the day on British tarmac, a whole new generation has grown up without ever knowing what life was like without them.

And yet somehow the novelty is still there. The passer-by in the street stops to watch as you park it, and chuckles "— Ow, these motorcycles nowadays . . . etc." You know the conversation. It's difficult to make them realise it's now a long time since we gave up all those traditional vices which went hand in hand with motorcycling — the raucous noise, the shattering vibration, the oil leaks, the difficult starting and all those perpetual, fiddling adjustments. We gave them up along with dirty hands, bruised knuckles, sprained ankles, blurred vision and premature deafness.

In place of them, we got motorcycles that didn't need a size twelve boot to prod into life, didn't deposit a greasy lake on the garage floor, and ran so smooth you could stand a threepenny bit on the tank (that's something else that got phased out). And a new word was added to our common English usage, though it's never found a

Honda 750K7

place in the Oxford dictionary: superbike.

Whatever it defines, there's no doubt it symbolises the sleek shapes of the seventies, and whatever the traditionalists say, they are here to stay with us for a long time.

In fact, in fifty years time I'm sure a new generation of traditionalists will be preserving and revering them as a magnificent piece of vintage history. By then, perhaps, they won't have the petrol to put in them, nor will some blindly benevolent government allow them to use such dangerous and anti-social machines upon the public highway. But if they do, and if they can, the one the veteran enthusiasts will go for is the CB750 Honda. The original, the classic, the definitive superbike.

Like the many thousands of riders today they'll put up with the faults, the flaws and the drawbacks, because it is *the* machine.

To recount that the CB750 has been running longer, has sold more and still sells more than any other seven-fifty on the market is merely to rehash bland statistics.

Now, after a near decade, and a little long in the tooth, it is ready to be phased out and replaced by a whole new range of Hondas. Compared to its newer rivals, it is generally slower, and doesn't handle as well.

It has a stop-gap super fast brother, the F2, designed to cope with the immediate rivals, but basically Honda are saving their big broadside for their next generation — bikes for the eighties. The present humble CB750, despite changes in style which designate it the K7, has changed very little from the first four which so shocked the two-wheeled world. But if it still sells, why not? People obviously still want it that way. Which brings me to the problem I found road testing the K7, or at least trying to put my impressions into words. When I ro   one of the originals, so many years back now, it was different and it was exciting. But it's not so any more.

Now almost everybody has a bike with the same specifications, and more. And if I were to compare it directly with some of its capacity class competitors, there are a number of points I could give damning criticism — but that's a trap which I note other recent road testers have leapt into all too keenly.

It's not enough to hold it up against it's newer, more advanced rivals. It's too easy then just to point to the lessons they have learnt from Honda's experience. You have also to remember what it was designed to do, and how it's likely to be used.

If you're in two minds whether to buy a CB750, I don't know if I'll be able to help you swing the balance either way. If you've already decided, there's nothing I can say that will dissuade you. It's an uncompromising motorcycle. It just is.

The most obvious changes Honda have made on the K7 have been in cleaning up the overall finish. Gone, for example, are the rust traps that acted as unsightly heat shields on the silencers. The latest quartet of noise suppressors are long and shapely, without reducing ground clearance. The rear footrests, by the way, have been moved up and forward onto the rear subframe, thus doing away with the need for ankle savers.

Gone too is the gaudy paintwork on the tank, replaced by a rich deep satin finish set off with a gold trim. Gone are the cobbly rubber fork gaiters, exposing clean chrome stanchions. The whole thing looks more luxurious, neater, if anything even more classic in its lines.

The changes underneath the obvious skin are straightforward. The new K7 is basically the heart and limbs of last year's sporty F1, but with the external costume of the tourer.

The engine unit is straight out of the F1, with the power boosted a couple of notches up the scale to 67 bhp. The front fork and rear dampers are off the F1 with another inch added to the suspension movement at both ends.

The frame it shares with the current F2 giving it, along with last year's long fork, another two inches on the wheelbase over the previous K6. A longer bike means more stability in a straight line, and more predictability through corners.

That does make it one of the lengthiest of the superbikes, getting into Z1000 dimensions and thus making it difficult to change direction quickly, or steer through tight turns.

But it's by no means unmanageable. It just has its own way of going about things. Just make up your mind where you're going before you get there.

The actual ground clearance has been improved on the new model, mainly with the taper on the silencers allowing the main stand to flip further back out of the way of greedy tarmac. But it's really a brave man who explores these possibilities to their limit.

The K7 gives you a feeling of security and stability, but it never encourages you to treat it with disdain. It will tackle most bumpy twists of English country road and shrug off excessive speed without complaint. But there just comes a point when it begins to squirm and pitch its head, letting you know that enough is enough.

What it really loves are smooth open surfaces, with sweeping cambers, where it glides gracefully at any throttle opening without the wallowing kangaroo pattern so much a part of the days before the Japanese learnt how suspension was supposed to work.

On its own preferred terrain it is quite magnificent. And even on roads it takes to with more reluctance it is no worse than average for a present day bike of its size and specification.

The round profile 4.50 x 17in Japanese Dunlop that comes as standard on the rear wheel did not appear to be too keen on white lines down the middle of the road, nor on those occasional lengthways ripples so beloved of highway engineers. But a faintly discernible weave was the only outward sign of incompatibility. And once you know it's there and what it does, you learn to ignore it.

One thing I found harder to ignore was the rear drum which would tend to snatch whilst braking into bumpy turns, causing the back wheel to patter. While never actually dangerous, it did make me a little nervous of my right toe.

The single disc on the front in comparison felt tremendously spongy at the lever, but was found to be excellent in use and very predictable. Treated, needless to say, with the required caution in the wet, it was quite adequate for hauling 650lb of man and motorcycle to a rapid standstill. Not overbraked by any means, but for all round security, I find the combination of a good drum and an adequate disc an ideal compromise.

If I had to live with the K7, I would probably swop the 11 inch circle of stainless steel for one of the cast iron conversions now readily available. But that's about the only modification I would consider on what really is, all round, an extremely well put together machine, perfectly suited to its task and on present rates, very good value.

One of the biggest impressions left after riding the bike is that of real comfort — that's after I'd tuned our test bike a little to fit. When I collected it from Honda's Chiswick headquarters the handlebar was set almost vertically in the yoke brackets, which, with its gull-wing profile, forced a riding position more suited to a chimpanzee. I should have altered it there and then, but in my hurry to get out on the road and make the most of a rare sunny day this summer, I persevered.

It was only after my arm muscles began to set in agonies, and my finger joints numbed that I broke into the tool kit and did the necessary. By tilting the bar back, and laying the levers flat, I discovered the nearest Japanese replica yet to a BMW flat stick. Just perfect. I'm sure it can't be just a question of personal preference. I've got quite long arms, but it really is so much easier to control the steering with the bar just that critical bit low.

Yet I'm continually amazed to see so many other riders on the road, on big bikes and small, with their wrists wandering about in the clouds. Well, maybe they think it looks good. It used to be so much a part of style, particularly influenced by the Americans, that standard bars on oriental bikes used to compel this posture. If you didn't like it, you had to find another that would, and accept the fittings for the controls.

Nice to see that such fittings have finally been tuned to suit we (more sensible) Europeans.

The seat is very comfortable, well padded, nicely finished, and with plenty of room for even a big pillion passenger. For those interested in vital statistics, it's 26 inches long, 9 inches wide at the tank, 13 inches at the waist, and 10 inches when it reaches the rear of its raised hump. With the bike off the main stand, your behind is 33 inches off the ground, and when riding solo you can slide it back to the start of the hump near the centre strap, and thus stop yourself slipping progressively rearwards. After six hours in the saddle at one stretch, I was experiencing no ill effects and could have continued for another six, I've no doubt.

The tank, slightly pear shaped towards the front, is not too large to be obtrusive, although perhaps could be a shade bulkier for long distance touring. Still, holding just over 3½ gallons, it gives you around 120 miles reasonably fast riding before you go

on reserve and start worrying about petrol stations.

The safety hood covering the tank cap proved a small irritant as it was a loose fit and tended to rattle in its mountings. Although now popular with manufacturers, this covering of the petrol filler does make it a bind if you happen to use a tank bag. Similarly, the oil filler cap, situated on the right side under the seat. While you can see it from the outside, you can't actually fill it without lifting the left-folding seat, unless you happen to carry a funnel with a kinked snout.

Perhaps not a major problem, as oil consumption over 1500 miles was negligible.

On the left side, below the seat, a rubber-mounted plastic side panel pulls off to reveal all the electrics you normally need to get at. You can check the battery level and replace, if necessary, any of three fuses placed in the circuits of the tail lamp (5a), headlamp (7a) and mains (15a).

Another good point as far as maintenance goes is the new rear chain, with its sealed rubber rings on the rollers, similar to those several other manufacturers have introduced. If you have to have chains on big bikes, this is part way to the answer. The full answer, of course, would be to have a completely enclosed chain, keeping it in a sealed bath away from the elements, and preventing it from contaminating everything around it.

But the dictates of style still apparently demand a simple one-piece chain guard which only covers the top run of the links.

This only stops the bike being sprayed by a film of road dirt and grease, and leaves the bottom of the chain free to collect it in the first place. No progress there, I'm afraid.

I wonder how many other riders find handlebar grips a problem, or are they just things you put up with? Only a small point, perhaps, but one on which I found a real revelation last year when I rode a CB750 F1 which belonged to scrambler Vic Allan. Vic had swopped the standard grips for a pair of soft plastic moto cross grips made in Sweden. They have quite large ridges, but being supple tend to mould themselves into the shape of the hand in use.

These proved to make a remarkable difference in sensitivity, when handling the bar and operating the heavy throttle of a big motorcycle needs a lot of physical effort in the palms. I have permanent hard pads on the top edges of my palms from the long time riding of other people's bikes, and I've no doubt that more

been said a thousand times before.

For all the innovations that have come since, it is still impressive. Mild, but meaty.

One or two little things still let it down. A few that I have mentioned, and one other, the horn, which was quite pathetic for anything larger than a moped.

But those being said, the humble and now much discounted CB750 still has a lot to offer for itself in its capacity class. No longer the market leader it once was, but still the original, and still the model from which others can learn.

And when, as must happen in the not-too-distant future, Honda phase the old faithful out to make way for their new generation of road burners, there will be a few tears shed for the passing of an age. I only hope the next one will be as good. . . .

Specifications
CB750 K7

Engine: Four cylinder 736cc (61 x 63mm) single overhead camshaft four stroke. Compression ratio 9.2 to 1.
Four Keihin piston valve type carburrettors. 28mm choke. Maximum claimed power 67bhp at 8500rpm.

Transmission: Toothed belt primary drive through wet multi-plate clutch to five speed constant mesh gearbox. Internal ratios: 2.50, 1.70, 1.33, 1.53 and 0.96 to 1. Chain final drive.

Lubrication: Pressure fed dry sump. Tank capacity 6.2 pints.

Fuel: 2 star minimum. Tank capacity 3.7 gallons including ½ gallon reserve.

Electrics: 12 volt 14 amp hour battery. AC Generator 0.21kw at 5000rpm. Coil ignition. Self starter.

Frame: Double tube cradle.

Suspension: Telescopic front fork, 5in movement. Rear by twin spring and hydraulic units, 4in movement, with five position adjustment for preload.

Brakes: Single 11in hydraulic disc front. Rear 7½in drum.

Tyres: 3.50 x 19in front. 4.50 x 17in rear. Japanese Dunlop Gold Seal.

Dimensions: Wheelbase, 59in; Seat height, 33in; overall length, 86in; overall width, 34in; overall height, 45in. Dry weight, 480lb.

Top speed: 112mph.

Fuel consumption: 40mpg.

Price: £1,335.

Concessionaires: Honda UK Ltd, Power Road, Chiswick, London, W4 5YT.

sensible grips would have prevented that.

The standard ones of the K7 are particularly nasty, having virtually no ridges, and so smooth that with leather gloves on I was continually having to re-adjust my grip on the throttle on long runs.

I didn't like the pull-on, cable-operated choke situated in the middle of the handlebar console. It was stiff in operation, and with a bike that needs quite a lot of coaxing to warm it up from cold, was more awkward to use than a simple lever on the side of the carbs.

But the nicest lever to use was the clutch, requiring just two fingers to pull it back to the bar, and slip it in again, although the actual action of the massive multi-plate unit tended to be a bit fierce on the transmission.

The transmission is one of the few areas where the big Honda begins to show its age. Still good, but compared to its newer rivals, the five speed box is rather clumpetey in use,

and coming down, it was possible to miss changes. The general running, particularly at slow speed does also tend to make rather a lot of noise, including the now familiar whine.

Going up the ratios are quite well chosen, though a slightly too large gap between first and second, with third taking you up over the legal limit and still another two notches to go. Top gear is very tractable, going down to less than twenty miles an hour while the impressively smooth engine provides sufficient pull from just over tickover.

Maximum power is rated at 8500rpm, with the red line a thou later, and the bike is geared to reach it readily. Cruising at 70mph in top means 4000rpm, although the engine speed at which it seems the happiest is just a shade higher.

What can I add though about that bulletproof power unit, so deceptively good mannered, which despite its age, is still a legend in its own lifetime? Very little that has not

BARGAIN OR BANGER?

History

BY any definition, the Honda 750 four has got to be one of the classic motor cycles of all time. The first of the current generation of superbikes, its introduction in '69 was the beginning of a new era in motor cycle engineering. Like it or not, you have to respect it; the Honda belongs on a pedestal alongside such machines as the first Triumph Speed Twin, the BMW R67, the B Series Vincent Rapide, and the first featherbed Norton.

Furthermore, it's a reliable piece of kit — which, in all honesty, is more than can be said for most of the previous great names. The CB750 has had its troubles, of course, but for one thing most of them have been comparatively minor, and for another Honda have usually been pretty quick about sorting out snags as soon as they rear their heads rather than waiting until they become major problems. The result is what the factory describe as progressive development and the cynics quite wrongly refer to as mucking about with the machine in order to confuse mechanics and spare-part emporiums. The fact of the matter is that the big Honda was reliable from the word go and the changes have merely been refinements. So far as the spares' situation is concerned there shouldn't be any major problem providing engine and frame numbers are quoted when buying bits.

Having said all that, let's now examine the bike bit by bit through the critical eyes of a potential purchaser.

A classic; fore-runner of the superbike generation but, more to the point, reliable. Honda's "progressive development" has taken care of the snags, but made the spares situation complicated.

No.4 CB 750 Honda

THIS feature is the fourth in our series on what to look for when buying secondhand bikes. In each we look at one particular machine — at its history, its good points and its bad points. The series is intended as a ruthless and down-to-earth guide for the person thinking of buying a second-hand bike. It deals with the known weak points of particular models and details the sort of problems the average owner may expect when he comes to live with the machine.

Chassis

THE first thing to look at is the general cleanliness and condition of the beast overall. A frame which is rust-besmirched and tatty can be an expensive business to clean up on any big bike, and the Honda is no exception. Likewise be wary of battered mudguards, tank, seat, etc; all these things can involve you in bigger money than you think. A not uncommon place for rust is around the area of the rear swinging arm pivot, which comes in for a goodly share of road muck and all too often not such a goodly share of the cleaning rags. Also grab the back wheel and yank it from side to side to test the swinging arm bearing. Excess play here (say, more than $^3/_{32}$ inch at the wheel spindle) means replacement of the pivot pin and bushes; not an expensive job, but if it needs doing and the previous owner hasn't done it then he's probably the sort of berk who will have neglected the bike in other areas as well.

Still down on your hands and knees, look for salt pitting in the alloy parts (which needs cleaning pronto if it isn't to become a permanent blemish), and bubbling and rusting of the chrome parts, particularly the exhaust. The four-into-four exhaust systems (the ones with the four silencers, as opposed to the F models' four-into-one set up) rust from the inside outwards, and the first signs of the rug are usually to be seen at the tail ends of the silencers and also underneath at their lowest point, near the front ends. Look for bubbling or outright rusting, especially on the left hand side, where rear chain lubricant gets thrown onto the underside of the exhaust and blocks up the little drain holes in the mufflers. The latest four-into-one systems can be fitted to earlier bikes, but they won't drop straight on; the mods may well be worth making if you have to renew a whole system, however, since the four-into-one pack is (a) cheaper and (b) longer-lasting, because the silencer runs hotter. With any exhaust change, either to a later pattern or to one of the proprietary hot-shop systems, the wise owner should check that the main jets are still suitable, either by making the conventional checks himself or wheeling the beast into a switched-on Honda dealer for analysis on their electronic fruit-machine.

However, we are getting off track a little. To come back to the frame and cycle parts, the next thing to look at is the state of the spokes, wheel rims and tyres. Wriggle the wheels to see if the rims move in relation to the hubs (which is rare but not unheard of) and ding the spokes with a screwdriver or something in the usual way to see if any of them play D flat while the rest sing A minor.

Check the tyre condition bearing in mind that boots for a thing like this ain't cheap. The original tyre sizes are 325/19 front

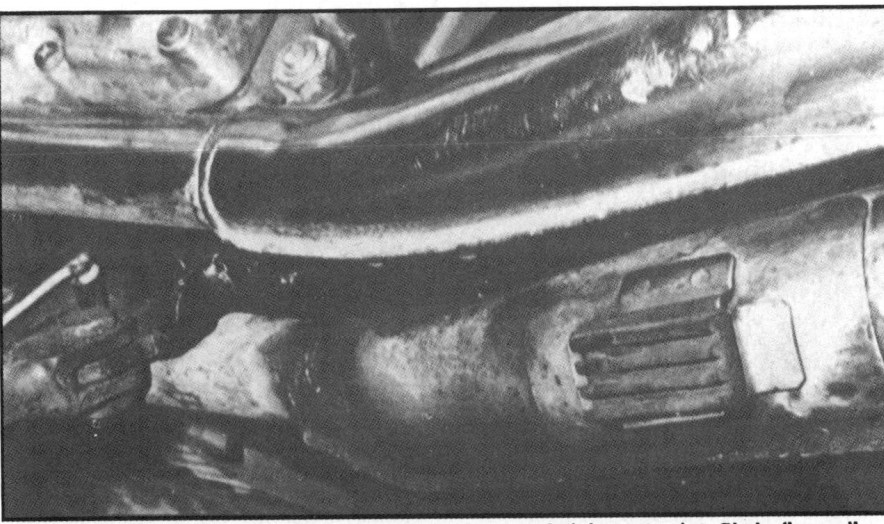

The 'four-into-four' exhaust systems start to rust here, at their lowest point. Chain-flung oil blocks drain holes and they rot from the inside out.

The first part to succumb to rust blemishes is usually the frame area round the swinging arm. Also check the pivot nipple has been greased, and test swinging arm for side-play.

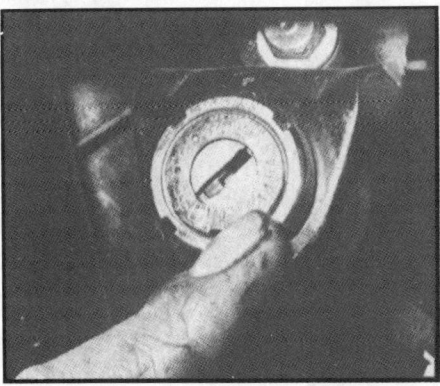

Good anti-theft tip is to file the number off the ignition switch. Just make sure you've noted it yourself, though!

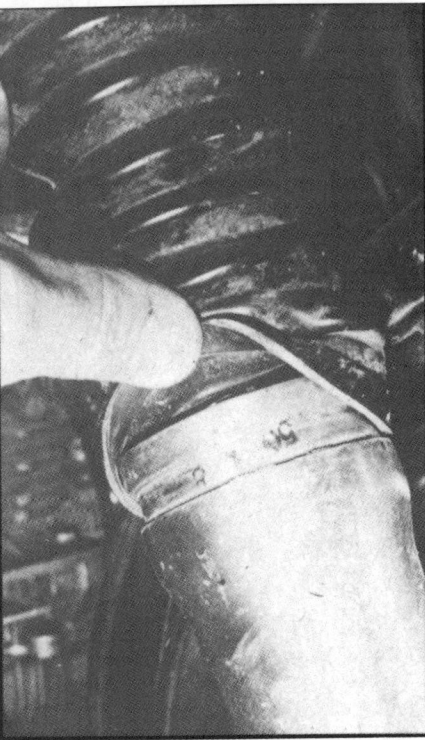

Fork slider bushes seem to be long lasting, but steering head races are not. Whilst on the forks, look for leakage from the slider seals; cure is to use latest double-lip seal, which fits all models.

and 400/18 rear (with the exception of the latest K7 model, which has a 350S19 front and 450S17 rear) so if you find anything different, be wary. So far as tyre types are concerned, it is difficult to comment since different boots are compatible with different riding styles to some extent. Some people have problems with Dunlop TT100s while others get good results from Roadrunners and Red Arrows.

Returning to the frame, probably the most common fault is pitted steering head races. These are fairly easy and not too expensive to replace, however, and Paul Dunstall does a taper-roller conversion which generally survives rather better than the original articles. Look, too, for weeping seals on the front fork sliders, which has also been something of a perennial problem; if you have to renew the seals, use the latest double-lip pattern. (Which means leaving out the backing ring used with some earlier seals.) Also check the front wheel bearings, and look for signs of the brake disc having rubbed the fork leg. This happens if the front wheel spindle is in the wrong way round.

Engine

BEGIN by looking for the usual signs of oil leaks and smoking; CB750 engines are not prone to either of these maladies, so one that does weep or puff should be regarded with the deepest suspicion. The only history of this sort of problem was a very occasional tendency for a small weep from the head gasket on pre-'74 models. The oil guide arrangement was changed from engine number CB750E 2352923, which knocked the weep on the head. Earlier engines can't be converted, but they don't really need to be; the problem is rare, and in nearly all cases a new gasket sorts it out with no problem.

The most important guide to a 750 engine's condition is the sound and the smoothness of it — and the judgement of that, unfortunately, is something you can't really put into words; either you have enough experience of the marque to know what the mill ought to sound and feel like, or you haven't. In the latter case, of course, the brightest thing is to take with you someone who has. The only thing we can really say is that there ought to be no obtrusive noises (apart from clutch clatter, of which more later), and that as you rev up gently the unit ought to settle down into its characteristic imitation of a

sewing machine without any single item particularly making itself heard. If it runs lumpily at tickover (which is best detected, apart from the uneven vibration cycle and an irregular knocking noise, by standing behind the bike and listening to the exhaust beat) you may have a minor mechanical or electrical problem, or it may simply be that the carbs need tuning. In the latter case you might be able to get rid of the knock and produce smoother running — and thus confirm that the lumpiness is unbalanced carbs — by resting a finger on each carb lifting rod in turn; it's a bit of a "maybe" experiment, however, and quite frankly we wouldn't expect to learn much from it unless we were fairly well accustomed to Honda fours. It's worth examining the throttle lifting shaft for wear and/or stiffness in any case, however; and at the same time, check that the throttle slide lifting rods all have about the same degree of axial play. If they haven't, someone's been a bit heavy-handed while they were balancing the carbs. The original CB750 had a four-into-one throttle cable arrangement instead of a lifting shaft, so they tended to go out of sync rather more easily.

If you have a very flat and rough-sounding engine, particularly in a bike which shows signs of having been dropped hard at some time, it is just possible that the auto-advance unit (or even the crankshaft, according to

some sources) has been slightly bent owing to being taken down the road on the timing or generator covers. The repairer obviously replaces the relevant cover(s) and anything else which is clearly damaged, but if the engine runs a bit flat and sick thereafter, what do you do? The inevitable answer will be to flog the damn thing quick. One or two experts make a point of whipping off the timing cover and watching the ignition cam nut go round to make sure it's not a-wobbling.

Still, all in all the main measure of engine condition remains its cleanliness, smoothness and silence. Mileage is nowhere near as important as the way the brute's been looked after; some engines have been known to run on for 150,000 miles without trouble while neglected ones have a very much shorter life. We would be generally suspicious of buying a big-bore converted machine for the obvious reasons, the major exception to this prejudice being the 812 Yoshimura conversion, which gives a bit more power without leaning too heavily on the bottom end.

One final word of warning: if you buy a late model 750, make sure you read the instructions about which fuel to use. Five-star has too much lead for the modern pollution-orientated engines, and can cause top-end trouble. Two-star is the stuff to burn in the more recent models.

On earlier models this oil feed pipe was prone to developing a kink which restricted the flow of oil into the engine.

If the engine runs lumpily, you can try light finger pressure on each carb lifter in turn; if it smooths out, problem is merely synchronisation.

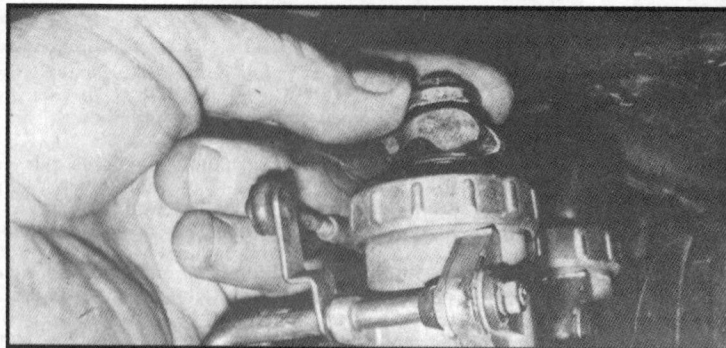

Check the throttle lifting shaft for play or stiffness, and also check the free 'twisting' play in the slide lifting adjusters. If one has more than others, someone's been heaving on it and you'll need a new slide and adjuster.

MODEL GUIDE

Model	Engine/frame nos. from/to	Remarks
CB750	Engine 1000001 - 1044847 Frame 1000001 - 1044825	First of the line, intro'd '69. High bars, four-into-one throttle cables, four-into-four exhaust.
CB750K0	Engine 1044848 - 1045147 Frame 1044826 - 1044947	Transitory model, very much the same as CB750. Only 36 were imported into Britain.
CB750K1	Engine 1044813 on Frame 1053399 on	Slimmer than previous models by virtue of seat, tank, and side cover changes. Crossbar lifting rod on carbs.
CB750K2	Engine 2000001 on Frame 2000001 on	As K1 apart from trim changes and detail frame changes.
CB750F1	Circa '75	First of the 'F range' sportster versions, running concurrently with K2. Suspension geometry changes improved handling, and power (which had been gradually falling off in the K range because of emission regulations) upped to 67bhp. Four-into-one exhaust.
CB750K6	Late '75	As K2 apart from detail changes.
CB750F2	'77	Replaced F1. Changes to carbs, head, porting, valves and cam upped power to 73bhp. Twin front discs replace single, and Comstar wheels introduced. Four-into-one exhaust slightly modded to improve ground clearance. Rear chain sealed-link type.
CB750K7	'77	The K range now being regarded as the 'touring' version. K7 has the F1 engine, a few frame changes from the K6, and spoke wheels, single front disc, and four-into-four exhaust. Has sealed-link chain.

Transmission

THE CB750 clutch has a fully justified reputation for being well-nigh indestructible — but what it isn't, however is completely silent in all cases. Clattering and squawking noises are common, but they don't matter a jot. If you really can't live with them, the answer is to fit a Gold Wing clutch plate — part number 22322/371/313 — and leave out one of the existing friction plates; but, as we've said, the noises are completely harmless so there's no need to do anything about them at all.

The other common clutch irritation on early models is judder on the take-up. This again won't do any harm unless it's so bad that it's obviously snatching the transmission heavily (which is most unusual), but if you want to cure it you can do so by fitting the later pattern of clutch oil feed metering jet and the clutch hub that goes with it. (Which has extra oil holes in it.) The change of jet and hub was made from engine number CB750E 1020826.

Something you do need to watch out for is a tendency to jump out of fourth and fifth gears on models prior to engine number CB750E 2304511. The fault was cured by changing the profile of the selector drum, and the later drum (part number 24301/300/040) goes straight into the earlier box and solves the problem. However, getting into the box involves a complete engine strip which you might not be envisaging ten minutes after buying the bike . . . .

Next thing on the transmission side is the bearing on the shaft which carries the final drive sprocket. Until it was replaced with a bigger bearing altogether on the K6, this race was occasionally prone to breaking up, with disastrous results on the gear cluster, the crankcases, and everything else in sight. So when buying a second-hand 750, we would recommend whipping off the sprocket cover (see pic), trying the shaft for up and down play or end play (always bearing in mind that the sprocket can rock on the shaft, so make sure you grab the shaft itself), and looking for weepage from the oil seal. If all this is okay it still doesn't guarantee that the bearing is a hundred per cent sound (the trouble is that the outer track splits, which happens with precious little warning if it's going to happen at all), but on the other hand it does have the merit of being the only sort of inspection we can make. The break-up isn't a common problem exactly, but looking for warning signs is certainly worthwhile.

The last area, naturally enough, is the rear chain and sprockets. Chain wear is inevitable, so if you find one that's a bit tired it's probably more a question of budgeting for its replacement — along with the sprockets as well if they're 'hooked' — rather than rejecting the bike as a possible purchase because of it: after all, who replaces a chain when they know they're about to sell the bike . . . ?

The latest 750 fours, the K7 and the F2, have sealed-link chains, which last considerably better than the older pattern. These chains do not fit the earlier sprockets, however, and nor can the sprockets themselves be changed for the sealed-link types. Lastly, Honda no longer recommend using a spring-link on the 750 chains, so bear in mind that a chain-change is really a job for a dealer, who has the correct link-crimping tool to fasten up the connecting link. Chains have been known to fracture if the battery breather drops fluid on them, and they obviously wear quicker if they haven't got the adjustable chain oiler which was fitted from engine number CB750E 1026144; so if you buy a bike earlier than that, reckon on investing in a chain oiler mod kit.

On pre-K6 models, remove the final drive cover (two screws) and check shaft for play and oil seal behind sprocket for leaking. (Sprocket itself will wiggle, but that doesn't matter.) Note undesirable spring-link on this final drive chain.

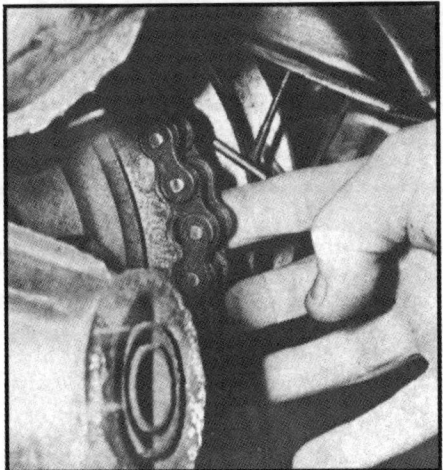

This rear chain is well worn, as many tend to be at selling time. Check also to see if sprockets are 'hooked'. Latest F2 model has 'O ring' rear chain, but you can't fit that to earlier versions.

Coming next

Number five in our "Bargain or Banger" series will deal with the Kawasaki 900-four.

HONDA CB750 F2

Test & Photography: Martin Christie

IF it works on the track, Honda say, they put it on the road. At least that's the message gleaming from all those multi-colour ads that have been gracing the press in the last few months.

And alongside a picture of Phil Read on his World Championship TT Formula Honda, is our Phil standing by the sporty looking CB750 F2, with the obvious implication of praising it by direct comparison.

Of course there are a few minor discrepancies in the comparison, notably the 997cc double overhead camshaft engine which powers Hondas formidable big-class endurance racers, each of which costing, on conservative estimates, £30,000.

But then if you're buying a bike for the road that costs only a shade over £1,300, you won't have to be too disappointed if it bears only a passing resemblence to its illustrious relative.

However, taking the claim at face value, it still is a little difficult to work out exactly what Honda found worked on the track and which has been put on the road. The only

obvious feature is the Comstar alloy wheels, built up by pressing two metal starfish inside an independent rim.

On close inspection these look disconcertingly flimsy for a five-hundred and fifty pound motorcycle, but of course they have been well tried and tested for a whole season in endurance racing without a failure. And having seen them in action at the Bol D'or, I'm prepared to accept that if they put up with that, they'll put up with anything.

Certainly the more complex bolt-

up construction of the Comstar wheels looks likely to suffer from structural fatigue which is one of the dangers of the more popular single-cast alloy wheels. And if you've seen one of the latter broken up, you'll know exactly what I mean. The other big plus from racing development is in the suspension department. The F2 is by far the best suspended Honda yet, with more movement, better damping and improved springing. The front fork itself is excellent, completely new and a direct result of the endurance testing. With a good five inches of travel, it has a superbly progressive action, and none of the wrist-breaking bottoming found on earlier models. The rear units, with five position adjustment, are also excellent, though hindered by the actual length of the bike.

The only other similarity to the raucous red racers is the four into one exhaust system with its massive bazooka-style silencer giving out a fruity but not offensive note — that and the natty matt black finish to the engine parts.

Honda have boosted the power of the F2 over previous four cylinder units by dropping bigger valves into the head, altering the shape of the combustion chamber and tuning the cam profile. This has given it more horses in the middle to upper range, and beefed up claimed bhp from 67 to 70. It would be difficult to claim this as a result of recent racing technology as old four-stroke hands like Honda have known all these tweaking secrets for a long time.

It's just that they've finally had to do something with the veteran 736cc mill to keep it in line with the sort of performance being produced by competitors like the GS750 Suzuki. This they have achieved without losing the tremendous flexibility and smooth running characteristics of the single overhead cam motor.

But it is essentially a compromise, and a stop-gap measure to update a basically long-in-the-tooth machine while a completely new range is being prepared for introduction next year.

For all that, it is still quite a nice bike, it's just that the short cuts taken to achieve this updating become apparent in use.

If you read the test of the F2's immediate brother, the traditional touring K7 in last month's issue, you may recall I drew similar conclusions about the bike, but was fairly ambivalent towards the machine as a whole. It didn't try to be anything more than a newer version of an old bike.

With the F2 however, I find it harder to be so forgiving, because it tries so hard to push a competitive image, and inevitably demands to be compared with its rivals. In that race, it doesn't come out so well. The fundamental problem is that it's too long. And the reason for that is the longer suspension, both at the front fork, and with the rear units. The front wheel obviously had to be thrown out further to stop the chrome mudguard slamming against the exhaust pipes under compression of the fork.

But there is enough clearance beneath the rear mudguard and backplate to take at least two inches off the swinging arm and thus compensate for that. That would bring the wheelbase back to the more manageable 57 inches and still retain the same excellent suspension movement.

As it stands, at 59 inches, it is so long that those very suspension advances are wasted because the whole bike is so difficult to take through corners. A lot of manhandling, and much lean is needed to get the machine to

HONDA CB750 F2

change direction at speed, and low speed handling and steering is inevitably heavy.

Altering the wheelbase a couple of inches may only seem like a minor operation on paper, but it makes a critical difference to the F2 on the road. And of course, on the production line in Japan, altering the swinging arm means a lot more work than just bolting on different suspension units. So that's why the stop-gap seven fifty stays the way it is — until they phase it out that is.

The other problem with getting more suspension movement is that the seat height tends to rise, unless there's considerable redesign to the rear sub-frame to accommodate the longer units, and the increasingly agile rear wheel.

Honda have kept the F2 still relatively low in the seat, at 32 inches certainly no higher than any of its rivals. Like any present 750 or over, if you've got short legs, you'd better invest in some platform shoes.

And while the overall height of the bike is kept quite low, again with the general length, pushing it around is no mean feat in itself. Although to be fair, as one of the expected refinements nowadays, getting it on and off the main stand, was very easy.

If Honda do carry on their stated policy of putting what works on the track on the road, it will be interesting to see what the brakes look like on the new bikes. For it is noticeable that though the F2 boasts massive twin 11 inch discs on the front, and a single 11½ inch on the rear, they bear little resemblance to those the real racers have been riding on. And I can't say I blame them.

In the dry the F2's brakes are horrendously powerful, but if the roads are even a shade greasy, the rear particularly is absolutely lethal. As with the drum on the rear of the K7, I found the brake tending to lock, and the rear wheel to patter if the surface was at all bumpy. Could it be, again with the long wheelbase of the bike, that there is not enough load at the rear in relation to the performance of the brake? I'm no brake technologist, but I do have a healthy respect for my own skin, and I scare easily. So I didn't enjoy riding the F2 in the wet very much at all.

I didn't get the solid-feeling front brake to lock up, to be sure, but in anything other than scorching sunshine my right hand hovered over that lever as delicately as if I was clutching a new-born babe. The all weather brakes on the endurance racers of course aren't made of trendy stainless steel, and they are extensively drilled to disperse water. So please, Honda, put a bit of that know-how on the road. We'd sooner settle for that than a matt-black replica engine.

It's also interesting to note that the racers mount the twin front brake calipers forward of the fork, when everyone in the last few seasons has been saying they had to be mounted after to counteract the natural steering inertia brought about by their very weight. The F2 has them aft of the fork, supposedly copying this trend. And the two units are conveniently marked left and right in case you should have any confusion about their intention. But perhaps Honda have now discovered this wasn't quite such a good idea after all.

Certainly the F2 has a marked tendency to shake its head when you shut off violently, and it's inadvisable to take your hands off the bar for too long.

High speed handling of the F2 in comparison is pretty good, where you can make the most of the predictable steering and the smooth riding. The standard Japanese tyres don't like white lines and other slightly slippery obstacles, but otherwise once a straight course is selected, it stays on it like a train. And it's at those times it's possible

to make full use of the fearsome acceleration.

In tighter turns, and in traffic, you've got your work cut out. And as the extra power of the F2 is mainly in regions unusable is such situations, boosted bhp is no help. Fortunately both the throttle and clutch proved light in operation, but after prolonged plodding in traffic, your wrists begin to tell you, if you didn't already know, that the F2 is a strain.

A pity really, because the engine is still so tractable and clean running. Top gear will run right down to a mere 15mph, only just over tickover speed, and pull away with only the slightest trace of a hiccup, and no hesitation. 30mph is 2,500rpm in top — with enough power on tap to take off without changing gear.

There's no real power stop on the Honda engine. If you roll off and wind it back on you get a first surge at about 3,000rpm, and a final boost over 6,000 when the accelerator pumps on the four 28 mm Keihins come into their own.

At sustained high speed running, over 6,000rpm, there is a tendency for another curious hiccup I have noticed on previous Honda fours. Just a very slight, almost imperceptible hesitation, which occurs occasionally. Perhaps it's a built-in safety device to keep the rider awake and alert, because the general running at speed is so smooth it's almost soporific. A tingling vibration is hardly noticed by the intrepid pilot, except that it virtually obscures all vision in the rearview mirrors.

The F2 is the most powerful, and with the present gearing, the fastest of the long line of Honda seven fifties. The ratios give the bike a top speed of 126mph, and the power curve such that it will surge up to that maximum 9,500rpm without any real difficulty. More power and speed, of course, than can be used safely on English roads, but such that gives you the confidence at lower, legal limits of all that potential on tap.

For all this extra power and speed, the F2 surprised me by returning an average fuel consumption of just under 50mpg — and that over a selection of riding between town use and high speed country cruising. With the present fuel tank that gives you a touring range of over 130 miles before you begin to consider where the next petrol station might be, and virtually another 30 before you have to start worrying.

Oil consumption over the period of the test was negligible, which is how it should be on a modern engine, and works out at topping up at the rate of a pint every 1500 miles.

On the debit side, however, one of the worst features of the F2 is the gearbox, which proved to be quite diabolical. Although the operation of the clutch lever at the bar was light, requiring only two fingers to feather it, the take up on the transmission was clumsy. Changing up, in fact, I found it smoother not to use the clutch after changing into second, and coming down the change between fourth and third was invariably missed at first attempt.

I soon got used to changing down about six times when I wanted to slow down, but then it would occasionally surprise me by going in properly on the way and leave me juddering in first.

The old toothed belt primary drive seems to be the main culprit and also makes the transmission excessively noisy at slow speed, but the gearbox itself, including the selection mechanism is long overdue for a rethink after ten years.

Once in, the ratios themselves are good, and well chosen for their purpose, it's just finding them that's the problem. Not that bad compared with things we used to put up with in the old days, but compared to the modern versions of slickshift selection, pretty awful. You can bet your bottom yen the racers don't have to juggle with that Pandora's box when they're doing 170mph.

Of course, to be fair, there are a lot of things, regardless of what they learn from racing, that Honda have learnt from the road already, and put into practice.

The handlebar layout and instrument console is excellently

HONDA CB750F2

laid out, easy to use and the speedo and rev counter themselves very accurate. The only thing difficult to operate is the dip beam switch which is on the wrong side of the left bar grip from your thumb. You have to crook your thumb at the join to avoid sounding the horn as well and it's an unnecessary distraction while night riding.

That being said, the horn, a twin unit, is excellent and up to the sound standards all bikes over the size of mopeds should have: enough to put the fear of god in offending motorists. And the headlamp with it's 60/55 watt bulb is one of the best in the business. It gives you a 60mph night speed on country roads in safety instead of luck.

Along with all the usual electrical gubbins, the headlamp flasher is useful, although slightly fiddly to operate on the same switch as the horn. Nice refinements under the seat are two helmet holders which are secured by the locking of the seat itself, and an ample toolbox in the rear hump which can also accommodate a puncture repair outfit and other little odds and sods that always seem to come in handy.

Overall the finish is of the high quality one comes to expect from Honda. The colour schemes are a deep two-tone red, or blue set off with a gold flash along the tank. That, and the matt black turnout of the engine gives it the compact racy appearance so very much part of the image.

Underneath that image, as you'll have read, it doesn't quite match up to the advertising campaign. But the shortcomings are based on the constraints of Honda's production programme. The word is that the new bikes which will replace machines like the F2 next year will be impressive. But then, no doubt, so will the price.

And at £1,379 the stopgap seven fifty still represents pretty good value for money on present standards, as long as you realise it isn't quite the bike Phil Read races on.

Our test bike, however, was exactly the one Phil appears with in the ads, and used briefly on the road. It currently belongs to Comerfords and many thanks to director Bert Thorn for making it available.

Specifications HONDA CB750 F2

Engine: 736 cc (61 x 63mm) air cooled single overhead camshaft in line four cylinder four stroke.

Compression ratio 9.2 to 1. Carburation four 28mm Keihins with accelerator pumps. Replaceable paper air filter. Dry sump lubrication system. Claimed maximum power 70bhp at 9,500 rpm.

Transmission: Primary drive through toothed belt through wet multi-plate clutch to five speed constant mesh gear box. Overall ratios: 14.2, 9.7, 7.5, 6.5 and 5.5 to one. Final drive by sealed chain.

Electrics: 12 volt 14 amphour battery and 210 watt alternator. Coil ignition. 7in diameter headlamp with 60/55 watt bulb. Self starter. Twin horns.

Frame: Tubular double cradle type.

Suspenison: Telescopic front fork with oil damping. Oil damped twin rear units with five position adjustment spring preload.

Brakes: Front hydraulically operated twin discs of 11in diameter. Rear single disc of 11½ in diameter.

Tyres: Japanese Dunlop Gold Seal 3.25 x 19in front, 4.00 x 18in rear.

Happy man! Keith Newton's CB750 shows how the model can be restored to spotless condition despite 68,000 miles and being ridden by the motorcycle press (horrors!) in its early years.

Honda CB750 Four

Fault it if you can.

Jim Reynolds savours the first, formidable, Japanese 'four'

HONDA'S CB750 is arguably the most significant model in the company's domination of the British market. The ubiquitous little 50cc step-through models may have put more of the world on wheels; the 125 Benly and CB72 250 showed the Japs could make reliable performance bikes; the CB450 'Black Bomber' may have caused worried frowns in the boardrooms of Britain's own manufacturers; but when Honda offered the world four-cylinder motorcycling with electric starting and a disc front brake, this was revolution!

The 750 four first appeared at the Tokyo Show in October 1968. It came into a world that had been regularly promised a roadster version of MV's racer only to have the 600cc shaft-driven version offered in 1967 – a determined attempt to keep ideas of racing beyond the ambitious private owner. And only the most short-sighted of MV Agusta aficionados could call the 600 good looking, with its rectangular headlamp contrasting

oddly with the elephantine curves of the bike. It was later that the graceful lines of the racing MVs was reflected in their road models.

Now, Honda's four-cylinder roadster was to be something within the average enthusiast's financial reach, and the world held its breath. A pair of the CB750s was shown to a dealer convention in Las Vegas and the price in the vital American market was pitched below the recently introduced three from BSA-Triumph. I can still recall a friend, who then worked in the development department at Meriden, looking very sick when he told us the news at a club night: "They've got a four with an electric starter, and it's cheaper than our bike with three cylinders and a kickstarter. Which would you buy?" The silence that followed the question was deafening. . .

The four reached Britain for the 1969 Brighton Show, when two pre-production models were displayed. Leaving the Brits with mouths

watering, they were whisked away to France but one returned for Bill Smith to ride a few TT practice laps and report back on its behaviour. 'Motor Cycle News' managed to get a ride on this pre-production model in September of the same year, and shortly after the bike was sold to Tippetts in Surbiton, and is believed to have been used by The Earl of Denbigh, today the President of the Motor Cycle Association.

The precise history of that bike is not clear, but it did fall into the hands of Keith Newton, well known in Vintage Japanese Club circles for his rebuilds of numerous Hondas. Keith swapped the prototype for a bike that he wanted even more – the original road test CB750 production model. Read the road tests of the day, look at Honda's leaflets, and the registration number you'll see is YLY 70H. That is the bike Keith has re-built, from the spoke nipples up, and he was the obvious man to talk to about the pitfalls and problems in bringing an early Honda Four back to full health.

Honda CB750

W E ARE concerned here with the earliest versions of the 750, the rare CB750, the even rarer CB750K0 and the CB750K1 that took the model up to the beginning of 1972. From that time the K2 was offered, with cosmetic changes and its engine and frame numbers starting from the 2000001 point – that first

The overhead cam and rocker gear is the most vulnerable area if a Four is neglected, with the oilways prone to clogging when the filter is not changed and the lubricant kept clean.

This engine is still on the original crank, bores and pistons, after a ring change at 40,000. The crankcase, barrel and cylinder head have been sprayed with Spectra 5 Wheel Silver, a good match for the Honda original finish – an alternative is Holts' DS100. Chrome on this restoration was applied by Custom Fasteners of Redditch.

digit is a handy point to watch in dating a bike that you might have doubts about.

The CB750 – note no model suffix on the very early version – used a one-into-four throttle cable arrangement, with a splitter box. This was changed to a single cable and arm linkage with the 750K.

While Honda are the most obliging of the Japanese makers regarding old parts, if one is obsolete and its successor will do the job, that's what they'll send. The fact they still supply parts for 20-year-old machines is to their credit but anyone rebuilding to original should know about that pitfall.

If you can find a copy of the parts list for the CB750 and its successors through to the 750K2 (there's no mention of the 750K0, just to confirm that it's very rare!) check reference number 1434105 on the back cover. If you have no luck finding one of these, Honda guru Dave Ayesthorpe at Honda Restorations in Gloucestershire can provide reasonably priced photocopies – see Services Guide at the end of this article. Another invaluable book to look for or have copied is the Shop Manual – reference

623001 – that will show dismantling and assembly sequences, even if some of the transactions are a little quaint, such as describing the handlebar as the "steering handle pipe"!

Colours on the CB750 are Candy Ruby Red and Candy Blue Green, no longer available officially but possible to match quite well; again, details in the Services Guide. But there are some parts that come under the heading of 'unobtainium': the earliest CB750s had mudguards with unbeaded leading edge that were updated to a beaded edge during that series' life and finding the early version is a major problem. Both the 750 and 750K models were fitted with a dual seat with a small rear hump that disappeared with the launch of the K1 in 1971. Order a seat from Honda today and you'll get the flat K1 pattern. Prices up to £200 have been offered for the genuine article, so if you have one on your bike, count yourself very lucky!

The CB750 also used a shorter form of the rear chainguard that later versions fitted, and whilst there are private operators

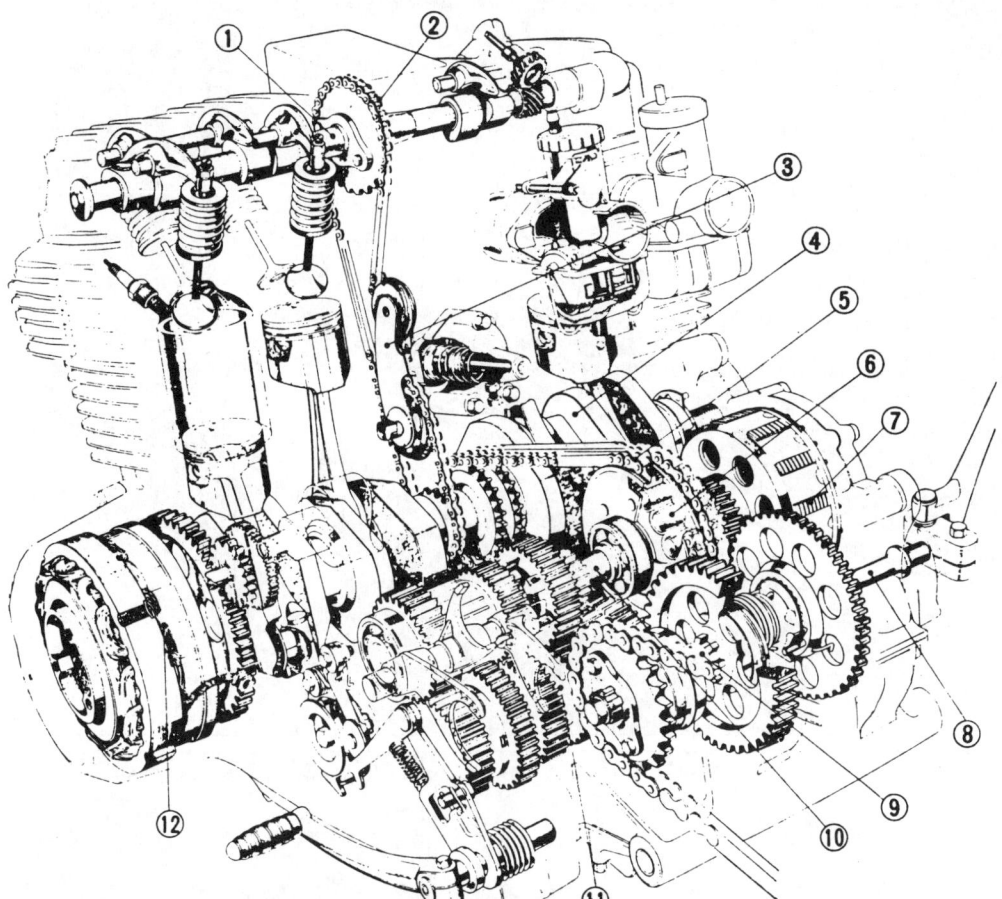

1. Camshaft
2. Camchain
3. Camchain tensioner
4. Crankshaft
5. Primary chain
6. Primary driven sprocket
7. Clutch
8. Kick starter spindle
9. Final driven shaft
10. Mainshaft
11. Countershaft
12. A.C. generator

Engine drawing from the handbook showing camshaft drive.

CB750 and CB750KO versions used speedo and rev counters with plastic bodies and glass; from the K1 they altered to metal bodies with real glass, and replacements ordered today from Honda UK would come to that specification.

willing to mould such items at moderate cost, they want enough orders to defray the cost of tooling so back to the autojumbles on that one. And if you're really keen to produce the original look, the correct sticker giving details of oil levels and types that went on top of the tank is not available. If anyone knows someone who could produce a small batch, Keith Newton would like to be put in touch. Letters can be forwarded via 'Classic Mechanics'.

Original tyres were Bridgestone or Japanese Dunlop, and again these are not made now. Most owners swapped to British or European rubber as a matter of course,

and unless you are building specially for concours detail, that is the obvious route to take. The four separate exhaust pipes are still available at around £68 each, while the small heat shields on the upper silencer (Part No. 18315-300-010 or 020) now come in bright chrome, whereas the very early ones were in dull chrome with black inserts. If detail is all-important, having new parts blasted and then chromed can give the correct effect, but do talk to your plater about this.

The CB750 used an air filter box painted in the colour of the main feature areas (i.e. blue or red) but during the production run

of the 'K' variant, this was changed to a ribbed black box that was less prone to cracking because it is more flexible. The original is available to order but the price may hurt at something over £100. (Or even try the Classic Mechanics *free* autojumble!). It's also worth noting that more early CB750s were sold in France (and more still in America) than we got in Britain, so if you're on holiday and see a breaker's yard in either country, take a look around.

Detail differences between each series is generally dictated by experience providing the chance to improve reliability, the air boxes being a prime example. Owners of the model stress the bikes ability to cover big mileage without major problems, provided the oil is changed regularly and kept clean with filter changes. "They do take a lot of abuse," Keith Newton confirms. "But if you go over the top and one goes wrong, it can be very expensive to put it right."

A shining example of getting it wrong is an engine Keith had in his workshop when we talked. The owner had used a pattern replacement for the oil filter housing centre bolt (Part No. 15420-300-010) that was slightly too long. When tightened it stripped off a fraction of thread. It entered the lubrication system upstream of the filter element and blocked off the oil jets that feed the camshaft and rocker gear. The camshaft bearings were shot, the cam lobes damaged and the hardening on two rockers broken through. This had happened two years ago, and the replacement parts had cost almost £200.

Next time you hear Honda telling the public to buy only genuine Big H spares

Early exhaust shields were in dull chrome with black inserts, and the rear chainguard was shorter than the K1 version. Find the latter if you can!

Crank journal dimensions are stamped under the front engine mounting and should be referred to when ordering new bearings.

The early ignition switch was recessed, with a collar on the key sealing the unit off when the bike was in use.

consider this! Keith Newton again: "There are good and bad pattern parts, but Honda's stuff is a known quantity and if anything does go wrong you've got a comeback."

Looked after and ridden sensibly, which means clean oil and not thrashing the engine from cold, the CB750 in its early forms was good for at least 40,000 miles before any real work was needed. If changes of oil and filter are neglected, the most vulnerable areas are camshaft and rocker gear, which on early models were lubricated via simple drillings, pumped up from the main oil gallery through two of the barrel studs. Dirty oil will lead to blockage

of these drillings and subsequent starving of camshaft bearings and the whole top-end assembly. Later CB750s and onwards used oil control jets in this area, which give more specific control of lubrication but makes the need for clean lubricant even more urgent.

If you are offered a bike that is noisy at the top end, consider it carefully unless it's a very silly price – and you make your own mind up about that!

The Honda cam chain problem didn't exist in these models and 40,000 miles is a reasonable life for the single row chain. If worn, replace it and the camshaft sprocket

along with the roller tensioner as a precaution. The chain is part number 14403-286-003, the sprocket 14321-300-010 and the tensioner 14500-300-000. Keith Newton showed us a tensioner assembly that looked pretty worn, but when he explained that it had covered 68,000 hard miles on the road test bike, we felt it could be excused!

The primary transmission, by two single row chains, is prone to rumbling when worn. If you hear this on a bike you are considering, try lifting the clutch – if the noise reduces noticeably, all you've been hearing is the backlash on the mainshaft splines. It should not be a problem in service – this

Keith Newton's 750 Honda, number YLY 70H as ridden by press road testers and actually surviving!

really is a case of "they all do that" – but the trick lies in correctly identifying the noise. If the carburettors are out of balance, the tendency for the primary trans to rumble is increased.

The gearbox is a strong unit that gives little or no trouble, apart from the traditional notchy Honda gearswapping. The output shaft bearing is the most vulnerable to wear, and any sign of a leak here should be closely looked at, checking for play at the shaft. If you are considering a K1 version, note that these had a rear chain oiler fitted on the output shaft, and oil leaks should not be confused with mist from the chain. The oil seal (part number 91205-300-003) tends to go before the bearing, and can be replaced without major disassembly.

If you are considering buying a late CB750 or the K0 and K1 versions, take the precaution of counting the teeth on the final drive sprocket. It should have 17 or 18, but if it only has 16 teeth it's one that slipped the dealer recall net after the original 16-toother proved to be too small and produced rapid chain wear. If you use a bike with the small sprocket, there is a real risk of the chain breaking and damaging the cases.

Reading the official shop manual, one is soon impressed by the precision of manufacture reflected in the use of internal and external micrometers to check parts for tolerance. "It does help if you're handy with a micrometer when you're working on one of these," Keith Newton acknowledges. Typical of this thoroughness is the stamping of individual crank journal dimensions beneath the front engine mounting, and the etching of journal and pin sizes on a flywheel after the crank has been ground. A lettered code is used and the shop manual explains this in detail. It enables an owner to order his bearings to a specific dimension, if he ever needs them. Keith Newton's own immaculate example of the breed has 68,000 miles behind it, including letting an assortment of the Press loose on it, yet it still has the original crank along with the same pistons the factory fitted some 18 years ago.

Bigots laugh too easily at the early Japs, not realising how well they were thought out and put together. Old dogs are about, most of them reduced to that state by a combination of ignorance and carelessness, but if an early CB750 can be rescued before neglect puts it beyond recall, it can be a straightforward rebuild with only a few parts unobtainable.

When Keith Newton's four was displayed at the 1985 NEC International Bike Show, it drew more attention than any other bike in the Classics display, and the Show organisers accepted his valuation of £5000 as a realistic figure for insurance cover. Definitely worth considering as a rebuild project!

● **Information:** Vintage Japanese MCC. Contact membership secretary Dennis Lodge, 65 Greenhouse Farm Road, Runcorn, Cheshire.
● **Reading:** Haynes' Super Profile on the CB750, by Pete Shoemark. Haynes' Honda 750 Four Owners Workshop Manual, by Jeff Clew. See also handbooks mentioned in the article.
● **Parts:** Dave Ayesthorpe, Honda Restorations, 1 Penarth Way, Aston on Carrant, Tewkesbury, Glos. GL20 8HL. Tel: 0684 72862. **Rex Judd,** 415 Burnt Oak Broadway, Edgware, Middx. **Cables:** T Johnson, 5 Laburnum Grove, Banbury, Oxon. OX16 9DP. **Paint:** Dave Ayesthorpe, as above. **Superbike Customs,** 0922 477285 – ask for Lee.

● **Frame and engine numbers of early models:** CB750 engine numbers to 1044847, frame numbers to 1044825. CB750K0, engine numbers 1044848 to 1045147, frame numbers 1044826 to 1044947. CB750K1, engine numbers 1045148 to 2000000, frame numbers 1044948 to 1053399.

When Suzuki's GS750 arrived, Big H had to do something

GOOD a run as the CB 750 has had, we could not get ourselves over-excited about the F1. Sound as it was, it somehow failed to live up to its Super Sport tag. When "Shopping for a 750" I remarked that the Japanese are better innovators than developers, but with the F2 Honda have certainly pulled out some big stops. It represents a considerable all round improvement over the F1 which updated but scarcely bettered the K series from which it was derived.

No doubt the F2, introduced last summer, has benefited from Honda's endurance racers but commercially the reason behind the many modifications has been the hot competition on the road. The Suzuki GS 750, right first time from a two-stroke manufacturer, had taken many by surprise and, as one Honda dealer confessed, "killed the CB 750 F1 stone dead" (surely the reputation of 10 years cannot die that suddenly?). While the Yamaha triple is not so directly

comparable, it is certain to attract the growing number of riders who appreciate shaft drive. Big H had to do something.

They have. This time it is more than a matter of looks although the F2 has gained here too. The styling is more aggressive and the Comstar wheels must quickly outdate spokes. This is not merely a point of fashion, since they need no maintenance. I wonder how many of today's young riders know or care what tunes spokes should play? Black on the lower forks should pock less than polished alloy but I am less in favour of blacking the engine — it highlights the dirt even better and usually chips.

With all their Japanese competitors joining them in the four-stroke camp, Honda have the deepest bag of experience into which to dip to keep in front and have rejoined the horsepower race, now aiming once more at 100 bhp per litre. Not new, you may say, at least on the small

bikes, but the progress in regaining these outputs is measured in the continued control of exhaust noise and emission and considerably broader powerbands than the 100 bhp per litre machines of a few years back.

Previously the 68 bhp Suzuki GS 750 was quicker than the CB750 F1 Honda by a greater margin than its stated one extra brake horsepower would suggest. Now Honda claim 73 bhp at 9,000 rpm, achieved by means of larger diameter inlet and exhaust valves and new carburettors. The result is more than a paper gain — enough to justify beefier con rods. There was a trace of pinking on the Bill Smith demonstrator at low rpm using two star fuel, even though the compression ratio has not been raised.

The feel of the motor remains the same: distinctly Honda. It is perhaps less exceptionally smooth than its free-spinning Suzuki counterpart but it does boast a flatter torque curve which has

750 FI

now been usefully extended upwards and there seems to be little if any loss of tractability at the bottom end compared with the F1. Red lines are creeping higher at Honda. This one starts at 9,500 rpm and can really be used. Our test machine happened to have a dead accurate speedometer verified as far as 110 mph, the speed at which the white BMW Escort got left behind (orange stripe and all – Ed.) leaving the F2 to attain 118 mph in rapid time with the rider in the normal sitting position. With the bike fitted with a nose fairing, a racing crouch may not have added much but since Honda reckon it takes 5,000 miles to loosen a bike and ours read only 1,200 it is evident that this Bill Smith F2 will have a true maximum well the better side of 120 mph. The Suzuki has been caught and the softer tuned Yamaha "Supershaft" slightly outpaced.

For most owners of larger capacity machines a maximum speed, let's be honest, is to be indulged

now and again when nobody's looking and subsequently worn on the belt as a matter of prestige. Of more practical daily relevance is the improved acceleration – the F2 is noticeably more eager than its predecessor above 5,000 rpm. Unexpectedly this comes with a definite improvement in fuel consumption. The F2 carburettors now run very lean, made possible by throttle-actuated petrol pumps which remove the flat spots. The results speak for themselves. The F1 would not come above the mid-40s even after being frightened by a Vascar machine. The F2, commuting briskly across country, returned a genuine 52 mpg. . . Most welcome. Unfortunately the 1,500-mile oil change interval remains.

One improvement that is not forthcoming concerns the weight stakes. This latest 750 is still heavy metal and when standing still retains a feel of some deadweight even compared with the Gold Wing. The seat height has gone up a shade but

thanks to revisions to frame geometry the handling is much less ponderous at low speeds. At the same time it is certainly no more twitchy at high speeds. The whole bike seems better balanced and inspires fine riding. Who says racing does not benefit the breed? The front forks are not as supple as they might be but the ride remains satisfactory. There are now two front discs, of course. They are spoked to save unnecessary unsprung weight inside the rubbed area and while braking is not particularly responsive, the stopping power is there in the dry but still disappears to some degree in severe wet. Some fault, probably in the alignment of one of the front discs on our example fed back through the brake lever and made the last few yards of retardation a jerky process. (The wife thought a Comstar wheel had gone oval.)

The Honda's long-distance potential has been improved by its longer range (up to 150 miles

HONDA 750 FI

before needing the one gallon reserve) and without any increase in tank capacity. The quartz iodine headlamp is not as effective as some of the better ones offered by accessory manufacturers, but it does greatly improve upon the previous unit and that of most of its competitors. Why it has taken so long for Honda to take this lead I cannot imagine. The idea has been going begging for years. Similarly the twin horns are a valuable improvement, long overdue.

The gearbox is unchanged so that the mere snicks of the F2 compared with the clunks of the F1 must be ascribed to individual variation. The overall ratios appear to be the same, a lowered primary chain reduction being compensated by an altered final drive ratio where a sealed grease "O" ring chain replaces the traditional kind and makes a lot more noise into the bargain. In fact chain noise is predominant during normal running. When one is riding in anger the engine begins to drown it, but it seems impossible these days to extract a genuine roar from any Honda. By definition, sealed chains must be endless, Which necessitates removal of the rear swinging arm for replacement, but experience of such a chain so far suggests that the innovation is worth it and may stave off the shaft on some bikes for awhile yet. (Mine has only needed 2½ flats of adjustment in the first 4,000 miles and has seen some very bad weather.)

A word about that fairing. I have always dismissed handlebar fairings as styling gimmicks to boost the speed image rather like those adhesive stripes that we used to see on hot Anglias and A40s whose owners could not afford the real thing. The Oxford fairing is better finished than most and its screen is tall enough to be o some use. Back at Bill Smith's the owner of the bike summed it up as "better than nothing". I was not ready to agree until reverting to an unfaired machine and yes, there was a difference particularly at high speeds. Whether you think i worth £33 (plus VAT) to keep the instruments dry and you a bit less wet is a moot point.

Has the Honda caught or even overtaken the Suzuki GS 750? That's a matter of opinion Before the F2 it wasn't. The Suzuki is regarded by some as having set new standards from Japan (in execution if not originality) and in my book i still wins as a first impressions bike. But the Honda F2 is now at least as fast, more economical and at high speeds handles comparably. It remains a sound proposition with excellent lasting properties for the serious high mileage rider that stem from its 10-year-old motor, which, as Bill Smith says, "Can't be bad" For the man who does it himself, it is worth a mention that while Honda, too, are turning to twin overhead cams, the present single cam and rocker arrangement does allow the owner to adjust his own valve clearances with only a spanner and screwdriver. (Happy days, fas disappearing.) The price has gone up, inevitably but Honda do offer a generous guarantee.

Whether or not this is the final version o Honda's famous 750 I cannot know. Rumour is unreliable but certainly Honda have not broken faith with the transverse four-cylinder formula. I it is, then the CB 750 like a good trumpeter i finishing on a high note, even if it is no longe alone in blowing it.   R.P